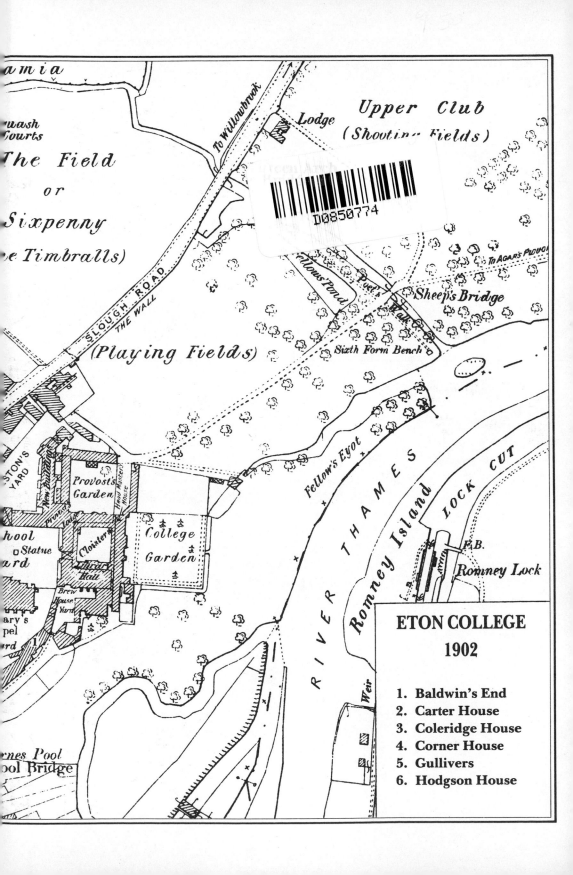

amia

wash Courts

The Field

or

Sixpenny

(e Timbralls)

Upper Club
(Shooting Fields)

To Willowbrook

Lodge

SLOUGH ROAD

THE WALL

(Playing Fields)

Fellows Pond

Poet's Walk

Sheep's Bridge

To AGAR'S PLOUGH

Sixth Form Bench

STON'S YARD

New Buildings

Provosts Garden

Provost's Lodge

Head Masters House

College Garden

hool

Statue

ard

Cloister

School Hall

Brew House Yard

ary's pel rd

Fellow's Eyot

RIVER THAMES

Romney Island

LOCK CUT

F.B.

Romney Lock

Weir

nes Pool
ol Bridge

ETON COLLEGE

1902

1. **Baldwin's End**
2. **Carter House**
3. **Coleridge House**
4. **Corner House**
5. **Gullivers**
6. **Hodgson House**

Eton Renewed

Eton Renewed

A History
from 1860 to the Present Day

Tim Card

JOHN MURRAY

© Tim Card 1994

First published in 1994
by John Murray (Publishers) Ltd.,
50 Albemarle Street, London W1X 4BD

A catalogue record for this book is available from the British Library

ISBN 0-7195-5309-1

Typeset in 11/13pt Garamond by Wearset, Boldon, Tyne and Wear
Printed and bound in Great Britain by The University Press, Cambridge

For Gay and Martin Charteris

Contents

Illustrations

The illustrations are drawn from the College Collections, reproduced where necessary by Eileen Tweedie. Many photographers are now unknown. However, the author and publishers would like to acknowledge the following: Plate 12, Howard Orme; 35 and 38, C.C. Gaddum; 40, Peter Opie; 43 and 45, Margaret Bourke-White and *Life* magazine; 51 and 61, Philip Mitchell; 55, Philip Snow; 60, Zissou Limpkin; 62, George Buchanan; 63, Mark Phillips. Plate 58 appears by kind permission of the Stewards of the Henley Royal Regatta.

Preface and Acknowledgements

IN FEBRUARY 1984 the Provost and Fellows authorized David Macindoe, the Vice-Provost, and Archie Nicholson, a retired Housemaster, to write an official history of Eton College up to 1963, the year in which Robert Birley retired as Head Master. The intention was to emphasize the more recent period, since a Victorian history of Eton College had been written by Sir Henry Maxwell-Lyte. Sadly two years later David Macindoe died suddenly, to be succeeded as Vice-Provost by Archie Nicholson, and he in turn died young, early in 1989. Archie Nicholson wrote two-and-a-half chapters covering the history from 1440 to the middle of the nineteenth century, and David Macindoe wrote a chapter on Edward Lyttelton, Head Master from 1905 to 1916. We are all losers by so little having been accomplished. Apart from any other consideration both authors illustrated by the excellence of their own English style one of the strengths of Eton's classical education. It fell to me, Nicholson's successor as Vice-Provost and an Oppidan trained in Mathematics, to take up the task started by two Colleger Classicists.

With these intimations of mortality before me, I determined to concentrate on the period from 1860. Little that Maxwell-Lyte wrote on the subsequent period is of much value. The year 1860 is a natural starting-point, on the eve of the Victorian Commission examining the public schools which was to bring considerable changes to Eton. At the other end, it seemed right to try to carry the story beyond 1963. So much has happened in the last thirty years, and Eton is now a very different place from what it was then. The reader will appreciate that the price for recounting the recent past is an absence of value judgements about those still living. Those who deserve praise go unrewarded.

The same anxiety to finish the appointed task pushed me towards at least relative brevity. It would have been possible, and in some ways easier, to write a work of twice the length – so vast is the accumulation of material about Eton. The archives are substantial, though certainly not complete. Something over one in a hundred Etonians in the eighty years from 1860 led lives of sufficient distinction to attract biographers or to have justified the publication of volumes of memoirs – most of which have contained material about their schooldays. Inevitably there had to be selection, and much has been omitted – with regret. Furthermore the reader will look in vain for an assessment of Eton in the wider context of education and social history – my own expertise is not adequate. Nevertheless what remains is, I hope, an interesting story in itself, and a fair reflection of the strengths and weaknesses of the most influential school in Great Britain.

The reader will observe that Eton is referred to as the School and its teachers as Masters, using capital letters, whereas other schools have masters. This is not Etonian arrogance: it is rather to help the reader know what is under discussion. Similarly, feminists should not complain that the term Masters now includes women; in the nineteenth century the Etonian term Dame included men. The Glossary is intended to guide readers through any linguistic problems. Two maps identify the buildings of Eton at different times.

The Provost and Fellows trusted me to use the Eton archives: this History is authorized, but in no sense official propaganda. My thanks to the Master, Fellows, and Scholars of Churchill College in the University of Cambridge for permission to quote from the Esher papers in their Archives Centre, and to the Master and Fellows of Magdalene College, Cambridge, for permission to quote from the diaries of A.C. Benson.

Many have helped me with their recollections, or by offering papers. I am particularly grateful to Nicholas Elliott for lending me his father's papers, to Sir William Van Straubenzee who transcribed for me the Eton memoirs of his grandfather, Alexander Nelson Radcliffe, and to Sir Edward Cazalet, who lent me the Eton diary of his uncle, Victor Cazalet. Lord Aberconway kindly lent me a copy of the first volume of the Captain of the Oppidans' Book, otherwise lost. Robin Macnaghten, Tim Connor, and Roger Hudson read the first draft of the whole work and offered advice, most of which I gratefully accepted, but they should not be blamed for shortcomings that remain. David Graham-Campbell, Lord Glendevon, John Roberts, Nigel Jaques, Michael McCrum, Eric Anderson, and Tim Rock read and offered useful comments on some chapters. My thanks to Paul Quarrie, Penny Hatfield, and Linda Fowler, who helped me in College Library, and to Michael Meredith and Helen Garton in School Library. The illustrations owe much to the work of Peter Lawrence in building up Eton's photographic archive, and to the help of Christine Vickers. Finally my thanks to Pippa McCullough who struggled with my unruly script and many erasures, and to Neil Flanagan whose assistance with the records of Old Etonians was invaluable for indexing.

Prologue

ETON COLLEGE WAS founded by a charter of King Henry VI on 11 October 1440. Two days later the parish church at Eton was transformed into a Collegiate Church, that is, a corporate body replaced the parish priest and had the right to hold land and collect revenues. The King endowed the corporate body, known as the Provost and Fellows, with considerable estates spread over the southern half of England, because he intended his foundation to be a great centre of pilgrimage as well as a great school, the religious and educational functions being at that date inseparable. For his purposes he planned the splendid buildings which still exist. Indeed, he wanted the Chapel to be more than twice its size. The school he modelled closely on William of Wykeham's foundation at Winchester, with a schoolmaster and an usher to teach. The two schools have continued to share many features.

Sadly in the civil wars that broke out soon after the foundation, Eton College nearly perished, but it was saved, according to legend, by the intercession of the new King Edward IV's mistress. Its religious function withered and pilgrimages stopped. Eton College survived these and other troubles, and by the early seventeenth century was the foremost school in England. There were seventy Scholars as decreed by the Founder, who were boarded and educated free, and who lived in the College, and more than 100 Oppidans who lodged in the town of Eton, and who received the same education. This was entirely in Latin and Greek. Schooltimes were long, with boys coming from distant homes, and conditions were hard. The schoolmaster and usher had become the Head Master and the Lower Master in charge of the younger boys.

During the eighteenth century the school grew erratically, its numbers varying with political and economic changes as well as with the quality of Provosts and Head Masters. The royal favour of George III certainly helped. Assistant Masters were appointed, and each boy had a Tutor to whom he paid a fee, who supervised his work and gave pastoral advice. The Tutors began to run boarding houses, though much of the boarding was still in the hands of Dames. Although boys often had rooms of their own, as they do now, it was not felt unreasonable for brothers to share rooms or even beds. A good lunch was provided, but otherwise boys catered for themselves – 'messing' together. The Oppidans were at least more comfortably off than the Collegers who all shared a sparsely furnished dormitory into which they were locked each night. There was little formal discipline among the boys, except that the habit developed of younger boys fagging for the older boys. School rules were kept by the Masters, but were not adequately policed: boys had much spare time and led a free life.

The culmination of this period was the rule of Dr Keate from 1809 to 1834. He tried to keep the old system working, controlling (or more frequently not controlling) some 500 boys with little help. He is famous for the numbers he flogged and rebellions that he provoked, but his rule was not all bad. He was personally popular with the boys and a good teacher, and the liberty that the boys enjoyed was used profitably by many. In 1811 the Eton Society was founded to debate, soon acquiring the nickname 'Pop'; magazines were published, and boys educated each other in their leisure time. The group of friends around W.E. Gladstone would have been a good advertisement for any school at any time.

Games added to the fun of Eton life. Eton Fives and two strands of football developed along with cricket and rowing, and boys organized these games themselves in clubs. Cross-country running and swimming were popular, despite the frequency with which boys drowned in the treacherous Thames. Prize-fighting was admired nationally, and boys settled their quarrels with their fists – on the most notorious occasion a son of Lord Shaftesbury was actually killed.

The toughness of Eton matched that of society in the Regency period; during the reign of Victoria manners softened and Eton changed too. Keate's successor, Hawtrey, introduced Mathematics to the regular syllabus and improved the staff. When Hodgson became Provost in 1840, the Collegers were rehoused and it became possible to attract more able boys by scholarships. By 1860 the school was thriving. Certainly it was a very different organization from what it is now, both in the curriculum and in the way of life of the boys. But increasing numbers of parents found it attractive to send their sons to the School.

CHAPTER ONE

Eton in 1860

IF YOU HAD come to Eton in 1860 as a tourist to see the largest and most celebrated school in England, or with a sovereign in your pocket to visit a young godson, you would have arrived at either of the Windsor railway stations, which both opened in 1848. Across the bridge over the Thames, the Eton High Street bore some architectural resemblance to what exists today, but the actual shops sold very different goods, serving the local community and the school rather than visitors. Thus you would have passed a shop selling angling equipment, a purveyor of small animals and a photographer, a watchmaker and tailors. The thirteen pubs were (mostly) not for the boys, but the food shops which were more numerous on the approach to the College were largely looking for the boys' custom.

The centre of Eton would have appeared rather different on the west side of the road, but much the same to the east, for boys' houses stood where there are now the Memorial Buildings, and other boarding houses which have remained were mostly smaller. Nor had the great block of schoolrooms known as New Schools been built. Eton was greener, with larger gardens, and mostly surrounded by the Lammas land which happily has continued to protect the town. The playing fields did not extend so far north as they now do, towards the small villages which have been engulfed by the growth of Slough.

If you had turned into the College Buildings you would have found them almost as they are today. The School Yard would probably have been fuller of boys, in their tall top hats and black clothes, playing about or gossiping. Under Lupton's Tower the Cloisters looked a little more enclosed; the walls were bare of memorials other than boys' graffiti; the doors gave access not so much to offices and stores as to the residences of the Provost and Fellows of the College.

Heading the College was the Provost, Dr Hawtrey, who was, as was normally the case, a former Head Master. By 1860 he was nearing the end of a useful life. Also on the governing body were seven Fellows, one of whom acted as Vice-Provost and another as Bursar. Unlike their counterparts at Oxford and Cambridge, they could be married. All were retired masters in Holy Orders and not, generally speaking, men of particular distinction, though John Wilder and Edward Coleridge were honourable exceptions, the former for the generosity of his not always discriminating benefactions to the College and the latter for his distinguished service as Tutor and Lower Master – indeed he would probably have been chosen as Head Master in 1853 but for High Church leanings.

The duties of Fellows were not exacting, yet their rewards were substantial. Henry VI had founded the College to meet religious and educational needs, but by 1860 the main purpose of the College was to govern the School, for the religious functions had largely disappeared long ago. The Fellows had to administer the College property. They were patrons of the College livings, the best of which they reserved for themselves; for Queen Elizabeth had allowed them to hold livings despite the Founder explicitly forbidding this practice in the Statutes. They were responsible for the Foundation buildings, including the very valuable College Library. They preached in Chapel. The Provost's job was more substantial, in that he was actually in control of the Chapel and Rector of Eton. His authority extended over the School directly, and he effectively could veto initiatives of the Head Master. In particular he had powers over the King's Scholars, who were partly financed by the College – only he, for instance, could dismiss a King's Scholar.

The Provost and Fellows lived in agreeable apartments around the Cloisters. They were not required to be continuously in residence even in schooltime and could pay some attention to their parishes. They were rich, for though their stipends were low (fixed since the seventeenth century, the Provost at £279, the Fellows at

£52 p.a.), yet they had their livings in their parishes, generating say £800, and they had a second even more striking source of funds. The College's property was in land, and rents inevitably would have risen in money and in real terms with inflation and economic growth. The increases in rents, however, were not always required when leases were renewed: instead lump-sum premiums were extracted, or as they were then called, fines. The fines were divided among the Provost and Fellows, the Provost taking a double share. The fines varied from year to year, but on average by 1860 provided £800 per Fellow. One can imagine a happy scene at the annual division of spoil in a good year. The only defence for this practice was that other corporations behaved similarly, and that it was not explicitly forbidden in the Statutes. But it had been criticized by a Committee of the House of Commons under Brougham in 1818, and Victorian sentiment turned very much against the abuse.

The consequences were that the Provost and Fellows were very rich, but that the College was not – indeed Fellows could argue that they sometimes had to put back money to balance the College accounts. The College's income, about £20,000, was a bigger endowment than most other schools', and it did cover the board and lodgings of the seventy Scholars, the provision of services in the Chapel, and the maintenance of the College buildings. It did not, however, provide anything else towards the running of the School. For example, Housemasters who occupied College property (and the College did not own all the buildings in which the School operated) paid rent to the College. Nor were funds available from the College to finance any desirable investment projects such as the building of new schoolrooms.

Besides having incomes equivalent to something like £60,000 p.a. in 1990 terms, the Fellows had enjoyed a further advantage, that they could often preserve their Fellowships within their families: a Fellow's son could progress from King's Scholar to King's College, Cambridge; back to Eton as Classical Master, and then Fellow. By 1860 this comfortable progress was threatened: scholarships to Eton had recently become more competitive, and King's College, which had been reserved entirely for King's Scholars from Eton, was about to open its door to others. But the Fellows in 1860 were still an inbred group from a very narrow common background. Life tenure enabled them to be very lazy,

and the affluent comfort of their existence made them long-lived.
For example, in 1860 one had been a Fellow for thirty-eight years
and another for thirty-one. The same year yet another died after
twenty-seven years, and Mr Balston, a popular Housemaster who
will figure further in the story, was elected in his place by the
Provost and Fellows.

The Provost was appointed by the Crown and could therefore
come from outside Eton, but seldom did. Dr Hawtrey had a
similar career to other Fellows. His income was naturally greater,
but he was expected to maintain a certain style as head of the
College, and his expenses were therefore also greater.

To be Provost or Fellow was to take a step towards the Elysian
Fields. The Masters, at least the Classical Masters, were also rich
but they were very far from idle. The Head Master was above all
the teacher of the top division of the school. On him fell the
responsibility for discipline, and even for examination of the boys.
He appointed his assistants, who were almost all drawn from
King's College (unless the Provost permitted a departure from this
rule when no suitable King's man was available). Naturally it was
not easy for a Head Master to give much time to long-term
development or creative innovation. The Head Master in 1860 was
Dr C.O. Goodford, an amiable West Country man with a trace of
a West Country accent, and a respected teacher. Though appointed
in 1853 at the age of 40, he had made little change in the
arrangements he inherited.

One disadvantage under which the Head Master laboured was
the lack of administrative back-up. The Bursar looked after the
College Estates, not after the School's finances. There was no
School Office to deal with the day-to-day regulation of the School
– reports of absentee boys, collection of punishments, and so on.
Absentees were checked by boys chosen weekly from each division, praepostors, who visited the houses to see who had legitimate
excuses such as sickness. Written punishments for the Head Master
were shown up to his butler, Finmore,* and failure to do a
punishment might escape notice. The Head Master was also short
of Assistant Masters. No doubt this was partly because he had to
finance some of their salaries himself. There was no real distinction

---

* Finmore also supplied birches, both for use on the boys and for purchase
(tied with a blue ribbon) by leaving boys wanting a souvenir.

between the Head Master's private finance and the School's. The Founder had provided in the Statutes for a Head Master and a Lower Master, with salaries that became inadequate. The Founder had also decreed that the Oppidans as well as the Collegers should be taught free. As the School grew assistants were needed, and the College was not willing to pay for them. Thus the Head Master charged boys a fee for his services (and the Lower Master charged the lower boys), and from this fee the Assistant Masters were paid, and of course a supplement to his own income was obtained. By 1860 boys were paying 6 guineas p.a. to the Head Master, an entry fee of 5 guineas, and were expected to give him a leaving present of £10. Noblemen paid double. The Head Master, however, paid 42 guineas to each of his Classical Assistant Masters, and he had other necessary outgoings. In practice his salary was about £4,500 p.a. net – say £160,000 p.a. in today's money.

The 42 guineas paid for teaching in school hours was scarcely more than a labourer's wage. Fortunately, however, the Assistant Masters had their own independent sources of income. They received tuition fees from their pupils for tutorial work, and they could also charge for boarding boys. Generally speaking they could charge 20 guineas to their pupils for tuition, but Collegers paid only 10 guineas. Most kept boarding houses, varying in size from thirty-eight boys downwards on which a profit of £45 p.a. or more per boy could be made. Consequently an Assistant Master with a boarding house and a full Pupil Room could make up to £2,000 p.a., equivalent to some £70,000 p.a. in modern money.

It is worth understanding the financial position for it does much to explain why Head Master and assistants should have had an interest in keeping the staff small; in the assistants' case, the fewer their number the more pupils and the easier to fill their boarding houses. It also explains why so great an emphasis was placed on tutorial work. The average size of classical divisions was about forty, which made teaching ineffective; and the Masters rated teaching, for which they were paid so little, as less important than tutorial work, which was so handsomely rewarded.

There was also a marked lack of schoolrooms. As the numbers in the School grew the boys were crowded into inadequate space, many of them in Upper School itself, where five divisions would be taught at once, and many more in the cramped rooms below, now used for offices and storerooms. Boys sat on benches with no facilities for writing, so that lessons consisted largely of hearing boys construe, or recite saying lessons; and as only a few could be tested it was important that the work should be gone through under the supervision of the Tutor when some real teaching was possible.

This took place in the Masters' Pupil Rooms in their houses, and many more hours had to be devoted to tutorial work than schoolroom work. Furthermore Tutors also saw their pupils in groups for Private Business, that is, instructional sessions off the narrow official syllabus. It will be realized that the Masters worked much longer hours than the boys. On top of this exhausting routine came the control of a boarding house, and a general responsibility for discipline. Eton Classical Masters were mostly well off, enjoyed a gratifying social status, and employed substantial households – but only by accepting for themselves a superhuman burden.

Not all Classical Masters were equally well off. William Johnson, possibly the most famous of all Eton Masters, only secured a small and inconvenient house at a high rent, so that he gave up boarding boys after five years. (He was thus able to concentrate on the tutorial role which meant most to him.) There was no central control of houses in those days, and some were not even leased from the College – so that chance played a considerable part in deciding how profitable a house would be. The starting-up costs of equipping a house were substantial, but if they could be raised, a new Master would seldom have to wait more than a few years to get a boarding house, and, if his first was small and inconvenient, he could hope to move to a better building in time.

The only subject to have been introduced in a small way alongside Classics in the official curriculum was Mathematics. Mathematical Masters were in general far less well off. Mr Stephen Hawtrey, who was appointed as the Mathematical Master, had indeed built with his own funds the Rotunda, a circular building in which Mathematics was taught. He appointed six Masters to assist him, who did not have direct access to the Head Master. Their lower status was noticed by the boys who normally misbehaved with impunity during Maths lessons. Even Mr Hawtrey himself could not keep order, and only one of his assistants, Mr Hale ('Badger', for the colour of his sideburns) transcended the limitations of his position. The salaries of the assistants were only some £200 p.a., which could be supplemented by giving mathematical extras at 10 guineas or by running a house.

The French Master was paid in the same way 10 guineas by those who learnt French. French was not taught in class, but only as an extra in out-of-school time. German and Italian were taught by natives lacking the status of Masters on similar terms to fewer boys. So too was Art. Science instruction was given by visiting lecturers. English, History, and Geography were only taught, if they were taught at all, by Classical Masters, though some of these, to be fair, were enthusiastic and communicated their enthusiasms.

The nine non-Classical Masters could run boarding houses and there were three men not on the staff at all who ran houses. Strictly they were known as dominies, but they were more usually simply regarded as Dames, along with the ladies who kept houses. The fees at Dames' were only £84 a year, in effect £15 less than at Tutors' (that is, Classical Masters') houses. For Dames' boys needed to have a Tutor costing £21, while the fee at a Tutor's house of £120 embraced board and tuition. The Dame's profit per boy was more like £10, compared with the £45 a year obtained by a Tutor with a boarding house. Easily the most successful Dame was William Evans, the Art Master. There was no enforced upper limit on Dames' numbers and his house contained about forty-five boys. By 1860 he himself was largely inactive as a result of a mysterious accident, initially treated by laudanum and then by alcohol:[1] his daughters kept him largely out of sight, and the house was in effect run by his remarkable daughters, Annie (until she died in 1871) and Jane. Despite the success of Evans's, the Dames (male or female) were less well placed to get a house or to fill the house they occupied. A Classical Master, asked to be Tutor, would sometimes tell parents that he would only tutor a boy if the boy were to board in his own house. Also Dames only had access to the Head Master via the Tutors attached to their houses, and in theory it was only the Tutors who could set punishments. The lower status and the lower rewards of the non-Classical Masters inevitably created jealousies.

Even humbler were the three Conducts, literally 'hired men', who read the services and acted as curates of the parish of Eton. They were not chaplains with pastoral care – pastoral care and preparation for Confirmation were the Tutors' responsibility.

They were paid only £120 a year, but they had the prospect of inheriting an Eton living, not however one of twelve richer livings reserved by the Fellows for themselves. One, Mr Kegan Paul,* was Master-in-College, i.e. Housemaster to the seventy Scholars, but he only received £350, less than some Dames.

The Conducts had, of course, to be clergymen; the other Masters did not need to be, yet the great majority were. It is hard to think that they had serious vocations – rather that education was still regarded, from Oxford and Cambridge downwards, as being in the sphere of the Church of England. The cynical might point out that for the Classical Master, clerical orders were essential for promotion to Head Master or to Fellow, and in 1860 only William Johnson among the nineteen Classics Masters was a layman – though during 1860 he was joined by Edmond Warre, not yet in orders. Probably it is fairer to accept that most of the Masters were conventional Christians, not humbugs, who saw themselves as schoolmasters rather than priests.

Even the less-rewarded Masters were better off than most masters elsewhere. The position of the Classical Masters was remarkable. Their high pay was not necessary for recruitment, since it was far better than they could achieve otherwise as, for example, rectors of a parish or Fellows of King's. It resulted from the limited number of Masters and the willingness of parents to pay high fees. In theory there was competition among the staff – the most successful Tutors, by attracting most pupils, earned most, and so did those who kept the most successful boarding houses. But the competition was limited: rates of pay were fixed, and it was not possible, for example, for a young man to try to get his house established by charging less. Also the small number of Tutors relative to numbers of boys ensured that even the least successful had enough pupils to earn a comfortable living.

It cannot be claimed that high pay went with a high quality of staff. The Classical Masters were certainly homogeneous in their uniformly Etonian backgrounds, but as men they varied in attainments and application. A few were gifted teachers with well-stocked minds, but many were boring. Some could keep order, and most were at least conscientious, caring for their pupils after their

---

* He soon left Eton for the College living of Sturminster Marshall, and later he became a successful publisher.

fashion. There were family men and there were bachelors, either from inclination or because they hardly had time in their lives to change. Though the Eton community was touched with genius, its general level must be rated unexceptional. Inevitably one must ask why the School was so popular with parents. There were good educational features, which will emerge as we look at the boys' lives; but the School's main draw was the desire of parents to have their sons in a school that enjoyed royal favour, and where they would meet the right company. Of course this was sometimes mere snobbery – but it was not foolish snobbery, for no education-al force in a boarding school matters so much as the interaction of the students on each other. Parents were prepared to pay fees which in purchasing power were a little less than they are at Eton today, but which were certainly higher in relation to levels of income of the time. Fees, unlike Eton's today, were much ahead of those at other boarding schools (except for some small houses at Harrow). Furthermore the extra costs imposed by the living style of Etonians were far greater proportionately than elsewhere, and certainly than they are now. Remember also that large Victorian families often had several sons to educate. Thus Eton was narrowly a school for the rich.

The boys were almost uniformly Anglo-Saxon and Church of England, a total contrast with the modern Etonians of many races and religions. In 1860 there were 820 boys in the School, but a hundred of these who were in the Lower School and even some upper boys were below the age (13) at which boys are now admitted. The register for 1859[2] reveals that sixty-six were either peers or sons of peers, and five were baronets: in 1990 the equivalent figures were thirty-three and nil among 1,278 boys. Certainly titles are inherited less early now, but there are also more peers among whom Eton could recruit. It is clearly the case that peers no longer patronize Eton in the same way, and that Eton for its part has become far less socially exclusive.

Etonians came from all over the British Isles – in particular more from Ireland and from Scotland than is now the case. The competition to be the senior Irish peer and give a shamrock badge to the Head Master on St Patrick's Day was considerable.

Many parents, who were not peers, had substantial estates. Other than landowners, parents were commonly clergy (often well connected), officers (mostly from the army, but also from the navy), or barristers. Very few were from business, even from the

City. Probably the social range was narrower than it had been in the past or was soon to become in the future.

Most Etonians followed the same sort of careers as their parents. Of the 1859 register, 80 were to be clergymen, 112 army officers (and others were officers briefly), 26 had spells as MPs and a very few entered the Civil Service, mostly the Foreign Office or the Indian Civil Service. Many became barristers, but most returned to the estates from which they came, often serving as Justices of the Peace. The picture is essentially of a closed community, not evolving socially. That too is something which (for better or worse) has now totally changed.

The Collegers were not so very different in background from Oppidans: there were three sons of baronets in 1859. Very many were clergymen's sons, no doubt because the clergy were able to coach their sons for the College Examination, which had become a genuine contest since the living conditions of Collegers had improved. A group of preparatory schools feeding boys for scholarships was emerging, but was not yet fully established. The clergy fathers of Oppidans may have had richer livings (or richer wives) than the clergy fathers of Collegers, but there was no clear class difference between Collegers and Oppidans as there would have been earlier. The Founder intended College for the poor; the only deference paid to his wish was to exclude boys rich in their own right from scholarships.

The hostility which was generally supposed to exist between Collegers and Oppidans – and with some reason – cannot be explained on Marxist lines. Rather it is a matter for the anthropologist. The Collegers, *'gens togata'* – the gowned race – were referred to contemptuously as 'tugs' by the Oppidans (perhaps tug is a corruption of toga). The Oppidans needed a tribe from whom they could be different, though College and Oppidans happily united for instance in playing against outsiders, such as the Harrovians at cricket. It is true that the Collegers did not take much part on the river – an expensive sport; but they did have their own pack of beagles, separate from the Oppidan pack.

One particular problem for all Etonians was that boys entered at different ages and with very different academic attainment, and the ages of boys in most divisions spanned several years. Collegers elected in 1860, for example, were between 9 and 15 years old.

John Maude, who was first in the College Election* that year, was 10½, and he must initially have been working with boys up to three or four years older.³ Friendships with Oppidans cannot have been easily established. It is remarkable that in his memoirs he does not complain at all of being bullied. Indeed subsequently he evidently acquired many Oppidan friends, but it has to be said that he was lucky enough to be a good games player.

The lowest level into which a boy could be placed in 1860 was the First Form (five boys aged about 9). There were only six boys in the Second Form, but the Third Form, which also was in the Lower School, was much larger and subdivided into four sets, Upper Greek and Lower Greek, where some smatterings of Greek were learnt, and Sense and Nonsense. The last two names derived from the English which was expected to be translated into Latin verse: in Nonsense the Latin words had to be arranged to scan, but the English was not required to have any meaning. These first three forms constituted the Lower School under the direction of the Lower Master – and it was possible to be three years in the Lower School. Although the curriculum was largely classical, Mathematics and handwriting were also taught. In effect the Lower School was a preparatory school.

Fourth Form, Lower Remove, Upper Remove, Lower Fifth, and Middle Fifth were blocks in which each boy spent a year. In each block the boys would be divided into three, not by ability but according to the different times of arrival into the block. Promotion, for example from the top third of Fourth Form into the bottom of Lower Remove, depended upon Trials, set and corrected (except for Mathematics) by the Head Master. The other two-thirds of the block simply had Collections at the end of the half, looked over by the division Master, on which nothing significant depended. After Trials in the Middle Fifth, those who were staying on reached the Upper Fifth and freedom from Trials: promotion thereafter into Sixth Form was simply by seniority.

Fourth Form were taught in Upper School, partitioned by curtains through which the noise of Mr Thackeray's unruly

* The Scholarship Examination led to the election of Scholars to fill vacancies; this process conducted by the Provost and Fellows was the formal moment at which Collegers were chosen, and those chosen in 1860, for example, became the 1860 Election.

divisions easily passed. The classical work was largely repetition of passages learnt (saying lessons) and translation of prepared passages from the Latin and Greek books. Boys were required to bring written-out derivations* to show they had grasped the grammar of the passages. Other work set to be done out of school included themes for translation and Latin verses. Also in the lower blocks they were required to produce maps and written descriptions of the classical world. These involved a fair amount of work, and were easy to correct. Sunday Questions, however, on a theological subject and done at the weekend, were as great a chore for Masters as for boys, though they did at least teach boys to get up and respond to subjects new to them.

The construes were prepared in the Tutors' Pupil Rooms, and here boys could get individual help and instruction. Their themes and verses were corrected by the Tutors and fair copies required, unless the work was good, before it was shown up, to be looked over again by the division Masters – a curious double check which persisted until modern times, and which was used by division Masters, often gleefully, to spot errors on the part of their colleagues rather than their students. Another curious feature was that all the Fifth Form did the same classical texts: although this simplified the Tutors' tasks, it did mean repetition of work, with what was simple for the cleverest being done and redone by the stupidest. Every Friday, for example, from the Captain of the School to the lag of Fifth Form, all boys prepared up to fifty lines of Theocritus (not an easy author).

The classical work was essentially linguistic, though some literary standards were set by choosing good models among the classical authors. Only the Sixth Form, taught by the Head Master, read widely. Few other division Masters taught around the books that their divisions were reading, and there was no official provision for studying Ancient History and Philosophy. Even the literary element could have been better fostered by quick and fluent translation, but the emphasis was on accurate comprehension, and the use of cribs was rigidly, though ineffectively, forbidden. The best teachers set themes for translation which were interesting in themselves, most notably William Johnson, whose verse textbooks had poetic merit; his *Lucretilis* was used for over

* For example: 'amas': 2nd person singular present indicative of *amo* – whence the current joke, 'Boys learn *amas*, Tutors amass'.

one hundred years. Many thought verses a particularly valueless exercise, and they are no longer fostered by the classical establishment in this country. Certainly there was a danger that good versifiers would do the work for weaker brethren. On the other hand it can be argued that this was the most useful part of the classical work since it trained students to fit words exactly to the constraints imposed, and it gave an experience of problem-solving. In general it can be said that the classical curriculum did train boys to be thorough and to know well what they were studying. It was, however, narrow even within the limits that concentration on the Classics implied.

There admittedly were the three weekly mathematical periods taught in smaller sets in Stephen Hawtrey's Rotunda. Here at least the boys had desks at which to work, but the Mathematical Masters, inadequately treated, were seldom effective. Extra Works were set for boys to do out of school, but there as always it was difficult to prevent collaboration. Boys with genuine ambitions to succeed at Mathematics – those for instance who wished to do well at Cambridge – needed extra tuition (for which they paid). It was also possible to learn French, German, Hebrew, Italian, Fencing, Dancing, and Drawing as extra subjects, by paying. Such extras had to be attended at times free from school or Pupil Room.

The boys certainly had the opportunity for they had not many lessons. In a regular week, and there were few such, Monday, Wednesday, and Friday were whole schooldays. On these days boys went to school at 7.30 a.m. (7.00 a.m. in the summer) 11.00 a.m., 3.00 p.m. and 5.00 p.m., nominally for one-hour periods, though in practice for rather less owing to the late arrival of Masters and early release of all but delinquent boys. Tuesdays were half-holidays, and Thursdays and Saturdays had play at four. In practice Saturday was normally a half-holiday, since a holiday in the next week for a Saint's Day also turned the preceding Saturday into a half-holiday. Furthermore, boys' distinguished work could be rewarded by being 'Sent up for Play', which secured release for all from the Saturday afternoon school. The holidays were numerous and involved changes in the timetable to ensure that there were three whole schooldays in the week. Into this shifting but relaxed scheme were fitted long periods of Pupil Room, where almost every Tutor would be working with some of his boys. Most days from 9.00 to 11.00, from 12.00 to 2.00, from 2.30 to 3.00, and also from 4.00 to 5.00, some construing would be in progress. In the evening verses might be corrected and Tutors would hold Private Business (theoretically to those boys whose parents paid 20 rather than 10 guineas, but in practice to all). This Private Business was sometimes the best educational experience of the week, in which a Tutor could informally introduce topics, not always classical, outside the syllabus. For Tutors, however, the load must have been crippling, the working day about fourteen hours. For the older and cleverer boys at least it was not so bad, as they could secure release from Pupil Room once they seemed to know their work. A Tutor might punish an older boy by requiring his presence at 1.00, when he would otherwise be free for games or social activity.

There were other sanctions available, and rewards. Boys could be required to write out a lesson, on which they had shown themselves inadequately prepared in school. Bad behaviour was normally punished by the writing out of lines. There were, on the other hand, prizes, including prizes for non-classical subjects (notably the prizes given by the Prince Consort to encourage the study of French and German, and many prizes for Mathematics). Good work was also very freely encouraged by Sending up for Good to the Head Master; a good copy of verses was the exercise normally rewarded. The honour three times earned secured a prize, as it still does.

It will have been noticed that Chapel does not figure in the whole schoolday timetable, and there was none. There was morning Chapel on Sundays, matins with sermon (then as now at 10.40 a.m.). On Saints' Days and other holidays there were also morning services. Furthermore there were afternoon services on Sundays, whole-holidays and half-holidays, which were designed to keep the boys out of trouble more than to foster religion. The Sunday evensong had to be at 3.00, for Eton shared a Choir School with St George's, Windsor; trebles and lay clerks had to be back to sing there at 5.00.

In no account of the period do the Chapel services appear to have been at all edifying. Behaviour was bad, the sermons almost invariably boring if indeed they were audible.* Some hymns and psalms, notably 136, were sung with great verve, but they were exceptional. Nor was the building as beautiful as it now is. Stained

---

* Coleridge's sermons were honourable exceptions.

glass windows were being added, all but the west window of lamentable quality. The roof and choir stalls were in the Victorian Gothic manner, the organ inconveniently poised on the south wall. Already the school had outgrown the Chapel and lower boys on weekdays worshipped in the Cemetery Chapel in the Eton Wick Road.

The leisure time of younger boys was largely occupied in and around their houses. These were kept by Tutors and ten Dames, each with its own idiosyncrasy. One house was indeed quite untypical of the rest; most lower boys boarded with Mr John Hawtrey, and his house was effectively a prep school. They ate all meals together and had their own playing field. They had no fagging, but were a good deal more closely supervised than their contemporaries in the other houses. In general Tutors offered slightly greater comfort, reflecting higher fees; boys had their own rooms, except occasionally for brothers, (as now) furnished with table, chair, bed, ottoman, and burry. Dames, who did not have to observe the same limit on numbers as Tutors, would try to pack in more boys. Mr Evans offered most comfort but also took most boys. In general the older houses were reckoned by the boys (then as later) to have the greatest charm, usually because the rooms were varied. Boys ate their main meal in the house dining-rooms at the end of a very long morning; a light supper was also eaten there but breakfast, as well as tea, were taken in messes in boys' rooms. For these meals little more than a slice of bread and butter and a kettle were provided. There were no bathrooms, but basins at points in the house, and boys could occasionally wash themselves down from basins of hot water in their rooms. In the absence of adequate washing facilities, of course, the School did not differ from even upper middle-class houses of the time, and bathrooms were introduced at Eton as elsewhere before the end of the century. In most houses of thirty-odd boys, two boys' maids looked after the boys' rooms, and their tasks were much heavier than those of their modern successors – for there was more food eaten in rooms, hot water to carry, fires to clear, as well as the tidying of rooms and repair of clothes. Then as now they were sometimes rewarded by real affection from their charges.

Tutors usually exercised better supervision over their houses than Dames. Each Dame had a young Master attached, occasionally resident, to deal with any disciplinary problem; but many

Dames preferred not to know when they had problems. The
Captain of the house, the senior boy by the School List, could read
prayers or call Absence in the house, but there was no formal
prefectorial system, and the influence of the Captain depended
very much upon his character. Swells within the School might also
exercise influence within the house, perhaps in organizing games,
but they had no responsibility. On the other hand fagmasters, who
were those in and above the Middle Fifth did have control over
their fags (those in Remove or lower). Fagging had developed as an
exchange of services, something like the feudal system, in which
the young performed tasks for their seniors in return for protection from bullying and help in need. Some fagmasters took this
responsibility, as in the agreeable anonymous novel, *Collegers v.
Oppidans,*[4] where the hero redeems his errant fag by example.
Robert Bridges, the future Poet Laureate, took his eccentric distant
relative Digby Dolben* as a fag so that he could look after him.[5]
But most fagmasters enjoyed the power and privileges of fagging
without giving any return. Fags would prepare and serve breakfast
and tea, and run messages. They were literally on call. Abuses did
exist: boys would be fagged illegally to fetch things from out of
bounds, or to read cribs to fagmasters working on construe. But
there is little evidence of resentment of fagging in memoirs – it was
generally accepted, partly out of natural deference to older boys
and partly no doubt in expectation of the good times to come. Also
in most houses there were many fags, maybe over half the house,
to share the work. Bad fagging might be requited by a blow,
perhaps from a convenient toasting-fork, but there was no formal
punishment within houses and little bullying – least of all of the
young by the old. If young boys did have problems, then as now it
was likely to be from isolation rather than active unkindness. It is
hard to believe, however, that boys who came to school young
were not heartily sick of fagging at the end of, say, five years;
doubtless they would be skilled at reducing their chores to a
minimum by perfunctory performance. Fags, of course, would
seldom appreciate that there was a useful, character-forming aspect
to this system, and that what had been learnt might well be quickly

---

  * Digby Dolben died in a swimming accident aged 19, but not before he and
his poetry had strongly influenced Gerard Manley Hopkins. At Eton he was a
tractarian rebel against College Chapel religion. Boys admired and copied out his
poetry.

lost a year later in the decadent and idle enjoyment of the attentions of their own juniors.

In College there were differences. The junior Collegers, roughly speaking the fags, lived in Long Chamber, a dormitory (reduced from its original size). The rest had their own rooms similar to Oppidan rooms. The midday dinner and supper were eaten in College Hall. Lodging and that amount of board were provided. Breakfast and tea, which were eaten communally except by the senior boys, were paid for by the parents. A Colleger also needed an arrangement with a Dame, who for a fee would look after money for him, provide orders for new clothes to his parents' account, and so on, and take him in if he were ill. There were, of course, many more senior Collegers and the ten most senior, Sixth Form, constituted a prefectorial body who might formally punish boys, usually by setting epigrams to be written, but occasionally by corporal punishment. Only Sixth Form and infrequently the Captain of Liberty (Liberty were the next six boys who had liberty from punishment) had fags, but even so the ratio of fagmasters to fags was higher in College, and fagging consequently sometimes harder.

Games were still largely informal, but in the Michaelmas Half the Field Game was played by houses. Most houses shared fields on the common land west of Eton, and the whole house would turn out for games. A house competition had recently evolved, and in 1860 one of the Housemasters, Mr Wayte, presented a cup for competition. The School Field XI appeared in colours, the red and blue shirt still used, white flannel trousers with a scarlet and blue stripe down them, and a pork-pie cap. House colours soon followed. For ordinary football games dress was, however, informal: any old pair of trousers might be used. In view of the absence of washing, it is perhaps as well that boys tended to put on clean clothes every day. The Field Game, except in formal matches, was umpired by the captains of either side, to whom appeals were made and granted by the offending side. It was a rough game, and 'shinning', that is, hacking opponents' shins, was particularly prevalent, but it was one in which even poor athletes could participate, and was accepted as *the* game against other rivals at this time.

In the Lent Half cross-country running, enlivened by jumping over the many streams that in those days ran cleanly around Eton, was the main sport. The exercise could be made more exciting by joining the beagles. Fives was popular, but there were only eight courts on the Eton Wick Road, besides the areas between the Chapel buttresses where the game had originated. The informality of the organization of games at this time is illustrated by the building of two new Fives Walls in 1863–4; it was left to the Captain of the Oppidans to raise £300 and commission the building.

In the Summer Half there was rowing and cricket, and bathing in the river. The hardier youth of those days swam for a longer season than is now customary – and as was then normal, in the nude. To row boys had, as now, to pass a swimming test. There was no need to make an absolute choice between rowing and cricket – some boys excelling at both sports – but rowing was the more prestigious and popular. Boys hired boats for sculling, or for pulling with a friend; there were house fours and eights; for pure leisure boys could hire a tub. Races existed within houses, often as sweepstakes, perhaps with older and younger boys paired together. There were school races and a house four competition by this time, and the winners would be hoisted on shoulders and cheered in the High Street. Also occasional races were held between the School VIII and outsiders – in 1860 a race against Westminster was renewed after a long break. Clearly the sport had already developed competitively, though the arrival of Edmond Warre as a master in 1860 was to transform rowing. Rowing also had a social life of its own. On the Fourth of June and Election Saturday the ten-oared boat, the *Monarch*, would lead eights in procession to and from Surly Hall, where a sumptuous meal with a great deal of champagne would be consumed.* Then on alternate Saturdays in June and July there would be Check Nights when the Upper Boats would row their eights to Surly and dine off duck and green peas, while the Lower Boats consumed champagne and cake back at the boathouses. It is surprising that there were no fatalities, but not surprising that rowing was an expensive sport.

In 1860, the Captain of the Oppidans, who arranged the Fourth of June and Election Saturday dinners, allowed about one bottle per boy for the eights and for the other senior guests, but (as he wrote in the Captain of the Oppidans' Book) 'committed a great

* Surly Hall was an inn on the Windsor bank above the site of the present Boveney Lock.

error in getting (Sparkling) Moselle for Champagne, as it is nasty sweet stuff'. On Election Saturday this mistake was corrected, but heavy rain wrecked the day.

> The rain, however, prevented anyone from sitting at the tables, and indeed rendered the greater part of the provisions nearly or quite uneatable, and the wine being attacked with all the greater ardour, the effects produced by its conjunction with wet, cold and hunger, were something dreadful. I never remember to have seen so many so thoroughly intoxicated in one day before; one boy, indeed, narrowly escaped with his life, being only saved from death by great exertion.

Somehow fireworks were still released as the procession returned, and the band played on.

Cricket was also organized by the boys into different clubs according to age and skill. Upper Club contained the best cricketers from whom the XI was chosen. Sixpenny was a club for younger boys, which was named for its subscription. There was a general shortage of grounds, since the College property was at this stage bounded by Pocock's Lane; nevertheless informal games were also played, often with wet-bobs as well as dry-bobs participating. On days when there were matches dry-bobs were expected to watch the XI in action – a curiously un-Etonian practice, which was probably not effectively enforced. The two main matches were against Winchester and Harrow. The Harrow match took place at Lord's, where it was already a fashionable gathering. Behind the benches around the ground carriages were drawn up and alfresco parties held; boys sat on the grass and kept up a constant flow of encouragement for their own side, chaff for the other, interrupted by occasional skirmishes.[6] At this time Harrow had for some while been dominant, partly because of the more professional attitude they took to training their team. The social life of dry-bobs was more abstemious than that of wet-bobs, consisting largely of teas, the most exclusive held again under the auspices of the Captain of the Oppidans on Poets' Walk.

In 1860 itself a new activity was introduced, the Eton Rifle Volunteers Corps. In 1859 suspicion of French aggrandizement under Napoleon III led to the formation of Volunteers at Oxford and elsewhere. Edmond Warre was a leader of the Oxford Corps, and it so happened that Warre was temporarily at Eton in February 1860 holding the house of his old Tutor, who was ill. It was probably no coincidence that that month the Eton Rifle Volunteer Corps was formed. About 300 upper boys joined, and leading swells became the officers. A grey-brown uniform was selected. Colours were worked by the ladies of Eton and presented by Mrs Goodford on the Election Saturday. The Head Master acquired muzzle-loading rifles, and ten sergeants were hired from the Guards to give twice-weekly drills. The initial impetus was powerful, and by 1861 a shooting team could be entered at Wimbledon.* The Queen and Prince Consort were enthusiastic and helpful, and at the end of November 1861 the Corps was reviewed at Windsor by the Queen and the Prince Consort – his last public appearance – which was followed by a grand lunch in the Orangery for all the Corps. Sadly, however, inadequate boy commandants were to lead to difficulties, until by 1866 it amounted to little more than a shooting team. In 1867 the Corps was firmly re-established with Masters in charge. Oddly, up to that moment, it had no official sanction from the military authorities.

Much of boys' leisure was spent then, as later, in eating and drinking. No account of Eton omits reference to the sock cads who sold their fare by the wall outside the College buildings. Often food was bought on tick, that is, on credit, which was supposedly illegal, but connived at on both sides. The vendors remembered all debts, and were prepared to magnify them when they collected at the beginning of a new half. The most famous cad was Spankie, who knew and was prepared to use the aristocratic connections of all who owed him money. Reputedly he became a rich man. There were also a number of sock shops, frequented by different age groups, where food could be bought to carry back to breakfast or tea, or where intermediate meals could be eaten. Mrs Trone kept a sock shop frequented by Collegers, and they, before going up the High Street, would leave their gowns, which they had to wear all the time within Eton, with her. Tap was a more or less tolerated establishment which sold beer as well as food, and its upper room served as a club for the older boys. Initiation to the inner circle was by drinking in one draught the long glass, a hollow globe at the end of a long neck, which held about a quart. The Christopher Inn,

* At that time the centre for rifle-shooting rather than tennis.

which had been located in the centre of Eton until 1842 and open to boys, still drew some custom, and some Masters turned a blind eye to those frequenting it, though visits were certainly not legitimate. Other pubs and tobacconists were wholly illegal, and boys were likely to be flogged if caught visiting them.

Strictly speaking, however, the whole of the High Street and Windsor was out of bounds, an absurd state of affairs, since boys passed along the High Street to reach the river, or to reach the Windsor Castle Terrace and St George's Chapel which were in bounds. This illogical state of affairs gave rise to a further absurdity: boys were expected to shirk Masters whom they met out of bounds, for example by retreating into a shop, and the Masters would then pretend they had seen nothing amiss. No serious attempt was made to defend these arrangements, but presumably the school authorities preferred to be able to say that the towns of Windsor and Eton, with their unknown temptations, were out of bounds in case a boy ran into a fight or other trouble. Shirking then became a form of good manners: the boys did not place the Masters in the position of being obliged to connive directly at breaches of rules. Some Masters certainly regarded boys who failed to shirk them as discourteous, to be flogged for their discourtesy, and thus boys would be punished severely for what no one seriously regarded as wrong-doing.

Anyway, no objection was really taken to boys visiting Windsor except during the Windsor Fair in October. This was strictly out of bounds and Masters made efforts to catch boys, who might then suffer demotion as well as flogging. The braver spirits found the challenge irresistible, and accounts of escapes feature in memoirs and more overt fiction. The principal temptation of the Fair seems to have been gambling.

After lock-up, which varied with the length of daylight, boys were expected to be in their houses – though boys in Dames' houses might need to visit their Tutors for Private Business. Some work would be done and there might be occasional theatricals or organized entertainment according to the individual tradition of houses. Mostly boys would socialize, mob about, or play passage football. The very active Alfred Lubbock arranged boxing nights in his Tutor's, but without great success.[7]

The evening was no doubt also the time for escapades, and we read of boys climbing out of their houses, perhaps to poach and occasionally to seek female company. In general sex plays a small part in Victorian memoirs, and references such as there are tend to be veiled: '. . . a strong taint of mischief and worse evil'. Boys' relations with girls were discreet. If known to authority they were taken as a sign that it was time for a boy to move on. Two boys driving through Eton in a tandem with two women (presumably of doubtful repute) were sacked.[8]

The unattractive habit of giving small boys feminine nicknames is suggestive but was not as prevalent as it seems to have been at Harrow. Sermons speak of immorality, but this would apparently often mean masturbation rather than homosexual practices. A letter from an Old Etonian to the *Journal of Education* in 1882 speaks of immoral habits as rife but harmless; it appears to refer to the 1850s.

> I have in my mind's eye a list – a long one, I regret to say – of those who at my school were unfortunately conspicuous (I mean only in this particular manner; I should have a different story to tell of those who were addicted to drinking, bad language, stealing, idleness, etc.) and what ought I to find . . . why, of course I should have to point to mental and physical wrecks, men who have dragged hitherto a miserable existence, preys (not martyrs) to consumption and atrophy and insanity or else to outcasts from all good society. Now what do I find? That those very boys have become Cabinet Ministers, statesmen, officers, clergymen, country gentlemen etc.; that they are nearly all of them fathers of thriving families, respected and prosperous . . . Happily an evil so difficult to cure is not so disastrous in its results.[9]

The development of sentimental relationships between boys was known as 'spooning' – the term also used for relationships between boy and girl; it did not necessarily imply anything physical in either case. Digby Dolben wrote poetry addressed to an older boy, Gosselin, but probably carried his passion no further. How much the attentions of bigger boys to the younger were sensual, how much they were merely platonic is hard to say. The latter was countenanced at this stage in Victorian times, though it was to be regarded with increasing suspicion as the century went on, and by 1860 moral attitudes were more censorious than they had been

during the Regency period. Some of the adult attitudes had reached
the young, and probably in the better houses the tone was
satisfactory; but it would be rash to assume all was well throughout Eton. At any rate there does not seem to have been any major
scandal such as occurred at Westminster and Harrow. If boys pass
through a homosexual phase it little matters provided heterosexual
attitudes are later established: the relatively tolerant mood of 1860
was probably likely to cause less guilt and fewer subsequent
problems to the young than the intolerance to be found later.

It would not have been wise to rely much on the senior boys to
keep order in houses. So far as sexual misdemeanours with boys or
girls were concerned, they were the most likely offenders. But
there was no prefectorial system, except in College. Older boys
might intervene to prevent bullying or theft (though certain things
like schoolbooks could be 'borrowed'). Such boys were effective
because they were swells, accorded status because of personality or
athletic skill, not because they were appointed. In the School at
large, there was equally no formal disciplinary body of boys. Sixth
Formers had little collective status, though the Captain of the
Oppidans was an arbiter in disputes about fagging. Pop, the Eton
Society, was socially élite, but with no collective responsibility.
The captain of each game was chosen within his own club, and
took full responsibility for it – games were certainly not run by
Masters. A group of important people of this sort, swells, met in
the inner room of Barnes' sock shop, but they were an informal
group to be joined by invitation; not all of Pop was welcome and
not all members were in Pop. Pop was nevertheless the goal of
most Etonians. It still held regular debates in its own room, but its
members were chosen for acceptability rather than rhetorical skill.
In 1860 its twenty-eight members included four Collegers, five in
the XI and three in the VIII, and the Captain Commandant of the
Corps. It was self-electing. The only influence that the Head
Master could exercise was to encourage a boy to stay on to be a
Captain (or to leave if it were thought better that he should not be
a Captain).

There were other groups that had a certain influence, but again
no legitimate authority, who perhaps set a tone; for example, the
smarter set would be the last to enter Chapel, and anyone who
lacked the credentials would be frozen out. In all of this, one
detects that peer group pressure was strong even by the standards

normally prevailing in schools. Masters did not seek influence, as a rule, let alone attain it, but the arrival of Edmond Warre in 1860 was to make a change.

It was also the case that the best of Tutors sought to influence the intellectual development of their pupils. Most obviously William Johnson did so, and there can be no question that he profoundly affected his favourites both by the great range of his intellectual interests and by the ties of sentiment which bound many of them to him. We discover what Eton could be in what he wrote, quoted many years later with approval by George Lyttelton, another famous Eton master:

At school you are engaged not so much in acquiring knowledge as in making mental efforts under criticism. A certain amount of knowledge you can indeed with average faculties acquire so as to retain; nor need you regret the hours you spent on much that is forgotten, for the shadow of lost knowledge at least protects you from many illusions. But you go to a great school not so much for knowledge as for arts and habits; for the habit of attention, for the art of expression, for the art of assuming at a moment's notice a new intellectual position, for the art of entering quickly into another person's thoughts, for the habit of submitting to censure and refutation, for the art of indicating assent or dissent in graduated terms, for the habit of regarding minute points of accuracy, for the art of working out what is possible in a given time, for taste, for discrimination, for mental courage, and for mental soberness.[10]

This is admirable, and it was not entirely unrealistic. The classical curriculum was indeed intended to develop the arts and habits described. There was merit in the thoroughness and in the analytical methods inculcated. Boys did acquire care for accuracy in the use of words, and even critical standards which indicated assent or dissent in graduated terms.* But only the best can have achieved such refinement, and the cribber, or the boy unlucky in division Master or Tutor, would not have gained much benefit from his studies.

* The mass of records kept by boys indicate that most wrote a stylish and precise English to a standard that few modern Etonians could match.

It was also the case that some Tutors were men of wide interest, and that Private Business could encourage intellectual breadth, but too often the Eton curriculum was damagingly narrow. 'It is greatly to be regretted that for so many years of early life the reasoning faculties should be almost entirely neglected' (Johnson again).[11] It was not an education for business men, but Etonians were not destined for industry. Classicists might argue that Latin was a language of a rational kind, and that anyway some Mathematics were taught. Yet William Johnson's anxiety was justified: the Mathematics taught were primitive, and the exercise in reasoning that (in different ways) Science or History might have provided was usually absent. It is remarkable that the 1859 School List contained four future Fellows of the Royal Society. Competition for this honour was undoubtedly less in those days, but the Eton education cannot have been wholly blinkered.

A more serious complaint is that too few were motivated, and they mostly Collegers. Collegers by 1860 almost invariably won the prestigious Newcastle Scholarship based on Classics and Divinity. They were less successful in the Tomline prize for mathematical ability. One of the ways in which Collegers were seen to be different was that they were saps who took their work more seriously than Oppidans. This is true enough in its way, but it would probably be wrong to exaggerate the gap between Collegers and Oppidans, particularly as they began to aspire to University; and Oppidans varied from house to house. Some Oppidans of real intelligence suffered from the concealment of ability – sharpening their wits more by the evasion of set work and by the management of their Masters rather than by academic work. The handicap of an assured inheritance was already widely recognized: Etonians would have been readier to learn if they had been less rich.

Already by 1860 some were saying that games counted for too much. It is true that the schoolboy heroes were almost invariably games players; but this was natural as boys admire proficiency, and proficiency in action was much more visible that proficiency at work. Yet the part of games at Eton was much less than it was to become there and at other schools. The authorities' attitude to games was one of neglect: they did not encourage athletes, and indeed they were culpable in not providing enough facilities for the ordinary games player. It was also regrettable that there was so

little other organized out-of-school activity – most notably that
the School really sponsored no musical life. There would be the
chance to sing at a Master's soirée, or to receive lessons in
Windsor, but nothing else. Certainly Eton did not give the
opportunity to achieve excellence in diverse fields that exists
nowadays.

At least on the games field boys could develop powers of
leadership and were given the opportunity for organization: by
comparison modern school games dominated by masters seem to
have far less educational value. Boys also had the chance to take
initiatives. For instance in 1860 the Captain of Boats accompanied
by the Captain of the Eleven approached Dr Goodford and
suggested some sensible reform: Check Nights and the Oppidan
Dinner (a party for swells at the White Hart in Windsor) should be
abolished, with their tradition of excesses; in return the High
Street should be in bounds in the summer (obviating the need for
wet-bobs to shirk on their way to the river), the top wet-bobs
should be given leave from Saturday Absence as the Upper Club at
cricket already was, and the VIII should be allowed to row at the
Henley Regatta. This triumph of good sense was apparently more
easily envisaged by the young than by their governors. Also boys
initially ran the Rifle Volunteer Corps, though, as already noted,
before long Masters were needed to provide continuity.

Again, it will be clear that despite many restrictions boys had a
remarkable degree of liberty, particularly as they grew beyond the
need to attend long hours of Pupil Room. This time must often
have been wasted, but it could be used to take extras in subjects
outside the normal curriculum and it could be used by boys to
educate each other. A much smaller proportion of a boy's time was
occupied by planned activity than any school would permit
nowadays – though of course modern schools face pressures from
external examinations. Johnson saw the value of freedom; boys
should not be moulded – in his *Hints for Eton Masters* he wrote,
'Do let them alone sometimes: trust them to the sun and air and
their chosen companions . . . I write my hints for men who love
freedom more than power . . . who in school are content to have
pupils, and do not aim at having disciples.'[12] A.J. Balfour, the
future Prime Minister, who was not distinguished as a schoolboy
but whose promise was discerned by Johnson, wrote, 'If Eton,
through my own deficiencies, failed to supply intellectual inspira-

tion, it did not fail to supply opportunities; and this from my point of view was perhaps even more important'.[13] Freedom with opportunities encouraged those who wanted to be educated.

Even in matters of dress the school was libertarian, but the pressure to conform almost created a uniform; new boys who arrived unfashionably clothed suffered grave embarrassment. Older boys wore morning coats and hats of varying styles – the School only insisting on a white tie (the academic symbol) and a hat. Younger boys wore jackets, again the characteristic upper-class fashion of the time, until such time as they thought size and status permitted man's attire. No school rule, only fear of mockery, dictated the transition. Boys for some odd reason did not wear overcoats, in any weather, until a few years later some individualists decided to challenge the taboo; there was no official policy and consequently no objection; the wearing of overcoats became general, and Maude KS, for example, arrived back with a dark green coat.[14]

The degree of liberty permitted inevitably was taken for licence by some, and the attitude to work meant that indiscipline in the schoolroom could also be a problem. In both cases the standard medicines of the School remained written poenas and flogging. There was certainly less flogging than there had been, and probably many boys escaped all chastising – not necessarily the most virtuous. Shirking, so trivial and technical an offence, could earn a flogging – though boys could escape by claiming that it was first fault (a ploy which might be successful more than once). Alfred Lubbock was flogged a good deal when he was about 14–15, but in almost all cases it was voluntary, in the sense that he preferred to play games than to do his work, and that he then preferred to be flogged than do the consequent poena. This suggests that most boys did not find the punishment painful. The Lower Master did indeed mean to hurt, but the Head Master apparently relied on the disgrace rather than pain as the deterrent. Probably the ritual accompanying flogging was more objectionable than the punishment itself: in the Lower School the floggings were public. Yet there was no particular shame in the boys' minds in being 'swished', and therefore the punishment was not effective with most.

One type of attitude which we would condemn was an arrogance towards those of lower social order. Boys would pick fights

with cads, or they would bombard passers-by from the immunity
of their houses; and this was thought to be amusing rather than
reprehensible. Boys did have warm friendships, for example with
individual shopkeepers, but in general outsiders were neither
respected nor treated with compassion. This was a regrettable class
attitude. Within the School, except for the distinction between
Collegers and Oppidans, attitudes were more egalitarian. A merit
in fagging was that it might place the son of a duke under the son of
a parson. Nor were boys' political ideas rigidly conservative; after
all Gladstone was an Old Etonian and much admired. There were
non-Tory Masters too, such as Johnson who was an unorthodox
(because sentimentally imperialist) Liberal. This element of political openness was not, however, matched by willingness to question
social conventions. That is illustrated by Etonians' subsequent
careers – even those who developed sharply critical attitudes and
became reformers operated within the accepted professions.

Yet the conventions which boys so readily picked up from their
peer groups were not by any means all bad. Boys did learn from
each other a degree of tolerance and an ability to get along with
each other. To quote Johnson again, from a passage hardly in those
graduated terms which he extolled:

No one, who has not known the modern representatives of
Eton, can easily conceive, how little masters have to fight against
in the tempers and habits of those who come to them from
refined and highly-cultivated families. Such is the gentleness and
serenity of their bearing, so fine is their perception of what is
due to others, so deeply impressed are they with the sense of
honour they owe to their homes, that a man may be tempted
almost to think, that there is no need of his vigilance and no
scope for his exhortation.[15]

It must indeed be a tribute to the School that boys were
generally happy there. We hear of occasional boys who ran away
and of others who were withdrawn. But when one remembers the
problems inherent in adolescence there would seem to have been
only light casualties. By the time boys came to leave Eton, there
was perhaps a danger of excessive nostalgia – particularly for those
who experienced the golden glow of a final summer half with its

pastimes and its parties, and everywhere around them the haunting physical beauty of Eton.

The expense of leaving was considerable;* contributions had to be made to pay for the festivities, books were exchanged with friends and with Tutors, money was given to boys' maids and to the Head Master, and a final 'Vale' might be written:

> I go, and men who know me not,
> When I am reckoned man, will ask
> What is it then that thou has got
> By dredging through that five-year task?
> What knowledge or what art is there?
> Set out thy stock, thy craft declare.
> Then this child-answer shall be mine,
> I only know they loved me there.†

* Robert Pierpoint wrote to his father, just as he was leaving in 1864, asking for £44 or £45 (say £1,600 today). This covered ten presents for adults, as well as paying off musketry and boating bills, and journey money.

† This is a cheat: the poem was written not by a boy, but for one by William Johnson ('A Retrospect of School Life', 28 July 1863, published in *Ionica*).

CHAPTER TWO

Reform

ETON IN 1860 may have been a complacent institution, but it was
soon to be shaken by criticism and enquiry. In May 1860 a letter
appeared in the *Cornhill Magazine* signed 'Paterfamilias' (in fact
one Matthew Higgins, an Old Etonian whose time at Eton had
been brief). This letter regretted that the improvements which
could be observed elsewhere in English education had not been
made at his old school, 'Harchester'. In December 1860 another
letter revealed the identity of Harchester. Eton was inefficient
because it was understaffed, and the high salaries of the Masters
were therefore only acquired by the deprivation of the boys.
Cheaper but better Masters could be hired if the School were not
tied to King's. Even fagging reflected the greed of the Tutors who
thus saved on servants' wages. Another letter followed in March
1861.

Apparently the Provost considered writing a reasoned reply in
the *Cornhill Magazine*, and a defence appeared in the *Saturday
Review*, possibly by Goodford.[1] On 2 February 1861 the Eton
Society debated the wisdom of responding to Paterfamilias; thirteen to twelve were against. There was, however, almost universal
condemnation of the tone and substance of the letters, though it
was plain that some members of Pop were aware that improvements to Eton were conceivable.

No doubt they were influenced in this by a much more
damaging attack upon Eton contained in a lecture delivered by the
Etonian judge, Sir John Coleridge, to the Tiverton Athenaeum.[2] It

seems remarkable that the citizens of a small Devon town should wish to hear about the state of Eton, but they did, and the publication of the lecture (3 September 1860) gave the criticism national circulation. Sir John was much more moderate than Paterfamilias, and spoke from a position of recognized affection towards Eton. 'I am its advocate, I own; but for the time its judge also.' The Tutors were overworked, and too much drawn from King's. The non-classical assistants had inferior status to the Tutors, and French, Maths, and Science (and perspective drawing) should be taught more thoroughly. Even classical scholarship was in decline: there was a poor standard among the Oppidans in particular. The number of Fellows could be reduced to save funds which could be used to build classrooms and a new library, or to provide more scholarships. In short, much though he admired Eton, he felt that it must examine itself to safeguard the standards to which the rulers of the country were trained.

For the defence, principally against Paterfamilias and to some extent against Sir John Coleridge, William Johnson published two pamphlets, acknowledging that Eton had its faults, but claiming that moves were being made internally towards reform. There was need for more Masters and new schoolrooms, and for enhanced status for the mathematicians. Collegers were more successful than Oppidans in Classics now, but this was because they were competitively selected rather than that the Oppidans' standard had declined. Regulation and control of the boys' leisure time and the pastoral relationship of the Tutor were carried as far as they could be carried without violating the principles of the School's constitution. This reply was not the official School line, but a moderate restatement of Eton's values, with directions in which Johnson himself would welcome reform. Interestingly he did allow that Rugby was a better school, at least in part because it provided systematic study of History.[3]

Other hostile authors followed into print, including Henry Reeve in April 1861, a contributor to the *Edinburgh Review*, writing anonymously. He renewed the criticisms of the Fellows made by Lord Brougham's Committee in 1818 – that they were effectively milking the College's funds, so that capital was not available for improvements. The attack on the Fellows was indeed well justified, and on 2 May 1861 the Eton Society, in a debate in which they showed a surprisingly complete grasp of the financial

positions of Masters and Fellows, voted unanimously that it would
be advisable to send down a Commission to Eton to enquire into
the uses to which the Eton funds were put. Clearly those dreary
sermons had alienated the boys from the Fellows, while they were
loyal to their Tutors.*

In the same year the *Westminster Review*, the principal organ of
the radical middle class, attacked Eton in a very different vein.
Eton was guilty of self-love: Masters taught that success at Eton
was an end in itself, and this induced a moral childishness and
snobbery. The social as well as the intellectual attitude at Eton was
at fault.[4]

The intellectual climate of the time meant that the criticism
found a receptive audience. The public were impressed by the
educational ideas of Dr Arnold, of which admittedly they often
had an inaccurate grasp – for his ideas were represented in a
distorted form in the immensely popular *Tom Brown's Schooldays*,
published in 1857. They realized that Eton had been less affected
by Arnold than any other great school, with its absence of a
prefectorial system and its indifference to direct moral training.

The Liberal government decided to appoint a Royal Commission under Lord Clarendon to enquire into the administration,
finance, and curriculum of the public schools. The newer schools
were not examined, rather Eton, Winchester, Westminster, Harrow, Rugby, Charterhouse, St Paul's, Merchant Taylors', and
Shrewsbury. These were all endowed schools attracting the sons of
gentlemen, which is the general sense in which the term public
school was taken at that time. They offered a liberal education –
directed to general intellectual culture, in the eyes of their defenders, rather than 'narrowly' technical; they lacked the modern
departments of some recently founded schools such as Cheltenham
and Marlborough. It was expected that Eton would be the
principal target of the Commission, and so it turned out.

The Commission lost no time in getting to work. Appointed on
18 July 1861, it met four days later. Besides Lord Clarendon, who
had been privately educated, there were two Etonian Commissioners, Lord Lyttelton and Sir Stafford Northcote, and four others.
The Chairman himself dominated the Commission, but he re-

* The President, R.A.H. Mitchell, a future Master, thought that the Fellows
should invite Commissioners down: 'If a man must take a shower-bath, the water
doesn't fall so cold upon his head, if he pulls the string himself.'

garded Lyttelton very highly. From Eton's angle Lyttelton was regarded as too impartial, and Northcote was known to be ineffectual: it was not thought that Eton would have any champions within the Commission.

First the Commission drew up a series of printed questions sent to all the schools, and they did not start examining witnesses until the summer of 1862. By then Provost Hawtrey had died (27 January 1862). At his last Founder's Day banquet in College Hall, he had expressed his mortification at the agitation against Eton, and it was perhaps merciful that he was spared the visitation of the Commission. He lies beneath a substantial monument towards the east end of Chapel.

Lord Palmerston apparently assumed that the Head Master should automatically succeed as Provost and, without consultation, advised Queen Victoria accordingly. Dr Goodford was reluctant to give up the larger income that went with the headmastership – he had a large family – and did not think himself ready at the age of only 50 for the more relaxed life of Provost. He felt, however, that he could not refuse the royal bidding, and thus he became Provost.

The choice of a new Head Master was difficult. The Lower Master, W.A. Carter, was not well enough regarded as a scholar, and knew his own limitations: an external appointment was not wanted. Instead the Fellows persuaded their latest recruit, Edward Balston, to take the post. He was 44 years old and of the Kentish middle class. He was a Colleger in Keate's time, and had a very happy and successful school career, winning the Newcastle Scholarship, playing in the cricket XI, and becoming President of the Eton Society. He returned to Eton in 1840 and was immediately successful as a Tutor. His house attracted an aristocratic clientele, and did well at games. His fine presence – Queen Victoria is said to have thought him the most handsome clergyman in her kingdom – his courtesy, his kindness, and his generosity enabled him to rule his boys without harshness, though it would seem he did not have the fire to bring out their best intellectually. His father urged him before he went to Eton: 'Always remember, Edward, that you are not a gentleman.' Yet in fact he was one of the most gentlemanly of all Head Masters, and recognized by the boys as such.

In 1850 he had married Harriet Carter, the daughter of a Fellow soon to be Vice-Provost, the brother of the Lower Master in 1862.

Thus he was connected to one of the ruling dynasties of Eton.
Indeed in 1853 his name was mentioned as a possible alternative to
Goodford, when Coleridge, his former Tutor, was ruled out as too
High Church. Coleridge and his family connections no doubt
helped to secure Balston his Fellowship, and now they leant on
him to resign his Fellowship and accept the Headmastership. He
was also the choice of *The Times*. Nevertheless, for all his qualities
he had one great disadvantage – he did not want the job. Yet he
yielded, and with unconstitutional speed was admitted Head
Master on 25 February. The speed was justified since he would
have to face the Commissioners, with whom he had no great
sympathy, in July.

On 3 July 1862 the Commission visited Eton. Bursar Dupuis,
said by Kegan Paul to have threatened to drive them off with a
horsewhip, was evidently restrained.[5] The next day questions on
the basis of the written evidence began in London, at first directed
to the Provost and Bursar, who were supported at different times
by the Registrar, who handled routine College business, and by Mr
Wilder. The management of the College property and the conditions of Collegers were the first subjects. It cannot be said that the
Eton team performed well: they seemed unprepared for the most
obvious questions.

The College authorities showed themselves lacking in professional managerial skills: the Fellows audited the accounts themselves; they did not show in the accounts the fines (premiums)
which they divided among themselves; there was little evidence of
active management. The Commission was aware of the potential
gains from the development, just begun, of Eton's Chalcots estate
on Primrose Hill in London, and was anxious that the College
should obtain the full benefit of it. Did the Fellows regard fines,
which would certainly be obtainable at Chalcots, as part of the
property they held in trust for the College? They did not. All they
could say was that the fines had been divided among the Fellows
since records were known. Though the Statutes urged the Fellows
to live by their stipends alone, the practice had not been specifically forbidden. When capital was raised by subscription for new
building they contributed. No reasoned defence of the financial
arrangements was offered: perhaps none was possible. It was with
some relief that the Fellows could answer questions about the
conditions of the Collegers – how generously had the hardships,

which they themselves had borne as boys, been ameliorated! But even on this topic it was plain that wealth had brought less improvement to the younger members of Henry VI's Foundation than to the Fellows. Furthermore, the distinct Choir that the Founder wanted had ceased to exist, the College only contributing to the Choir shared with St George's.

The Commission turned to the position and powers of the Provost and Head Master. Both Goodford and Balston claimed that the Provost was not a limitation on the Head Master's freedom, but that the presence of the Provost resulted in useful consultation, and was not a real barrier to reform. Later witnesses from the ranks of the Assistant Masters argued on the other hand that many useful proposals had foundered on opposition from the Provost. No doubt a Head Master sometimes found it convenient to tell his staff that he could not do what they wanted, not because of his own conviction but because of the Provost's, regardless of whether the direction and strength of the Provost's views had actually been tested. Still the weight of evidence makes it clear that the Head Master consulted more with the Provost than with his assistants, and paid more attention to the Provost's wishes. This inevitably made for inertia.

The Provost also had to answer questions which might have been reserved for the Head Master had he been of longer standing. Eton had relatively fewer Masters than the other schools investigated: could he defend the understaffing? He replied that for recent appointees he had introduced limitations on the number of pupils a Tutor could take, though he had respected the vested interests of senior men. He thought divisions of forty no problem, but he admitted that taking a large number of pupils was more taxing. When Commissioner Vaughan argued that consequently understaffing was more objectionable in a school where tutorial work was so important, he had no answer – indeed, he pretended not to see the relevance of the point.[6]

Other matters were then brought up to which the Commission was to return with subsequent witnesses: the limitation of Tutors to Etonians – the Provost would approve the appointment of a non-Etonian if there were no good Etonian available, but he knew the Eton men and they would know the character of the boys; the low status of the Mathematical Masters – he felt that they did not command more status, and they were not all Etonians; the arrangements for French; the moral tone of the school; and the near-absence of a monitorial system.

The Head Master followed. His answers loyally supported the Provost's, and it was clear that at least between Goodford and Balston there would be no awkward division. In some respects he presented a more positive defence of Eton *vis-à-vis* Rugby; his answer when asked why he did not follow Dr Arnold's example of regular preaching in Chapel seems wise to modern readers, less uncritical in their view of Arnold:

> If I may be allowed to express an opinion, I should say that Dr Arnold was not an everyday man; and it does not follow that what he achieved is attainable by all other Head Masters. I should also be disposed to question the results of his preaching, eminently successful though it is said to have been. I think the religious character formed by it was not so genuine as it should have been... What I have noticed in Eton men has been an absence of all mannerism, if I may so call it, a freedom of ostentation in the conscientious discharge of what they consider their duty as Christian men.[7]

Balston could speak with some authority, for he had two Rugbeian brothers.* He also offered a defence of the tutorial system as against the monitorial system of discipline – in that it allowed boys scope to lead without the possibly corrupting effect of power, and gave the Tutor a real individual influence with his pupils.

There were some matters on which Dr Balston was open to change. He did not like the system of 'leaving money' as a source of his income. He was willing to countenance curricular change. Perhaps it was more important to introduce the teaching of English than of French, which could be learnt away from school, though he was not averse to making French compulsory in the Upper School. It was more necessary, however, to raise the level of Classics first, and there was a problem of 'want of time' available into which French could be introduced. That was a routine excuse offered by all conservatives: perhaps it was more relevant to note the want of time in the Head Master's week to think creatively about the possibilities of change. Probably pressure of time was

---

* Balston was a poor preacher, and constantly needed to clear phlegm from his throat.

also responsible for the limited managerial grasp shown by the Head Master, who seemed curiously uncertain of what was happening throughout the School, though perhaps that was also a consequence of the independence of the Tutors in so many areas.

Other witnesses were to offer another reason why French could not be introduced compulsorily – there was no one who could teach it, for Englishmen would have bad accents and Frenchmen were frankly not up to it. 'Is there not something in the disposition of English boys, and especially of Eton English boys, so utterly repugnant to Frenchmen that it would be impossible to teach the French language in class?' So said Edward Coleridge to Provost Hawtrey shortly before his death. 'Sorry as I am to own it, I am obliged to confess that I think it so', replied the Provost.[8] If this seems blimpish, consider that Coleridge's testimony also includes this moving credo, which explains how Eton education may have transcended the system of the time and how the tutorial relationship could have meant much to so many:

> There must be a constant conviction that there is hope for any boy whatever he may say, whatever he may do and whatever he may think. That conviction of hopefulness breeds a necessary sympathy between the teacher and the taught; that sympathy once inspired begets influence, and influence good. You thus possess a power of drawing out whatever elements there may be in the boy's nature, and not only by bringing them out by your own exertion, but of putting into him as it were a power of teaching himself, which I consider to be one great end, if not *the* great end of public instruction, namely, to make the boys teach themselves.[9]

Coleridge also displayed readiness to reform in some sensible directions.

There is no need to rehearse the evidence, written and oral, given by Assistant Masters. They offered recommendations for reform that have later been adopted, together with a defence of the best aspects of Eton which does credit to the intelligence and open-mindedness of many, particularly among the young Masters. This in turn indicates that Goodford made some good appointments, and it also probably witnesses to the influence of William Johnson, whose own evidence shows a clarity of thought lacking in his superiors. His suggested reform to the governing body was an

approximation of what Eton now has, as indeed was his proposal
that the Provost should be a retired statesman. Generally speaking
the Masters registered their own particular interests, the Mathematicians wanting a higher status for themselves, and Mr Tarver
wanting better conditions for French. He described himself as 'a
mere objet de luxe';[10] he saw the need to teach both grammar and
oral French, but he made no particular claims for French literature.
Perhaps the most critical was Mr Walford, recently returned to
Eton after teaching at Harrow. He wanted reforms in the classical
syllabus, with more emphasis on argument and on essay writing –
and in this he was tackling a serious embarrassment to Eton, that
despite the near-monopoly of Classics, Etonians did not stand out
as classical scholars at University.

There were other matters that the Commission pursued tena-
ciously, not only with Masters, but with young Old Etonians and
with a Colleger in his first year. What was the moral tone of the
school? Was there much drinking? Was fagging abused? Was there
bullying? How great was the division between Collegers and
Oppidans, and how harmful was it? The witnesses, almost to a
man, defended the school. Henry Macnaghten KS maintained that
fagging was not intolerable, even in College where there were few
fags, so long as the fag did not mind having his meals late; the
Commission was very reluctant to accept his lack of complaint. On
other matters they found more adverse evidence: boys' opinion
was not hostile to drinking though it was to drunkenness; boys
could lie to Masters in small matters (have you prepared your
construe?) though not in large; Oppidans and Collegers were
enemies when young, but the fault was on both sides, and they
grew together. Oppidans respected clever Collegers, but with the
sad result that they did not think to compete equally in classical
prizes. On bullying the Commission did have one clear complaint
– an MP's son was bullied, but the damage inflicted on him was not
helped by his removal from Eton against his wish, and the
misinterpretation of what seems to have been fairly characteristic
teenage rebelliousness. Other witnesses, adults and boys, knew of
the occasional case – the most quoted being, as they pointed out, in
monitorial College rather than among the tutorial Oppidans.
Public opinion was said to be decidedly against bullies, but some
Masters agreed that an improvement would result from the
dismissal of over-age boys working in divisions well behind their

contemporaries. If they were weeded out, that would also improve the motivation among Oppidans.

External evidence did not really cancel the internal evidence. The Dean of Christ Church regretted the idleness and ignorance of some Etonian students, but acknowledged that the Etonians suffered more from the temptations of wealth. On the other hand a Tutor of Trinity Hall distinguished the happy and natural relationship he had with Etonian pupils. At Sandhurst Etonians performed well enough, but they often lacked the Mathematics needed at Woolwich.

In its report the Commission was kinder to the schools than the critics had hoped. The final paragraph of the general report showed that the public schools had won round their judges, though individual comments make it clear that Eton scored less credit than other schools, in particular Rugby:

Among the services which they have rendered is undoubtedly to be reckoned the maintenance of classical literature as the staple of English education, a service which far outweighs the error of having clung to these studies too exclusively. A second, and a greater still, is the creation of a system of government and discipline for boys, the excellence of which has been universally recognized, and which is admitted to have been most important in its effects on national character and social life. It is not easy to estimate the degree in which the English people are indebted to these schools for the qualities on which they pique themselves most – for their capacity to govern others and control themselves, their aptitude for combining freedom with order, their public spirit, their vigour and manliness of character, their strong but not slavish respect for public opinion, their love of healthy sports and exercise. These schools have been the chief nurseries of our statesmen; in them, and in schools modelled after them, men of all the various classes that make up English society destined for every profession and career, have been brought up on a footing of social equality, and have contracted the most enduring friendships, and some of the ruling habits of their lives; and they have had perhaps the largest share in moulding the character of an English gentleman. The system, like other systems, has had its blots and imperfections; there have been times when it was at once too lax and too severe –

severe in its punishments, but lax in superintendence and prevention; it has permitted, if not encouraged, some roughness, tyranny, and licence; but these defects have not seriously marred its wholesome operation, and it appears to have gradually purged itself from them in a remarkable degree. Its growth, no doubt, is largely due to those very qualities in our national character which it has itself contributed to form; but justice bids us add that it is due likewise to the wise munificence which founded the institutions under whose shelter it has been enabled to take root, and to the good sense, temper, and ability of the men by whom during successive generations they have been governed.[11]

Certainly there were general recommendations made, some of which seemed particularly applicable to Eton. Most important was the reform of the governing bodies, and a new definition of their powers and responsibilities. This is roughly the area controlled by Eton's present Governing Body:

(a) the terms of admission and the number of the school;
(b) general treatment of the foundation boys;
(c) boarding-houses; the rates of charge for boarding, the conditions on which leave to keep a boarding-house should be given, and any other matters which may appear to need regulation under this head;
(d) fees and charges of all kinds, and the application of the money to be derived from these sources;
(e) attendance at divine service; chapel services and sermons, where the school possesses a chapel of its own;
(f) the sanitary condition of the school, and of all places connected with it;
(g) the times and length of the holidays;
(h) the introduction of new branches of study, and the suppression of old ones, and the relative importance to be assigned to each branch of study.   (General Recommendation III)

The Headmasters on the other hand were to have:

the uncontrolled power of selecting and dismissing assistant masters; of regulating the arrangement of the school in classes or divisions, the hours of school work, and the holidays and half holidays during the school time; of appointing and changing the books and editions of books to be used in the school, and the course and methods of study (subject to all regulations made by the Governing Body as to the introduction, suppression, or relative weight of studies); of maintaining discipline, prescribing bounds, and laying down other rules for the government of the boys; of administering punishment, and of expulsion.   (V)

The Commission recommended a broadening of the curriculum while retaining the primacy of Classics. French, History and Geography were to be compulsory at least in part of the schools. Music or drawing were to be available for the young. All these were at any rate represented in schools – only Eton had no compulsory French. Also Science was to be included, which was not taught within the official curriculum of any public school. The Commission was impressed by the example of German education, and did not believe that the subject was as unteachable as the classical establishment asserted.   (VIII–XXII)

With one member dissenting the Commissioners recommended a qualifying Entrance Examination and regular broadly based examinations which would have to be passed for promotion, and where failure to achieve promotion by a particular age would lead to a boy's removal.   (XXIII–XXV)

The Commission also suggested a general simplification of fees, with the abolition of the special charges, so much a feature at Eton.
(XXVI–XXVIII)

Many of these points were taken up in Special Recommendations for Eton. Most importantly they recommended a new Governing Body – a Provost and fourteen Fellows, of whom five would be paid a salary and thus carry on an element of the existing body. The Provost should not need to be a clergyman and should not be responsible for the parish of Eton. A small choir, with education for the boys in it, should be re-established. College livings might be given to Assistant Masters in orders as a pension for meritorious service, but there should be no automatic claim. Most importantly, 'The practice of granting beneficial leases should be discontinued as speedily as the means at the disposal of the College will permit, and . . . all fines received hereafter should be brought into the general accounts of the College.'

(Special Recommendations 1–15)

There were small improvements recommended for College, narrowing the age of entry, abolishing charges, improving the diet.

(17–19)

Turning to the School, they recommended a School Council to ensure consultation between the Head Master and his assistants. They recommended a small reduction in the number of boys to 650 in the Upper School (and 150 in the Lower School); they thought the size of the School encouraged factions. They wanted a systematization of the entry of Oppidans, and (in effect) a competitive entry to the Upper School, with no preference to those already in the Lower School. Sixth Form should be increased from twenty to thirty, and the Upper School subdivided with competitive promotions. No divisions should be more than thirty. The choice of textbooks and course of study should be revised, with a reduction in the time spent on Saying Lessons. The position of other subjects was defined and improved. External examiners should be invited in. Widespread reforms were suggested in the prizes and scholarships available, with the introduction of Exhibitions to stimulate the Oppidans.   (20–52)

There should be a daily morning service in Chapel, and the curious timetable could consequently be reformed. The choice of preachers should be wider.   (53–56)

Classical and Mathematical Masters should have equal chances of being Tutors in charge of boys' houses. Junior Masters should be given rooms, but not allowed houses until they had proved their competence.   (57–62)

Finally they recommended that the system of shirking should be abolished.   (64)

All in all, it was a striking package of reforms, and the Commission took some trouble to prove that it was financially possible, and that a timetable could be constructed to include the new subjects without overloading. The most surprising element, in the sense that it was not foreseen by even the most forward looking of masters, was the recommendation to introduce Science.* The

---

* W. Johnson, who was himself an amateur of science, and who presented a fine telescope to the school, thought that boys could not actually study a science because of the demand for time and for expensive laboratories; perhaps Botany was an exception. He did, however, think boys could make a literary study of scientific knowledge and theory – except that experience had taught him that Geology 'cannot be received by mere boys without a violent disturbance of their religious belief'.

difficulty of finding teachers for modern subjects, which had been widely discussed, was really only to be resolved by introducing the subjects, and thus training men for the future.

Though the Commissioners had endorsed the way of life to be found in public schools, and had not ruled between the tutorial system so dear to Eton and the monitorial system for which other schools claimed advantages, they made proposals that by implication almost totally condemned Eton in other ways. Paterfamilias for one was delighted. In another article for the *Cornhill Magazine* he wrote that:

> Their verdict as respects Eton is simply this: that of all the public schools of England, it is one at which the British parent pays the most for the education of his child, and from which he receives the smallest educational return for his money. The great majority of the Eton boys are stated to lead easy pleasant lives spending their time chiefly in the playing-fields and on the river, and not a little of it in the public houses and taps of the neighbourhood – and if they are so minded, but not otherwise, acquiring a faint smattering of the classics in the intervals of play.[12]

The Eton Society was less impressed. In a lengthy debate on 26 April 1864 they particularly opposed the suggested reduction of the size of the School, and what they assumed would be a consequent reliance on a competitive entry system to the School. Perhaps the dislike of intellectual competition was to some small extent evidence that the Commission was basically correct. Yet the Commission, and Paterfamilias, did miss the opportunities for self-education that existed in the old liberal arrangements. As Pop saw, the ever-rising popularity of the School was an indication of the virtues the Commission could not see. The boys also thought that they were not ill-taught in Classics, and were particularly angry with the hostile evidence of the Dean of Christ Church, 'famous for two things, one his antipathy to Eton, the other his being totally unable to keep any sort of order in his own college'.

The attitude of Fellows and Masters was doubtless mixed, and they were not obliged to react straightaway. For the Commission had only power to recommend, and legislation was needed if

Public School Statutes were to be amended. A short Act required at once approval by the Commissioners of new members of governing bodies. Then a Bill was introduced into the House of Lords early in 1865, but it was sternly resisted by Conservatives led by Lord Derby, now Prime Minister, who felt that such little reform as was needed could be left to the schools themselves. By the time the Bill had passed through a Select Committee it was much amended, but eventually in 1867 it reached the Commons and became the Public Schools Act of 1868. Rather than legislating change directly, the Act adopted the softer option of establishing Special Commissioners, headed by the Archbishop of York, to oversee the creation of new governing bodies and new statutes.

Thus direct change as a result of the Clarendon Report was slow to occur. Nevertheless Balston did introduce some desirable changes, which strengthened the hand of Lord Derby in the Lords. The most necessary improvement of all was begun by Goodford in 1861 but carried through by Balston: the building of thirteen new schoolrooms – which constitute now the front of New Schools. Balston himself contributed generously. The Classical Masters gave up their salaries for five years (remember the salary was only a small part of their emoluments) in return for a hand in the design. Balston also, in line with the priorities stated in his evidence, began some revision of the teaching of Classics: the *Eton Latin Grammar* which had been in use for 300 years disappeared.

When the Report appeared, meetings were held with Classical and Mathematical Masters which resulted in some small measures. French was introduced into the Lower School; Stephen Hawtrey as head of Mathematics was placed with proper seniority among the other Assistant Masters. Summer Trials were moved from May to July, with an end to the chaos that used to occur when promotions were made at the Fourth of June. Shirking was abolished despite the opposition of die-hards, and the bounds were relaxed.

In the summer of 1867, the decision was made to separate the Choirs of Eton and St George's and a Dr Hayne was appointed as organist. This was something of a personal triumph for a very remarkable lady, Miss Maria Hackett, who had been campaigning for fifty years for choristers in cathedrals and schools. Her pamphlet, *A voice from the tomb seriously addressed to all Etonians who revere the memory of the Founder*, pointed out that the choristers had been given much the same rights as scholars and a promise of preferential promotion for able boys into College. The Public Schools Act did not include the clause placing choristers statutorily on the Foundation for which Miss Hackett lobbied so hard, but nevertheless by 1869 arrangements had been made at Eton which satisfied her. Sixteen choristers were boarded in Dames' houses and given a good education in French, Latin, and Mathematics, besides religious and musical instruction. The boys were also given a stipend. Miss Hackett was delighted. For Etonians there was some improvement in the music in Chapel, and more importantly the post of Precentor, responsible for the music, henceforward attracted a better class of applicant.[13]

While this reform was going forward a more significant change was occurring. Dr Balston decided to retire. He had only accepted the headmastership as a stopgap. He could see that uncongenial reform would inevitably come, and his temperament was averse to a fight. He handed in his resignation at the end of June 1867 to take effect at the end of the year, and this was successfully kept secret to the great advantage of the Fellows in their search for a successor. There was no obvious Old Colleger and King's man to appoint from within the staff, and the most distinguished outside the School, Thring, Headmaster of Uppingham, was not interested in a school where he could not know all boys personally. So the choice fell on either Warre, aged 30 and recently ordained, or Dr Hornby, aged 43 and newly Second Master at Winchester. They had much in common, both Oppidans who had gone on to Oxford, both distinguished rowing men, and they were indeed already friends, though very different in character, as was to become clear. The Fellows selected Hornby, probably on the grounds of his greater maturity, but no records of the discussions remain.

Hornby had been an Oxford don and was therefore a good enough classicist to continue with the primary traditional function of teaching Sixth Form, but nevertheless he was also known to favour some changes in the curriculum. With the Public Schools Act nearing the end of its legislative journey, and with public opinion widely expecting some reform, there were indeed advantages in choosing someone with a different background from recent Head Masters. On the other hand, Hornby was not really by nature a radical, and those who liked the old ways could feel that he was not going to alter the character of Eton. That character was indeed going to change before the end of the century, but Hornby at least was one who responded only to outside pressures and then reluctantly. Warre, as it transpired later, would have been more ready to impose his own vision, his own version of educational excellence.

Hornby proceeded to reform timetable and curriculum. First of all he introduced a short daily morning service in Chapel, and abolished the afternoon Chapel on whole-holidays and half-holidays. At 9.45 a.m., after Chapel, a new period in school was substituted for Pupil Room work. This permitted the introduction of two compulsory periods of French in all but the top blocks and two periods of Science in some lower blocks. Most imaginatively the senior boys (the First Hundred, as they were to be called) were allowed to select their own Extra Study from a variety offered; thus it came about, for example, that Political Economy was taught by William Johnson some eighty years before Economics became regarded as a suitable school subject. History, Chemistry, Italian, German, and Geography were also available.

The broadening of the curriculum for the First Hundred was admirable. The school notebook of Reginald Brett* in his last year contains notes on Ancient History, on French History *in French*, on the Art and History of sixteenth-century Italy (and much other History), on Economics, and on George Elliot [sic]. It is clear that the abler boys were given a wide cultural background along with the Latin construe and verse composition which remained their main diet. There is some Mathematics, but it is Algebra at a fairly rudimentary level.[14] The education of the less able who did not reach the First Hundred was not so inspiring. As in many other schools, an Army Class was started to prepare boys for the competitive entry to Woolwich and Sandhurst, with rather more Mathematics taught. It was really pure cramming, and even so, many boys still needed to be coached after leaving Eton to reach the army's level.

The more varied curriculum required more Masters, and some improvement in the conditions on which the non-Classical Masters

* Later the second Lord Esher. More about him in the next chapter.

were employed. Hornby raised the number of Assistant Masters from thirty to forty-four, and made a little progress towards putting all on equal terms. Unfortunately most of the new Masters and new subjects were not a total success; they needed careful fostering in their early days, but instead they were still graded as second-class by most of the Eton establishment. Dr Hornby also abolished leaving money and some extras. No longer did noblemen have to pay double entry fees. Instead a fee of £8 per half for 'School Instruction and Charges' was substituted. The expensive practice of boys giving leaving-books was also forbidden.

While these reforms were being introduced, the Fellows were continuing to negotiate the nature of the new interim Governing Body with the Special Commissioners. On the whole the ideas of the Fellows were acceptable, but they did not secure the promotion of several of their own number as they hoped, and the Provost of King's was included against their wishes, despite the absence of any Eton representative on the King's Governing Body. The composition of the interim body approved in 1869 was thus:

the Provost;

the Provost of King's

four members appointed by Oxford University, Cambridge University, the Royal Society, the Lord Chief Justice;

one member appointed by the Head Master, Lower Master and Assistants (but not one of themselves);

four co-opted members.

It was not immediately evident that the paid Fellows were doomed, for the interim Governing Body wanted at first to replace itself by a Provost and Fellows who would include four residential, paid Fellows as well as the Provost. This expensive scheme was countered by other schemes proposed by the Special Commissioners. From May 1870 to July 1871 plans proliferated, some of which attempted to unite College and School by giving Masters a greater say in the governing of the College. The Head Master stressed the principle that the ordinary management of the School should be in the hands of himself and the Masters, subject only to the ultimate control of the Governing Body. That could be a Provost and a Bursar, both paid, together with a number of unpaid Master-Fellows. This scheme would have been too cosy. The Assistant Masters, when consulted, thought that there was no need for the

Provost to be in orders, and that the office of Visitor could be abolished.*

Cutting through the arguments, the Special Commissioners finally revived an earlier idea they had not previously approved, that the Governing Body, to be called the Provost and Fellows, should in future be the existing interim Governing Body, with Fellows unpaid, and this was finally agreed and approved by Her Majesty in Council in November 1871. For some time it was necessary to speak of the New Governing Body, because the old Fellows were left as a parallel but powerless body, drawing their stipends, occupying their residences, and preaching their sermons. Balston and the Lower Master, Durnford, were allowed to join them. Only the Provost and W.A. Carter, the Bursar, were included in the New Governing Body. The Winchester Governing Body has the same pattern as Eton's.

At the same time new statutes were approved which defined the College officers, including a Vice-Provost who was to be elected annually. The Provost could be a layman, though he was still to be a member of the Church of England. The Head Master was to be appointed by Provost and Fellows† and entrusted with running the School. His discipline was to extend over the Collegers, as had not been the case previously. New rules were created for the election to King's Scholarships – open to all British boys between 12 and 14. The Provost and Fellows were empowered to award pensions to Masters, an important provision since the old reward for Masters of the paid Fellowships and College livings would no longer be generally available.

Once the new statutes were approved, the next step was for the New Governing Body to draw up regulations for the framework within which the School should be run, and these were issued at the end of July 1872. The first regulations established rules for admission of Oppidans: a boy had to be aged between 11 and 14, to be able to pass papers in Latin, French, Arithmetic, English, History, and Geography (and the Head Master had discretion to

* The Visitor, the Bishop of Lincoln, had power to deprive the Provost if he were guilty of disgraceful conduct or grave neglect of his duty. About this time the Bishop of Oxford, 'Soapy Sam' Wilberforce, endeavoured to acquire the role of Visitor, Eton having been transferred from the diocese of Lincoln to Oxford. He was defeated.

† Initially by the New Governing Body.

1. 'A Bird's-Eye' view of Eton about 1860. The Head Master's house backs on to the Slough Road in the left foreground. Beyond it is the triangular Weston's Yard, with the Collegers' New Buildings and the School Library on the left, and Lower School with Chamber above to the right. Barnes Pool can be discerned below the Church; in 1860 it was the supposed boundary of the School.

2. Dr Goodford

3. Dr Balston by George Richmond

4. Dr Hornby

5. Rafts in the nineteenth century with the Brocas beyond. Boathouses were privately owned until the Eton College Boat House took them over in 1910.

6. A swimming passing, *c.* 1870. The artist may have allowed himself some licence with top hats, but contemporary photographs confirm the accuracy of the depiction.

7. William Johnson

8. The original score for the Eton Boating Song sent home from
India by Algernon Drummond (AHD) to William Johnson

9. Leaving portrait of Edmond Warre
by George Richmond

10. Oscar Browning

11. Boys gathered around the newly installed Burning Bush, *c.* 1865

12. A boy in the School of Mechanics, 1993

13. The Carpentry Shop in the School of Mechanics, 1886

14. Dr Warre by J.S. Sargent. 'Warre, booming out our names from the Chapel steps, is entirely a great and fine, not entirely a solemn sight – and he is Eton.' Percy Lubbock

15. W. Evans's House Group, 1871. 'Beak' Bickersteth sits to the right of the table adjacent to the right-hand pole of the pergola. Behind him is Edward Lyttelton. Robert, the sixth Lyttelton brother, stands above the table and Alfred, the eighth, most loved and most brilliant, sits second from the right. Three other future government ministers are Herbert Gladstone, seated left of the table, Charles Lacaita, next to him in the centre of the picture, and Henry Hobhouse on Gladstone's right.

16. Harcourt Gold's Room in 1895. He was Captain of the Boats, and therefore the grandest boy in the School. The Ladies' Plate is displayed among many other trophies.

17. Cricket on Sixpenny, *c.* 1900. Beyond the Fives Walls (built in 1871) can be seen the Drill Hall and the old Gas Works.

18. Lord's, just before 1900

19. Shooting – wholly illegal. This group of friends poached 2,260 head of game between October 1908 and July 1910. It is good to record that rather more than the average number survived the War, perhaps because of their skills, and became related by marriage.

20. A Shooting VIII in Corps Uniform in the late nineteenth century, posed in front of the colonnade of School Yard

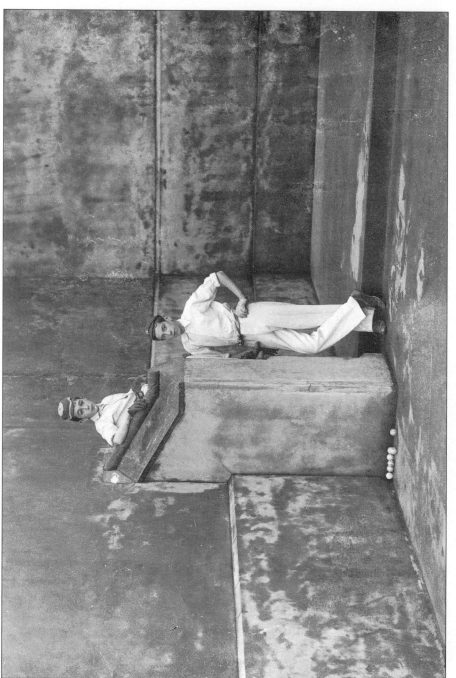

21. Two boys in a Fives Court. Though two can play, it is properly a game for four.

22. The Eton College Hunt in 1888

23. The Head Master's Schoolroom, c. 1881. The flogging block on which boys knelt for punishment is on the left.

24. The first laboratory at Eton, c. 1895. Dr Porter is on the extreme left.

25. Royal Gratitude. In 1882 Queen Victoria was attacked outside Windsor Station by a lunatic. Two Eton boys, Gordon Wilson and Murray Robertson, rushed to her rescue, and one quick-wittedly knocked the revolver upwards with his umbrella (which is preserved at Eton) – so that the shot passed harmlessly through the roof of her carriage. The Queen summoned the entire school to Windsor to express her thanks. No adults were present other than her ladies-in-waiting. The heroes stand behind the Queen. The Captains of the School and the Oppidans are before her, thanking her for her words. The sketch was made by a boy, H.H. Robertson-Aikman, at the request of a newspaper.

add other papers). Boys had to progress to Fourth Form and Fifth Form by certain ages, and had to leave not later than the end of the schooltime in which they were 19. The First and Second Forms, and thus the old Lower School, were abolished in 1871. The Lower Master was left in charge initially of the Third and Fourth Forms.

Regulations then laid down rules for the boarding of Collegers, which was to be free, and of Oppidans. Oppidan boarding houses should in future be kept by Masters only, and should be opened or extended only with the consent of the Head Master and sanction of the Governing Body. The number of boys in a house was not to exceed thirty-five, except with special permission, and each boy was to have his own room, except that on application two brothers might share. The Head Master was to nominate new Housemasters, taking account of seniority. Charges for boarding were fixed at £99 or £85 p.a. according to the quality of the houses (rather than as to whether they were run by Classicists or not). Boys were to pay through the Housemaster £24 p.a. to a newly established School Fund, and a 5-guinea admission fee. The Classical Tutor was to receive 20 guineas per pupil, but was limited to forty pupils.

A committee of three Masters ran the School Fund, and reported annually to the Governing Body. The School Fund had to pay the Head Master 6 guineas p.a. per boy and the admission fee for each boy. Other sums were allocated for classical, mathematical, modern language and Science instruction. The School Fund had also to bear various costs such as Rates, though it was the intention of the College to pay these expenses when their funds permitted, as also to pay to the School Fund and to Tutors the approved fees on behalf of the Collegers. The College finances were not yet, however, in a position to allow this, since income was not rising quickly and the old Fellows were still entitled to a salary.

Chapel services remained under the control of the Provost, though the Head Master had the right to preach or appoint preachers. Holidays were regulated (fifteen weeks for lower boys and three extra days for Fifth and Sixth Form). A programme of instruction was approved, and an examination for the First Hundred boys was set up each July, which came to be called the Grand July. This had external examiners appointed by the College, and numerous prizes depended on it. (Also from 1875 boys began to take the Higher Certificate which enabled them to matriculate at Oxford and Cambridge.) The Head Master had power to expel boys for misconduct, but had to report each case to the Governing Body. He had under his authority all the Masters, and there was to be not less than one to every thirty boys. His control over the teaching and management of the School was reaffirmed.

To a considerable extent these regulations confirmed what was the existing practice. They did not entirely satisfy the Public Schools Commissioners, for in 1874, when new Statutes, Schemes and Regulations were approved by the Queen in Council for the seven great public schools, regulations were added, the main force of which was to ensure better provision for Science. A proper proportion of marks in Trials was fixed for Maths and Science (except for the senior boys). There was to be at least one Mathematical Master for each one hundred boys in the School, and one Science Master for each two hundred taking Science. There should be facilities for some specialization. The Governing Body was to provide Science laboratories, and so on. Similar regulations were enforced at the other public schools.

The authority of the New Governing Body was immediately challenged. There was an agitation by Housemasters and Dames to raise their boarding charges by £11 p.a. Costs had risen a little, and improved standards were being introduced. They claimed that parents wanted these and were willing to pay. They gained the Head Master's sympathy, but their case was rejected by the Governing Body. The Masters now proposed to send a circular to parents suggesting that they pay an extra £12 p.a. The Head Master reported this to the Governing Body, who again refused permission. The Housemasters nevertheless went ahead with their circular. The Governing Body thereupon caused their Clerk to write a frosty letter simply headed 'Reverend Sir' to the Head Master for allowing this circular; after a summary of the facts came the message:

> The Governing Body cannot but express their surprise and regret that . . . any such circular . . . should have been issued, and if possible, they still more regret that this should have been done with your knowledge and consent . . . As this Circular cannot now be formally withdrawn, it should be considered as issued without authority, and of no effect . . . Any application for an increased charge for the Board and Lodging of the boys should be made in the first instance specifically to you, and, if approved

by you, should be communicated to the Governing Body, without whose sanction it will be dereliction of duty for anyone connected with the School to take independent action.[15]

The episode was important, for the Governing Body had successfully asserted their control, and were never again directly challenged. After a discreet interval the Governing Body met a deputation of Masters, and at the end of 1873 the Provost wrote accepting some of the case for higher boarding charges, but pointing out the danger of luxury and the higher costs at Eton than at other schools. A £6 annual increase was authorized.

Of all the changes that had been brought about the reform of the Governing Body was the most significant.* It permitted the administrative reform of the School as well as of the College itself. The College did not immediately become richer, but its income was to grow with the development of the Chalcots estate, and its wealth was in future to be used for the benefit of the School rather than of the Fellows. A source of funds for capital expenditure became available. Also as the College gradually acquired the buildings in which the boys were boarded, the Head Master was able to extend his control over the Housemasters.

The Finance Committee which operated the School Fund did a good job. The new changes permitted the Classical Masters to be paid increased salaries, an initial £300 reducing to £150 as they acquired pupils (who still paid their Tutors 20 guineas) and took on houses. A pension fund was also soon established. The Finance Committee could report that a young man 'with a full pupil room at Eton, is in a much better position than he could hope to be in any other profession within the same time, and better off than most of those senior to him in the same profession'.[16] Considering that his pay before taking on a house would be in excess of £30,000 in today's values, we can accept their judgement.

Larger salaries were paid to the modern Masters, as they came to be called. These were now no longer in receipt of the same volume

---

* The Governing Body was able from the first to secure good men to serve on it. The third Earl of Morley deserves particular mention. As Lord Boringdon he was one of the most eloquent speakers in the Eton Society of 1860, and he gave evidence to the Clarendon Commission. He served devotedly on the new Governing Body from its inception until his death in 1905. He was a much respected politician.

of fees for extras since their subjects had entered the timetable. Their salaries ranged from £400 to £600, that is up to about £20,000 in current terms. The inferior position of the non-Classical Masters reflected their continued lower status, and the widening of the curriculum was not therefore an immediate success. Boys generally thought the modern subjects less well taught and frequently behaved badly in school. It was possible for Oscar Browning, at first an advocate of curricular reform, to argue that the change had caused an overall loss.[17] Width of education meant shallower education. He also argued that some of the freedom that the best Tutors had to direct their cleverer pupils individually into wide courses of reading had been sacrificed. The curriculum was not so loaded, however, that boys could not still find time for private study. Some of the individuality was preserved in the Extra Studies for the First Hundred, which must be judged the most successful innovation.

The early progress of Science in particular was disappointing. In 1869 a Chemistry laboratory was built where James Schools now stands, said to have been modelled in brick on the Abbot's kitchen at Glastonbury. This was built by the generosity of Dr Hornby. In 1875 a Natural History Museum was started from the subscription of the Science Masters; into it was moved a magnificent collection of British birds bequeathed twenty-five years previously by Provost Thackeray of King's, and up to that point kept in the School Library. Then in 1879 Professor T.H. Huxley, the great champion of the theory of evolution, became the Royal Society's appointed member on the Governing Body, and Science gained enhanced prestige. In 1881 new Physics laboratories were built on South Meadow Lane. Though many boys laughed at Science, an increasing number began to be impressed.

The new professional choir also struggled to gain acceptance. Hornby was against it, largely because he would have liked to use the funds supporting the choir for other purposes. Initially the lay clerks were not available for all services and Hornby tried to set up a voluntary choir. The records are very incomplete, but Dr Hayne apparently met with such obstacles that he resigned, and his successor did not last long. Only when Dr Barnby came in 1875 was Eton music properly established. It seems likely that the plan to board choristers never came to fruition. The abolition of the Lower School in 1871 would have made their presence in boarding houses anomalous. Later there was pressure to set up a boarding house for choristers, but it was never successful, and the boys therefore lived locally and were not educated by Eton.

From the Etonians' angle, what was notable was how little their lives had been changed. They had to go into daily morning Chapel, but they were spared the afternoon Chapel on holidays and half-holidays. They had more schools but fewer saying lessons. To their relief their freedom was largely unscathed. For some time yet Eton was to be what the boys themselves, not their Masters, made of it.

CHAPTER THREE

Fresh Beginnings, Sad Ends

WHILE THE REFORM of institutions and curriculum made its slow progress, new initiatives were being made within the School, none more fruitful than the foundation of the Musical Society. This occurred in a manner typical of unreformed Eton. A group of enthusiastic boys in Evans's arranged a singing class: Spencer Lyttelton, E.W. Hamilton and Hubert Parry were the leaders. With the help of two Masters, William Johnson and C.C. James, an organ was purchased by subscription in 1862 and placed in the largest room in New Schools where the Society could practise. They engaged a new Music Master, John Foster, the alto at Westminster Abbey, who by degrees raised the standard of the music performed. From Hubert Parry's account the practices were often larks, and perhaps for that reason did not enjoy Dr Balston's approval, let alone support. Nevertheless a School Concert was put on at the end of 1864.

By this time Parry was already composing music fluently: 'October 30th [1865]. By God's mercy I got into Pop today. Eddie [Hamilton] and I played right through my Sonata, it being now finished.' With the encouragement of Sir George Elvey at St George's he secured his musical degree at Oxford before leaving Eton, and the Cantata which he wrote as a degree exercise was performed at his last School Concert in 1866.

December 8th. My Cantata was performed this evening. When we began one of the violas had not appeared, so we had to do without him, which was rather a pity. I couldn't induce the 'cello and basso to begin the 1st chorus properly, and in the bass solo, my soloist did not begin for two bars after the proper time. Next came the tenor solo, but unfortunately Gibbons, who was to have sung it, was nowhere to be seen. We waited some time and at last a message came that he was in bed. Stephen Hawtrey made a speech, and we had to go on to the soprano solo, which was a great blow to me, and moreover the said solo was well murdered.

However, my misfortunes were redeemed in the last chorus which went like bricks, and when we got to the end the audience were very good and applauded furiously and the consequence was that the whole thing was encored.

This time the Overture went quite to perfection – our viola had also come back – the first chorus went well, the bass solo very respectably and the 2nd chorus pretty fair, and then Snow,* in the most gloriously kind way, came and sang the Tenor solo from my score. He sang it delightfully and was encored. Then came the soprano solo, and then the last Chorus went like nothing ever went before. It was perfectly sublime conducting it, and it quite astonished me it went so well.

Then the audience applauded furiously and the last chorus was again encored, and this time all the audience stood up. It was so jolly. And then when it was over, everybody came and shook hands with me and congratulated me. Such a row, such an excitement. Dr Elvey was delighted, and talked about playing again when I have it done at Oxford.

And Mr Cornish was very kind about it, and said it was quite a pleasure to sing in it. So passed off the first performance of my Cantata, and I hope it won't be the last.

Parry's diary catches the amateurish spirit of this first revival of Eton music. We should not think of Parry as a pious musical prodigy: by his own account he could misbehave and abuse trust – as other boys might do:

October 10th [1864] . . . then we sang Mendelssohn's *Nightingale* which is quite lovely. Altogether I spent a most enjoyable

---

* The Revd H. Snow, a Master, was physically large. He subsequently changed his name to Kynaston, and became Headmaster of Cheltenham.

evening, which I ended up with wine and sandwiches and biscuits in my dame's room. When everybody else had gone Lyttelton and I stayed on and finished the bottles and afterwards adjourned to bed. I had a smoke while I was undressing and went to bed, contented if not perfectly happy.

Later in his last summer, returning from watching the Winchester cricket match, '[we] smashed the window of the carriage, and we tore our blinds to pieces and threw lemonade bottles out of the window'. The next morning the Station Master appeared to complain, but the Head Master (shamefully) took no action. Parry's animal spirits gave him the energy to work hard and read widely, as well as play and compose music. And yet perhaps his greatest joy was in games. 'November 8th [1865.] When I was changing in my room Phipps came up and told me I might get my Field shirt!!! Glorificous!' Next year he was Keeper of the Field:

November 17th. The School played the London Amateur Athletics. A most magnificent match. We were in splendid form and won by two goals and two rouges to nothing. Sturgis, Sally Alexander, Jim Tait, and Calvert all played sublimely. I kicked a goal by a shot. Ferguson got a most awful shin from Mitchell, which bared the bone of his leg, and I fear he will not play again ... Sally got kicked all over the face, and came out of a bully with his face streaming with blood, and most of us got shinned and considerably knocked about.

Parry's school days are characteristic of the unstructured life of Eton in Dr Balston's time. Although it was many years before Eton music reached its present eminence, the School continued to produce a remarkable number of notable composers. The arrival of Dr Hayne as organist in 1867 to replace Mitchell, said by Parry to be deeply incompetent, was not in itself a great improvement, but Hayne's successors must have had some gift of inspiration.

Parry's triumphs both in the concert hall and on the games field were recorded by another innovation, the *Eton College Chronicle* which first appeared on 14 May 1863. Although there had been many Eton magazines before, nothing previously had achieved the continuity of the *Chronicle*. Intended at first to be issued fortnightly, it developed into a weekly magazine carrying up-to-date accounts of activities at Eton. The first editorial announcement was charming: 'To parents of Eton Boys our Paper will prove an especial boon, as it embraces the whole School, and will in great measure supply the place of letters, which often from press of circumstances and time, Boys omit to write.' Early editorials discussed the Report of the Clarendon Commission, and defended the level of scholarship in the School. There were lists of prize-winners, reviews of plays and concerts and of Speeches.* There were letters, which were sometimes used to further causes, for example, by inviting subscription to the new Fives courts in 1864 or to a rackets court in 1867. Inevitably, however, a large part of the paper carried reports of games; indeed in the Lent Half when there were few games, the editors could not always produce fortnightly numbers. It would be absurd to blame the editors for writing more fully about the final of the house sides than about the Newcastle Scholarship, but one impact of the *Chronicle* was undoubtedly to lionize the games players, and to increase the orientation of the School towards games rather than work.

At this time too the most loved, the most nostalgic celebration of any school's sport was written – the Eton Boating Song. On 9 January 1863 William Johnson wrote to his brother: 'I could not get to sleep last night, being engaged in making a half-humorous, half-sentimental boating song for the 4th June; and when I wake I find it burning to be written out.' On 5 June 1865 (actually that year the day of celebration of the Fourth) a periodical called the *Eton Scrapbook*, edited by two of Johnson's pupils, printed seven stanzas under the title, 'Song for the Fourth of June'. Meanwhile Johnson had sent the poem to another old pupil, Captain Algernon Drummond in the Punjab, who composed the famous tune (with help from a cousin, Miss Evelyn Woodhouse). Originally a barcarole, it became widely known as a waltz before the end of the century.[1]

Another lasting institution had its origins in the final half of Balston's reign: a decision was reached at Mr Warre's house on 1 November 1867 to found the Ascham Society, initially of fifteen Masters (including mathematicians as well as classicists). Its purposes were the discussion of 'the theory and practice of Education with a view to the improvement of existing methods, and the discussion of literary and scientific subjects with a view to

* Speeches are recitations by Sixth Form, designed to show off their abilities to the Provost and Fellows.

self-culture'. In turn members read papers which were then debated with varying zeal, the interests of the subjects discussed fighting against the extreme lateness of the hour – for the meetings began somewhat unpunctually at about 10.15 p.m. after House-masters had put their houses to bed (remember the first school had been at 7.00 or 7.30 a.m.). The first paper was read by Johnson on the teaching of Ecclesiastical History, and there were others which related closely to the work of the schoolmaster; in general these stimulated most discussion – Cornish's paper on the admissibility of drawing and music to the Eton curriculum ended after mid-night. Early papers aimed at self-culture were surprisingly often on scientific topics, and they testify to the width of interest of the best Masters at this time. The Ascham Society continues to this day, though it does not meet as frequently as in the early years. Its influence in stimulating the Masters has certainly been consider-able, and thereby the Ascham Society has enriched the boys, though most boys remain unaware of its existence. At the twen-tieth paper, again from Johnson and this time on the teaching of Political Economy, the reader entertained the Society at Mr Skindle's inn at Maidenhead, and it has subsequently become the practice of the Society to accept gastronomic as well as intellectual refreshment from its readers: thus the Society has brought pleasure as well as improvement over the years.

At the end of 1867, as mentioned earlier, Balston resigned the headmastership and took up the living of Bakewell. He had retained his popularity with the boys. The leaving portraits by George Richmond of his pupils, which still hang in the Head Master's dining-room, testify to the affection he aroused. When Alfred Lubbock came to say goodbye to him: 'I had a long talk with him, and when I had deftly secreted the bank-note on the table, and had received his leaving-book, I felt quite down in the mouth, and shall never forget his "God bless you, Lubbock", as I shook hands with him for the last time.'[2] This reaction would seem to have been typical. Yet he is not usually regarded as a notable Head Master. Generous and benevolent, a good teacher himself and successful in appointing new masters, friendly to acting as well as to sport, it might seem that he deserves kinder judgement. He ran Eton on perhaps too light a rein. He should have been more aware of what could be advantageously reformed. Ultimately, however, it is his abdication which has condemned him. He believed, with some reason, that certain values that the old Eton represented were threatened by reform, but he was not prepared to fight for what he cherished.

That much survived was partly owing to the accident of a certain similarity in character between Hornby and Balston. Yet where they differed the comparison is nearly always favourable to Balston. Certainly Hornby handled the immediate problems of reform successfully. His management of the introduction of daily morning Chapel won especial praise: some of the Masters favoured prayers in their schoolrooms, which would have been a very poor substitute. But it soon became clear that Hornby was lamentably idle and irresolute. At the end of his first Summer Half he left Eton to pursue his favourite sport of mountaineering with much undone, including the payment of the Masters' salaries – still his responsibility. Johnson wrote to his brother:

> The worst of him is that he is dilatory and ever idle ... He is a makeshift creature, a jury mast, not an organiser, easily pushed to and fro. He set to work resolutely in Trials to change [places] according to marks: then he [had] three sons of noblemen plucked. [So] the Tutors go and press him to reverse the decision, giving reasons for excepting their lordlets, and he gave in, after it had been made public that the brats were plucked.[3]

Luckily Hornby enjoyed the support of Warre, not at all jealous despite the disappointment of his hopes. In Johnson's words: 'He takes it heroically and is a Vesuvius of zeal, throwing out a new core of project and fervour every day.'[4] It was generally judged that most of the good initiatives of Hornby's time owed much to Warre. Yet Hornby did rouse himself at times.

Most dramatically he brought about the departure of William Johnson. Enough has already been said to indicate that Johnson was in many ways the outstanding master at Eton. He required high standards of his pupils, encouraged them, and wrote perceptively about them. His tutorial letters set a new standard and have been the pattern for others to follow.* His extraordinarily well-

---

* The long series of letters about Dalmeny, later the Prime Minister, Lord Rosebery, survive and are extensively printed in Robert Rhodes James' biography. In a letter to Cornish, who was teaching Dalmeny, Johnson wrote the famous judgement, 'He is one of those who like the palm without the dust'. His letters to the boy's mother were equally perceptive.

stocked mind enabled him to teach on several layers at once; in a classical division he could illuminate the text with historical or literary comparisons; his critical judgements were stimulating if eccentric. He was the subject of anecdotes such as endear Masters to the young: how he shortsightedly chased a black hen down the street thinking it to be his hat; how if the Windsor garrison marched past his Pupil Room, he would rise and cry to the small boys, 'Brats: the British army!' (As he engagingly wrote in his diary, 'Love me, love my England'.)[5]

Yet this man who could so profoundly influence boys within his sphere was known to have faults. He had favourites, and with these boys his conduct was often foolish. It was not just that he easily fell in love with boys whom he was looking after, but he had a voyeuristic delight in encouraging the affections of boys towards each other. It was possible to rationalize his behaviour by reference to the Platonic conception of the younger boy learning wisdom and good behaviour from the reciprocated love of an older boy or man. Johnson, however, was honest enough with himself to know that his own feelings were disturbed by sexual passion. His story is of considerable interest in itself, but it is also a case-study of the many schoolmasters who have been great teachers because they have been romantically drawn to their pupils. How are we to weigh possible emotional damage against the encouragement to achievement? Johnson's story also throws light on sexual mores at Eton, at a time when homosexuality was coming to be regarded as far more of a problem than it had been even as recently as 1860. Furthermore the story can be traced surprisingly fully, though not completely, through Johnson's fitfully kept journal and through the records of Reggie Brett. In 1868 Johnson's great love was for Francis Elliot, the son of the British Ambassador in Constantinople, but he was also drawn to Brett (who was not in fact his pupil) and to Williamson, a younger boy known as the Chatterbox, and subsequently as Chat. Both Elliot and Brett also loved Chat, who certainly returned their affection. On 25 January, when Elliot was away delayed sick in Thrace, Johnson records:

> I have been cheered by the inexhaustible charms of the Chatterbox. [After a day in London] we dined snugly in the Mousetrap*

* The Mousetrap was his study, named from Frederick (Mouse) Wood, an earlier much-loved pupil.

-- then did I lament a little that I had to go to pupilroom. Chatterbox became prettily weary and half silent, having a touch of sore throat, and he was altogether in the minor key: but I went to bad Latin, and he to his bath, the first use of the new bathroom; he looked in upon us when at work, in dishabille: I heard Edward Lyttelton observe to his brother that I was in an unusually good humour.

In the summer when Elliot was cox of the VIII and in the shooting XI, Johnson could write of 'domestic happiness with Elliot'. On 29 May: 'He looks as well as a seraph, he lives that serene and precious life of pleasure without passion which is so strange and adorable to me.' During the summer holidays, he stayed with the Williamsons. '[I] wish they would not put on the dinner table two candlesticks in a line between me and the boy.'[6] He wrote to Brett: 'I long to dream of Elliot. I adore him more every week.'[7] He warned Brett that indiscreet letters were a problem with mothers – advice that he hardly heeded himself.

In October 1868, Brett recorded in his diary:

After supper at the Trap Elliot and I lay together on the long morocco sofa. He put his dear strong arms round me & his face against mine. Chat, not very well, sat near the fire ... WJ in the big red chair close to our sofa. We kept calling for Chat, & finally he was lifted on to us, nestling in between Elliot and me. My arms were round him, & Elliot's were round him and me. Chat liked our both breathing in his ears. We kept on repeating this. All things must end.[8]

Jealousies were unknown in this unusual ménage, and Johnson apparently took pleasure in Elliot and Brett kissing. Whether in fact Johnson himself embraced his young friends is uncertain – probably he did not.

By July 1869 when Elliot was again in the VIII but grown to be an oar, Johnson could look back:

I can't conceive how any one can love a son or daughter or wife more than I love [Elliot] and I get away from myself in thinking about him much more than I could if he belonged to my family. I have seen him this last year, as I never saw any other person, openly and unreservedly loving his two boy friends and enjoying their love: in truth we have all of us lived together in such intimacy and joyousness as never was described or thought possible: he has been the central object, the greatest of us, in the greatness of courage, endurance, unselfishness, self-control, righteousness, temperance, severity of taste, simplicity, plainness of speech, frankness, reserve. Day after day his lovely countenance has been getting more expressive and more tender and kind.[9]

But now it was time for Elliot to leave – the tragedy of the romantic schoolmaster.

Just possibly the intensity of life with Johnson was more than some boys could stand, because the number of his pupils was falling off. We should not read too much into this; he was not well placed to secure pupils since he was not a Housemaster, and anyway he was now 46, no longer so young. Johnson wondered whether it was time to move on. He recalled the possibility in 1860 of his becoming Professor of History at Cambridge. 'I had rather if a professor at all, profess political economy. But I am really a triple professor here – and get good classes and good pay – why go to Cambridge for so little.'[10]

In April 1870 Brett left. 'I am now no longer an Eton boy. Yesterday, I left the dear old place for ever as one of her members, not as one of her sons. The events of a sweet half have been leading up to this. I could hardly stand the last chapel . . . So many new friendships opened this half; to be dropped and lost for ever.' But not all were dropped, for he and Chat were to be guests together at Halsdon, Johnson's holiday home. On 12 April Brett records: 'I have kissed [Chat] in every room in Halsdon.' There were to be other visits to Halsdon and Eton in 1871. Then at the end of March 1872 Brett again visited Eton and Halsdon.

All was not well at Eton. There had been a number of sexual scandals. A boy in his first year, Probyn, had been sent away with four admirers. A friend of Brett's, Reggy Parker, was sacked with a young boy called Quicke, when Cornish, Quicke's Tutor, 'opened a foolishly written, affectionate note from Reg'.[11] It seems hard that the younger boys, presumably more sinned against than sinning, should also have been dismissed.

Chat and Beak (E.E. Bickersteth, a boy at Evans's of quite exceptional good looks) who both had left Eton during 1871 were also staying at Halsdon. On 9 April, a bleak note in Brett's journal records: 'Tute [Johnson] talked to me all the morning. He has resigned his Eton appointment and has offered to take me on here until June, then send me to Avranche with Elliot.'* Brett proved to be a good friend. 14 April: 'I am to stay with Tute and give up my Cambridge term. Tomorrow I go to town and Eton to arrange Tute's affairs.'

What had happened? We shall never know for certain. If Johnson was keeping a journal at the time, it was destroyed. Henry Salt, who revered Johnson, says that an indiscreet letter which Johnson had written to a pupil was brought to the notice of Dr Hornby. If so, it is unlikely to be a letter to any of the pupils mentioned here, for they continued to keep company with Johnson, which their parents would certainly have forbidden. Possibly, in the context of boys being sacked from the school, a parent argued to Hornby that his son could not reasonably be penalized when one of the Masters was encouraging similar behaviour, or even acting similarly; he may have had documentary support. At any rate, Hornby must have demanded Johnson's resignation. Earlier doubts about his future may have returned, for it seems that Johnson did not contest his case. He went quietly. At the beginning of the Summer Half, boys simply found that he had left. The Socrates of his time had drunk a gentler cup of hemlock.†

Some have thought that Warre pushed Hornby into action, others that Warre wished to save Johnson. It is not necessary to take either side. Certainly Warre had admired Johnson – the two men shared many values and Warre tried out ideas on Johnson as a rational critic. But years later A.C. Benson recorded that Warre spoke coldly of Johnson: he must have learnt and disapproved of what was happening in the Mousetrap. Indeed, if Hornby knew the truth, he could not have acted otherwise. There was moral danger in Johnson's conduct: Chat never escaped to a normal sexual life, Brett married the sister of a contemporary at Evans's but he continued to have homosexual leanings (even towards his second son). By contrast Reggy Parker, of whom Brett recorded at

---

* The resignation was known in Eton a few days earlier – as soon as most Masters had left.

† Brett's notebook contains a translation of Plato's Apology done with Johnson on 24 April. The Socratic comparison must have occurred to Johnson himself.

the time, 'Reggy Parker writes from Derbyshire where he is reading with the customary reverend mister ... he will probably die in India or live gloomily in semi-poverty',[12] was soon married. The difference was between the passing fling of a perhaps highly sexed boy, and the establishment of a sexual pattern encouraged by an influential figure.

Johnson's life moved into the shadows. In the summer of 1872 there was another tragedy; when he was on holiday in Germany with Chat and Beak, Beak died at the age of 18 of galloping consumption. Johnson, and still more Chat and Brett were devastated (though Brett when he heard the news first dashed to Beak's rooms at Cambridge to destroy any embarrassing letters, showing a glimpse of his future as political and social operator). In October 1872, Johnson resigned his Fellowship at King's, and changed his name to Cory. He became a non-person at Eton, his name removed from his textbooks, but many of his friends and pupils remained loyal. At the age of 55 he left Devon for Madeira for the sake of his health, and there he found a young wife who looked a little like Beak. They had a son and returned to England. He taught some girls who found him still a magical teacher, and he died with reasonable contentment in his seventieth year.

> And when I may no longer live,
> They'll say, who know the truth,
> He gave what e'er he had to give
> To freedom and to youth.[13]

The early 1870s were marked by what Edward Lyttelton, a boy in the School then and later Head Master, called 'a hideous amount of vice'. No preventive measures were taken; new boys were never warned; and then if detection came, expulsion followed. Boys' opinion was often on the side of those convicted. In 1871 a club called the Hallelujah Club was organized – 'the conditions of its membership are not fit for publication'.[14] Less harmfully there was an epidemic of pornographic photographs, presumably of young ladies.[15]*

The worries about homosexuality were doubtless behind other changes at Eton which were made by Hornby, and which were

---

* Alexander Radcliffe was asked by his Tutor, Warre, to open a suspicious envelope. Fortunately the photographs were of a different type, also popular at that time – they showed Masters' heads on animal bodies. Warre, mightily relieved, took them off to Chambers to entertain his colleagues.

generally regarded as evidence of his philistinism. Theatricals were stopped; games took on an increasing importance. Whether athletes are any less liable to adolescent homosexuality seems doubtful, to put it mildly, but that view was widely accepted at the time. Certainly on this matter Warre would have been entirely with Hornby. He had already used his influence to promote rowing, and to prevent punting and excursions up backwaters because of the moral hazards that he suspected.

Warre and other games-playing masters were soon to form a camp, opposed to another camp of intellectuals. The conflict between these groups was to continue, and was to cause a damaging deflection of energy. Athletes on the one hand, and intellectuals and aesthetes on the other, should rather see themselves as complementary in education. There is no necessary conflict for boys' time or interest. Boys who do well at games are often those who do best at work, and, as Parry's career demonstrates, musical excellence can coexist with a passion for sport.

The most active opponent of athleticism, however, Oscar Browning, thought that the tide in favour of the athletes must be stemmed. 'I give my opponents full credit for thinking that the manliness and even the morality of the school depended upon the adoption of their principles: but I thought then, and I think now more than ever, that they were mistaken, and that the only road to morality and good conduct lies in the recognition of the supremacy of the mind.'[16] Unfortunately Browning, usually known as O.B., was not an ideal champion of any cause. He was kind and generous but somewhat absurd – snobbish, tactless, and too humourless to see his own weaknesses. In practical terms he most usefully established a Literary and Scientific Society, to entertain distinguished lecturers (mostly literary figures such as Ruskin) from outside the School, and to hear papers written by the boys themselves. He stimulated music and debates in his own successful house, but more dangerously encouraged boys from other houses with cultural pretensions to find a haven with him.

One tutor, Wolley-Dod, who ran an indifferent house, complained to Hornby about a bright boy of his, George Curzon, being taken up by Browning. In fact, though O.B.'s instincts were homosexual, there is no suggestion that they were not at this time sublimated; indeed Browning was trying to raise moral as well as intellectual standards. But the Head Master tactlessly began his interview with Browning: 'So I hear Mr Wolley-Dod has a good-looking pupil'. Although Lord Scarsdale, Curzon's father, sided with O.B., Hornby ruled that Browning must have no further relationship with the boy during term-time. This episode in 1874 was not the first occasion of friction between the two men. Already Hornby had accused Browning of idleness in neglecting some of the routine tasks; there was some justice in this complaint, but only in the sense that Browning devoted more time to bringing out the latent talents in his pupils and those to whom he taught History. The Head Master even faulted the History teaching, because O.B. covered such dangerously modern topics as the French Revolution. Again in the earlier debate over boarding charges, though O.B. had supported Hornby against the Governing Body, he later prevaricated over the acceptance of the compromise settlement which it was Hornby's duty to enforce. He had also made unauthorized entry charges for furniture and so on. On individual issues the blame varied but Hornby could reasonably feel that Browning did not meet the Assistant Master's primary duty to assist his Head Master; on the other hand a bigger Head Master would certainly have found his way to mould this gifted schoolmaster into his team.

In 1875, a relatively trivial issue led to a final split. O.B. was guilty of exceeding the number of pupils and boarders allowed. It seems that he did fall into line but again prevaricated, for little reason other than that empty rooms were costing him money. In an explosion of pent-up anger Hornby sacked him. A friend of Browning's had recently been convicted of a homosexual offence, and Hornby continued to suspect Browning; but the reasons were never adequately stated or clear, and much sympathy remained with O.B. Some of the Governing Body felt that though Browning must go, Hornby should also offer his resignation. Others, including the Provost, felt that the Head Master's power over his staff, newly affirmed in the 1868 Act, must be maintained. Three of Browning's friends threatened to resign but were dissuaded.* Even a sympathetic judge such as Hugh Macnaghten could not but feel O.B. was responsible for his own downfall. 'He talked very injudiciously, and seemed to take a positive pleasure in risky situations.'[17] Austen Leigh, one of Warre's party, was less charitable, noting in his diary, 'I always thought him very insubordinate

* The Masters, Cornish, Luxmoore, and Ainger, were three of the best.

and unscrupulous, playing with honesty and sailing very near the wind, but his last offence seems to have been premeditated rather than executed'.[18]

So Hornby stayed and Browning left without any financial compensation. His income, he claimed, dropped from £3,000 to £300 p.a., and his excellent mother who had helped run the house was also inevitably turned out. Newspapers debated the issue and Knatchbull-Hugessen, whose wish to get a second son into Browning's house had helped to occasion his downfall, raised the matter in Parliament, but to no avail. Browning, lastingly bitter against Eton, was to play a valuable part in raising academic standards at King's, and in fostering adult education. His increasing obesity and undiminished snobbery made him too much a figure of fun to be a good martyr for the fight against athleticism. But where others gained, Eton had lost. Furthermore, even those who had welcomed Browning's departure were left uneasily aware that their security in their jobs was diminished.

Besides the conflicts between athletes and intellectuals, there was another possibly even more acrimonious divide – which came to be called the tutorial question. The Classical Masters, by acting as Tutors, enjoyed higher pay and status than others. The Mathematical Masters holding houses resented this, wishing to act as Tutors to boys in their own houses – with the control of boys' time, the right to send a boy to the Head Master for discipline, and the right to prepare boys for Confirmation. It was indeed illogical that if a boy had a Housemaster in orders and a lay Tutor, he should nevertheless have to look to the Tutor for spiritual instruction. In 1871 the Mathematical Masters expressed their grievances in a Resolution to the Governing Body. This was answered by a vigorous response from the Classical Masters: the tutorial system was a central feature of Eton education, the Tutor must be a man who could instruct in the boys' main curricular work, and that meant that the Tutors must be Classical Masters and have priority in controlling boys' moral and intellectual education. It would appear that some concession was made to the Mathematical Housemasters on discipline, but in 1873 and 1875 they were complaining again: parents regarded Tutors' houses as inherently better, and too often in conflicts between Tutor and Housemaster over a boy the mathematical man was having to give way to someone much his junior.

In 1881 the non-Classical Housemasters were complaining again: they should be the medium of communication with parents; their names should be printed ahead of the Tutors' in the School List; they should arrange religious instruction; they should supervise boys' work other than Classics, and have the right to switch boys from classical Private Business; they should receive reports of boys' work in school; and they should have the independence and right of access to the Head Master enjoyed by Classical Housemasters. The Classical Masters once more objected, and Hornby sided with them, particularly rejecting the claims to control non-classical work, and to provide religious instruction. Nevertheless, the Governing Body did direct that the Housemasters should be the medium of communication with parents, and that Housemasters should be informed of their boys' progress and conduct, and they should have control in their houses. These regulations were circumvented by the Classical Tutors still writing directly to parents, and by punishment tickets still going only to the Tutor. The Governing Body resorted to asking the Head Master to appoint a committee.

The committee proposed an uneasy compromise, giving the Housemaster more rights to information, and actually suggesting that a non-Classical Master could act as Tutor to boys in the top of the School who were not pursuing a fully classical curriculum, with some of the consequent financial advantage. (This was a small concession because it applied to few boys.) The Head Master was entitled to allow religious instruction to be in the hand of the Housemaster. From this compromise, it became Eton language to talk of a House Tutor and a Classical Tutor, who might be the same. The soothing use of the same word 'Tutor' was fruitful of much confusion – when a boy spoke of his Tutor it was not necessarily clear who was intended.

The compromise did not command general assent, and Hornby still sided with the Classics. He did allow the House Tutor priority in matters which were essentially House matters, but the Classical Tutor was to retain the direction of a boy's studies and the disposal of his time. In special cases only, for example with a boy of great mathematical ability, or in the Army Class, the Classical Tutor could be partly replaced by a non-Classic. In his letter to the Governing Body Hornby added his private convictions: that the tutorial system depended upon the boy being in contact with a man of superior character; that the Mathematicians frankly taught badly; that this was not a matter of status, and that they should not be fussing about status but improving their performances; and that Classical Masters should never be in a position where they might have to be subordinate to Mathematicians. It was easier to appoint Mathematicians than good Tutors, and the good Tutors with whom he had to work were in practice Classics. Hornby's views carried the day, but they did not end the dispute. The non-Classics retained their grievances, and so far as most boys and parents were concerned the Housemaster was always likely to be the more significant figure, since the house not the Pupil Room was the focus of boys' social life.[19]

Nor was this the end of Hornby's struggles with his staff. An almost farcical episode led to the loss of two of the more interesting Masters. The Revd J.L. Joynes, the Lower Master from 1878, was a quirky old Tory, who bred an even more eccentric radical son with the identical initials, who followed his father's career through Eton and King's, and then back to Eton. He and his brother-in-law, Henry Salt, were both good Tutors but were regarded suspiciously as freethinkers and radicals – not only about Eton but about the political economy of the country. Still more reprehensibly, they were vegetarians and fond of tricycling. In summer 1882 young Joynes, greatly influenced by the maverick American economist Henry George, met and travelled with him in Ireland. The Irish police arrested them as conspirators. The Government had to apologize to George as an American citizen, and Joynes wrote a brilliant account of the fiasco for *The Times*. When Joynes proceeded to go further by writing a book, *Adventures of a Tourist in Ireland*, Dr Hornby told him that he must choose between his mastership and the book. He accordingly resigned his post at the end of 1882 and published.

Salt did not follow at once, but when Hornby was replaced by Warre, and Salt foresaw no change in the character of Eton, he too resigned. Salt was the greater loss, a humorous man with views about education (such as opposition to corporal punishment) that would nowadays command fairly general assent. On the specific issue, the only excuse for Hornby was that Eton had already learnt to fear publicity in the press, on which Joynes was thriving. On all other grounds, the action was illiberal and Eton lost valuable diversity of opinion. Young Joynes and Salt were to become founder members of the Fabian Society. They were not Eton's only contributions to Socialism but, at this stage at least, Socialism was a polar reaction to what Eton taught. The only mitigating circumstance is that then as almost always the School did encourage individuality and allow boys to grow in different directions.

It was not only with Masters that Hornby had troubles. The early 1870s saw discipline as well as sexual mores in the School at a low ebb. On the Fourth of June 1871 revellers knocked down a shop sign near Barnes Pool in the shape of a ship. The shopkeeper, already unpopular, replaced it, with the word '*Resurgam*'* written on it. The boys regarded his act as one of impertinence, and on Election Saturday the sign and the shop were again attacked by drunken oarsmen returning from the Procession of Boats. When two Masters tried to intervene, one, the unpopular but respected Mr C.C. James, was subjected to yells of 'Stiggins' (his nickname), was hit over the head by one of his own pupils, and would have been thrown into Barnes Pool had he not been rescued just in time by his large and powerful companion, Snow. Boys were certainly punished on this occasion with lines, and in some cases flogging, and the Election Saturday celebrations were cancelled thenceforth with little loss.

This episode was partly premeditated lawlessness, though the attack on Stiggins was mob action under the influence of drink. It reflects no credit on the School, but at least Hornby took some action. He was not, however, an effective disciplinarian. He flogged fairly often and set lengthy poenas, but the poenas were seldom completed since it was still left to his manservant to check them. Sometimes he failed to act at all. A boy called Brooke had not written a Georgic set as a punishment by the Science Master, Madan, and was so abominably rude that Madan hit him. Thereupon Brooke knocked Madan backwards into his own chemical phials, and went off to report him to Hornby. Result: Brooke escaped scot-free, and Madan was required by Hornby to apologize to Brooke! It was surprising that Madan survived to become in time a successful teacher.†

---

* I will rise again.

† This story may be the origin of a lasting myth among Etonians, that they are entitled to hit back at a Master who strikes them. No doubt masters should not strike pupils, but a provoked master's blow is far more forgivable than a schoolboy's.

Meanwhile trouble was particularly prevalent at Mr Rouse's* small house where a number of disreputable characters were contemporaries. Their leader, 'Mad 'Unt', was the son of a Cabinet Minister. He was a great hunter, once catching a squirrel which he then released in Chapel; it climbed to the pinnacles of the gothic canopied stalls. His skill must have been considerable, for nocturnal excursions resulted in copious supplies of game which were strung up outside his windows, 'Hunt's larder'. He was as deadly with catapult or even a thrown stone as with a gun. On one occasion out after ducks or ducks' eggs at Ditton Park, he stripped to swim to an island. Interrupted by a keeper, he swam hastily to shore and ran, naked and pursued, the several miles back to safety at Eton. The popping of corks and other sounds of revelry frequently disturbed the night at Rouse's; and then one day these were outdone by a loud explosion when a room was destroyed by a booby trap, perhaps humorously intended for Pecker Rouse himself. Shortly thereafter Rouse's gang tried to protect one of their number who not surprisingly had missed school by over-sleeping, and they were eventually proved to be lying. Mad 'Unt and the worst offenders had to go. In a mock funeral with black crepe and a black flag flying, boys mourned their departure. It was also the end of Rouse's house.

Another well-attested but less dramatic failing was the addiction of Etonians to gambling. Boys frequented the races at Windsor, and felt it a challenge to go to Ascot and even to Epsom. Hornby did little to curb these breaches of School rules. Indeed he was, himself, increasingly absent from Eton except to teach and attend Chapel, or to call Absence, a half-holiday roll-call which had traditionally been undertaken by the Head Master, but which had little value when the Head Master knew few boys, so that absentees had only to arrange for a friend to answer. Hornby in fact left Weston's Yard, where Head Masters had lately resided, for Black Potts, the fishing cottage of the seventeenth-century Provost Sir Henry Wotton, situated half a mile down the Thames.

One problem in controlling the school was that there were still inadequate facilities for games in the Lent and Summer. A few new

---

* Rouse was a mathematician, a Fellow of Trinity College, Cambridge, but his scholarship was not matched by any practical ability as a schoolmaster. He was nearly always late for meetings of the Ascham Society, no doubt as he tried to ensure some sort of order in his house.

Fives courts were built on Sixpenny in 1870, and a new cricket ground was opened beyond the Jordan in 1873. Even then only some 150 boys could play cricket, and they were mostly the swells.[20] The boys of only modest ability who were not wet-bobs had little to do except window-shop. It was a legitimate criticism of the intellectual party that the best athletes spent excessive hours at games, without the School providing the generality with the exercise necessary for their health.

The Field Game in the Michaelmas Half did provide for all, though it was so rough as almost to be a danger to health.* Surprisingly the boys remained totally loyal to the game although the best footballers did participate away from Eton in the newly formed Association Football. Thus it came about that the Old Etonians not only entered the FA Cup but reached the final six times between 1874–5 and 1882–3, beating the Clapham Rovers in 1879 and the Blackburn Rovers, a professional club, in 1882. In 1883 they lost to another professional club, Blackburn Olympic, and thus were the last amateur team to reach the final. They used Field Game tactics of dribbling, concerted rushes, and ferocious tackling. When these tactics were countered by more sophisticated play, the Etonians nevertheless found themselves still in a position to help the development of the national game – most notably Lord Kinnaird, who became president of the FA.†

It is curious that the Old Etonians' football triumphs did not stimulate any serious playing of soccer at Eton. The year 1879, however, saw the development of a different useful leisure activity. By the generosity of Warre, a new School of Practical Mechanics and a Drill Hall were built. The School of Mechanics, which depended upon the subscriptions of boys, did not easily establish itself, but it survived and offered Etonians the kind of training on a voluntary basis which was to become fashionable for all a hundred years later.

The laxity and absence of leadership from the top in Hornby's time did encourage the development of boys' responsibility. From 1875 there seems to have been an improvement in the tone of the

---

* A game between Warre's and Browning's was apparently the bloodiest of matches, reflecting the animosity between the Tutors.

† Kinnaird was a terrible shinner; when his mother feared that he might one day come home with a broken leg, one of his fellows replied grimly, 'Never fear, ma'am, it won't be his own'.

School, and this was caused by the emergence of a monitorial system in the houses and in the School as a whole. It was in Evans's that the new pattern for running a house appeared. William Evans had always encouraged his boys to take responsibility; he had also provided his house with a library. When his daughters assumed control of the house, the managing committee of the library gradually grew in importance, and came to be called 'The Library'. The anxiety of the boys to prevent Balston and later Hornby imposing another Master on them appears to have pushed the boys towards managing the everyday affairs of the house and taking responsibility for its discipline. When Annie Evans died in 1871 and Jane Evans took sole charge of the house, she developed the institution – having The Library to breakfast with her every morning. Although The Library were self-electing, Miss Evans would influence their choice. A system of self-government had developed, which, even though it retained elements of barbarism, allowed the house to be one of the best run in the School, and bred a tremendous *esprit de corps*. In 1876 when Jane Evans was very ill, the house conducted itself with a success that astonished some of the Masters. When William Evans died on the last day of 1877, Hornby rightly decided that the house should continue as Miss Evans's, despite the Clarendon Commission's recommendation against Dames' houses. Gradually the Library system of control was adopted by other houses. A durable pattern of government had evolved.[21]

Meanwhile there were changes taking place in the boy management of the School. Pop was beginning to acquire more monitorial power and the Captains of the School and Oppidans were gradually losing such prestige and influence as they once possessed. George Curzon, Captain of the Oppidans in 1877–8, analysed the position in a long magisterial account of the duties of the post. The shift to more competitive examinations had led to the accelerated promotion of young, clever boys. Thus the top of the School List and Sixth Form tended to be occupied by a less mature, less influential type of boy. There were exceptions, of course, such as Curzon himself, who gave considerable thought to the reform of the School, bringing about, for instance, the publication of the various School funds for which boys were responsible (and they were not negligible in those days when individual boys still ran so many activities).

One questionable accompaniment of the developing monitorial system was the increasing use of the cane by boys in authority. There had always been cuffs and blows delivered, often on impulse, but the judicial, formalized beating was new, at least among Oppidans. It was probably an import from other schools. Often it was used effectively and responsibly, and the existence of an available and accepted sanction undoubtedly encouraged senior boys to act against bad behaviour. As early as 1867, in Balston's last summer, the Captain of the Oppidans was writing 'the best punishment for [refractory fags is] in my opinion, a good kicking, or a liberal use of the cane'. The good kicking was traditional, the use of the cane was not.

In 1875 a somewhat absurd episode ended with a probably illicit use of the cane. Two Eton parents (one Mr Quintin Hogg) arranged a service for the American revivalists Moody and Sankey, to be held in a tent on South Meadow. Mr Knatchbull-Hugessen, Oscar Browning's ineffective champion, complained to the Provost and Head Master, and indeed caused the matter to be raised in Parliament – surely, he said, the religious instruction given in College Chapel was adequate? Hornby declined to stop the service: such a course would be inconsistent with Etonian liberty. The senior boys were worried, not so much by the religious issue as by the fear of a disturbance. Some boys had got up a petition against the service; more alarmingly a boy in the VIII had torn down the petition, and was thought to be planning to lead an attack on the preachers with rotten eggs. The Captains of the School and the Oppidans arranged for this oarsman to be kidnapped by some strong boys in Sixth Form, since they did not believe he would obey unless forced; they then proceeded to assert their authority by each giving him twelve strokes. Meanwhile the service was at the last moment shifted to Windsor. Nearly two hundred Etonians turned up, but the service passed off without any trouble.[22]

The attitude of Hornby to the growth of monitorial authority, and to the use of the cane, was by no means clear. Evidently he shirked making a firm decision. In 1876, for instance, he encouraged the Captain of the School to carry out an investigation of another case of poaching in Ditton Park which led to the offender confessing and accepting a beating. It is also said that he permitted Pop to carry canes. In 1878, Curzon reported that members of

Sixth Form were entitled to cane boys in their houses with their Tutor's consent, or even at his wish; and that the Captain of the Oppidans and the Captain of the School could deal with cases of ungentlemanly behaviour, bullying and so on among the Oppidans and Collegers respectively. But in 1879, Curzon's successor states that:

> the head-master forbids caning or corporal punishment of any kind, yet when actually a case comes before him, he cannot help seeing the folly of his rule & has to shuffle out of it somehow or other. The pusillanimity & folly of this is only too apparent; fortunately very few know that he does not allow caning, so do not dispute it.

This Captain, King, regarded the diminution of old authority as actually being Hornby's work.

> Nobody regrets more than I do the present head-master's policy and the results it has led to. It has made the nominal authorities of the School [Sixth Form] quite distinct from the real authorities [Pop] & put Sixth Form and Pop in a sort of antagonism to one another. Whether the evil can ever be repaired is hard to say, certainly the present head-master will do nothing to mitigate the harm he has done.

One year later, the next Captain, W. Hobhouse, found himself in trouble when two boys in a certain house were accused of illegal fagging. The offence was proved, the Tutor appeared willing that action should be taken and the Captain accordingly gave the offenders seventeen cuts.* The Tutor then complained to the Head Master, and wrote a furious letter to the Captain of the Oppidans. In the end the Head Master supported Hobhouse, the Tutor and Hobhouse apologized to each other, and the matter passed off after causing some sensation in the School. Most boys apparently sided with the Captain of the Oppidans. He explicitly acted as Captain

---

* The punishments seem stiff, but the boys were tough. About this time a boy was given twenty-seven strokes by the Lower Master, which aroused complaints from the Masters but not (to his credit) from the boy himself.

of the Oppidans rather than as a member of Pop, but it was thought by many that this was a matter for Pop (and the Captain of the Oppidans might not always be in Pop). That should be taken as a sign of the way power was moving.

The official attitude to boy power was displayed further when the Eton Mission was founded, and the Trust Deed of 1882 set up a Council to have absolute discretion in managing the Mission. The Council comprised ex officio all Masters, all boys in Sixth Form, all Captains of houses, the Captain of the Boats, the Captain of the Eleven, the President of the Eton Society, the President of the Eton Literary and Scientific Society (Oscar Browning's child), and all boys holding commissions in the Eton Rifle Volunteer Corps. In addition, one boy was to be elected from each house. Thus the boys were in a majority. An executive committee was appointed, which no doubt guided the crucial business of the Mission; boys were at least equally represented on this with Masters. Today the Charity Commissioners would not allow boys to have votes in such a body, let alone to be in control. But at that time large sums of money were, in effect, entrusted to boys, as for instance in the running of games and the Fourth of June. Boys were treated so much more like adults in some ways – but so much less in others.

The Eton Mission was the last important innovation of Hornby's time. Mid-Victorian England had woken up to the realization that the Church had hardly touched the life of the urban working classes. In March 1880 W.W. How, Bishop of Bedford, addressed a meeting, already predisposed to undertake some good work, and the meeting ended with a resolution 'to connect the school distinctly with some charitable work in London'. With commendable energy, derived no doubt once again from the influence of Warre (who became one of the first three Trustees), funds were raised, a plot of land in Hackney Wick acquired, and a Missioner appointed. The first service was held in October 1880.

The first Missioner was William Carter,* of the family who had provided so many Fellows of Eton, a straightforward and courageous character. He was another of those Etonian footballers, one of the founders of West Bromwich Albion. So attractive was his personality that the congregation quickly outgrew the undertaker's shop, its first venue, and by June 1881 a corrugated

---

* Later Archbishop of Cape Town.

iron church for 200 was erected. In those early days Old Etonians would come down from the West End to help, and clubs were started. The whole apparatus of social and welfare activity was soon established.

From the start there were criticisms. Stewart Headlam, the Old Etonian Christian Socialist, was openly contemptuous. Christian Socialists saw the movement of which the Mission was part as an attempt to impose upper-class views on the masses. What they felt was required was a fundamental change in the social system that imposed the misery that the Mission sought to relieve. There were Socialist Masters at Eton in 1880, Salt and young Joynes, but they played no part in the foundation of the Mission. The view that relieving the worst afflictions of the capitalist system, by passing on a small quota of its benefits, could make that system more acceptable was widespread. E.M.S. Pilkington's attractive memoir of the early days is called *An Eton Playing Field*. Hackney Wick was to be the field on which a new Battle of Waterloo was to be won, and the victory would be over the problems that poverty, ignorance and crime so persistently raised. By implication the class war would be avoided if the poor were given some of the advantages and attitudes inculcated at public schools. The lads of the Boys' Club 'are ready to be led, but not by one of themselves, as is the custom of public school boys. I want you to go and make friends with the young working classes not as their masters but as their equals. They will appreciate your help, but may not express their feelings till they have grown up into men, when they will do so freely.'[23] No doubt many who gave their money or gave their time were motivated by vague feelings that such giving could justify the social status quo and assuage the feeling of guilt that their privileged position engendered. For some there was indeed an element of benevolent picnicking – it was good work and it was fun. But those few who gave most to the Eton Mission clearly came to realize that they were receiving more than they were giving. The Mission was to be a significant, even if inadequate, force towards wider awareness at Eton.

On 9 May 1884 Provost Goodford died. Although he does not figure prominently in Etonian memoirs during his time as Provost – apart from references to his accent slightly alleviating the tedium of his lengthy utterances in Chapel – he had performed his job acceptably. Certainly he did not press Hornby towards any reform, but he carried through the recommendations of the Clarendon Commission fairly, if not enthusiastically.*

It was no surprise when the Crown, on the advice of Mr Gladstone, appointed Dr Hornby to succeed as Provost, thus ending his headmastership. Although it is clear that under Hornby some worthwhile changes occurred at Eton, he cannot be rated a great Head Master. As time went on he became more incapable of initiative – Edward Lyttelton, who knew him both as boy and as Assistant Master, remarks that 'The attempt made by a few progressives on the staff to goad Hornby into further activities of administration were resisted with a courteous immobility to which educational history affords no parallel.'[24] Lyttelton attributed this to the workload which he attempted to carry, which effectively overwhelmed him. Salt, less charitably, summed him up as a pleasant but weak and obstinate man.

In his duty as teacher of Sixth Form, to which he seems to have attached most importance, he was barely adequate. Even the Sixth Form would attract numerous poenas, which took little effect since they were seldom fully written. M.R. James reports that boys were sometimes legitimately excused verses, but that sometimes they excused themselves. '"I haven't had your verses, have I?" says Hornby. "No, Sir, I'm skipping this week." "Skippin'? Didn't you skip last week?" "Did I, Sir?" "Yes: I think there's been too much skippin' lately: I can't have boys skippin' week after week in this way."'[25] Though M.R. James presents a picture of a slack regime, he does, however, say that he loved Hornby dearly and that his interest was captured. Probably most boys liked Hornby. One of his best qualities was a vein of irony, which later helped him as Provost to become an accomplished after-dinner speaker. Once a group of boys, led by Curzon, Captain of the Oppidans, approached Hornby in hot weather with a request to wear white top hats. It was probably a sham request, though Curzon had tried to prevent the practice of nude bathing, gaining Hornby's support, but foundering on the opposition of Warre.† Anyway, Hornby handled the top-hat deputation deftly: 'Don't you think you would look rather like book-makers?' Gilbert Coleridge, one of the deputation, recalling the incident, remarks: 'We protested

---

* His memorial brass in the Antechapel records that he 'patiently endured' the changes ordained by Parliament.

† Bathing drawers were only donned in 1893.

against such a sumptuary law, but he was firm, and some of us regretted that we hadn't adopted the fashion without leave, for then perhaps he would not have interfered'.[26] Probably Eton was a better school in 1884 than it had been in 1868, but this owed more to an increasing seriousness in society as a whole, and to the efforts of the best Masters, than to the Head Master. Hornby even recognized the second point in a generous letter to Warre (July 1884): 'You have done a quantity of things for the School which I could not have done, and for which I have often had the credit.'[27]

CHAPTER FOUR

Doctor Warre

FOUR NAMES WERE canvassed to succeed Hornby: Dr Percival, the President of Trinity College, Oxford; Kynaston, who was the former Assistant Master Snow with a new name and now Head Master of Cheltenham; Welldon, an old Colleger who was to be Headmaster of Harrow; and Warre. Some correspondents in *The Times*, old Collegers, tried to disparage Warre. A letter on 25 July 1884 signed Academicus argued that Eton was made up of two schools, each with very different characteristics, the seventy Collegers and the 800 Oppidans.

> The smaller section has proved itself every year more moral, more industrious, more distinguished in academical honours; the latter has become by degrees more idle, more extravagant, more self-indulgent, more entirely devoted to athletics and less to literary pursuits ... The choice of the new headmaster will determine which of these two principles is to triumph ... [For] the last quarter of the century [Mr Warre] has made no mark as a scholar, a preacher, or a man of letters. His name is associated with no questions of educational reform; on the other hand, he is well known as the best rowing coach in England and as an able field-officer of Volunteers. He is an oppidan of the oppidans. The ordinary Etonian character, for good or for bad, has received a strong impression from his energy and strength of will.

The implication was that the strong impression was for the bad, and critics of Warre will still say that Academicus was correct. But

Warre did not lack defenders in *The Times*, and when on 29 July the Governing Body met, nine of the eleven votes went to Warre.

No one should lightly disparage Fellows of All Souls, but Dr Warre (he at once acquired a DD) was not a very clever man. The Collegers in his first Sixth Form chose to perpetuate the hostility of Academicus by boorish rudeness. Dr Warre, showing a surprising vulnerability, wrote one night a letter of resignation to the Provost; but after sleeping on it, he tore up the letter, determined not to be beaten by a pack of boys.[1]* Warre had, however, an exceptionally active mind that compensated for any lack of depth or originality. He immediately set about some long-needed reforms, which brought down on him the wrath of the most conservative Etonians and Old Etonians who feared that the new Head Master would raise the intellectual standard. He had indeed done that when he began his house. Sir William Anson, later Warden of All Souls and a Fellow of Eton, contrasted him with Balston as Tutor:

> I was at the House of the Rev E. Balston, a man whose charm of manner endeared him to generations of pupils. But it was not a working House . . . In 1860, Mr Balston became a Fellow . . . and I became the pupil of Mr Warre . . . Warre even now seems to me whenever I meet him, to impart to me some of his overflowing life and vigour. The impression he made on us boys was remarkable. We all began to think it creditable to work . . . and when I left Eton I formed a strong determination to do something for the credit of Warre's House and of my old school.[2]

The first letter that Warre wrote to the Governing Body in October 1884 was by implication a most damning indictment of his predecessor's reign, and it cannot have made pleasant reading for Dr Hornby. Discipline and academic standards were too low, and a comprehensive programme of reform was required.

Extra hours in school were added; there were now to be twenty-five periods a week, with more Maths and French, and some reduction in classical Pupil Room work. Trials, instead of being a yearly examination, were set to all boys each Half, replacing the ineffective Collections. Educationalists would now-

---

* It was typical of Warre that he should later have appointed Goodhart, one of the ringleaders, to the staff.

adays say that Etonians were over-examined. But nothing at the time did more to improve standards among the less ambitious boys; nothing else could have so effectively permitted the reduction in flogging that followed.

Other changes were organizational. The Absences where the Head Master had called over the whole School were replaced by Absences for smaller groups to be called over by Assistant Masters. A School Office was created under Sergeant-Major Osborn of the Volunteers to keep a check on the presence of boys in Chapel and schools, a job which had been inefficiently done by boy praepostors from each division. Only the Head Master's two Sixth Form praepostors were retained, to call offenders in the Bill. A school messenger helped the school clerk by collecting and delivering notes between schoolrooms, houses, and the School Office. School punishments were now more competently collected. Tardy Book, to be signed in the School Office before early school, was instituted as a goad for unpunctual boys. Records could now be kept of boys who had failed in Trials or of malefactors. It was even possible, as never before, for Housemasters to check lists of would-be entrants to the School, to see if there were boys listed for other Housemasters besides themselves, or boys requiring a Housemaster.

From 1885 also a much fuller School Calendar was produced which showed where boys should be at all times. Masters could obtain from the School Office copies of their division lists, and appropriate numbers of copies of work which they might need to set. The Calendar showed a new organization of the boys by blocks, each roughly corresponding to a one-year stage in the School.* Upper boys included Sixth Form and First Hundred, now known as A Block, and Fifth Form; the latter had always been in three 'divisions', which now became Blocks B, C, and D. The Remove were transferred to the Lower Master's jurisdiction as lower boys, and known as E Block; Fourth Form and Third Form became F Block. Collegers started in D and were likely to spend more than a year in A; Oppidans started in E or F – the lowest in Common Entrance spent one half in Third Form and then a further year in Fourth Form. The School Calendar showed the

---

* The Calendar contained a wealth of other information: School rules, lists of past winners of scholarships and the major prizes, records of all prizes and honours achieved by current Etonians, rules for examinations, and a map showing where Masters lived.

divisions within each block, their weekly programme, the books set, and the syllabus to be studied.

This tremendous advance in efficiency, attributable to Warre's gift for delegation as well as to his attention to detail, appalled those who had enjoyed the laxity of Hornby's rule. Where was the fun that older Etonians remembered? There was even much less fear of flogging, which had added spice to remembered adventures. Perhaps it is not surprising that conservatives complained.

Dr Warre also immediately took steps to improve teaching standards by visiting Masters at work. There were a number of uncomfortable episodes when he surprised groups out of control. Even if all was well the alarm felt by many a Master did not escape the delighted notice of his division. The most skilful Masters managed to get Warre to teach himself, perhaps on his favourite topic, the trireme. On one never forgotten occasion, Warre, meaning to leave a schoolroom, walked into a cupboard.[3]

In the same first letter to the Governing Body Dr Warre also put forward a programme for building. Here his proposals were less happy and fortunately less successful. He wanted to create new sick-rooms for the Collegers (remember that the youngest did not have separate rooms, and that sickness was a more serious problem in those days). His planned way to achieve this was to transfer the School Library, which was then housed in part of College's New Buildings, into Upper School. This in turn meant that he wanted a new big schoolroom where the whole School could be assembled, and Speeches performed. Furthermore, he wanted to pull down Savile House in Weston's Yard, where Head Masters had resided since Hawtrey was appointed as Head Master. Warre disliked the noise of traffic from the Slough Road (even in those days), and he wanted to build bigger.

The Governing Body appointed a committee to consider this new building programme, and as soon as the scheme became known opposition grew.* By the end of 1885 a lobby had emerged

* In January 1885, *Macmillan's Magazine* published an 'Ode on a Near Prospect of Eton Chapel' in which Dr Hawtrey supposedly speaks:

> These changes, to an Eton mind
> So rude, so needless and unkind,
>   I might perchance condone,
> If but the vandal's ruthless hand
> Would let thine ancient buildings stand,
>   Would leave thy walls alone.

against the idea of transforming Upper School, and for the preservation of the buildings in Weston's Yard. By December 1885, a petition had appeared in *The Times* and in February 1886 Mr Gladstone wrote to express his hostility. The most remarkable document, however, was a slim volume by H.E. Luxmoore, a Housemaster, published in 1885 and subtitled, *Some views and opinions of Sparrow on Housetops*. After a melancholy survey of the work of recent improvers in College and town, the Sparrow compared the beautiful chimneys and brickwork of Savile House with recent building. 'There have been incredible rumours of its intended destruction by those who have the care of our buildings. Perhaps to destroy it is better than to maul it.' The pamphlet ended with some general principles of conservation, ahead of their time, which few now would fault.

Eventually Savile House was saved, and it was determined that the Head Master should move in due course to the Cloisters, once death had cleared enough Fellows' houses to provide him with the space he needed.* In June 1886, the Fellows defeated the plan to turn Upper School into a Library by six votes to four. In March 1887, the Committee for the Improvement of Buildings recommended that the Library should be moved to a part of New Schools adjacent to Common Lane, which was at that time occupied by the Drawing Schools. Thus the sick-rooms for Collegers could be built, the one part of Warre's plans to come quickly to fruition. By then, however, new demands had arisen, for a Lower Chapel, for new classrooms, a Museum, a Physics laboratory, and new Drawing Schools. These were eventually to be built: the Lower Chapel was dedicated in 1891 and the foundation stone of Queen's Schools was laid by Queen Victoria in 1889 (after the old Mathematical Schools on that site had been demolished).

The Lower Chapel was widely supported by Masters, but some of the Fellows wondered whether it would not have been possible to stagger the hours of teaching so that two services could have been held in College Chapel. The building itself in the Perpendicular style has never enjoyed the esteem in the Eton community which perhaps it deserves – probably because of its secondary status. It is dark, but is built of good materials with distinguished

---

* Warre immediately built Colenorton as a guest house. Both it and the boys' house which he had earlier built (Penn House) suggest that Warre's disappointment was Eton's escape.

detail, and it is in harmony with the neighbouring Queen's Schools.

The programme of building was a reflection of Warre's energy, as well as of increasing demands from an expanding and developing school. Five new Masters were appointed straightaway, and the staff was to rise from forty-four to sixty-one during his time, while the number of boys increased from 894 to 1,021. Needless to say, the Governing Body did not accept the consequent expenditure without dispute and hesitation, and private finance was still required for many projects. Hornby, who had himself been denied finance by the Governing Body when he was Head Master, was cautious, but enough Fellows as a rule were carried along by Warre's enthusiasm and insistence. The College raised mortgages on the Chalcots estate, and in doing so they reduced the Foundation's net income, causing financial problems that were to persist for sixty years.* It would have been wiser in the long term to have kept the size of the school down, and to have concentrated available funds on improving facilities for a smaller school; it might also have been possible to induce the parents to contribute to the building programme by a higher fee.

In one respect Warre was at heart conservative: he was not keen to dilute the classical curriculum. He did, however, quickly allow German as an alternative to Greek for the weaker boys (hardly an easy option). He was better disposed to modern languages than to Science. Believing that modern languages should be taught by natives, he employed two Frenchmen on the staff, whom he liked, M. Roublot and M. Hua. The latter could not pronounce Warre's name, nor Warre his, but it is recorded that in their attempts they made exactly the same noise.

He himself was not a particularly good teacher, and critics have argued with some justice that he was more interested in training character than training the mind. His sermons were pedestrian; but when he spoke to the boys briefly about some particular disciplinary issue, the very clear distinctions he would draw between right and wrong were effective. He had the gift of appealing to boys'

---

* Until 1900, Eton suffered from the amateur guidance of the Revd W.A. Carter as Bursar, the only one of the former Fellows to continue on the Governing Body after the reorganization. By 1900 he was an octogenarian. Then after a brief unsuccessful first appointment, the Governing Body chose Mr Hollway-Calthrop, who provided more effective management.

better nature. Undoubtedly he was helped by his tremendous physical presence.* His majesty was such that it conquered even incoherence in his speech. There was an occasion when he addressed the school about 'an evil elephant' at large – 'element' presumably intended, since it was smoking and drinking – without provoking a titter. Masters too, even when unhappy with some change, could recognize the idealism and aspirations for Eton that guided his every action. He once rebuked in a kind enough way a Master who had avowed that he was looking out for an opportunity to set some troublesome youth a Georgic: 'You should look out *not* to set him a Georgic'. This was characteristic of the more enlightened relationship between Masters and boys which Warre encouraged. It had certainly existed between the best Tutors and their pupils, but had not been general. In his first letter to the Governing Body Warre had expressed a desire to reduce the amount of punishment in the School, and he succeeded.

The first decade of Warre's headmastership was an impressive period, in which he stamped his mark on the School. The School had become more regimented, but it had also become more purposeful. The academic standards of the weaker boys had improved. Discipline was better. The School's reputation stood higher than ever. But in 1896, when he was in his sixtieth year, Warre's health began to give him trouble, possibly the first symptoms of Parkinson's disease which was eventually to disable him. The second half of his long headmastership was to be less successful than the first; he never lost his hold on the boys but Masters became more critical.

There was no obvious change of course. Warre continued to bring before the Governing Body schemes of improvement, and building continued. The Governing Body found itself drawn into the provision of capital for boys' houses. Though rents were charged to the Housemasters, these did not provide a full economic return. Undoubtedly the growth of the School and the rising expectations of parents were major reasons for new houses and for financing improvements to existing houses, but the old random difference between the size and state of houses created problems when a Housemaster retired. The Housemaster gave up his lease on his retirement, and it would normally go to another existing

* It was reputed that Warre's top hat would fit over two lower boys' heads simultaneously.

Housemaster who would move with his boys, probably from a smaller and less desirable building. The new Housemaster might well not have room for all his predecessor's boys when he moved in. Consequently houses tended to break up on the retirement of Housemasters. This was a peculiarly Etonian problem, caused by the private ownership of the leases on houses and the attachment of boys to their Housemasters; in most other schools, boys were allocated to a school-owned house, and stayed there even if the master changed. Warre thought the existence of some small houses convenient, as suitable appointments for younger Masters, but the Governing Body was aware of the unpopularity caused by the dispersal of houses, and knew that boys sometimes left early when their Housemasters retired, with consequent drops in School numbers. It was agreed that smaller houses should hold thirty-six boys, and larger houses forty boys.

This and other changes were not in the financial interests of Masters, who had to wait longer before becoming Housemasters (typically twelve years), and who had to pay higher rents for improved houses, and higher running costs. The increase in the number of Masters also reduced the number of pupils per Master, on which their earnings depended. One advantage to Masters achieved at this time with the help of the Vice-Provost, their representative on the Governing Body, was a pension scheme to produce guaranteed pensions on retirement at age 55. This also was in the interests of the School.*

Meanwhile Masters felt that many of Warre's reforms added to their labours for less and less obvious educational advantage. His genius for administrative detail became irksome. For example, in September 1901, A.C. Benson, an excellent teacher and Housemaster, who started on Warre's side, was writing in his diary of a bad Masters' meeting at the beginning of the half: 'Warre has broken out again with pink and blue books, foils & counterfoils, forms & memoranda. If he is asked any question about the absurdest detail, his voice goes down into his belly & he says "it makes for the good government and therefore for the good morality of the school".'[4] Clearly Warre knew that he was not carrying his staff, for in October he lectured them again during Chambers 'like a Colonel dragooning his men. "We must remember that the strongest part

---

* The first two Masters to benefit were Stone and Broke.

of a chain is its weakest link." Always just wrong in all his oratorical effects', Benson comments.[5]

In April 1901, the Prime Minister enquired of Warre whether he would accept the Deanery of Salisbury – perhaps an indication that friends thought it was time for Warre to move on. He refused, however, saying that he felt he still had work to do at Eton. In particular he wanted to make some changes in the curriculum.

In 1899 French had become compulsory for all the First Hundred (A Block), and there followed a number of concessions to public opinion. In 1900 Classical Masters eventually persuaded Warre to allow streaming in classical divisions. He had always favoured mixed ability teaching, thinking that the presence of a few clever boys stimulated even the dimmer divisions. But most Masters saw the interests of the cleverer boys being sacrificed to those of the stupider. Then there came the first possibilities of able older boys, not just the Army Class, moving away from their classical specialization. History at once attracted boys, because it was well taught by C.H.K. Marten. Boys began winning scholarships to Oxford and Cambridge in subjects other than Classics.

The diminished importance of classical studies revived the tutorial question. Was it possible to justify the privileged position of the Classical Tutors when a boy's principal work might be done with a non-Classical Master? The re-emergence of the tutorial question in 1902 and early 1903 was to trouble Warre severely. He saw that there was a case for further concession to the non-Classical Masters if this could be kept fairly nominal, but he was determined that Eton was to remain primarily a classical School. The Classical Tutors worked with their boys from the time they arrived in the School, directed most of their work, met them in Private Business, and developed a sympathy which was worth preserving even if at the end of their time boys might regard History or Maths or Science as their primary study. The Masters' Representative, Warre Cornish the Vice-Provost, was also placed in a difficult position. He too instinctively sympathized with the Classical Tutors, having been one. The Governing Body looked to him for impartial advice, but did not really find it, though he did move towards a more neutral stance under pressure from the non-Classical Masters. A few Classical Housemasters, notably Benson, had sympathy with their non-Classical colleagues; he perceived that the financial disparity was at the base of complaints.* He also saw, however, that someone in the Eton system needed to do the work of the Classical Tutor: were the Housemasters prepared to guide boys' intellectual development in the way that Classical Tutors did?

The Governing Body heard representations from the rival camps, and adjourned their discussions. In May 1903 they made a small change to the regulations to allow boys who pursued German, Science, or History instead of Greek to be distinguished by a mark in the Calendar, and a small portion of the Classical Tutor's fee to be reallocated. It was such a small change that it resolved virtually nothing.

Almost as much can be said about Warre's curriculum reform. In the autumn of 1903, the Head Master formed working parties to consider the curriculum in each block. The majority of Masters supported his view that Eton should remain a classical School, and should not have a modern side, such as many schools had by then acquired. Furthermore, Warre wished to retain Greek with Latin in the main 'trunk' of educational growth. The Classical Masters would also teach Divinity, History, and Geography. French, Maths, and Nature Study were to be part of the general curriculum lower down the school. In the end, the key questions of when alternative subjects were to be allowed into the curriculum, and whether some subjects, such as French, might be remitted for a time in a boy's career and studied more intensively at other times, were not resolved. Some groundwork was done for whoever was to succeed Warre, and some deficiencies in the existing programme were exposed. It does not seem that German had been a success with the less able boys. Some Masters perceived that the four languages (Latin, Greek, French, and German) attempted by some boys were too many. Those who defended Greek were able still to rely on Oxford and Cambridge requiring Greek for entrance. But even among the Classics Masters, some were questioning whether the classical curriculum could not be reformed.

By then, however, it was clear that Warre's resignation must be near. On 1 June 1903, a terrible disaster occurred. About 4.00 a.m. a fire broke out at Kindersley's house.[6] This building, Baldwin's

---

* In 1906 the average income of the ten Classical Masters below the standing of Housemasters was £774 (over £30,000 in today's terms) and of the ten equivalent modern Masters was £591 (about £23,000 now).

End, was about 200 years old, a three-storied house largely built of wood, lath, and plaster, with low ceilings. A boy, Jackson, was luckily awoken, found a cloud of smoke and fire in the passage outside, but was able to break his window and escape, alarming others. Many boys managed to climb out, and escaped down a massive old Wistaria.* The Kindersleys rescued many, including their children and servants, and neighbouring boys and Masters were heroic. Unfortunately there was no adequate roll-call, but it was noticed that a young boy called Horne was missing. He had been unable to get out of his window which was blocked by iron bars designed to keep boys in after lock-up. It seems he appeared at his window but fell back overcome by smoke. Lucky were those boys who had loosened their window bars – one, Bligh, only that very night. Jackson had called the fire brigade who now controlled the flames. But only then was it discovered that another boy in the middle of the School, Lawson, was missing. He was found in the ruins by his bed: he probably never woke up.

Lawrence Jones, Captain of Kindersley's house, recalled in his memoirs that Warre appeared early on the scene, and took in a number of boys, including himself. He remembered watching Warre shaving, the tears rolling down his cheeks, as he himself wept in the Head Master's bed. He also recalled that Warre made a mistake in sending two telegrams to the fathers of Lawson and Horne: 'Very grave news. Come at once. Edmond Warre.' He knew that Warre should have said that the boys had died. This was just the first of a number of moments at which Warre failed.

The celebrations of the forthcoming Fourth of June were quickly cancelled. By 11.00 a.m. a letter of sympathy arrived from the King, and once again Warre broke down. Many of Kindersley's boys went home, and others were billeted around the houses. Mrs Warre Cornish, the Vice-Provost's wife, heroically washed the bodies of the dead boys – Lawson's almost unscathed, but Horne's sadly burned – and laid them out among flowers, so that they should not look too distressing when the parents arrived. A Memorial Service, conducted by The Provost, was held at Eton, but the School was not properly represented when Lawson and Horne were buried at their homes. Warre had collapsed – and it must be said that self-pity seems to have been the main cause. At an

---

* Among those who survived the fire was Hugh Dalton, subsequently Chancellor of the Exchequer in Mr Attlee's Labour government.

inquest the next week his evidence was entirely self-exculpatory: he did not take the responsibility for what had occurred.

Certainly it was true that Warre had been aware of the dangers. In 1891 there had been a fire at Radcliffe's house without casualties, and a conflagration was always possible in those days of open fires and matchbox houses. Instructions had been issued, and reports made to the Governing Body. It was a case where the independence of the Housemasters worked very disadvantageously, for the College was not keen to pay for precautions, and the Housemasters knew that they would be tenants for only a few years. Warre had sent round instructions, but he had not ensured that Housemasters had carried them out.

Then ten days after the fire, there was an extraordinary sequel. A very young boy in Rawlins's, Levett, woke at 4.00 a.m. and found a 17-year-old boy called Moore, boarded out from Kindersley's house, lighting a fire under the boys' staircase. With astonishing calmness Levett put out the fire, returned to his room and worked, checking every so often to ensure that all was well. He did not think it proper to disturb his Tutor. When Rawlins interviewed Moore, the boy's reactions were not consistent – at one time claiming he was sleep-walking, at another appearing to confess all. There was a disposition to believe that Moore might have simply been deranged by his previous experience, but circumstantial evidence emerged that Moore had been about earlier than most others in the Kindersley fire, and dressed; he had said to a boys' maid, 'Isn't it a jolly blaze?' Furthermore he had earlier fired ricks, something his parents knew but had not mentioned. He was withdrawn from the School, but not prosecuted. Nevertheless, it must be assumed that he had deliberately started the fire in Kindersley's: a quiet, slow but friendly boy, doing reasonably well in the School – but apparently a pyromaniac.*

Though a deliberately started fire would always be a hazard, conditions in Kindersley's were at fault. There should have been alternative exits, there should have been an immediate roll-call. But there was sympathy with Kindersley: other Masters knew how easily this might have happened to them. He continued with his house, but he never got over this disaster. Nor really did Warre. For some days after the fire he still lay in bed, weeping and reading

---

* A businessman's son from Liverpool, he went on to a reasonably successful career as a journalist.

Dickens; to Benson he and the Bursar together were like two mock-turtles. Others were left to carry through fire precautions. All bars were removed from boys' windows, nightwatchmen (hitherto only employed in Evans's) became general, and fire escapes were more generally provided. Another fire in 1905, caused by an electrical fault, suggested that the new arrangements would work well.

There were many who behaved well, but one must mention the magnanimity of the Lawsons. They had an extension built to the Natural History Museum. There is a Latin inscription in the Antechapel, composed by Hugh Macnaghten: 'The boys who were his friends had this tablet put up to the innocent memory of Lionel George Lawson. He was a keen watcher of birds, and God who Himself remembers the sparrows took him in his fifteenth year from peaceful sleep to his own bosom.'

Thanks to the building programme, Kindersley's house could reopen in a different building in September. Despite the growing debts of the College, this programme was to continue. And there was now in hand the grand project that Warre desired – the Memorial Buildings to the 129 Old Etonian officers killed in the Boer War. This was to provide the great room and the School Library that were closest to his heart. The College was willing only to give the site, and effectively to replace the two houses which were currently there, one of them of unusual ugliness. Otherwise the funds were raised by subscription. Warre's determination carried the project forward almost single-handed, and before he retired as Head Master he saw the foundation stone laid. There was a competition among Etonian architects, and the building is indeed lavishly ornate. But in this, and in the brick and stone alien to the traditional materials of Eton, it is in Pevsner's judgement, 'the only building in Eton that seriously jars'.[7] Neither the great hall nor the library proved practical – the acoustics in the hall being too difficult to allow the whole School to be addressed together before the acquisition of an adequate loud-speaker system, and the library initially wasteful of space.

By the autumn of 1903, Warre was increasingly showing signs of fatigue. Hornby was worried enough to talk to Benson. Warre was so idle! (He did not attach the same importance to teaching Sixth Form as Hornby did.) If Hornby did criticize Warre, Warre 'with a kind of triumphant air' would say, 'You have given me a sleepless night.'[8] In the summer of 1904 pressure grew on him to resign. The Vice-Provost wrote, and was supported by two of Warre's best friends on the Governing Body, Lord Morley (himself dying) and Anson, the Warden of All Souls, a former pupil of Warre. In October his resignation, to take effect at the end of the Summer Half 1905, was accepted, and the Governing Body, transmuted at this time back to the Provost and Fellows, wrote to express their 'high appreciation of his long and distinguished services to the School'.* Whatever the discontent that had been felt at some times by some Masters, all could be united at this moment in appreciation of a Head Master who had so dominated the life of the School. And as the moment of departure came, the tide of sentiment grew: all recognized that a great and widely loved man was going, that an era was ending.†

It is certainly true that Warre's headmastership determined the nature of Eton over the next sixty years. When the Memorial Buildings were complete, the centre of Eton took its present form: changes since have been on the periphery. The programme of building had no precedent, and was not to be matched until the 1980s. Almost all that Warre really wanted he obtained, except a new Sanatorium (he hoped to turn the old Sanatorium into a Choir School). For Eton with its separate rooms, a large Sanatorium is not really crucial. We may regret that much of the new building was of no great merit, but neither the College nor Warre should be too much blamed since they employed leading architects of the time. Also the resources of the College were seriously depleted. Wild's Estate in North London was sold, for the development of Hampstead Garden Suburb and the Hampstead Heath Extension, and the College had to borrow something like £10 million in present terms. Furthermore, although Housemasters were charged rents, the new buildings and playing fields were not income-earning assets with as good a yield as the property sold.

Warre also set up the administrative framework and the balance

---

* Luxmoore, the senior Master, spoke nobly in Chambers when the Masters were told. Next morning Warre had to read the Epistle for St Luke's Day: 'The time of my departure is at hand. I have fought a good fight. I have finished my course, I have kept faith.'

† Luxmoore wrote to an old pupil, 'He certainly did the leave-taking well & people who a year ago w'd superannuate were now almost fulsome. [His qualitites included] simplicity, a very vigorous & active vitality of mind, straightforwardness, affectionateness, goodness.'

of work and play which were to persist for sixty years. In the next chapter we shall see also how a lasting character was set upon the social life of the boys. In a School the size of Eton, with so many Masters of personal distinction, no single individual could determine the ethos of the place. But Warre was a man of vision, and his vision was to a remarkable extent realized during his rule.

He was above all a typical Englishman of his time, drawing his strength from his West Country roots. He loved gardens and animals; he was happy in his family. He was no theorist, but a practical man. A great patriot himself, he wanted Etonians to take their places as leaders of the country, upright in the service of God and their fellow men. It is often claimed that his vision was anti-intellectual and philistine; and it is true that he disliked boys just sitting and talking, that he was not really sympathetic to eccentricity. But he did value intellectual activity. In 1898 he induced Pop to reform its membership so that the Captains of the School and Oppidans were ex officio members, and that the Society should always include five Sixth Formers. Furthermore he wanted, but did not secure, a special room in the Memorial Buildings for Sixth Form to enhance their prestige. Certainly Warre had his failings: he was slow to act against bad Housemasters; his concept of the curriculum was excessively linguistic, and his interpretation of a classical education was narrower than it should have been. He was a great democrat, but one who expected everyone else to share his views; and to a considerable extent they did.[9]

If we ask why Warre was so successful in imposing his vision, it must be said that the British of his class and generation were like-minded, and therefore predisposed to value the store that Warre set on high-minded achievement. But ultimately Warre's greatness rests on his personality. His magnanimity, his fairness, his friendliness were characteristics that boys could appreciate. They experienced, in the words of *The Times*, 'the contagion of his zeal and energy'.[10] The intellectual Percy Lubbock wrote of him that, 'whatever potency there was in the idea of Eton, it was manifest in the figure of Warre towering above us. He *was* Eton before our eyes; and so the idea of Eton struck home in a young imagination – splendidly, illustriously, with the ample and generous dignity of Warre himself.'[11] A.C. Benson, who did not by any means share all Warre's views, and who became increasingly critical, nevertheless wrote in his diary in 1902: 'The more one thinks of him the more *his greatness* emerges – when I am in his presence I am entirely dominated by him.'[12] Warre's reputation and Eton's excellence might have been higher had he started and finished his headmastership earlier. But even as things were, the stature of Warre makes him stand out as one of the great headmasters in the history of education.

CHAPTER FIVE

The Golden Age?

THE PERIOD EITHER side of 1900 was one in which the public
schools enjoyed a high noon of prosperity and popularity, though
with hindsight it can be seen that the condition of British society
was not so assured as most Britons assumed. Economically the
Americans and Germans had surpassed the British, and this began
to stir questions about the quality of British education. The
apparent triumph of imperialism was marred by criticisms of its
aims, and by the Boer War which demonstrated its underlying
fragility. This too was the period of the rise of Socialism, and with
it came criticism of the class system on which public school
education was based. Yet most of those involved with the schools,
teachers and particularly pupils, believed in the perfection and the
permanence of the arrangements of which they were part.

The years between 1873 and 1896 were marked by falling food
prices, and so by declining agricultural rents. The agricultural
depression was not bad enough to alter the social fabric dramatically, but it did mean that the traditional Eton parents were less
affluent. Because the School had grown since 1860 and because
boys spent on average perhaps a year less in the School, the
number of Etonian families had increased. The landed classes were
still represented, but new families, with wealth based on the City
of London or prosperous cities such as Liverpool, had enlisted
their sons. The count of noblemen and sons of noblemen in 1899
was similar to that of 1859, with seventy-five peers or sons of peers
(including two members of the royal family) and three baronets

out of just over 1,000. Fewer boys came from Ireland, but there were some from the United States and from the Empire, including a few Indians.

Many Etonians were still destined for the same sort of occupations as in 1860, and a number could still expect a short career in the army before returning to run family estates and to act as local Justices of the Peace. A study of 1899 Etonians carried out in 1910 (when they would have been not more than 30 years old) is incomplete in two senses: careers were often not always fully developed, and not all were properly recorded. Where occupations are given, the army, the church, and the law appear more significant than they probably were. Still, there is no question that the most common career was to be an army officer. Other traditional careers continued: fifty-five of the 1899 Etonians are reported to have become barristers, though probably not all practised, and it was now common to be a solicitor; twenty became clergymen; and thirteen had already by 1910 been elected Members of Parliament. But about 125 are reported as in the City* or businessmen, and a surprisingly high proportion of the latter were engineers of various sorts. Some thirty-five appear to have remained in academic life, while some sixty entered public service, most commonly as diplomats but also as Indian, Sudanese or Egyptian Government officers. Farming and land agency had become common careers, and quite a number farmed overseas. There were a few doctors (and one dentist), artists, actors, architects, and authors. Dr Warre reported in 1902, and his figures roughly tally with the 1899 register, that of 1,400 recent Etonians 600 had gone on to the University and 400 to the army. The army figures were inflated apparently by those volunteering for the South African War, but there were also many Territorial officers whom Warre probably did not count. Eton was a notably military school, but it had become much more diversified both in the homes from which boys were drawn and still more in the occupations to which they went. Not surprisingly the Etonians of 1900 were more purposeful than those of 1860. The great majority expected to have to earn a living.

* The first Old Etonian, at any rate in recent times, to be elected Lord Mayor was Sir Joseph Dinsdale, 1901–2. He gave the College a fine silver-gilt and enamel cup to celebrate this achievement. His appointment was symbolic of Eton's close connection with the City in the twentieth century.

It was still not cheap to send a boy to Eton. The fees were slightly higher than in 1860, though prices in general were lower; it would seem that charges for extras and tradesmen's bills varied from some 25% of the fee for a young boy, to some 50% for an older boy. Compared with 1860, the cost of an Eton education showed little variation. If in real terms the parents paid more in fees, at least boys were, for example, now given breakfast at most houses.

In other ways, too, parents had more for their money. The pupil–teacher ratio had been almost halved: by the end of Dr Warre's time it was seventeen to one. Classical divisions, which were the largest, contained on average just over thirty boys. By then all subjects were taught in adequate schoolrooms – rather dour places by modern standards, but functional. The classical schoolroom, where most of the schoolroom week was passed, might contain a map of the classical world and the occasional reproduction of an ancient sculpture. Classics Masters taught Divinity, History, and Geography, and were in effect responsible for ensuring that boys learned to write English. There was also an odd arrangement by which French literature was taught as a construe by Classical Masters ('Classical French'). Younger boys still spent much time with their Classical Tutors, and if they were with a non-Classical Housemaster, they would go to Pupil Room in a young Classical Master's schoolroom.

Fortunately there were some excellent Classical Masters, who figure prominently in later memoirs, such as Cornish, Luxmoore, Macnaghten, and Benson. These men were bred in the liberal tradition established by William Johnson – the oldest had been taught by him and knew him, the youngest had heard of his methods, and were reminded of his virtues by the publication of a collection of his letters and of other works after his death. Even those whose methods were more authoritarian could be appreciated and successful, for example Austen Leigh, the Lower Master; for most young boys value the sense of progress that comes with a lesson well learnt, and a part of the syllabus mastered. The failures were the dull and narrow men who could not even exact a proper standard of industry. Few boys were lucky enough to meet only the stars, and some suffered under a succession of dullards. Lord Berners, for example, claimed that he was only once lucky, when he was up to Benson.[1]

In other subjects the general standard was lower. French teachers of the time won few favourable comments, though all liked Monsieur Hua. The Scientists were erratic, but Dr Porter's unruly schools were fun for most – he was touched by genius – and Biology was very well taught by M.D. Hill.* The Mathematicians were mostly said not to be good, though some better younger men were appointed by the end of Warre's time. Non-mathematical boys quickly despair in that subject, and some at least learnt some Maths at Eton – J.M. Keynes, for instance, won his Cambridge scholarship in Mathematics as well as Classics, and the large group of Etonian engineers must have had some tolerance for Mathematics, though one suspects that their enthusiasm was fired more by practical work in the School of Mechanics.

It is not easy to estimate how hard Etonians worked. The clever but idle no doubt got by with very little; some were clever enough to attain distinction in later life and report their idleness in memoirs. Yet many boys did work hard, particularly in College and the best run houses, and at the other end of the scale, the dull who came into the lower divisions on entry were kept busy by the pressure of Trials and possible superannuation. Within good houses the scholarly, unathletic boys achieved positions of eminence, but there was little evident reward in the eyes of the school at large for those who worked hardest. By the 1890s, the Eton Society had become notably unacademic, and the quality of its debates piffling. But Dr Warre's reform of Pop in 1898 certainly brought about some improvement – Keynes, for instance, was elected to Pop after winning his scholarship.

Games undeniably counted for too much. Matching the progress of muscular Christianity in public schools generally, they had come to play a larger part than in 1860, as more playing fields and better facilities were provided. Large areas of land were acquired towards Slough. First Mesopotamia was added and then, crucially, in 1894 a number of Old Etonians and Masters noticed that the land west of the Slough Road was for sale for housing development. They quickly raised enough money to purchase and present it to the College, and then the College itself acquired the large farm east of the Slough Road known as Dutchman's Farm. Thus a vast

---

* In 1900 the Eton Science Masters, inspired by Hill, founded the Association of Public School Science Masters.

area, less liable to flooding, became available for games and, equally important, a green space safeguarded Eton from the expansion of Slough.

By 1900 there were new activities to occupy leisure in the Lent Half, once so little catered for. Soccer established itself in the 1890s, but an attempt to start Rugby football failed. Boxing and fencing became recognized sports, with occasional matches. A rough golf links was laid alongside the Thames beyond the railway. Fives, rackets, beagling and shooting remained important, and athletics took place in a rudimentary fashion. The sports were run as sweepstakes, with entrance fees and many prizes. In the other halves, the Field Game retained its prestige, and cricket and rowing were equally esteemed by boys. Boys continued to organize and run their own games under an Athletics Committee chaired by the Captain of the Boats. Cricket teams and rowing VIIIs did rely on coaching by Masters. C.M. Wells, a scholar who helped Dr Warre with the top classical division, was himself a most distinguished cricketer, but he could not ensure that Eton had the better of Harrow. The Lord's match enjoyed astonishing prestige neverthe-less, and was watched by large crowds, many only tenuously connected with either school. At the end of the match ritual rioting took place – a tribal encounter which would not be tolerated these days. The VIII was coached by R.S. de Havilland with astonishing success. Victories in the Ladies' Plate at Henley Regatta against the older crews of the University Colleges were achieved regularly, and the times recorded seem extraordinarily fast: recent advances in boat-building technology and in scientific training have only cut them by some 5%. Both de Havilland and Wells insisted that the boys were still in charge, and they expected to be asked to help (and of course to be thanked). The Ninth Man in the *Monarch* became the organiser of internal racing; even though he now has more help, he remains one of the most responsible boys at Eton.

The Master of the Beagles also had great responsibilities. In 1877 a versatile athlete called Rowland Hunt had put the beagles on a better financial footing; he found an improbable kennel huntsman called Lock who kept a Turkish Bath in the High Street, and who, except when he was hunting, always wore a very brief pair of scarlet bathing drawers; the hounds were kennelled at the back of his premises. In 1899 Francis and Riversdale Grenfell, who were

twins,* inaugurated a period of outstanding success; with great
energy they raised money to build the kennels which are still used,
they acquired a new pack of hounds, and they recruited George
Champion who proved to be an outstanding kennel huntsman.
The Eton College Hunt regularly attracted fields of well over a
hundred boys, and was managed with little help from any Master
except a Treasurer.[2]

By 1900 it was general for houses to keep books recording their
annals. These are almost exclusively concerned with games, though
full accounts of debates were also preserved. Even the College
book, which does record prize-winners and scholars, is mostly
concerned with College's sporting record. This emphasis on
games, part of a national obsession, was no doubt welcome to the
School authorities. Masters were involved in games, not to run
them but to participate with the boys. Attitudes were well
encapsulated in an exchange of verse between Julian Sturgis, an
Old Etonian author, and his friend Arthur Benson, his sons'
Housemaster; Benson, very much not an athlete, was disturbed by
the dominance of games:

> 'Ode by a Schoolmaster' (by J.S.)
> Oh, better far the flannelled fool
> Than those who neither play nor work at school,
> Better the muddied oaf
> Than boys who loaf.

> 'Ode by a Parent' (by A.C.B.)
> I am quite of your opinion, Sir, that cricket
> Is an excellent recipe for hand and eye,
> And a boy who can successfully keep wicket
> Is a better sort of boy I don't deny.

> But today a British jury if empanelled
> Would pronounce that boys are criminals who loaf,
> That a fool becomes a hero if he's flannelled,
> And an oaf, if he is muddied, not an oaf.[3]

By 1900 games for all were not just possible, they were
mandatory. House Captains of Games would insist upon exercise

---

* The Grenfell twins were killed in the First World War; Francis was awarded
a VC.

being taken at least during the Michaelmas Half. Young boys who
shirked risked punishment, and idleness was only tolerated in
older boys of proven incompetence.

Non-sporting leisure activity was becoming adequate. Acting
was still regarded as dangerous – just occasionally to be permitted
in a foreign tongue. Art was not so vigorous as it had been, since
Sam Evans, William's son, was 74 by the time he retired in 1903 (to
be succeeded by his son Sidney). Music was in a healthier state,
with concerts regularly presented. Both Sir Joseph Barnby (as he
became after leaving Eton) and Dr Lloyd were highly respected.
But to set matters in perspective, one in ten boys was learning an
instrument in 1892 when Dr Lloyd was appointed, while over half
learn one or more instruments a hundred years on.

The Musical Society was only one of a number to entertain and
educate the boys in the evening. The Literary and Scientific Society
collapsed, but was replaced by the Essay Society which lasts to this
day, with boys reading papers to each other, and by a School
Debating Society. First a Natural History Society and then a
Scientific Society were formed. A Photographic Society catered for
enthusiasts. The Shakespeare Society enabled boys to read plays
together. There were also many visiting lecturers to talk about
literature or public affairs. Furthermore boys could use the School
Library and Natural History Museum, both exceptional by the
standards of the time.

The Corps was now strongly established, with nearly 400
members. Naturally it enjoyed the support of Dr Warre, who had
been involved from its inception. Field days were held away from
Eton, sometimes with other schools, and the annual camp was an
important event. On big occasions such as royal visits, the Corps
in its distinctive grey uniform enjoyed pride of place.

Eating and drinking continued to be important activities for
most boys. 'Sock cads' were still to be seen, but were less visible,
having been cleared from the front of the College. They were now
called Jobies, after one Joby Powell, who also supervised the Fives
courts and some of the playing fields, and they took their buns to
cricket matches or wherever they could hope to find custom.*
When Powell died in 1899, his business was purchased from his
widow, and School Stores were founded in 1900 to provide sock,

---

* The last Joby died aged 93 in 1953.

and then eventually other services to boys. It was initially run by a committee of Masters and boys in the interests of the boys, though when it grew in the 1920s it was reorganized under a committee of Masters with a professional manager.

Tap remained a club where boys could drink beer, and in 1900 a new club became available for wet-bobs at Queen's Eyot up the river. The island was first leased to Eton at a peppercorn rent, and then an attractive clubhouse was built, supplying food and beer. Queen's Eyot became a favourite wet-bob excursion. Both Queen's Eyot and the School Stores had the backing and interest of Dr Warre.

Inside boys' houses, debating societies had become general, and these did indeed debate. Members of Debate also enjoyed certain small privileges and exemptions from punishment. Election to Debate became the first step up the hierarchy within the house, and aroused passionate competition. The political manoeuvring was a subject of conversation to rival games. Members of Debate gradually acquired small responsibilities, but authority rested very much with the Library. This was normally a self-electing group of five or six boys, always containing the Captain of the House and the Captain of Games. The former was the top boy academically.

It was quite normal for boys to stay until their nineteenth birthday – but occasionally permission could be obtained from the Head Master to stay an extra Summer Half, at the end of which a boy might be 19½ years old. Mature moustachioed boys must have been frightening figures to the young. Boys who did not see themselves reaching positions of power or achieving success in their chosen field were liable to leave earlier, and they normally secured nothing but a token taste of authority. Also a Housemaster might persuade a boy whose influence he thought undesirable to leave early. The right to fag was normally confined to the top blocks of the School, unless a house was very short of senior boys. Fagging was expected of all boys for a year at least, and those who were lower boys for seven halves fagged for seven halves. Academic success gained practical advantages, even if sporting success meant more socially. A clever boy might be out of fagging by his fourteenth birthday, a lag could still be fagging when he was nearly 16. Even so reminiscences speak of even early days at Eton as happy ones, and fagging as a very tolerable chore.

Fags were liable to be punished by the Library for failures in their duties, and this often meant corporal punishment or 'smack-ing' as it was called. Younger boys would also be beaten fairly readily for failure to take exercise, or for breaches of house rules. This was a frightening experience enough, but worse was reserved for older boys who sinned more seriously. Bullies, for example, would be severely beaten by a principal School authority with a nobbly Pop cane. *The Eton Glossary*, published by boys as a guide to newcomers in 1902, says of the Pop cane: 'For purposes of chastisement it has a peculiar poignancy'. Lesser punishments, such as fining, were available and used with little compunction. Punishments usually seem to have been accepted without resent-ment, but there are cases of Oppidans appealing to the Captain of the Oppidans, which was thought more justifiable than appealing to the Housemaster. Dr Wingfield-Stratford, who was briefly at J.P. Carter's, wrote that:

> flogging [at Eton], and the endurance of flogging, were as much a form of athletics as compulsory football. There was no particular sense of shame involved, and hardly any of justice and responsibility. The upper boys quite frankly enjoyed beating the lower boys, and were proud of whatever skill they possessed in doing it so as to inflict maximum pain. The appetite naturally grew by what it fed on. Any or no excuse were considered good enough for the command 'Bend over'.[4]

This verdict may be justified of some houses, but Wingfield-Stratford was not himself beaten, and to Sir Harry Luke who was in the same house, this judgement was a travesty.[5] At some houses boys were unlikely ever to be beaten.

Clearly sometimes Housemasters did not know what was going on in their houses. House discipline and house games were regarded as matters for the boys. There was a good deal of difference between the tone of the best houses and that of the worst. One suspects that punishment was most freely given and least effective in the worst houses, but apparently a boy called Keppel was beaten ten times in a half in Evans's, which was certainly a good house. One of the worst houses was Allcock's, Sir Shane Leslie's house evoked in the novel, *The Oppidan*. Allcock, he later recorded, was far from a gentleman, and had a very bad Dame. At the end of 1902 a scandal broke just after Shane Leslie left which led to six boys being dismissed. Apparently a young boy returned home having nearly failed in Trials – 'You won't be able to stay at Eton unless you are a good boy', said his parents. 'I shan't be a good boy if I do stay at Eton' was the reply – and an unpleasant tale of brutality and (presumably) sex emerged.[6] Warre was deeply shocked, and toyed with a foolish scheme of having groups of vigilantes in each house; but he did not immediately take Allcock's house away. Dr Porter did lose his house because of rule-breaking. At one amnesty fifty-two packs of cards were surrendered. Narayan, his Indian house Captain, who was wildly in love, regularly climbed out at night to visit the lady in London. Porter's vanity apparently prevented him from seeing the evidence that all was not well.[7]

Happily there were many excellent houses, with Luxmoore's outstanding. The shy but upright and artistic Tutor inculcated civilized virtues in his boys. Perhaps they became priggish, for certainly Luxmoore's regarded themselves as a race apart. As Miss Evans observed, 'I think poorly of any Master who does not believe that his own house is the best of all'.[8] Many Housemasters no doubt did do so, and their views were usually shared by their boys. One of Macnaghten's boys offered a definition of a good house: 'The best houses are the ones where the boys manage themselves, where the master never seems to take any notice of what they do . . . The upper ones do what they think he would like, and the under ones do what they are told.'[9] It can be seen that Eton's prefectorial system was very different from Dr Arnold's conception, by which the prefects were the channels for the headmaster to reach the younger boys with his Christian message. At Eton the boy leaders emerged by election from their own peers, and the Housemaster's guiding hand could only be lightly applied, though certainly his need for vigilance was all the greater on that account.

An understanding of the working life of a successful Housemaster can be gleaned from Benson's diary. He also wrote books about schoolmastering, but the diary is spontaneous and not dressed for public consumption. A typical day in the winter began with 7.30 a.m. school. The morning was occupied continuously either in teaching or in writing letters (3,000 a year) until 2.00 p.m. dinner. At 3.00 p.m. he might take a bicycle ride or walk with a colleague. Then there would be more school or Private Business, which

might, if for example it was concerned with History, require
preparation. At 8.00 p.m. he might find himself helping boys with
work and going round the house. At 8.30 p.m. he would perhaps
be at a small supper party, but by 9.30 p.m. he would be going
round the house again to talk to the boys individually in their
rooms. Thereafter there might still be business to transact with
colleagues or an Ascham Society meeting, and Benson himself
would also try to carry forward his literary work or write up his
diary before bed at midnight.[10]

Benson's observations about the boys illustrate his understanding of them and the enduring characteristics of boys. We can learn
of the problems that fatherless boys, or (very occasionally) physically attractive small boys or bullied boys, suffer, and 'of a little
picking and stealing, which baffles me'. But boys' problems could
be discussed with prospect of amendment: 'I don't think boys *ever*
dislike being talked to about themselves, if only one is *fair*, & does
not suppress all the good points, as one feels inclined to do'.[11]
Then gratifyingly there would be progress to note – for example in
1899, George Lyttelton 'vexes me. He cares for nothing but
cricket'. A little later, 'The Lytteltons v. selfish – their convenience
the only consideration. But George may mend.' Soon after he is
reported to be keen on his work and he becomes house Captain: he
is $\alpha+$. By the autumn of 1901, Benson records his laughter at
discovering George Lyttelton (by then a 15-stone giant) in a bath
towel dispensing justice to lower boys. With Lyttelton and his
successor Alec Cadogan, Benson was extraordinarily blessed in his
Captains, but no doubt he had worked for his good fortune.
Certainly then and thereafter the character of a house could be
largely determined by its Captain.

Despite his success, which must have often been its own reward,
Benson found the grind too much. 'We are here (1) a maitre
d'hotel, (2) a clergyman, (3) a lecturer, (4) a coach, (5) a policeman
– most of us are athletes too – & Warre has made many reforms &
all have added to the masters' work & responsibilities.'[12] Policing
was the worst duty, and he did not think it proper that Masters
should indulge in espionage. In any case, Benson thought the scale
of sin – worst immorality, then cruelty, then dishonesty, then lying
– was wrong. He gave up his house and left the staff in 1903. Other
Masters did not have an alternative literary career to pursue. They
stuck with their tasks, more or less successfully. They were well

paid, but even the bad Housemasters worked long hours at their job.

College was a special case. There even stronger traditions of self-government had developed, but the Master-in-College was meant to exercise pastoral care. His position was even more disadvantageous than that of the non-Classical Housemasters, since the entire direction of Collegers' work rested with the Tutor, who submitted reports direct to the parents. The Master-in-College was still inadequately paid, and really the job was only tolerable for a young man with better expectations ahead. It was not easy for him to influence the older boys – the normally anodyne College Book records a sharp rebuke for Goodhart, the Master-in-College in 1896, for unwarranted interference.

Perhaps because Collegers lived closer together, particularly when young, more rules and customs regulated their lives. The Captain of Chamber, where the youngest boys lived in stalls which partitioned the old dormitory area of College, had had power since 1877 to maintain order with the siphon whose other function was to enable baths to be filled from a tap. Even when Collegers had rooms of their own they still ate tea together, and only the oldest boys messed like Oppidans. The Captain of the Tea Room kept order with a toasting fork. Any boy in Sixth Form or Liberty could beat any boy below him with the Captain of the School's permission. This was known as 'working off', the College equivalent to the Oppidans' smacking. Thus the 16-year-old Keynes reported in his diary: 'I was worked off very gently by Chute for throwing one pellet in hall last Thursday. He said I was going to throw more. He could see it in my eye. It gives him a great deal of pleasure and does not do me much harm.'[13] In fact when the senior boys were of a tolerant disposition, and they often were, the regime was not harsh. Sir David Scott, a few years younger than Keynes, avoided being caned throughout his time.[14]

Collegers still did not have altogether easy relations with Oppidans, particularly when young. One frequently reads that 'Collegers and Oppidans get on better than they did', and the only reasonable explanation is that young boys on both sides continued to be at odds, but as they grew older they learnt kinder ways. There was still some deliberate separation: Collegers did not enter the house competitions at football and cricket, and the St Andrew's Day Wall Game against the Oppidans remained more a trial of strength than a game; indeed College had acquired in J.K. Stephen* a hero to embody the myth of College superiority. But at least some Collegers were uneasy about their distinct culture: in 1893 the Captain of the School reflected in the College Annals:

> It is a pity that College does not hold the position in the school to which performances entitle us, owing largely to the way in which Collegers keep to themselves and do not try as a rule to get to know Oppidans until their last year. Of course no Colleger would doubt that College is infinitely superior to any house and most of all socially. But if we were less exclusive we need certainly not lose our *esprit de corps*, and College would have a better chance of taking its proper place as the leaders of the School socially and in athletics as well as in work. We need never degrade ourselves to the level of a house by entering for house-competitions, but it rests with us to do away with any ill-feeling which still remains between Collegers and Oppidans.

There may have been differences between houses, but there were strong forces working towards uniformity in the School. It seems to have been very much an age of conformity, with Etonians accepting the pains and pleasures of their lives unquestioningly. At this period many customs developed the force of the law. For example, dress became codified: Eton jackets for boys below 5 ft 5 ins; then tails, with stick-ups worn by Sixth Form, Pop, Upper Boat Choices, the Eleven. Pop took a number of other petty dress privileges to itself.† Although Dr Warre did intervene occasionally, most Masters allowed rules and regulations to develop at the boys' will, and the boys chose to impose standards which modern youth would find unacceptable. These standards were enforced, largely by the Eton Society who were keen to defend their own privileges, but who were not always ready to assist the Masters in the larger preservation of order.

---

* Collegers still drink to his memory. A gifted versifier, he was possessed of phenomenal strength. After leaving Eton he became mentally unstable, and one author even alleged that he was Jack the Ripper.

† Some privileges were rational, such as compelling other boys to walk on one side of the street, which kept one pavement clear for adults; but others, such as claiming an exclusive right to turn down overcoat collars, were irrational. The right to carry Pop canes in public, which should not have been permitted at all, was disputed; the Captains of the Oppidans felt that they as well as the Athletics Committee should be thus privileged.

In the area where Masters were responsible for order, there were more varied gradations of punishment, established by Warre. Tutors could sentence idle older boys to PS, Penal Servitude, which meant that they would have to work in Pupil Room with lower boys if their work was consistently bad. This sanction was a powerful incentive since boys were confined when they could otherwise be social, and they were slightly humiliated by being treated as juniors. Division Masters could not only give standard punishments for minor offences set out on 'tickets' which had to be signed by Tutors (both Tutors, when the Housemaster was not a Classic). They could also signify especial displeasure by using a Yellow Ticket. Cumulative or grievous sin would lead to a boy being complained of to the Head Master or Lower Master, when he might be placed on a White Ticket which not only imposed restraints on liberty but set a period in which the boy's work and behaviour had to be regularly approved. It was undoubtedly effective at a time when so much freedom was normally allowed. Failure to improve on a White Ticket or disgraceful behaviour would lead to a flogging. At Dr Warre's hands this was simply a shameful ceremony, but Austen Leigh undoubtedly intended to hurt.* In his years as Lower Master he apparently flogged some 300 boys (some more than once), about one boy in ten. In their different ways both men were effective, both respected and both liked.

At this time also the business of reporting on boys to Tutors was systematized. Classical reports were full and informative. Other reports, based on a smaller contact, were perfunctory.

If the Etonian polity sounds repressive, there were saving graces. The most important positive influence was the generally high level of civilization prevailing among the Masters. For example Sir Lawrence Jones says that he acquired from the coach of the VIII, de Havilland, enthusiasm for Georgian architecture, which was not widely appreciated at the time.[15] The friendship which often developed between Masters and boys was in itself an educational force.†

---

* Austen Leigh was known as 'the Flea', a name he acquired when he was a diminutive but physically active boy; but many Etonians supposed that the name was derived from the gusto with which he drew their blood.

† For example, Maurice Baring tells how his literary interests were encouraged, and how some Masters became very much his friends.

Two women also exercised a disproportionate influence. One was Miss Evans. Even in her seventies she was respected beyond her own house. She had acquired great wisdom about boys, and insight into character, and the simplicity and sanctity of her own life gave authority to her advice. She could not naturally exercise the control that she had done, but she was still close to her Library who tried to run the house as she would wish. Also at the end of her life her nephew, Sidney Evans, helped her. Some parents did feel that she was too old, but it is a remarkable fact that her house remained full and continued to enjoy a high reputation right up to her death.

The other remarkable woman was Mrs Warre Cornish, the wife of the Vice-Provost. (She appears in Shane Leslie's *The Oppidan* as Mrs Thackeray.) Boys were invited to her beautiful drawing-room with its William Morris wallpaper, to be entranced as much by the quality of the company they would meet as by the brilliance and unexpectedness of Mrs Cornish's own conversation.* They might also be taken to see the riches of College Library by the courteous and cultivated Vice-Provost. Some Masters regarded Mrs Cornish with alarm and thought her unfeeling and *posée*; to others she was an inspiration. As Leslie said, she was a *grande dame*, Miss Evans a great dame.

Certainly the generous hospitality of the Cornishs far outran the Vice-Provost's stipend.† It was no doubt a tribute to him that the Vice-Provost was first the Masters' Representative on the Governing Body, and then ex officio on the Governing Body – a better arrangement since it was difficult for him to represent the staff impartially when, as in the tutorial question, his past experience and bonds of friendship predisposed him to one view.

Sadly the Provost was not the same force for enlightenment. Now a widower, Hornby lived an even more reclusive life than he had as Head Master. The Vice-Provost had to rebuke him about his failure to discharge his duties, and he had lost the friendship of Warre. His inactivity was demonstrated over tree-planting on the newly acquired Dutchman's Farm: it was left to two Masters,

* Her recipe for a happy life: '*Quarante ans* – faith and a pack of hounds'. She could be disconcertingly unkind even to boys: 'Good evening, Mr Gay. What a pleasure it will be to hear you talking to us again about eschatology.'

† The Vice-Provost received a stipend of £25 and his house, and had a pension of £400 p.a. The family conferences on economy might end only with the conclusion that the parrot's seed ration should be cut.

Benson and Tatham, to acquire 500 trees – and then Hornby forbade planting on the grounds that he had not been consulted. Benson burst out in his diary: 'A pig-headed selfish man, the most unconscientious indolent official in England who spends nothing on the place, sees no one . . .'[16] and so on. But Hornby did make amends on this issue, and he could still charm away wrath when he aroused himself.

It was the Head Master rather than the Provost who took the initiative in organizing some of the great occasions that marked this period. Indeed Warre would plan every detail himself. The Queen's Jubilee in 1887 was celebrated in style, with the boys performing a torchlight tattoo in the courtyard of Windsor Castle. Dr Wilder, the Vice-Provost of the day, had actually also taken part as a boy in the Eton celebrations of George III's Jubilee in 1809.* In 1889 the Queen was in Eton to lay the foundation stone of the new Queen's Schools; and she returned in 1891 when her daughter, the Empress Frederick, unveiled the statue of her there over the archway. In 1891, also, her grandson the Kaiser inspected the Corps, an occasion when a boy discharged a blank under the Kaiser's horse. The boy, Cunliffe, survived to become Captain of the Eton and Oxford Elevens, and indeed Fellow of All Souls, but he was killed in the First World War. The Kaiser on the other hand lived on to write to the *Chronicle* in 1933 to deny that his horse had reared or that he had asked Dr Warre to expel the boy. Visits of other royal personages were less exciting, but led to the embarrassment of the Eton authorities who found themselves subjected to over-many requests for an extra week's holiday.

The Diamond Jubilee brought a repetition of the torchlight ceremony. Next year the School was represented at Gladstone's funeral. He had not been entirely happy on various visits to lecture at Eton. Once on going to the Pop room, he was dismayed to find a picture of a Derby winner. Another time he nearly found his own portrait turned face to the wall. Yet his devotion to Eton did not waver; on his last visit to lecture in 1891 he said, 'As I know your hearts are full of love for this glorious School, I may venture to say that I think my own heart is not less full'.[17] Then in 1901 at the Queen's death, Etonians lined a part of the route for her cortège, the Volunteers in front and the rest of the School behind them. All

* Dr Wilder, who was Vice-Provost from 1885 to 1893, was born in 1802. It will be understood that the post of Vice-Provost is not taxing.

were deeply moved. The new King, who insisted that Etonians had a privileged position at the funeral, proved to be as good a friend of the School as his mother. The King allowed the Boats to sup in the Home Park on the Fourth of June, Surly having closed in 1899. The royal visit in 1904, however, was not a success. Edward VII arrived in a bad temper and spent only a few minutes with the boys. In the Head Master's schoolroom, little Prince Eddy was made to kneel on the flogging block, while Queen Alexandra wielded an imaginary birch – an unedifying scene.[18]

The celebrations of the Fourth remained the principal School festival of the year. In 1891, there was a special celebration for the 450th year of the College, which was wrongly supposed to have been founded in 1441. Previous anniversaries of this kind had not been marked. Other events might excite Etonians – none more than the great flood in November 1894, which caused the School to go home for a few days.

At the end of the century Etonians found themselves caught up in the disasters of the Boer War, where so many had friends or relatives serving. Boys indeed left early in eagerness to enlist. Soon the *Chronicle* was recording the deaths of young OEs, and of one much loved at Eton, Major Myers, who had been appointed Adjutant to the Corps on retirement from the Sixtieth, but who re-enlisted and was quickly killed by a sniper's bullet. His generosity to the College included the bequest of his Egyptian collection, which remains one of the most glorious treasures of Eton. It is hard now to realize how the deaths of so many fine young men could be regarded as almost as much an occasion of pride as of sorrow. Hugh Macnaghten's epitaph on those who died in South Africa is moving, because it seems to have been true:

> Possessing all good things, at duty's call
> We died for England; that was best of all.[19]

Yet when better news came of the war, the Etonians fully shared it. There were near-riots after Ladysmith was relieved, and again when the Siege of Mafeking was broken. The boys *en masse* were ill-behaved, though their energies were sensibly channelled into an evening procession to Windsor to march past the Queen who appeared at a window in St George's quadrangle. Keynes reported back to his parents:

Feelings were first let off at Mr Broadbent's House, and it was found that windows and exuberance were quite incompatible. When there were no more left to break, the Eton Society (there is nothing like Pop keeping order on these occasions) drove off the mob . . . We do not break windows because we are mad with joy, but because we think that under the circumstances we can do so with impunity.[20]

Warre wished the boys to have a broader sense of responsibilities than this, and the Eton Mission continued to draw large sums of money from them, and to be fully reported in the *Chronicle*. In 1898 Eton House was built to accommodate a larger staff at Hackney Wick, and to permit boys to stay overnight on visits. Most boys no doubt gave only a passing glance to the little welfare state that was run in their name, but a few were permanently affected. Attempts were also made to involve boys with the Melanesian Mission. Heroic Old Etonians, some of whom had taught at Eton, had led the Mission work in New Zealand and the South Seas,* but the current Etonians were quickly surfeited by tales of their exploits; when yet another mention of Bishop Selwyn brought an audible groan from the congregation in Chapel, Warre had to deliver one of his effective little homilies.[21]

Chapel services had not improved all that much, and the sermons were not widely appreciated. Sir Lawrence Jones indeed only remembered with any favour Dr Porter's sermon in Lower Chapel – he was so amusing that he was not asked again – and the sermons of a new young master, Dr Alington, who really knew how to talk to boys. But Keynes is not so universally critical in his diary entries. The singing, both by Choir and congregation, was improved, thanks no doubt to the efforts of Barnby and Lloyd.

The interior of the Chapel itself was being improved after much mishandling. A new organ screen was built in 1882 as a memorial of the Afghan Wars. Then Luxmoore acquired and presented tapestries by Morris after designs of Burne-Jones. The centre panel was at first hung on the south side of the Chapel but, as part of the

---

* Bishop George Selwyn, the apostle to New Zealand, had been a Tutor who with William Evans instituted the swimming test; Bishop Abraham had been the first Master-in-College. Bishop Patterson, martyred in Melanesia, and Selwyn's son, also a bishop, were both Old Etonians.

Boer War Memorial, the east end was entirely reorganized. The
floor was repaved in black and white marble, a new free-standing
altar erected, and the tapestries hung behind. Once again Luxmoore took a leading part in this restoration, which did at least pay
some respect to the original plans of the Founder.*

Eton in Warre's time offered in general a picture of a well-
ordered enterprise where improvements in the fabric were being
matched by improvements in the product. Outside comment is
mostly favourable – but the remarkable fact is the extent of public
interest. The works of Nugent Bankes, written in Hornby's time,
were best sellers. *A day of my life or every-day experiences of Eton*
was written while the author was a 16-year-old boy in Cornish's
and earned him £100 for the copyright. It was reprinted many
times, and sold 10,000 copies between 1880 and 1889; together
with a companion volume a year later, *About some Fellows*, it must
have done much to disarm anxious parents with equally anxious
sons about to embark on an Eton career. The Eton it presents is
not a hard-working place – much talk of work but little action –
but it also is friendly and happy. The author returned to rework his
mine in 1901 with *An Eton Boy's Letters*. A better work of fiction
is *Tim*, written by Howard Sturgis in 1891, which explores the
relationship between two boys against an Eton background. In
that their friendship was romantic rather than physical, and largely
one-sided, it was probably true to life. At this time reminiscences
of an earlier Eton were appearing, and receiving reviews in the
Chronicle, which itself commanded a considerable circulation
outside Eton. So too did boys' literary journals, though perhaps
the best of these, the well-written *Seven Summers*, ran into a Head
Master's ban. An amusing spoof, *Eton as she is not*, commemorates
a deception played by some boys on an over-curious but credulous
journalist; they sent in accounts of spurious events such as
'Slunching the Paddocks' which were all printed. The journalist
proved to be the future Lord Northcliffe.

Many readers of Etoniana naturally were Old Etonians, and it is
no surprise that such a volume of sentiment for their old school
should have led them to follow the pattern of some other schools

---

* The tapestries conceal the verticals inherent in the architecture of the Chapel,
and a sculptured reredos, such as there once was, might have been preferable.
Luxmoore was also anxious to acquire a copy of Watts' Sir Galahad: the artist,
much moved, gave this freely.

and found an Old Etonian Association in 1897.* The choice of a colour for the tie proved more troublesome than the founding of the Association, but in 1900 the present discreet blue stripe on black replaced a more flamboyant blue on white.

The pride of Old Etonians in their school extended to the boys. One or two American visitors were struck by this, as by the absence of luxury, and by the fact that games took place without supervision. But did pride narrow minds? In Hornby's time and earlier, boys lived very independent lives and thought their own thoughts. Was it now too conformist a society? Lawrence Jones wrote that he was never again to experience the glory, the power, and the patronage that he had as Captain of the Boats.[22] Is this an indication both that Eton was too self-regarding and that it sapped ambition?

Certainly Etonians grew up in an extraordinarily leisured way. By the time they left, they should have outgrown boyish things, and Lawrence Jones claimed that this was the case more than with other undergraduates he met at Oxford.[23] Boys who enjoyed Eton were more agreeable because of it: happiness helps. Even less obviously successful boys like Lord Berners, who left young because of ill-health and who saw danger in one's golden age coming too early, 'never regretted having been to Eton, although I left it as Antony left Cleopatra, with more love than benediction'.[24]

We have already met J.M. Keynes, but think also of Arthur Villiers, born the same year (1883) and a fellow member of the Eton Society. Here was a boy who cultivated style in a way which some have seen as characteristically Etonian.† With the confidence born of success he would lead the Ram into Chapel sporting a large

* Lord Rosebery, the first President, said that he knew only one Old Etonian who had not liked the School: was this Lord Salisbury, his successor as Prime Minister? He was known to have disliked Eton, even though he sent his sons. The next President was A.J. Balfour, Salisbury's successor, who had a Cabinet of whom half were OEs.

† The Hon Arthur Villiers was at Donaldson's. Donaldson's brother, the future Bishop of Salisbury, was Eton Missioner, and his wife, Lady Albinia, had also devoted her formidable powers to organizing women in the Mission. As a young boy, Villiers, in trouble with his Tutor, said, 'Sir, I have been praying hard about this and I know that God has forgiven me. I assume that in the circumstances you will too.' That worked. Later in the XI he failed to score in either innings at Lord's; Lord Jersey was greatly distressed, but Arthur said, 'I am most awfully sorry, father, but after all it's only a game'.

dahlia in his buttonhole.[25] But he was to settle at Eton House in Hackney Wick when he began his career in the City, and throughout his life he was to work actively for, and to devote his fortune to, the people of Hackney Wick and Leytonstone. Keynes and Villiers, one by intellect, the other by action, were to tackle the problem of economic deprivation. Clearly the experience of Warre's Eton did not prevent the growth of social conscience, nor its effective operation.

Etonians of Warre's time contributed richly to the national life of the first half of the twentieth century, and they were not as stereotyped as Warre's critics claim. But was it a golden age? Perhaps it was easier for Etonians to dominate their fellows than it is now, for reasons which have origins outside Eton. Viewed objectively Eton did have faults. The curriculum remained imperfect, despite the academic success which Etonians achieved, for example, in Science. The quality of teaching was variable for a school which claimed to be a leader, and which paid such high salaries. Above all, too much depended upon the particular house in which a boy boarded. Warre's Eton had considerable virtues but it was by no means perfect.

CHAPTER SIX

Edward Lyttelton and the First World War

CONSIDERING THAT THE Governing Body had been nerving itself to push Dr Warre into retirement for some time before he told them that he would leave in July 1904, it is remarkable that it should have given such inadequate thought to his possible successor. True, a decision had been made that the new Head Master should be paid £4,750 instead of the £6 per boy that made Dr Warre one of the top earners in the country (with just over £6,000 or roughly £250,000 in modern money). As to the actual selection, no steps had been taken, and a different appointment with considerable bearing on the headmastership was made first.

In July 1904 Warre Cornish ceased to be the elected Masters' Representative on the Governing Body, and was co-opted as Vice-Provost. (The Vice-Provost became from that time ex officio a member of the Governing Body.) It is unlikely that this lovable man would have been re-elected, in view of his partisan handling of the tutorial question. At any rate, Somerville,* an Irishman who taught Maths and French to the Army Class and was not a Tutor, conceived the idea of running Arthur Benson as Masters' Representative. Benson was still resident at Eton, working on the editing of Queen Victoria's correspondence in Windsor Castle, though he had just been invited by the new Master of Magdalene College, Cambridge, his old colleague Donaldson, to become a Fellow there. Benson had on the whole supported the non-Classical Masters, and yet most of his close friends were Classics. It seemed

* Later MP for Windsor.

that he would be a well-informed Representative who might push the Governing Body towards a solution of this troublesome dispute. Furthermore, Benson wanted the job, for which he felt well qualified. Unfortunately some of the younger Classical Tutors, led by A.B. Ramsay, were determined to stop Benson. They wished to preserve the dominant role of Classics in the curriculum, and the position of the Classical Tutor as controller of a boy's educational progress – together with the associated financial advantages. They enlisted M.R. James, a Fellow of King's, as their candidate for Representative. Benson had no taste for competitive election, particularly with James who was a friend. He and James agreed to withdraw to avoid a contest, and the Masters, after sounding some twenty other possible Representatives, eventually selected Eldon Bankes, a KC. Benson believed that he would have won (though Somerville did not campaign well for him), but he was hurt by an unpleasant letter from Ramsay and the knowledge that some of his oldest friends would not have voted for him. Such were the ugly consequences of the tutorial question.

Benson, then aged 43, was thought by many, including most of the Fellows, to be the obvious successor to Warre. He had himself always had doubts about this, and his rejection turned him more powerfully against seeking the headmastership. He was a good teacher and had run a very successful boys' house (despite an aristocratic clientele, which has often proved difficult to manage). His father had been Master of Wellington as well as Archbishop of Canterbury; he was an Old Colleger, he was the author of a number of books and of poetry including the first, less jingoistic, lyrics for 'Land of Hope and Glory', and his literary circle was wide. To the outside world he was the most distinguished Etonian schoolmaster. Yet, like other members of his gifted family, he was a depressive and homosexual. In his diary he wrote that he admired Johnson whose affection ruled his great intellect, whereas he had allowed his own intellect to rule his affections: we may think his was the better way. Certainly while he was at Eton he kept pederasty and depression at bay. It is possible that had he been Head Master, he would have found himself too occupied to be depressed, but in fact he was to suffer a breakdown in 1907 and another ten years later. His black moods, his bachelor state, and his sensitivity to criticism would undoubtedly have made a Head Master's life difficult and solitary.

The other candidates were not outstanding – four Headmasters who had taught at Eton, Edward Lyttelton of Haileybury, Lionel Ford of Repton, Sydney James of Malvern (brother of M.R. James), and Charles Lowry of Tonbridge. F.H. Rawlins, who was to succeed Austen Leigh as Lower Master and later Warre Cornish as Vice-Provost, was the strongest candidate on the existing staff – an amiable (if loquacious) and competent man, he was already 52 and had been rejected by Marlborough; the young Master-in-College, Cyril Alington, was an outside possibility. The Provost and Fellows do not seem to have considered anyone at the Universities or any schoolmaster without an Eton connection.

The four Headmasters and Rawlins were interviewed on 15 March 1905, but Benson did not appear. On 6 March he had written to the Provost to say that he did not think he could form a ministry – in other words he realized that some key members of the Classical Department would not support his programme. On 7 March he had stated conditions in a letter to the Vice-Provost: that he would only accept if he was really *wanted* by the Provost and Fellows, that he should have a real chance of being supported by the staff, and that it was put to him that it was his duty to accept the headmastership. He did agree at the instigation of Sir William Anson to write a paper setting out what needed to be done at Eton by way of reform. The minor suggestions that verses might be dropped by less able boys and some work transferred from Tutor to division Master were enough to alienate the Vice-Provost. Nevertheless, the Provost and Fellows did not reach a decision on 15 March and the Provost wrote to Benson to ask him to an interview on 29 March. At that meeting, where Hornby was very much in command, the tutorial question remained an issue. Anson and probably the majority of the Fellows were anxious to have Benson, but he was clear that he would only say yes if asked unreservedly by all.[1]

It was hardly surprising that the Fellows turned away from Benson – he had required too much. This second rejection wounded Benson again – he would not revisit Eton until Warre Cornish was dying in 1916. Yet was he not himself to blame? Luxmoore wrote to Monty James on 2 April:

I am not sorry that he is not to be Head Master, as I think the standards wd have been relaxed, & also that he wd have hated it

& not lived his real life. but I wd gladly have served under him. nevertheless I don't think he has shewn all along so much sagacity & practical tact as I expected in so quick & experienced a man. he ought to have stood or not stood. there has been too much shilly shally & not enough reticence ... but he is hurt & disappointed & that goes to one's heart, for his kindness and frankness do not deserve such wounds.[2]

The Fellows still had to choose from the other candidates. Warre Cornish, who had been Rawlins' Tutor, apparently thought that he was not up to the headmastership. Lord Cobham was able to press the claims of his brother, Edward Lyttelton, and on 5 April he was selected. When the news reached Eton, Alington saw Rawlins coming across School Yard, obviously quite broken; he ran out to offer sympathy, and Rawlins said: 'They have made the biggest mistake of their lives'. But before the day was over, he had pulled himself together. As Lower Master he was to do much of the Head Master's work for him, and no one ever heard a disloyal word.[3]

The Honourable and Reverend Canon Edward Lyttelton may have lacked Benson's intellectual distinction, but he was still a considerable and unusual personality. He had acquired a scholarship at Trinity College, Cambridge, and had originality as a thinker. He was a most gifted athlete, captaining the Cambridge Cricket XI which beat the Australians in 1878, playing soccer for the Old Etonians in an FA Cup Final and for England against Scotland. He was an enthusiastic musician with a fine bass voice, and his wife was also a notable singer. Furthermore he belonged to a most distinguished Eton family, the seventh of eight famous brothers, sons of Lord Lyttelton who served on the Clarendon Commission.

All these advantages would have recommended Edward Lyttelton – but he also had prepared himself (after two years at Wellington) by apprenticeship as a successful division Master and Tutor, when he shared accommodation with Benson, and as Headmaster of Haileybury for fifteen years, in which time he did much for the school and enjoyed the goodwill of boys, parents and staff alike.

Lyttelton was also a man of the strongest principles and deeply religious. He regarded teaching as a Christian vocation. As Benson remarked in his diary: '[Edward] has great courage, great honesty, great high-mindedness – indeed he is perfectly fearless and honourable'.[4] Sometimes his regard for truthfulness made him less than charitable, and the quirkiness of his mind made his judgement suspect and sometimes unfair. Indeed there was lack of sensitivity as well as misjudgement in two letters which Lyttelton wrote to Benson even while the headmastership was undecided. The first merely asked, 'Am I wanted?' when Warre's retirement was announced, and that was difficult for Benson to answer, aware as he was of Lyttelton's shortcomings as well as of his qualities; and it suggested that Lyttelton was quite blind to Benson's own possible claims for the job. The second was even more tactless. Written on 22 March 1905 after Lyttelton had been seen by the Fellows and before Benson was interviewed, it was a scarcely veiled attempt to induce Benson to withdraw – he should not go for the job unless he was sure to accept, because the Governing Body would be embarrassed by a refusal.

More seriously, Lyttelton lacked intellectual coherence. His mind would pursue fads about hygiene, such as liking to sleep in the open air. (He was also a vegetarian; luckily his wife shared these enthusiasms.) At Eton the administrative problems demanded closer attention than he cared to give them, and his inattention to finance led some acrid critics to doubt whether he had ever fully grasped the difference between capital and interest. P.A. Macindoe had been appointed Junior Bursar in 1902 with the specific task of administering the School Fund, which was the Head Master's responsibility; he used to relate, without rancour, how difficult it was to persuade Lyttelton to concentrate on financial matters. Even his nephew, George Lyttelton, a distinguished Eton Master, stated many years later that he had 'a head full of feathers'.

He was not a first-rate scholar, and this was a serious handicap considering that the Head Master always taught the Sixth Form. He ought no doubt to have refused to do so. It was already partly entrusted to C.M. Wells, a brilliant scholar and teacher, and another Master could certainly have been co-opted. He had a gift for finding interesting things to say off the main subject, and there was no lack of effort on his part. He won the devotion of his Sixth Form, but inspired great mistrust in what he taught. Geoffrey Madan recalled: 'Whether in classics or theology, his teaching was positively corrosive of sound learning and only less so of religion.' On one dreadul occasion a boy misconstrued 'Rex Pheras progressus est' ('the king advanced to Pherae') as 'King Pheras advanced', and was uncorrected; another boy, spotting the howler, asked 'Sir, will you tell us about King Pheras?' 'One of those old Macedonian kings. Tell you about him another time.' Nor could he keep the Sixth Form in order. Geoffrey Bridgeman who was up to him in his last four halves looked back on the Brown Man, as he was universally known because of the bronze complexion engendered by his enthusiasm for open air, with a mixture of affection and amusement. 'The amount of tomfoolery which B.M. tolerated was well-nigh incredible. Whether he observed it all with secret amusement or never noticed it will never be known – almost certainly the latter.' The three senior Collegers occupied a bench and desk which were movable, 'and a favourite antic was to inch both desk and bench imperceptibly forwards until they reached the middle of the room where they remained for a short time and then equally gradually retreated'. He also records the following dialogue between the Head Master and Ralph Gamble KS, a very good-looking boy killed in 1918. At an early school on a hot summer day, Gamble was clad in greatcoat and purple cricket scarf. B.M. was of course known to be keenly interested in health and hygiene.

B.M.   Take off that coat.
R.G.   Sir, I'm feeling rather chilly this morning. I'd rather . . .
B.M.   Oanh,* take it off.
R.G.   Sir, I . . .
B.M.   OANH, TAKE IT OFF.
       [R.G. complied and was seen to be stark naked from the waist up.]
B.M.   Oanh, put it on.

Lyttelton was not always so tolerant. He was interested in boys' pastoral welfare and maintained the observance of the School rules on the whole effectively, but without losing boys' goodwill. Yet his lack of judgement was evident from time to time; Geoffrey Chance, when almost in Sixth Form, was taxed with another boy over some misdemeanour in Luxmoore's garden. The Head Master proposed to cane them and was surprised that they did not

---

* A curious grunt with which Lyttelton frequently prefaced remarks.

willingly accept his punishment. Why? 'First of all, we did not do it. Secondly, we are too senior to be beaten.'[5]

Boys forgave Lyttelton his shortcomings, recognizing his transparent goodness. Masters, less immediately warm-hearted, felt more acutely his incompetence. Yet Conybeare, one of the best young Masters, argued that it was right to have Lyttelton as Head Master rather than Rawlins: Edward was very inefficient and Rawlins very efficient, but Edward had so much soul and Rawlins none.[6] His years as Head Master were to be years of conflict, but his quality as a man outweighed failure as a Head Master.

Immediately on Lyttelton's appointment, he had an unpleasant case to handle. The Captain of Williams's house was found to have been systematically corrupting younger boys. He was sacked, and Williams's, which had reached the final of the house Football Cup, were obliged to scratch. This justified firmness seems to have helped to bring about some improvement in the tone of the School.*

His first year was made more troublesome by the dominance of a very clever cluster of boys at the top of the School: it is sometimes easier for Head Masters to have more straightforward athletes in charge. A group managed to produce six numbers of an ephemeral called *The Outsider* during the months of June and July 1906 – it was both amusing and more irreverent than was customary, with jokes for instance at the expense of the pretentiously named Committee of Taste which was presiding over the construction of the Memorial Buildings. Of the seven Editors, five, Charles Lister, Julian Grenfell, Patrick Shaw-Stewart, C.A. Gold, and Edward Horner, were to die in the World War, their brilliance and promise rendered unassailable by death, any youthful tiresomeness condoned.†

Gradually Lyttelton increased his control on the School, however, helped by the replacement as time passed of some of the weaker Housemasters by better men. The first replacement was

---

* P. Williams was a bad Housemaster, complacent because of the athletic success of his house. C.A. Elliott, the future Head Master, boarded there for two halves in 1902–3. He was beaten on his first night as a fag – and he later used this experience as a cautionary tale when talking to house Captains. At the time he felt, 'This was just the kind of thing one must expect in life. But there were certain things which I could *not* stomach and against which I did react.'

† Ronnie Knox was also an Editor, possibly even more gifted. He and Robin Laffan survived.

poignant for him. In January 1906, Miss Evans died just short of her eightieth birthday. He was one of her Old Boys. There was an agitation not just limited to members of the house that she should be succeeded by her nephew Sidney Evans, the Drawing Master, who had helped her a good deal in later years. Warre had warned Sidney that he would not succeed, claiming that he was not senior enough (he was not technically a Master since his subject lacked sufficient status). Lyttelton stuck by this decision, a position made much easier for him by the commendable restraint of Sidney Evans. Evans's had been something of a self-governing fiefdom and the School rules were not so punctiliously applied there in all respects. M.D. Hill succeeded to the majority of the boys, and was to prove a successful Housemaster. He had to move to Gulliver's, a small house, 'ideally unsuitable for its purpose'; it was rat infested; in two of its dark ill-ventilated boys' rooms the ceilings had collapsed.[7] It serves as a reminder that Etonians did not live in great luxury.

Lyttelton managed to tame some of the more arrogant manifestations of school life – for example 'hoisting' winners of School events, particularly on the river, was stopped, and so were Mediterranean-style promenades of boys in the streets on summer evenings. Some other tiresome frolics of Pop were also restrained. Of course, boys would still get up to the old escapades, and modern technology brought new opportunities – boys kept motor bikes in Windsor, for instance. Yet the general tone of the School seems to have improved from its low point at the end of Warre's reign. Lyttelton also urged Housemasters to curb beating in their houses.

One useful reform was the reorganization of Leave. Boys could previously take Leave away from School, a Long Leave, and Short Leave, at their convenience, provided they did not miss more than an acceptable number of School periods. Lyttelton arranged that the whole School should take a rather longer, co-ordinated Long Leave at the same time. In the summer, Leave coincided with the Lord's match against Harrow.

Reform of behaviour was seldom controversial but reform of the curriculum was to occasion Lyttelton much trouble on two fronts. First, it was not easy to persuade Masters, particularly the Classics Masters, to accept any change. Secondly, it proved even more difficult to induce the Provost and Fellows to provide the funds needed to finance change. This was partly because they seem to have become more aware of their financial difficulties after Dr Warre's empire-building, and partly because Lyttelton lacked his predecessor's force and skill in dealing with the Governing Body.

Straightaway it was accepted that Greek need not be compulsory for entering the School, though it was still expected that the better boys should take the subject, which remained a qualification for entry to Oxford and Cambridge until after the First World War. Another organizational improvement was to make boys take Common Entrance in an examination at their preparatory schools: it had been the practice for boys to arrive at Eton and then take an examination on which they were placed – which made it more difficult to fail those who were not of required standard.* Further up the School, boys who had acquired the School Certificate introduced in 1910 were more free to specialize, when they could abandon all study of the Classics. At the same time less use was made of the Higher Certificate Examination; instead Eton's own July Examination was the final test of Etonians. This remained no very compelling goal for those who did not choose to work hard.

Unfortunately Science was seldom chosen for specialization, and after a few years it transpired that Eton was doing less Science than the law required. Sir Henry Roscoe and his successor as Royal Society Fellow, Sir Henry Miers, were active to improve this shortcoming. An outside report was invited, which suggested wholesale change, including notably the appointment of a Head of Science. Up to that time the five Science Masters had never been adequately co-ordinated. The excellence of M.D. Hill in Biology, the brilliance of Dr Porter in Chemistry, and the eccentricity of the young Physics Master, John Christie,† were unharnessed. It is nevertheless true that several of the few boys who persevered with Science proved to be exceptional: Moseley, who died at Gallipoli,

---

* Even then exceptions were made: Tom Harley, having failed for Winchester, arrived in September at Eton but was judged to have failed again. His father asked Lyttelton, 'Do you never make exceptions?' Lyttelton, who could not lie, admitted that he had for Prince George of Teck. 'Then why not for my son?' In this case the result was successful for Eton and for the boy.

† He brought with him Bertie Wolfe as a laboratory assistant, who served quite admirably at Eton until 1959. He himself was a less successful teacher and in later years would send his butler to early school for him – 'Captain Christie will be along presently, gentlemen'. Known to Benson as the musical motorist, he was later to found Glyndebourne Opera.

was probably the greatest Etonian discoverer after Robert Boyle. Egerton, one of the founders of the Scientific Society at Eton, was a most distinguished Fellow of the Royal Society; J.B.S. Haldane and Julian Huxley were to pay tribute to the inspiration of Hill's teaching. It would seem that Science suffered, not because of its own teachers, but because the other Masters did not encourage boys into what they regarded as not an Etonian subject.* Furthermore, there was little opportunity to attract boys lower in the School, since little Science was taught, and it was not possible for more to be taught unless more Masters were employed. Yet Dr Lyttelton, willing though he was for reform, could not obtain from the Provost and Fellows funds to hire the Head of Science whom he wished to employ, let alone to increase the numbers of the Science staff.

Not long after this failure, he was able to appoint a new Classic, but Classics Masters, drawing most of their salary from pupils, were less of a burden on the School Fund. The Provost and Fellows should no doubt have increased the fee, but they were extremely reluctant to do so, and the basic annual school fee payable in 1916 when Dr Lyttelton retired was only 1½ guineas more than it had been in 1905; parents were paying more, but only as extras for new services and a larger house fee. Nor could the College subsidize the School. The agricultural estates remained poor investments. Something like £10m. in modern money had been borrowed against the security of the Chalcots estate. The sale of land required the permission of the Ministry of Agriculture which was charged with ensuring that Charities did not sell property improperly; the College was, however, able to sell another portion of Chalcots to the railways just before the War.

In two areas Lyttelton was able to bring about reforms dear to him. First, physical education was introduced into the curriculum for boys who did not do Greek, and all lower boys had some training. The instruction in the Gymnasium, completed in 1907, was given by ex-military instructors who were paid by special fee. Along with the Gym, an indoor rifle-range was provided in its roof, and facilities for fencing and boxing were added. But the Governing Body was not prepared to countenance an indoor

* Some Classicists claimed that boys naturally 'preferred Henry's holy shade to Huxley's shady hole'; but they biased the boys' choice.

swimming-pool – arguing that the charges for its use would be unacceptable to parents.

Secondly, the arrangements for Music were made a little more generous. From 1906 boys could leave morning schools to be taught Music. Dr Lloyd, the Precentor, was principally employed to play the organ in Chapel and to train the Choir, but he did give Music lessons, with one official assistant, Dr Morsch, and other instrumentalists according to need. Dr Morsch had no guaranteed pension, and what the College offered hardly permitted him to retire. Eventually an adequate sum was found and Morsch returned to Germany; the onset of War gave an excuse to stop his pension, which was only grudgingly restored in 1920. By the end of Lyttelton's time, however, Mr Basil Johnson, who succeeded Dr Lloyd in 1914, had six official assistants. The School Concert was moved to the new School Hall – a popular occasion well attended by the boys who also cheerfully joined the Musical Society, but it must be admitted that the programmes lacked the serious quality of modern concerts, and orchestral standards were low.

Lyttelton also doubtless supported the Vice-Provost's scheme of 1909 for reopening the Choir School. A small day prep school was in effect opened, so that boys in the Choir could receive not just musical training but an all-round education. There was provision for sixteen choristers and twelve probationers; dinner was provided in College Hall; and some provision was made for further training of the musically gifted (by way of two £25 exhibitions) and for placing boys in apprenticeships. This scheme recaptured some of the Founder's wishes, even though it was not quite all that Miss Hackett wished.

Lyttelton was also responsible for the introduction of Oppidan Scholarships (OS) in 1909. These entirely honorific titles were given to boys who were successful in the College Examination but who chose not to go to College. They were still placed one year below those who did go into College, an illogicality which persisted for more than fifty years. The title may have had some slight influence in creating academic prestige, but it could be an embarrassment to the young OS.

The overall condition of the curriculum and of boys' academic performance was recognized among the Masters to be unsatisfactory, but there was no agreement about what should be done. For some the solution was the adoption of a modern side; others felt there should be a return to the classical core and fewer subjects. It was quite widely argued that in order to solve the salary problem – the inequality between Classics and others – the staff must be *reduced*, which could be done by allocating less time to subjects which had to be taught in smaller groups. The Head Master must be blamed for not taking a clearer lead.

In 1910 an inspection of the School added to the criticism of academic affairs. The team of dons found fault with many aspects of classical teaching – for example that it was excessively literary, and that Pupil Room work was not systematic enough and was dropped too abruptly when boys left the Lower School. English standards were not good enough – too few essays were written. Teaching by the Classical Masters of History was careful rather than stimulating; of Geography it was with one exception inadequate. Arrangements for Science were still unsatisfactory. Too many boys over 17 were under-motivated, and they would have left school had they come from less wealthy families. The final judgement of the Classical Inspectors was indeed two-edged: 'If we have laid stress on certain things which seem to us to be defects, we do not forget that Eton's highest service to the nation is that she educates boys whose circumstances make it difficult or impossible for the school work to be as important in their eyes as it is in the eyes of less fortunate schoolboys.'

At this time there was also a significant drop in the numbers in the School, for the first time since the 1830s. In 1908 there were 1,045 boys, but by 1912 the number dipped to 998. Whereas in 1906 a peak number of 414 had been entered, of whom 224 came to the School, in 1910 only 301 were entered, of whom 195 actually came to the School. In early 1912 there were, surprisingly, only 301 sons of Old Etonians. Lyttelton thought that the fall in numbers might be attributed to the School's inadequate provision for boys who did not shine socially or athletically, and who were not motivated by their schoolwork: even if too many remained for the academic health of the School, too many were lost for its financial health. Lyttelton also thought that the disunity of Masters might be responsible. Certainly the unequal attraction of different houses must have had considerable effect; parents who could not secure the Housemaster of their choice would not necessarily place sons in what they saw as a second-rate house, but would move to another school. A scheme of bursaries for sons of OEs was considered, but since it was suggested that the bulk of the remission should be financed by the Housemasters themselves, it was not attractive to them. The Provost and Fellows declined to be drawn into any such scheme, adjourning discussion *sine die*. Numbers recovered slightly after 1912, and no more was heard of the problem, but its existence even temporarily was an indication that all was not well.

Eton remained a very closed community in which the interests of the boys were above all in their own world, and particularly in sport, as examination of almost any issue of the *Chronicle* shows. The editors were quick to defend any treasured institution, for example the beagles which were attacked by Henry Salt, the former Master, in his pamphlet, 'The Eton Hare Hunt'. They would not have been free to question anything very fundamental about Eton's position, even if they had wished to do so, but they were very willing to criticize any behaviour of the boys which would reflect on the School – boys loafing in the streets, slouching about, or behaving badly during an outside lecture, and so on. The outside world was, however, impinging more seriously on Eton. Charles Lister* was probably the first Etonian to be a Socialist at School, his radical views if anything adding to his prestige. When in February 1908 a deputation of unemployed, on their way to present a petition to the King at Windsor, were allowed to hold a meeting in School Yard, many boys were present and cheered wildly at intervals. The friendliness of the boys was probably aimed more at upsetting authority than demonstrating sympathy, and it was not echoed in the correspondence to the *Chronicle*, where protests from present as well as past Etonians complained about the desecration of the Chapel steps. There certainly were voices at Eton raised on behalf of the disadvantaged, but it seems likely that they were not much more numerous than in Warre's time.

The Eton Mission remained the approved vehicle for awakening boys' social consciences, and in Lyttelton's time it perhaps reached its zenith. Much money and energy poured into Hackney Wick, with the result that boys sometimes complained that the area was now too prosperous:† should not Eton transfer its activities to

---

* The Hon Charles Lister KS, a son of Lord Ribblesdale.

† But not so sanitized in the eyes of authority: boys were inoculated before they visited the Mission.

another part of London? The congregation overflowed, and the Missioner wished to extend his church (in accordance with Bodley's original plan) and to build a tower. At that time there was resident a young OE, Gerald Wellesley, running the Boys' Club; it too was overflowing. Wellesley became convinced that the boys should not be turned away at 18, and started an Eton Old Boys Club, which also outgrew its premises. So funds were needed for a new building. At Eton, the Council had to resolve the rival claims, for both projects could not be financed. Some boys (to judge from letters in the *Chronicle*) did realize that a club was more important than the tower, that the work of a mission is with people; but the establishment view prevailed, that the Missioner was best placed to determine what the parish needed. Gerald Wellesley decided then to raise the money he needed himself. By 1913 the Eton Manor Clubs were established in fine premises,* but they were separate and secular. The summer camps at Cuckoo Weir,† started by Gerald Wellesley, were continued, and Eton boys could help. The Manor was to be a remarkable creation, still more perhaps when Arthur Villiers, who had always been at Gerald Wellesley's right hand, took command. But the Mission suffered, through the fault of the clergy both in the original conflict and in allowing a breach to continue for some thirty years.‡ Mission and Manor were both great institutions in East London, but as one they would have been more than the sum of their parts; and the split certainly lessened the appeal of the Mission to Etonians.

While conflict marked so many issues at Eton, nevertheless there were public events on which all could unite. The School Hall was opened in 1908 and the Library in 1910. Between these occasions Provost Hornby died in 1909 at the age of 82, physically active and a good chairman and speaker to the end. His funeral was an impressive occasion, marked by traditional ceremony. The gates of School Yard were kept shut until his successor, Dr Warre, was chosen by the Crown, and he was quickly admitted in December. No other man was likely to be chosen, but Warre was too old and too ill to be an effective Provost, though he still was a commanding presence in his first few years. He was able to enjoy another two

---

* Designed by Goodhart-Rendel, best of Etonian architects.
† One of the School bathing-places, on a backwater of the Thames.
‡ The view of the Missioners seemed to be that the Manor was a respectable half-way house which actually prevented the young coming to Christianity.

royal visits, on the second of which George V declared his intention of sending his son Prince Henry to the School.

Another splendid occasion was the Pop Centenary Dinner held in School Hall. A remarkably high proportion, 405 out of a possible 1,310 old members, attended. Lord Rosebery, by now a Fellow, presided; there were seven courses, six wines, and six speeches; and a special train conveyed the revellers to London. 'Phrases such as "the aristocracy of merit and distinction at Eton", "Eton the heart of Empire", "the tradition of Eton to produce leaders", were proclaimed amid cheers, and all departed with conviction that they had shared in the apotheosis of the Eton spirit.'[8] But A.C. Benson, who was not present, remarked in his journal that it was so vulgar.

Two deaths perhaps encapsulated the Eton spirit rather better. In 1912 Captain Oates walked out into the snow to give his comrades a better chance of return from the South Pole, an act commemorated in the colonnade of the new Memorial Buildings. Alfred Lyttelton, the Head Master's youngest brother and a former Tory Cabinet Minister, died suddenly in the summer of 1913: gifted with every talent and universally loved, he was what every father wished an Etonian son to be.* He too was commemorated by a portrait in School Hall. Both men were seen by the *Chronicle* as examples to their successors.

At least one young hero, however, emerged from the School itself, Fowler, the Eton Captain at Lord's in 1910. The victory that Eton achieved that year lived for long in cricket history as *the* example of how a game could be retrieved from the depths of adversity. Harrow had scored 232 in their first innings (Fowler, 4 for 90), and Eton collapsed – all out for 67 (Fowler, 21). Following on, they lost 5 wickets for 65, and all seemed lost. Fowler, however, stood firm – scoring 64. Nevertheless, Eton were only 4 runs ahead when the ninth wicket fell. A gallant last pair added 50, but what sort of target was 55 runs after Harrow's first innings? Yet Harrow were soon reduced to 32 for 9. Their last pair also showed courage, adding 13 runs, before the final wicket fell and Eton were left victorious by 9 runs. Fowler had taken 8 for 23. The excitement of the crowd, the delirium of the Eton supporters, surpassed all previous occasions, and enthused the country as a

---

* Indeed, what every English father wished his son to be – as Asquith said in a famous tribute paid in the Commons.

whole in a way that now seems incomprehensible. Fowler was a national figure – a telegram addressed to 'Fowler's Mother, London' was successfully delivered. C.M. Wells, coach of the XI, remarked with typical understatement that Fowler was not a bad fellow.

The last few years before the War saw Eton at length begin to assert a superiority over Harrow in a number of excellent matches. Perhaps some cricketers were inspired by the brilliant final innings they saw their Head Master play on Upper Club in 1913. But it was as a social gathering rather than as a cricket match that Lord's flourished. In 1914 in perfect weather another splendid game brought another Eton victory from behind. The total attendance over two days was 38,000. In the years that followed, that golden occasion became the romantic epitome of the world that was lost.[9]

A little more than three weeks later, while the OTC (as the Corps had become in 1908) was at camp, war was declared. The camp broke up hurriedly on Bank Holiday Monday, 4 August, and many boys rushed to enlist: some who were expected back at School in September did not return, eager for service, and if they had the OTC's Certificate A they quickly became officers. A few others, mostly resident abroad, were also absent. Five Masters had also already enlisted (M. de Satgé with the French army); three, George Fletcher, Eric Powell, and Charles Gladstone, had been specially recruited to serve as liaison officers. When the challenge came, Etonians, like so many contemporaries, responded as their traditions and ideals required. Already in the second *Chronicle* of the Michaelmas Half, a list of forty fallen was published under the heading *Etona Non Immemor*, and similar lists were to be published in every issue throughout the War. Sometimes a poetic epitaph appeared, in Latin or Greek as well as in English. Often a letter from a friend or a short obituary by a Tutor would be published, speaking of the courage and cheerfulness with which the young officer had met his end. Pride tempered by sorrow is the predominant note. Nothing quenched the eagerness to reach the front line. As Julian Grenfell was to write in his poem 'Into Battle':

> He is dead who will not fight;
> And who dies fighting has increase.

Inevitably the life of the School was profoundly affected. So

many unexpected leavers left the School short of boys, but twenty
Belgian boys, led by Prince Leopold, arrived in November to fill
some of the empty rooms. The finances of the School would have
been seriously affected, but for the departure of nine Masters, not
all of whom were replaced, and for the system of tutorial fees
which meant that the Masters shared directly in the shortfall of
income. Masters were recalled, new Masters found (including, for
instance, George Fletcher's father). The life of the School could
continue with little variation. The Corps had increased recruits,
and there was more training – replacing games on Thursdays. Also
boys worked in a munitions factory in Slough. Some Housemasters valiantly wrote a steady stream of letters to their old boys –
and Rayner-Wood enrolled his lower boys to copy his letters for a
wider circulation. Macnaghten's warm letters would have cheered
their recipients even had they been read in happier circumstances.
Weekly services of intercession in Chapel made a deep impression.
A list of names of the dead was kept in a glass case on the outside
wall of College Chapel: 'We watched the list grow and wondered,
not morbidly, nor yet enthusiastically – just in a detached way –
whether ours would be there one day and whether it would have a
little Victorian Cross printed beside it.'[10] Yet it would seem that
most boys, while being aware of the implications of the War,
continued to live in the present: for them house ties and Trials
continued to matter: the 16- and 17-year-olds simply took up the
responsibilities which had so suddenly descended on them; discipline in houses seems to have in no way relaxed; the imminence of
death did not breed hedonism.

The usual festivities of the Eton year were cut – no Fourth of
June extravaganza, no Lord's, no Founder's Day Feast. The money
saved went to charity. But the School also benefited from a number
of charitable concerts, most notably a recital by Dame Clara Butt,
who had a son in the School; her rendering of 'Land of Hope and
Glory' must have perfectly matched the School Hall. On this
occasion Pop turned themselves into ushers, a new departure for
these privileged grandees, but it had been organized by Victor
Cazalet, their very musical President.[11]*

* Cazalet, later an MP and Minister, died in the Second World War. He kept a
diary which records the astonishingly full social life he led at Eton even six
months into the War. Often he was invited out for all four meals on a Sunday.
Possessing every schoolboy gift, he was yet one who did not like Eton.

With the New Year of 1915, awareness of the horror of the War grew. In the letters of a young Old Colleger Master, George Fletcher, the excitement and fun of the first weeks gave place to a stoic determination to see the struggle through. Yet Fletcher did not lose the sense of playing a game for high stakes. As a competent linguist he would crawl over to listen to the talk in the German trenches. Arriving at a different part of the front in March 1915 he found a captured French tricolour displayed on a tree behind the German front line. One night he crept through to rescue it, and it now hangs in College Chapel. Two days later a sniper shot Fletcher dead.[12]

When so many were heroes, perhaps two should be specially mentioned. George Schack-Sommer was a mining engineer in Russia when the War broke out. Determined to get into action he enlisted in the Russian cavalry and won *three* St George's Crosses, Russia's premier award. When he was killed in July 1915, he was a Corporal, with a recommendation for a Commission. Henry Simpson, 'a young American of infinite daring came back to help England for love of Eton in November 1914', and served for two years almost continuously before he was killed with the Royal Flying Corps.*

Considering the great emphasis on literature in the Eton curriculum, it is sad that there is no great Etonian War poet. Patrick Shaw-Stewart's lines written at the time of Gallipoli do, however, show the classical background as well as the increasing pressure on the soldiers:

> Was it so hard, Achilles,
> So very hard to die?
> Thou knowest and I know not –
> So much the happier I.
>
> I will go back this morning
> From Imbros over the sea;
> Stand in the trench, Achilles,
> Flame-capped, and shout for me.

Shaw-Stewart survived Gallipoli to die on the Western Front, a most distinguished Battalion Commander only 29 years old. If

---

* He is commemorated by a tablet in the Cloisters.

Eton poets disappoint, the Old Colleger George Butterworth was the most promising English composer to fall. He was killed in 1916.

By 1916 Eton itself was facing new problems. The Provost, debilitated by Parkinson's disease, was by now hardly able to play any part, and the Vice-Provost was dying of cancer. An increasing burden was placed on the Fellows, and particularly on Dr M.R. James, the Provost of King's and Senior Fellow. Decisions were taken to raise a War Memorial Fund to provide bursaries for the sons of Old Etonians killed in the War, and to dedicate the colonnade under Upper School and the Cloisters to memorials.

The Head Master's position was a particular problem. In March 1915, he preached a well-intended and indeed Christian sermon at St Margaret's, Westminster, in which he suggested that we should be cautious in condemning the whole German nation (remembering our own history of expansion), and that in a final peace we should be ready to act generously: if, for example, the Kiel Canal should be internationalized, so perhaps we should surrender Gibraltar to international control. An avalanche of fury descended upon his head. The papers, led by *The Times*, were sharply critical; a large volume of letters was sent to the papers and to members of the Governing Body, mostly hostile, and often demanding that Lyttelton be sacked. The King was angry.

A few more temperate letters were written in Lyttelton's support, including one from the President of Pop, Captain of School, and Captain of Oppidans, in which they said that they, and Etonians generally, knew that the Head Master's patriotism was beyond question; and it is clear from Cazalet's diary and from the Captain of the Oppidan's book that they did genuinely side with the Head Master. Yet such was the wave of anti-German hysteria at the time that the friendly voices were drowned. The Editor of *The Times* had perhaps the last word by reporting (correctly but maliciously) at the foot of the correspondence column that the Etonians had been sent home early owing to an outbreak of German Measles.

There is no doubt that Lyttelton was foolish in not foreseeing the public reaction, but he had never even supposed that his sermon would be reported. Even if the sentiments were commendable, the timing was ill-considered. The problem in 1915 was to win the war, and the time was not ripe for appeals to magnanimity.

Also the reference to Gibraltar had the effect of stirring up Spanish opinion, which was in any case inclined to be pro-German.

The Fellows convened a Special Meeting, on 22 April 1915. Lord Cobham, who was placed in an awkward position by his brother's insensitivity, did not attend. Cecil Lubbock, who was the Masters' Representative (and the Head Master's representative too) had the important job of reporting feelings among Masters (they were divided), and of securing fairness to the Head Master. Lyttelton was heard in his own defence, but (according to a note taken by Rosebery, the Fellow most hostile to Lyttelton and the most anti-German) he did his cause no good. Unanimously they agreed a note of rebuke: 'The Provost and Fellows cannot but regard the Headmaster's recent speech and letters as detrimental to his authority and the welfare of the School. They feel bound to add their confidence in him as Headmaster of Eton has been seriously impaired.' Some of the Fellows, who had lost confidence before this trouble, hoped that he would resign. Others thought, as Lubbock had represented to them, that the Head Master would resign shortly. In fact he only wrote an abject letter, so abject indeed that it is hard to see how he could write in such terms and not resign. It was agreed by the Fellows that they could not dismiss him, and they thus had to wait until the end of 1916 before he departed.[13]

Two incidents of the time recapture the atmosphere of extraordinary hysteria in which Lyttelton could hardly hope for any balanced treatment. In the spring of 1916 it was found that a boy called Schroder who had been in the School since September 1914 was of German parentage, and the Fellows only reluctantly agreed (with Lord Rosebery and Lord Halsbury dissenting) that he need not leave the School; and that summer a German maid who had been long employed by Mrs Lyttelton was prosecuted for espionage on the grounds that she had sent a perfectly innocent letter back to Germany not through the Royal Mail (and thus avoiding censorship).

Lyttelton's departure was almost universally regretted by the boys. Two small changes illustrate the ways that boys saw him as liberalizing as well as good: he managed to get the windows in College Chapel opened, reducing its stuffiness; and he abolished the stiff dickies that boys wore with their tails in favour of aertex shirts. To quote a Macnaghten letter:

You will have heard that E.L. is giving up at Christmas. The boys are sorry to a man, or rather to a boy. I am personally very sorry indeed; for I think that in spite of a few 'blazing indiscretions', he is one of the very best men alive, and though perhaps not supremely good in any of a headmaster's duties, such as preaching, teaching or organisation, by sheer force of character he wins the affection (I know) and (I think) the respect of all the boys.[14]

He himself left without rancour, though his wife, who had been ill throughout his headmastership, felt bitter towards the Governing Body, who neither by expression of words nor by financial generosity over pension paid any great tribute to Lyttelton. Yet many of his failures, and there were failures – for example to reform the curriculum as thoroughly as he meant or to bridge the gap between Classical and non-Classical Masters – could be attributed in part to lack of support from the Provost and Fellows.

In April 1916 the College found itself needing a new Head Master and a new Vice-Provost. The Bursar was almost blind and had to retire the following year, with a more generous encomium than the Head Master attracted from the Fellows. And the Provost should most certainly have retired, though no Fellow felt inclined to press him into resignation at that juncture despite his inability to write and his near inaudibility. He was a tragic figure, hardly seen except when a fine day allowed him to be wheeled in his bath chair into the playing fields. It was said that spring that 'the Head Master was mad, the Provost ill, the Bursar blind; the Vice-Provost all three'.[15]

There was a thought that F.H. Rawlins, who had done well as Lower Master, might be a stopgap Head Master and he wanted the job, but he was in his mid-sixties. He was instead preferred to Walter Durnford, a former Housemaster who was the Cambridge University representative on the Governing Body, as Vice-Provost. A committee considered a number of possible candidates for Head Master and fixed a new salary at £4,000 p.a. (Lyttelton's had been increased to £5,000) but took away some expenses previously borne, such as the cost of Leaving Books for boys. They were fortified in this parsimonious decision by the discovery that Eton pay was still well ahead of that at other schools. It was also sensibly agreed that the Head Master should retire after fifteen years or on reaching the age of 65 unless requested to continue. The short list contained six names – one of them Ramsay from the staff. The full Governing Body selected Dr Alington of Shrewsbury, who had been the Master-in-College previously at a brilliant period, by six votes to four ahead of Dr Vaughan of Wellington. The choice had been well made.

It fell to Lyttelton to select a new Lower Master for his last six months, and he appointed Ramsay ('The Ram'), a forceful man but one of the most die-hard Classics.

> When he asked me to be Lower Master I felt ashamed, in view of the disputes I had had with him, and I told him so. He was quite obviously surprised by this aspect of the position. The very idea that such things could be remembered was simply contrary to his nature. I felt that I was in the presence of the truest Christian nobility, and from that moment I would have done anything to serve him.[16]

Certainly Edward Lyttelton was more probably a saint than any other Eton Head Master. At his last School Concert he was presented with a large cheque by the boys, which was given by him to fund Edward Lyttelton Addresses each year in Lent. In his last sermon he chose the text: 'henceforth I call you not servants . . . but I have called you friends'. 'Let us think before we part of the beauty of friendship' were his last words to Eton as Head Master.[17] It was no special eloquence in the sermon that made its effect, but the awareness of the congregation that many among them called *him* friend.

He was later to write of 1905–16 as 'dark times', but possibly speaking more of his wife's illness than of the worry and conflict that came with headmastership: he certainly always loved Eton. But he was glad to be relieved of administrative work. Typically he found employment first as a curate at St Martin-in-the-Fields, later very successfully as Chaplain and Lecturer at Whitelands, a teacher-training college for women in London. He was much in demand as conductor of retreats and as preacher – 'Well, it's certainly a rum thing, but I never go into a Church without visualizing the spin of the ball up the nave'. He died in 1942, active to the last. Wherever he went, he inspired remarkable affection by his unselfishness, his wit and humour, and his simple goodness.

It was not easy for Alington to follow someone so widely loved by the boys, but the brilliant success with which he spoke to them soon won him acceptance. Even though the rigours of the War had intensified, boys and Masters welcomed the grip that the new Head Master demonstrated. Measures of voluntary rationing of food and fuel were taken. Long Leave was suspended and the holidays lengthened to reduce travel. Potatoes were cultivated on the playing fields. Boys even accepted at the request of the Ministry of Agriculture the temporary end of the beagles. (They were not put down, let alone served at Boys' Dinner, but simply not hunted so that no one could say they were damaging crops.) The years 1917 and 1918 were to prove dreary indeed, and the boys often felt cold and hungry. A dish invented by Henry Marten's formidable twin sister to make use of any last scraps of fat, known as Miss Marten's pudding, was often to be recalled later with horror.[18]

Yet the numbers in the School increased. By Michaelmas 1918 there were 1,077 boys, and in addition seven Belgians, one Russian, and one Serb. This was the largest number ever. The Provost and Fellows had temporarily relaxed the rules limiting numbers in houses to help Housemasters who were facing higher costs. They had also permitted at the end of 1917 a voluntary extra £5 per half to be added to the house boarding fees, which parents proved willing to pay. The increased numbers of boys also permitted an addition to the Science staff which had already been augmented by the return of a wounded John Christie. Aldous Huxley, an old Colleger, was also recruited as a temporary Master: his experience of correcting holiday tasks appears in *Antic Hay* and Eton is revisited in *Brave New World*; Harold Acton recalled him wearing a long orange scarf and looking like a juvenile giraffe escaped from a zoo.[19]

The casualties did not cease. One rather different casualty, from an earlier brilliant group of Collegers, was Sir Cecil Spring-Rice, a pupil of William Johnson and then Luxmoore. He had as British Ambassador in Washington patiently and successfully fostered Anglo-American friendship only to be relieved in favour of a more political appointment when the USA entered the war. It seems that on his last night in Washington he reworked an earlier poem, which was found among his papers a month later when, a broken man, he died: 'I vow to thee my country'.[20] Royalties from it helped to sustain the Eton Mission for fifty years. It is remarkable that Etonians have contributed so much to the anthems of our nation: Arne composed 'Rule Britannia' and first set 'God Save the King'; Benson wrote 'Land of Hope and Glory'; Parry wrote the music of 'Jerusalem'.

Another victim in 1918, but not this time of battle, was Dr Warre, who resigned as Provost that summer. He lived on until 1920 at Colenorton, the guest house he had built when he was Head Master. No one doubted his services to Eton, but it was sad for Eton as for himself that he should have suffered so long a decline. Happily M.R. James was persuaded to come from King's to Eton; he had been *de facto* Provost since 1914, and he recognized Eton's great need. The move to Eton was very much to the College's advantage. He was not a former Head Master, nor a clergyman, but he was to make the Provost's Lodge a positive rather than a negative influence on Eton's life.

Soon after his installation on Michaelmas Day 1918 came the Armistice. Some of the scenes that occurred during the Boer War recurred, but not to the same extent. Everyone was too tired: there was relief rather than rejoicing. It could hardly be otherwise: 1,157 Etonians had been killed, more than one-fifth of those fighting, and a still larger number had been wounded. Perhaps one-third of those who took leave of Edward Lyttelton were dead. Some public schools had even higher casualty rates, but Eton was well above the national average of 12.5% of combatants killed. There was, too, a feeling that the best had died. As Luxmoore wrote:

> it wd seem as if the very pick & best of all are marked for death & the blows come so steadily, how the nation is to recover in the next generation I can't see at all, since all the fittest do *not* survive. one is marvellously proud of them, almost amazed to see to what heights of courage & sacrifice our fellows rise, but pride does not clear the future, so only faith is left.[21]

To a considerable extent it would seem that Eton had educated its pupils exactly to such an end as befell them. Of the wisdom of Etonian generals, there may indeed be doubt, but of the regimental officers (and Etonians must have fought in every regiment of the army – not just Guards, Greenjackets, and Cavalry, though they certainly had most) there is great evidence of courage and of leadership. Etonians received these awards for gallantry: 13 VCs; 548 DSOs (including 44 with one Bar, 4 with two Bars) – this award was sometimes for gallantry, sometimes for successful leadership; 744 MCs (including 37 with one Bar, 4 with two Bars); 10 DSCs (including 1 with Bar); 16 AFCs; 4 DFCs; 1 DCM; 2 MMs; and 591 foreign decorations, some of which rewarded courage. No doubt selfish cowards existed, but most letters suggest anxiety not to survive, but to die properly if that was necessary. The young Etonians were able to care for their men, encouraged to do so perhaps because at home and at school they had always been treated as individuals themselves. One letter from a rifleman about an ordinary Etonian, Dick Levett, must serve for very many:

> No one will ever be able to say that the upper classes have not given their All in this just cause. The best and bravest have given their lives freely. I am not sure it is us who suffer so much as those who are left to mourn their loss. Mr. Richard was so unselfish – always thinking of the comforts of his men and was admired and respected by them. They would have followed him anywhere and if possible given their lives to save his.[22]

It could be said that other schools exhibit parallel records of self-sacrifice, but the Etonian culture of the pre-War period was exceptional. It was the creation of Warre rather than of Lyttelton. Warre saw Etonians as doubly privileged, in their country and in their School, and boys were trained that privilege brought obligations. Lyttelton too was acutely aware that there was a call to service. Eton may not have provided the preparation needed for peacetime service as leaders of industry, but in the War Etonians saw that there was something precious to defend and their duty was clear. Eton was not militaristic in the years before the War – the Corps was a voluntary institution, which only just over half the boys joined. Lyttelton, less favourable to the Corps than Warre, allowed the Commanding Officer in 1912 to write to parents distributing a War Office circular designed to recruit officers for the Territorial Army, and that seems to have confirmed a rise in Corps numbers to about three-quarters. Yet once War came the Etonian response was complete, and immediately another 100 who had not been members joined the Corps.

Their Eton heritage and Eton friendships evidently sustained many of them. Henry Dundas, Captain of the Oppidans in the summer of 1915, was just one of many who formed deep, but not physical, relationships. Victor Cazalet reported in his diary (30 June 1915) that 'HLD loves me', and this was a friendship that lasted until he was killed, holder of the MC and Bar, in September 1918. After his death, Cazalet wrote of Dundas' depth of feeling and his 'honest, frank confession of sentiment'. Still warmer was Dundas' affection for Ralph Gamble (who was also very close to Cazalet); when he died in August 1918, also having been awarded the MC, Dundas wrote of the perfection of their friendship – 'I thought I'd forgotten how to cry'.[23] Such love was freely compared to that of Jonathan and David, and it meant much. Even the less emotional regularly gathered for Fourth of June dinners behind the lines – there were eighty-five together on the Mount of Olives in 1918. Occasional Field Games or the shared perusal of a copy of the *Chronicle* apparently also helped morale. No doubt the fact that many Etonians still had strong territorial links based on rural estates counted, but Eton was an important part of what had to be defended.

There were Etonians who died with the word Eton on their lips. And Eton did not forget them. Their names were inscribed in the colonnade under Upper School, and some are recorded in memorials in the Cloisters. Fine tapestries, designed by Lady Chilston and woven at the Morris Works at Merton Abbey, hang in Lower Chapel. They relate the life of St George to the education in patriotic duty of the Etonian. The largest part of the sum collected was not used for any triumphal expression such as the South African War Memorial but to found bursaries for the sons of the fallen. Another moving and practical memorial was the Old Etonian School at Ypres commemorating the 324 Etonians who died in the Ypres Salient, which educated the children of those who tended the War Graves in Flanders until 1940.

Etona Non Immemor.

CHAPTER SEVEN

Doctor Alington

CYRIL ARGENTINE ALINGTON was born in 1872, the son of a clergyman. He was a scholar at Marlborough, where he returned to teach the classical Sixth Form after holding a Scholarship at Trinity, Oxford and winning a Fellowship of All Souls. In 1899 Dr Warre had attracted him to Eton, and he quickly made his mark as one of the most stimulating of teachers and the best of preachers, a man who could also play cricket, Fives, and rackets with the most gifted boys. In 1904 he was appointed Master-in-College and he presided happily over a particularly distinguished period. He secured the removal of partitions from Lower School, and transferred College Prayers there from what is still called the Prayer Room. He initiated what Collegers call Secular Singing, a rather higher-brow variety of sing-song. From College he was appointed to the headmastership of Shrewsbury – eight more happy and successful years.

The ease with which he reigned at Eton concealed the extent of the problems which he faced when he arrived in 1917. He was the first non-Etonian Head Master for over two centuries, and the boys, devoted to his predecessor, regarded him with suspicion. The circumstances were adverse, with the staff short of young men, and some inevitable, even if surprisingly small, deterioration in standards of scholarship and discipline. Yet Alington overcame opposition with courage, good humour, and generosity of spirit; and problems were solved by his quick and fertile mind.

Richard Martineau,* writing on Alington, quoted Thucydides on Themistocles: 'by his innate intelligence, having had no time to weigh his decisions and asking none, he had the best judgement in a sudden crisis, and was infinitely shrewd at calculating consequences'.[1] In contrast to his predecessor, he was clever with people, and undoubtedly he handled the Governing Body with skill. He dominated the daily meetings of Masters in Chambers with ready replies which turned indignation to laughter. The speed with which he would dictate beautifully turned answers to his morning mail was as impressive. The excellent Bendell, his secretary, also had time to be an ever-helpful School Librarian.†

Yet he was not a scholar in any true sense. From his Oxford years 'he retained a loyalty to the classics, a feeling for what Greece means for humanity. And he knew more Latin than one sometimes thought.'[2] He was better equipped to teach Sixth Form than Lyttelton, but he too would have been wiser to delegate that traditional task – in which his efforts were to compare so unfavourably with those of C.M. Wells. Apparently he took trouble to prepare construe lessons, knowing that his Classics were shaky; but he thought he could teach English and Divinity without preparation, and the result was 'pitiable'.[3] Even as a young man his teaching was rapid, superficial, jocose, at any rate in the eyes of a clever boy, Geoffrey Madan. His system of marking would appeal to many an idle schoolmaster. 'There was a maximum of nine marks for everything, whether construing or written work. But the only alternatives to scoring full marks were to score five, or else to fail altogether.' He could on the other hand put on a virtuoso performance: 'as a class of pupils collected for some ordinary school work, he put aside the books that had been brought, distributed copies of Virgil, and himself translated the whole of the sixth Aeneid to them, making it once again what it was in the Middle Ages, a dark and jewelled oracle, heavy with fate and romance.'[4]

In his earlier days he had indeed been better suited to the tutorial

* R.C. Martineau, taught by Alington, was appointed by him to succeed C.M. Wells with the top division; thus he had also a colleague's insight. The sentence quoted below, 'And he knew more Latin than one sometimes thought', is as revealing about Martineau as Alington.

† At Shrewsbury Alington appointed a young cricket professional, Neville Cardus, as his part-time secretary.

26. Miss Evans by J.S. Sargent. 'My Dame was, or professed to be, terrified of meeting a great portrait-painter who had been painting "everybody who was anybody" for some time; and Sargent afterwards confided to my mother that at first his knees felt like water. No doubt he expected an appalling old dragon who had been controlling some fifty untamed young savages for an indefinite number of years. Needless to say, when they met, they fell completely in love with one another.' (Charles Lyell)

27. A.C. Benson

28. The old Baldwin's End, *c.* 1890. Note the bars over the boys' windows.

29. Baldwin's End on fire, 1 June 1903

30. Speeches on the Fourth of June, 1902. A scene from *Much Ado About Nothing*. J.M. Keynes leans on a stick. W. Hope-Jones, 'Hojo', is seated on the right. (For photographic record the scene had to be restaged out of doors.)

31. Speeches on the Fourth of June, 1937, in Upper School

32. Sidney Evans's studio, *c.* 1906

33. The present Drawing Schools

34. The Field Game. Marindin's are playing Luxmoore's in 1886.

35. The Wall Game in 1938

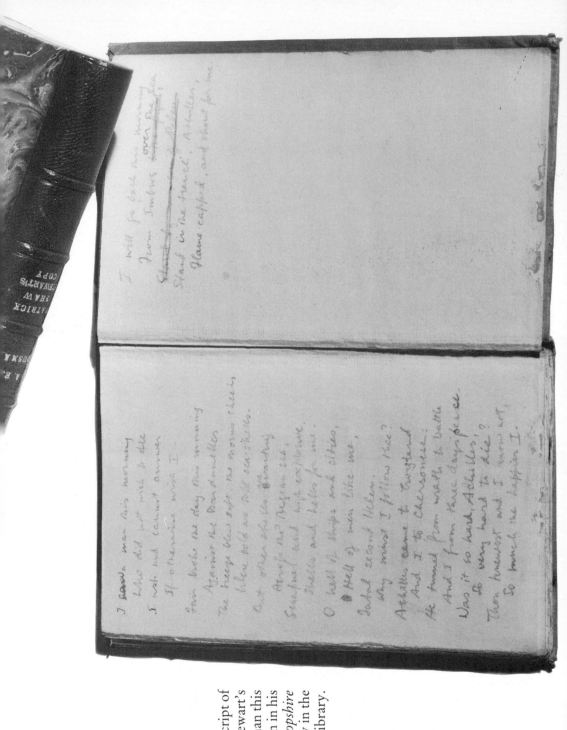

36. The manuscript of Patrick Shaw-Stewart's poem 'I saw a man this morning' written in his copy of *A Shropshire Lad*. It is now in the Macnaghten Library.

37. The dedication of the Memorial to those who fell in the First World War, Founder's Day, 1921 (the 500th Anniversary of Henry VI's birth)

38. Claude Elliott photographed with his predecessors Cyril Alington (on his right) and Edward Lyttelton

work. For instance, again according to Madan, instead of the approved religious Sunday Private, Alington,

> one of whose most reliable qualities was his readiness to be bored and his detection of impostures other than his own ... would range about the room, taking down a book here and there – he had a large miscellaneous library, badly kept, of four or five thousand volumes – all the time talking with high brilliance, more or less connectedly, on questions of the day, with no definite subject and not even a text, as it were, for his discourse. Such was his ease and variety of mind, that he could continue this astonishing performance week after week with three different sets of boys, never repeating himself.[5]

Alington also encouraged his pupils to read, to learn by heart and to write* – and he himself had a prodigious memory and wrote fluently. His light verse was rather good, though outshone by the work of his pupil, R.A. Knox. His detective stories were no match for the best. His more serious work is more notable for quantity than quality.

These gifts and defects he carried into his headmastership: he could stimulate, but he did talk too much, and was superficial and flippant. He was to make his biggest mark on the School as a preacher, yet he preached much too often, frequently in the form of fables which came as second sermons at the end of evensong. Normally it was the manner rather than the matter which impressed: his striking presence, his melodious voice, the theatrical tricks. His Holy Week addresses, delivered whenever this fell during the half, were by far his best sermons. He had thought out the characters of those who failed – the crowd, Judas, Pilate, St Peter – and he made them utterly convincing. The packed congregation had come voluntarily; it was not disposed to be critical; but it was moved and it did not forget.

Apart from his cleverness, his most distinguishing quality was his kindness. He knew surprisingly many boys, and:

> however shy or dim they might be, however badly they might have behaved, he tried to win their confidence by shewing his

---

* His anthology of this work – *Poets in Pupil Room* (1908) – was his first publication; it is quite entertaining.

interest in them. He was very generous of human weakness, very tolerant of youthful impertinence. No one who was never up to him will believe how patient he could be with Collegers of a certain type. Lesser men would have crushed them and forgotten them; Alington endured with a smile, and made some of them friends for life.[6]

He was particularly fortunate in his wife. He had married Hester Lyttelton, a daughter of that philoprogenitive Lord Lyttelton, a half-sister of Edward Lyttelton. Of Mrs Alington it is impossible to find any comment but affectionate praise. The Alingtons kept open house in the country, and amazingly found time even in the half for boys or for Masters and their wives to tell their troubles. 'If some could not quite overcome their alarm of the Head Master, they could tell Mrs Alington anything.'[7] As a host, Cyril Alington had grave faults. He would talk all the time (just as he would play every hand at bridge). He was a snob, harmlessly but ridiculously; in 1921 he became a Chaplain to the King, and, 'when he had preached at Court, he would tell us all about the King. Yet how well he took it when we laughed!'[8] Mrs Alington knew Cyril's failings, and occasionally rallied him on them. But she recognized that the best in anyone (not just her husband) was all that mattered. Her steadfastness, her joy in life, and her originality ensured that she was loved by the whole community of Eton. She was the perfect wife for Cyril, and always devoted to him as he to her.

Alington was also fortunate in the Provost under whom he served for almost his entire headmastership. Monty James had been at Eton from 1876, when he was 14, to 1882 – his twentieth birthday actually fell just before he left, and he may have been the oldest boy ever in the school. He was one for whom the relaxed life of Eton before Warre worked wonderfully well. Occasionally mischievous or idle, he eventually achieved the goals that Eton offers to the gifted: in his last year he was elected to Pop, obtained a scholarship to King's and won the Newcastle Scholarship; and he used the freedom of those days to read widely, including a first exploration of College Library; he was an editor of the *Chronicle* and president of the Literary Society. Undoubtedly he owed much to his Tutor, Luxmoore, a debt that he never ceased to acknow-ledge; and interestingly among many distinguished contemporaries within College, A.C. Benson was a powerful influence. At King's he established his scholarly reputation for biblical studies and as an antiquarian, but he also began to write stylish ghost stories, and he became a central figure socially in the College. The sudden death of the then Provost in 1905 led to his election as Provost of King's before his forty-third birthday. In this role he renewed his contact with Eton, becoming ex officio Senior Fellow. He also discovered a talent for chairmanship and, despite his office, managed to continue to be approachable by the young. Perhaps his gifts made everything come almost too easily: Monty 'with his amazing knowledge & power of absorbing learning without seeming to work, with his boyish & untidy humour & his unruffled goodness is a dangerous model for young men who have to make their way in the world', to quote Luxmoore.[9] Warre's incapacity thrust the burden of chairing the Governing Body on to the Senior Fellow, and he presided so skilfully that it was natural, when Warre eventually retired in 1918, that many wanted him to be Provost. There were other candidates – Dean Inge of St Paul's, and even Rosebery – but the choice of Dr James was quickly made and gave much satisfaction. Perhaps it was more surprising that he should be prepared to move from an ostensibly more important job. Possibly reformist dons at King's (led by J.M. Keynes) made the atmosphere there less congenial; possibly he thought that he would have more leisure for scholarship at Eton; more probably it was simply a matter of sentiment – Eton commanded his heart to an even greater extent than King's.

Inevitably his view of the world had been darkened by the tragedies of the War, but he remained a most accessible man. He loved the company of the young, and took an especial interest in the Shakespeare Society, which Luxmoore ran. Despite the handicap of being unmarried he also entertained Masters as well as personal guests in the Lodge more freely than his predecessors. And he cared for the various charities and historical links that bound College and town together. He also displayed a great gift for writing services for use in College Chapel* and for reviving ancient customs, such as Boy Bishop's plays to be performed by the Lower Chapel Choir at Founder's Feasts. If he thought his own scholarship would be more productive because of the move, he deceived himself; for in fact his serious writing diminished. Yet

* He had been mainly responsible for the memorial scroll sent to the next-of-kin of the war dead.

certainly he was to return to College Library with valuable results for our knowledge of the early days of the College: he was able to impress, for example, Robert Birley as the most scholarly man that scholar had ever met.

He was most importantly able to establish a happy working relationship with Alington. The mere fact that he was not, as his immediate predecessors had been, a former Head Master must have helped him. Only occasionally was he tempted to interfere in what the Head Master regarded as his proper sphere of influence, and even then any serious conflict was averted. In the meetings of the Provost and Fellows a greater readiness to support the Head Master – who in any case needed less support – was evident.

Dr Alington's first conspicuous achievement was to ease the long-running conflict about salaries. During his first year he secured an agreed new ten-point scale which more or less equalized the rewards between the Classical Masters and the rest. It halved the element of pay for tutorial services: a Classic would lose income if he had fewer than thirty pupils – which was regarded as the normal number – and could gain if he had up to forty pupils. Similarly other Masters were expected to take pupils or boys for extra tuition – a relic of the old system by which any special interest in anything other than Classics had to be pursued out of school. By now, with schoolwork in these subjects increasing, the aim was rather to help the weakest boys over their hurdles. It remained difficult for young Masters in non-classical subjects to attract a full quota of pupils and boys for extras, because there were not enough to go round, but potentially at least non-Classics could be almost as well paid. One who was not a Housemaster could effectively reach a top salary of £900 annually if he were a Classic, £850 if he were not. There were reductions of up to £200 taken by the Classics, and conversely the others gained similar amounts. Compensation was paid to the losers from the surplus accumulated by the School Fund.

In real terms salaries had suffered through wartime inflation, so that Masters were no longer anything like so wealthy as they had been. By 1920, however, a new inclusive School fee was established at £230 p.a., and this permitted an improvement in salaries up to about £1,200 p.a. – something like £20,000 a year in 1990s money. A Housemaster still could profit from the boarding fees, and might typically make another £1,200. After 1920, as prices fell, real

real incomes rose, and no further significant salary adjustments were needed in Alington's time.

Credit is due to the Head Master, and no doubt also to the Finance Committee, for settling this tedious problem. Attitudes altered during the War: selfishness was abated and the need to stand together replaced old sectional interests. Fortunately also the rise in numbers had built up a reserve in the School Fund, which permitted the compensation payments. The Governing Body did not involve itself in this settlement – the Masters were able to make their own arrangements, provided that they could do so within the School Fund. The new scheme did of course have the Fellows' blessing, as did the new increased comprehensive School fee.

The Head Master was less concerned to balance the educational claims of other subjects against those of the Classics. He himself was ignorant of Maths and Science, and though he ensured that more Science was taught than in Lyttelton's time, the provision remained unsatisfactory. There were still too few Science Masters even though he doubled the number of teachers, and their quality did not match the great men of earlier days. Some Science was taught to lower boys in lectures supervised by the Classical Division Masters – a curious and unsatisfactory arrangement even if the lectures had been uniformly good. But one Classical Master recalled waking up to hear his scientific colleague intoning that 'the luminosity of the galaxy was somewhat impaired by the proximity of the metropolis' – and if that was the standard, the system must indeed have hampered the development of Science. Furthermore, the allocation of hours in the timetable suited Classics: Scientists did not have long enough sessions for proper practical work. Not surprisingly, by the end of Alington's time, examination reports were commenting adversely on the standard of Etonian Science.

By contrast Alington favoured History, and actually wrote two historical works himself.* The inter-war years saw a considerable expansion in the number of History specialists, partly because of the attraction of the subject to Etonians, but also because of the excellence of the Masters, led by Henry Marten. Lord Rosebery, himself a distinguished historian and still a Fellow, founded a scholarship for historians which almost matched the prestige of the Newcastle Scholarship.

---

* He did try to teach the historians in the School, but bored them by talking too much with inadequate knowledge.

Teaching below the School Certificate level was still strongly classical. Alington at once floated the possibility of making Greek, with its richer literature, the compulsory classical language, but this was not really practicable when preparatory schools were geared to teaching Latin. So in F Block, at the bottom of the School, Latin remained the staple fare. There were five periods for Maths, three for French, one for Drawing; the other sixteen were taught in classical divisions, by Classics Masters, but they also had to teach English, History, Geography, and Divinity. Physical Training, which died in the War as instructors returned to active service, was not revived.

In E Block about 40% took both Greek and Latin, and the fifteen periods taught by their division Masters were composed of six Greek periods, five Latin periods and one each of English, History, Geography, and Divinity. 'Non-Greekers' had more Latin and English subjects and continued with Drawing. All E Block were taught four periods of French, four of Maths, and attended the curious Science lecture plus a note-taking period operated within the classical divisions. For E as well as for F there continued to be long sessions of Pupil Room devoted to classical work.

In D Block, authentically taught Science was introduced, four periods being allocated to this; Maths and French continued with four and three periods respectively. For 'Greekers' there were still six periods of Greek and six of Latin, with History and Divinity also taught in classical divisions: for 'non-Greekers', there were four periods of English, with more Latin and History. In C Block, the School Certificate Block, boys could select between Classics, History, German, and Science. In that block only did Eton begin to offer a fair chance to the non-Classical Masters.

Even after School Certificate, a remnant of general education was preserved for those doing Modern Languages, Maths and Science, for they were compelled to take History or English, as well as an Extra Study. Only sixteen periods were devoted to their main studies. The classical specialists, on the other hand, who had twenty-three periods each week, spent all but three with their Classics Masters, though they did keep up some History and English. Historians spent all but three on History and a language. The three periods were for Extra Studies, which did offer a wide choice. It will be noticed that English was not regarded as a specialist subject, though it was a popular Extra Study, brilliantly taught by George Lyttelton. These arrangements, established by Alington on the basis of what he received from Edward Lyttelton, were to last basically unchanged until the 1960s. For those with a mathematical or scientific bent they offered a very good broad education, even if boys were handicapped by the parsimonious allocation of time in their first years to Science. But for other Etonians, education remained essentially literary, with History at least offering a popular alternative to those with limited linguistic skills.

The results produced in examinations were not impressive, with School Certificate successes not much above average. The Head Master could argue to the Provost and Fellows that Etonians were not crammed for their Certificates – indeed not. But it is not clear that very much took place outside the Certificate syllabus. Certainly a fair number of scholarships to Oxford and Cambridge were won, suggesting that the ablest boys were well catered for. Yet for many Etonian specialists, life continued to be undemanding: if doors were opened for them, it would be by contact with a stimulating teacher, or by the Tutor who corrected exercises for his pupils and saw them three times a week for Private Business (twice only in the summer).

The School prided itself on not being academically selective, but in the early 1920s the Common Entrance Examination had to be used to filter the over-large number of entries. The School's growth of numbers continued, with boys staying on longer than they had in the War but never so long as previously. Alington found himself obliged to control the entry lists more effectively than before: Housemasters were limited to a fifteen-year tenure, and were only to guarantee eight boys places in a year. The School was full some years ahead, but it was not at that time necessary to register boys at birth.

School numbers were helped by the existence of the War Memorial Bursaries. About nine or ten were awarded each year to the sons of widows or veterans who needed help. A much greater number of boys had lost their fathers, of course – perhaps 15%; but grandparents and stepfathers could often help with fees, which, though increased, were not relatively so high as before the War.

The School Fund was very tight. It could not help, for instance, with an unfortunate problem that confronted the Head Master himself. He had come from Shrewsbury with an overdraft, and this increased rapidly at Eton. His household (with its still growing young family) contained twenty-two people, and the Alingtons entertained generously. In 1920 he was obliged to place his circumstances before Masters, but the Finance Committee – though sympathetic – could not raise his salary; nor could the College find extra money for him. The School Fund did, however, make him a loan, which subsequently was written off; this loan and the income tax implications of its write-off must have been a recurrent irritation to Alington.

More seriously, the College had no spare funds to finance new investment. It was true that Eton benefited from a number of gifts commemorating the fallen, apart from the main War Memorial Fund, but these were not always practically useful. Indeed the main fund financed not only the impressive frieze listing the fallen and the improvements in Lower Chapel, but the blood-red stained glass of the War Memorial Chapel within College Chapel, which was a less happy expression of the taste of a committee on which Luxmoore and Provost James were most influential.* Still more questionably it paid for a life-sized statue of a naked boy by Mackennal symbolizing the Offering of Youth.

To enlarge Lower Chapel and to build new Drawing Schools, in 1921 Dr Alington launched the Head Master of Eton's Fund in co-operation with the Old Etonian Association. The Head Master's letter explained that the aim was to provide essential construction which could not be financed by the College with its static income from rent on property, or from increasing the School fee. No target was stated, but the result appears disappointing. The War Memorial Fund had by then reached £150,000 – approaching £3m. in present money. But the Head Master's Fund produced only some £25,000 more. This, however, with some generous memorial gifts, met the immediate objects of the Fund. In June 1925 the King and Queen attended the morning service in Lower Chapel and then formally opened the Drawing Schools.

This was a development that improved the appearance of Eton, for redundant gasworks had stood on the site of the Drawing Schools. Alington cared for the appearance of Eton. It was his energy that secured a long lease of the island on which Luxmoore had created a fine garden, thus providing Eton with a lasting

* The window was designed by James himself.

amenity. Similarly when the King of Siam, an Old Etonian, revisited Eton and gave £2,000, Alington was able to persuade the Fellows to sweep away the old stables which had masked the view of the College from the north, and to lay out the King of Siam's Garden.

In 1929 the College was itself to launch a more successful appeal to establish a Land Fund to purchase property which would protect the Eton environment. Some £50,000 was raised, and farms were acquired at Cippenham and Chalvey, south of Slough, which were later to provide most valuable saleable assets when the M4 sliced through this land. Other farmland was acquired west of Eton at Boveney and Dorney.

Another environmental anxiety was increasing – the build-up of traffic through Eton. At this time plans for a new road to Windsor, east of the College, appeared, and for bypasses round Eton, west of the College, and round Slough, along lines which were subsequently built. Interestingly the College was at first hostile to an Eton bypass, perhaps because it did not wish to disturb its newly acquired green land. In 1929 also the College had to go to law to reassert its control over the Brocas,* where an illegitimate Brocas Association had begun to authorize fairs and other unwelcome entertainments.

The College was able with the help of a large bequest to build ten new schoolrooms and a new School of Mechanics, where Warre's Drill Hall and old School of Mechanics had been. These, known at first as Drill Hall Schools, were renamed Alington Schools after Alington's death. Most other improvements, notably the construction of thirteen covered Fives courts and four squash courts, were privately financed. Nothing effective was done, however, to renovate the boarding houses, and Eton's main plant was becoming increasingly inadequate and in disrepair. The General Purpose Committee of the Provost and Fellows had to be convinced before they would even agree to add another bathroom or lavatory to a boys' house – unless the Housemaster himself would pay for the work. They even refused £200 from a parent who wished to instal an extra lavatory in his son's house!

The administrative and financial routine was not Alington's natural ground. It was in dealing with boys and Masters that he

* The Brocas is the open space by the river immediately west of Eton town, and just upstream of the boathouses.

displayed his great abilities. He was a disciplinarian, and 'no one', in the words of the hostile Madan, 'ever felt that they could get the better of him, and moreover he had in his armoury that other heavy weapon, that he was not really what is called a gentleman'.[10] Certainly he was a traditionalist, which no doubt made his relations with boys easier. He reintroduced birching, and required the presence of two Sixth Form praepostors – practices which his predecessor had dropped, but which added to the solemnity of inquisition and punishment by the Head Master. If he felt that his own enquiries would not disclose the identity of a perpetrator of some crime, he would transfer the problem to the President of Pop, or the Captains of the School and Oppidans, who could exercise a more effective moral blackmail. In attempting to reduce smoking, he tried punishing the Library of an offender's house, as well as the offender himself – an unscrupulous and oddly mistaken experiment. In another miscarriage of justice, he suspended the sale of alcohol in Tap, thinking (wrongly as it eventually transpired) that Hobbs, the manager, had supplied spirits. He was ready to dismiss boys from the School, particularly if they added lying to an initial offence. Yet he could temper his severity, and boys in trouble might benefit from the understanding and humour with which he comprehended school life, or the kindness which he brought to a particular individual's problems.

Masters were also dealt with firmly but discreetly. Rayner-Wood was sexually indiscreet with a boy; Alington quickly had him absent as sick, and he retired a few years early without publicity. He was also able to encourage John Christie to retire to the life of a country gentleman, when it was clear that his financial generosity was outweighed by his relaxed attitude to his teaching.

Alington made many good appointments to his staff, particularly considering the difficult situation that confronted him, with a motley collection of wartime replacements, and younger men limping back, a diminished group, from the War. Further, the staff was growing in numbers, though only proportionately to the increase of the boys, and it was difficult to provide enough housing. Robert Birley always claimed to have begun his Eton career living in a bathroom. Nevertheless, good men were attracted to Eton, including a number who had come under Alington's influence while they were boys at Shrewsbury.

The haphazard manner in which appointments were sometimes

made towards the end of his time is illustrated by a young historian, Christopher Gowan. Invited to lunch in May 1932, he found the Head Master late because he had been playing rackets (in his sixtieth year). Alington explained that there was no History vacancy – could Gowan do anything else? 'Well, I did German and French in Higher Certificate, and have kept them up a bit since.' 'That's fine, I need a linguist in September. Go to France in the vac., come along in September and you can teach French until a History vacancy turns up.' It may seem odd that Alington had left filling the post so late, but perhaps not so surprising since the Head of Modern Languages did not even realize that he needed a man at all. Gowan returned to Oxford to report to his Tutor and his Principal that he thought he had a job. 'Have you got it in writing?' each man asked. Evidently Alington's reputation for reliability was not high. But a confirmatory letter did come, on the strength of which Gowan announced his engagement. Alington was not pleased: he thought it easier for a bachelor to learn his job, and bachelors were more easily housed.[11]

Whatever his shortcomings, there is no doubt Eton's standing grew during his headmastership. There were a number of public events which he enjoyed and which marked the esteem in which Eton was held. In 1921 Crown Prince Hirohito came from Japan to be received in School Yard; Alington's notice advised the boys: 'In shouting Banzai they will take their time from the Captain of the School.' In 1925 King Feisal of Iraq visited. The Captain of the Oppidans recorded:

I should have described him as looking weak & untrustworthy, but Mrs Alington, for whose opinion I have great respect, considered him an 'ideal Gilbert & Sullivan monarch'. The Head Master's suggestion that the field Mesopotamia should in future be called Iraq, in Feisal's honour, seemed to me distinctly one of the better jokes.

Among other famous visitors Gandhi caused rather different problems. He was accompanied as usual at that time by Miss Slade who insisted on sleeping across the threshold of the Mahatma's bedroom or in his dressing-room: 'No, my dear, not while I am a member of the Mothers' Union', said Mrs Alington.[12]

On some more solemn occasions the Provost, with his gift for words and ceremony, held the stage with the Head Master. One such occasion was the Memorial Service in School Yard on Founder's Day 1921, the 500th anniversary of Henry's birth, at which the frieze in the colonnade of School Yard recording the War Dead was dedicated by the Provost.*

The Provost's enthusiasm led to the removal in 1923 of the stalls along the sides of College Chapel, exposing the wall-paintings which had been covered at the Reformation. The canopies were given to Lancing College Chapel when an Eton Housemaster, C.H. Blakiston, went there as Headmaster. The technology of cleaning and restoration was not very advanced at that time, and forty years later Professor Tristan's work on the paintings was superseded by a second restoration.

It was the Provost too who led the mourning for H.E. Luxmoore, who died in 1926, active to the last as the moral and aesthetic conscience of Eton. He had lived on at Baldwin's End after he ceased to teach, still receiving old friends and boys in his garden, and presiding over the readings of the Shakespeare Society.† The Provost inherited this agreeable responsibility: occasionally his censorship alerted boys to indecencies in the plays that they would otherwise have missed. All boys joined with Masters in their pleasure when the Provost was honoured with the Order of Merit in 1930.

Luxmoore could have been Vice-Provost had he wished, but instead the post went in 1920 to Hugh Macnaghten, a man who enshrined the classical virtues of Eton with almost comparable distinction. By the summer of 1929 he was suffering increasingly from depression: Richard Martineau recalled Alington in Chambers asking Masters if they had the chance to try to talk to and cheer 'that great and good man, the Vice-Provost'. During the holidays he drowned himself in the Thames. The remarkable Library of signed volumes and other records of the Great War, collected by Sir Eugen Millington-Drake, was to be a memorial to his Tutor as much as to the fifty-three boys from the house who fell fighting.

Departures of the living were regularly marked in the *Chronicle*

* His inscription at the beginning of the frieze reads in translation: 'Let us thank our Lord God for these our brothers who fighting for their country passed through darkness into holy light.'

† There are a number of stories of ghosts at Eton, perhaps because of Provost James: it is claimed that Luxmoore could be detected in two photographs taken after his death, one in College Chapel and one in his garden.

by verses written with consistent felicity by the Head Master himself. Then it became Alington's turn to go. Early in 1933, when he was 60, he accepted the appointment to be Dean of Durham. And at the end of the Summer Half he was to leave with more of the customary parties and presentations than usual. At a floodlit ceremony in School Yard, he received the boys' gifts – a silver cup and a car.*

Neither boys nor Masters agreed in their judgement of the Head Master. He was never universally loved by the boys, and many regarded him with some reason as a sanctimonious fraud – referring to him as 'Creeping Jesus'. Yet those in favour would certainly be a majority. And Eton in 1933 was a more confident institution than it was at the end of 1916. Alington had been a successful leader.

Perhaps he should not have become a Dean, particularly after being a Head Master, for even fewer of those he dealt with were ready to interrupt or contradict him. His friends generally agreed that his failings became more evident, and yet when he revisited Eton to address the boys in Holy Week the old magic held. A very last memory of him at Eton was on one of those occasions: Alington, returning to the Head Master's house, observed a senior boy and Housemaster outside the study, both in tears; divining the situation at once, Alington explained to the boy that, whatever he had done, dismissal was not the final end that it seemed at that moment, and he offered his counsel to the boy after he had left.

He died in May 1955. Richard Martineau wrote a fine obituary in the *Chronicle*, addressed to the current Etonians who knew him only in old age. It ended, as was right, where his influence was greatest, in College Chapel.

Those who watched that bowed figure limping slowly through the hushed and crowded chapel, and who heard echoed through a loud-speaker those matchless cadences, will never forget the spell that was on them, as the eloquence of age appealed to all that was generous in youth. Can they imagine what it had been to listen to him when his voice disdained mechanical help, when he stood in the pulpit as lively and quick, almost it seemed as young, as the boys about him?

* The Head Master's son, Giles, later a much respected Oxford don, had a part in the farewells as Captain of the Oppidans.

CHAPTER EIGHT

Eton between the Wars

INEVITABLY THE GREAT WAR affected the character of Eton and of
Etonians. So many of the traditional parents had died; the economic circumstances of the country, and particularly of the landed
gentry, had changed; new industries led to new wealth, and created
a new demand for Eton education. Psychological changes were
more significant still: the old certainties had perished, the young
were more willing to question the traditions by which their
predecessors had lived – and died.

Considering all of this, it is impressive that so much continuity
was retained. In 1919 many of the upper class consciously wanted
to go back to what had existed in 1914.* Boys still came from
long-established Eton families; over half were sons of Old Etonians. The count of boys from the peerage is not much less in 1930
than in 1900, with sixty-four boys either peers or sons of peers in a
School some seventy-five boys larger. There were also ten baronets
(perhaps an indication that baronets, in particular, died at the
forefront of their troops). Another sign of continuity was that
there were still twenty-five sons of clergy. Naturally there were
fewer Irish boys from the Free State, but about 6% lived in
Scotland. A sprinkling came from overseas. Yet Etonians in-

* Lord's in 1919 revealed the general determination to defy the years since
1914. The Head Master made himself unpopular by forbidding boys in jackets the
right to wear white waistcoats as they had before the War – a practice he
considered expensive and exclusive. Otherwise the scene resumed its traditional
aspect, and it was graced by the presence of the King.

creasingly were based in London, and the connection with the City continued to grow.

Nor was there a marked difference in the careers which Etonians followed after they had left. Over the period 1927–33, Alington's final years, the average number of boys leaving was 211 p.a.: 57% went on to Oxford and Cambridge, 20% to the army, 16% straight into business. Those who went to University were not always the cleverest, and it is remarkable that Colleges were prepared to accept so many.

In Eton the institutions of Warre's time persisted. Boys in Oppidan houses continued to progress from being lower boy fags to upper boys, then to be elected to Debate and the Library. The Captain of the House, selected by the Housemaster, and the Captain of Games still exercised considerable power. Just how authoritarian they were varied with the traditions of the houses: the better Housemasters could influence the wisdom with which their houses were governed, but they would skilfully leave the boys with the impression that they were making their own decisions; with the weaker Housemasters the Library ruled untrammelled. Beating remained a standard punishment, but it, and fagging, were generally accepted. Bernard Fergusson's *Eton Portrait*, published in 1937, which gives an excellent account of Eton at this time, treats fagging and beating as open and accepted matters – not needing apology. Boys regarded such hardships as were to be undergone as rites of passage and, although abuses certainly did occur, normally both fagging and beating were quite tolerable initiations to the roughness of life. Wilfred Thesiger, for example, only quotes one injustice that rankled: he was giving tea to a boy from the Eton Mission before a boxing match, and had forgotten to ask his fagmaster to excuse him fagging. He was beaten and then later, for the only time in his life, was knocked out – a bad day.[*] When boys eventually found themselves in positions of responsibility, most had learnt that it is better to manage people by encouragement or reproof rather than by over-ready resort to punishment.

The strength of the houses lay in their cohesion. Christian names were normally used between contemporaries but seldom by boys

---

[*] Wilfred Thesiger, the explorer, enjoyed his time at Eton in the mid-1920s. He was a boxing Blue at Oxford, as well as a regular winner in the School Boxing Competitions.

of different ages. Houses had no common-rooms at that time, but there was no need. Boys could freely wander into their friends' rooms. The passages were available for gossip, as well as for passage football, a sort of indoor Wall Game for all ages, popular on Saturday evenings. Only the house library was in any sense a club room, but it was by now largely devoid of books, and only available to the Library who might typically be six in number; there justice was administered, and from it the house was run. Debate, perhaps twelve to fifteen boys altogether, would occasionally gather there to hold elections or to debate. These debates were not normally of any profundity, but they were solemnly written up in house books, along with records of the house's triumphs and troubles. The latter tend to be more interesting; here is a sample quotation: 'That the Under $14\frac{1}{2}$ had to be punished for their behaviour in their tie was a pity indeed, for punishments for games at once introduce an entirely wrong spirit ... but in this instance, I'm afraid, it was very necessary.' Most house books also contained character studies by house Captains of boys leaving, and these sometimes show a sensitivity which does credit to the authors and suggests that many Captains really understood those for whom they were responsible. Witness the following account of a future Queen's Private Secretary and Provost:

Martin Charteris came to Eton in Michaelmas 1926 and left at Christmas 1931 after an eventful and varied career. Intellectually he was undistinguished, but it was only laziness which prevented him from displaying his abilities. He was quick-witted, intelligent and possessed of a strong sense of humour, but as I have said before, intolerably idle. This idleness was only shaken off during his last year, when he made a sincere and successful effort to pass the army examination. Though by nature indescribably dirty and untidy, he had great charm and irrepressible optimism. His friends were numerous and his enemies non-existent – for he refused to dislike anyone or to treat any unpleasantness seriously. He will doubtless be benefitted by Sandhurst – but the house will miss his cheerful influence.*

* The writer was Jasper Ridley, killed while escaping from a prisoner-of-war camp in Italy during the Second World War.

The College Annals also contain 'obituaries' of boys leaving, but written by themselves. These are in an odd mixture of styles: factual, facetious, introspective, thoughtful, sometimes uncharitable. That Collegers should write their own accounts is an indication of the stronger tradition of independence in College. This did not necessarily make for humane government. Collegers were almost always more competitive than Oppidans and often cleverer – but not always, because the scholarship examination was biased towards Classics and did not attract large fields; forty candidates would be normal, boys from a limited range of preparatory schools, who had demonstrated ability to learn and had a good linguistic memory, but not always great analytical or logical gifts. Many Collegers came from characteristic Etonian social backgrounds, and fairly frequently had Oppidan brothers, but others were genuinely needy. When they arrived they found themselves isolated and still very differently placed from Oppidans. They were welcomed by the Provost, with a Latin form of admission, which appears to have originated with M.R. James – 'Be a good boy, teachable and truthful, being so pure and wholehearted among your fellows that you may in the end become an honourable citizen, serviceable to your country.' Very many indeed fulfilled that early injunction.

The young Colleger would find himself part of an Election that might be as few as ten or, one year, as many as twenty-two strong, the figure depending entirely on the need to keep numbers to seventy, and disturbed by the large number of leavers in 1914 and the smaller number in 1919. Regardless of whether they came in September or later in the year, all worked together. At first they lived in Chamber and could be liable to rough discipline from the Captain of Chamber, who was entrusted with more power than was wise for one so young. A romantic figure, Godfrey Meynell, terrorized Chamber in Cyril Connolly's day – not simply a bully, because he was also a leader of great courage, the sort of boy always likely to win an MC or a VC – and indeed he did win both.[2]* But others lacked his saving graces. After the first year with its fagging a quieter period might follow, but then Collegers faced a crucial set of Trials, before they took School Certificate,

---

* Godfrey Meynell was awarded a VC posthumously in 1935 serving on the North-West Frontier.

which determined their order for the rest of their schooldays. After that a Colleger would compete socially to be a member of College Pop, but he might relax slightly at his books until he contested the major prizes that were on offer towards the end of the Eton career. The Collegers were almost invariably victorious over Oppidans, at least in the Newcastle Scholarship – this was partly because it tested just those skills in which they had already excelled at their entry. It is usually asserted that Collegers worked much harder than Oppidans, but this may not be wholly true: they could, for example, co-operate over the difficult mathematical problem papers set to the select mathematical divisions, whereas the Oppidan would normally lack a companion in his house to consult.*

At the end of their careers, Collegers might blossom. Those who were good at games met Oppidans earlier, but others too began to spread their wings and acquire Oppidan friends. (Readers of this history will not be surprised to hear that the records continue to assert that relationships between Collegers and Oppidans are better than they were a few years earlier.) To Sixth Form and the Captain of the School belonged authority, probably even greater than that of the Library in an ordinary house. The use made of it might be liberal or it might be harsh. Fashions swung, but it would seem that College became more humane in the 1930s than it was in the 1920s. Highly political campaigns were waged, and on the whole the liberals made gains. College Pop was closed down, beatings became rarer. For a sane opinion of discipline, the words of Michael McKenna as Captain of the School writing in the College Annals in 1929 can be commended:

> [Beating] is useful first for diminishing the brightness of those sparks who prematurely become too splendid to be borne, and secondly for dealing with behaviour which strikes those in authority as being too abnormal to be overlooked. All the same I think there should be a fair margin of sin and bumptiousness allowed, into which nobody should make it his business to inquire too closely: otherwise College will tend to turn into sixty rabbits hunted by ten weasels. Also I am sure that the word

* Anthony Powell, in *Infants of the Spring*, claims that lower boy Oppidans worked hard – longer hours than their German contemporaries; whereas Collegers passed straight into the Upper School. He also says that Oppidans were not universally wealthy, but that this did not breed any sense of inferiority in the poor; the same would be true of College.

of mouth is the best way of dealing with 75% of offences committed.*

This would have been the view of wiser Oppidans too. In one respect, however, College remained different: Collegers built their social lives around their Elections. They were expected to draw their friends from their Elections; Elections would get a reputation which branded whole groups of boys, sometimes undeservedly. This was a limiting system contrasted with Oppidan houses where boys of different ages were thrown together more since they entered the School at different levels. Nowadays, it is true, all Oppidans also are in year blocks, but the social life of both Collegers and Oppidans is much less stratified. Oppidans between the Wars did not always regard the College system of government as much of a tribute to their intelligence: Collegers, on the other hand, while differing sharply among themselves, were almost united that whatever party was in power, College was superior.

In the School at large Pop remained the effective boy authority, though the Head Master might refer disciplinary problems to the Captain of the School and the Captain of the Oppidans. Critics could reasonably say that Pop did little to deserve its privileges, but it did at least monitor the public behaviour of boys and their dress. It ceased to debate during this period, and it met as a collective body only to hold elections. These were bitterly contested and might last for several hours as candidates were black-balled. The process, not altogether wholesome, was at least some preparation for political life, as boys learnt where power and patronage lay. Most Etonians aspired to be members. Even Cyril Connolly, a Colleger without athletic prowess, with only the Rosebery History Prize to distinguish him, but with a gift for amusing his contemporaries, suddenly discovered the attraction of a place in the sun; in one half he made the right friends.

The door burst open and about twenty Pops, many of whom had never spoken to me before, with bright coloured waistcoats, rolled umbrellas, buttonholes, braid, and 'spongebag' trousers, came reeling in, like the college of cardinals arriving to congratu-

---

* Michael McKenna was the son of Reginald McKenna, formerly Chancellor of the Exchequer. He unfortunately died after a long illness aged 21.

late some pious old freak whom fate had elevated to the throne
of St Peter. They made a great noise, shouting and slapping me
on the back in the elation of their gesture. I had got in on the
first round, being put up by Knebworth,* but after they had left
only the faint smell of Balkan Sobranie and Honey and Flowers
mixture remained to prove it was not a dream.[3]

The Eton Society did not offer role models which more puritan
schoolmasters would commend. Yet Joe Grimond, President of
Pop in summer 1932, writing in one of the best of all ephemerals,
Change, could argue:

> It is often in danger of being ridiculous, it is sometimes offensive
> and often useless, but always picturesque. Once having reached
> its haven boys, though assailed by many temptations, do at least
> become pleasant; and its very excellence lies in the fact that it is
> open to every danger and could never have originated in the
> brain of a schoolmaster.

Denys Wilkinson, a young Master in the 1930s, hostile as other
Masters sometimes are, changed his mind because of John
Boughey, President in 1938 and killed in the Second World War:
'In the boy of strong character with a sense of responsibility, Pop
does not engender conceit, but teaches him in the microcosm what
should be the behaviour of the public servant.'[4]

The number of societies of a more conventional pattern increased all the time. They catered for a wide range of interests, and
in most cases boys participated rather than simply listening to
distinguished outside lecturers. The Essay Society and the
Shakespeare Society remained intellectually the most prestigious.
To them was added the Archaeological Society, whose members
read their own papers on general artistic matters and made
expeditions, as well as hearing visiting speakers; it had a junior
counterpart. The Political Society received men of varied political
persuasions, from the Prince of Wales downwards, and the sessions of questions could be lively. After Sir Oswald Mosley's

---

* Viscount Knebworth became an MP before dying piloting his plane aged 29.
His father's biography of him, *Antony*, reveals him as an intelligent athlete with a
love of boxing, and a passion for Eton almost throughout his time in the School.

speech, Michael Astor asked: 'Will you tell us, Sir Oswald, whether you chose black for the colour of your party's shirts for motives of economy?' Mosley lost his temper, and the cause of Fascism at Eton was wrecked in the general hilarity.[5] There was also usually a School Debating Society, and the Cercle Français would sometimes debate in French. While the Scientific Society continued, the most vigorous growth in the 1930s was the Natural History Society which had over 300 members, and which cared for the Museum and a bird sanctuary by the Thames as well as arranging lectures and expeditions. The Photographic Society flourished, and a Film Society developed from the film shows which were laid on by the Captains of the Oppidans in the 1920s.

The biggest society numerically was the Musical Society which provided a School Concert each half. The standards were not what are obtained nowadays, but the numbers of boys participating were higher, and more boys were keen to attend concerts. The Precentor from 1926 to 1945, Dr Henry Ley, was well loved and his organ recitals were popular; and a number of distinguished outsiders gave concerts. Etonians were equipped to become patrons of music rather than performers, and in some houses playing music was not thought a suitable activity for boys. Other Housemasters encouraged music, notably A.M. Goodhart, who was a fussy, ineffective man but a respectable minor composer, and the excellent S.G. Lubbock who out-wooed Goodhart to marry the pianist, Irene Scharrer.

The Shakespeare Society was the approved vehicle for dramatic interest, but Alington did permit the production of plays – an activity which had been forbidden since Balston's time. In 1920 *Twelfth Night* was staged in College Hall – the first of a run of College plays; Luxmoore wrote: 'much as I disapprove, there were some most beautiful things in it & the acting extraordinarily good. the Viola not to be forgotten but it ought to be holiday work not school time.'[6]* Subsequently there were regular school productions, in School Hall, and house plays were occasionally mounted in the privacy of the more liberal Housemasters' rooms. It was possible for William Douglas-Home to get his first one-act play

---

* The Viola was not forgotten. He was G.H. Rylands (Dadie), who as a Fellow of King's exercised considerable influence on the course of English drama.

produced at the School while he was at Eton.[7]* Yet there was no encouragement for drama from the Head Master – it is uncertain whether it was Alington or his successor Elliott who gave permission for a play with the proviso that 'it should not be too good', for the story is variously related, but the remark has the authentic ring of official attitudes.

The Drawing Schools had a chequered history between the Wars. In 1922, Sidney Evans was still teaching in the cramped studio in Keate's Lane. On his retirement Alington appointed Eric Powell from the languages staff, who was a good amateur watercolourist. He was an effective personality and no doubt should have some of the credit for the new building, and his personal popularity drew some boys to it; but he was a good schoolmaster rather than an artist. When he died in an accident in 1933, his assistant, an amiable but quite mad man, Menzies-Jones, known universally as Mones, succeeded him. Even the presence of Robin Darwin (later Sir Robin, head of the Royal College of Art) as second-in-command did not make this an altogether happy period for Eton Art, and there was some feeling that painting and drawing had been pushed aside for pottery and marionettes – though the marionette theatre built by boys was in itself a remarkable achievement.[8] In 1938 Mones had the first of a number of psychotic attacks. The School welcomed him back with commendable tolerance, but from that time Wilfrid Blunt became effectively in charge, and a new regime was established.

There were certainly boys who became accomplished artists between the Wars, but the most remarkable outpouring of talent occurred at the end of Sidney Evans's time. Under his presidency the Eton Society of Arts was founded by Brian Howard and Harold Acton, with members chosen from those who took extra drawing at Evans's studio. Its purpose was aesthetic rather than artistic, though a number of the eleven founders were to have some link with the arts in later life. The subjects discussed included such topics as Post-Impressionism, the Decoration of Rooms, and Oriental Art. The Society produced a magazine, *Eton Candle*, which enjoyed surprising esteem outside Eton; it was to be the high spot of Howard's melancholy career of self-advertisement, the subsequent decline charted in many memoirs of Oxford in the 1920s. What was most remarkable, however, was that four of the

* He had to cede the principal role to Giles Alington.

members were authors of distinction: Henry Yorke (the novelist Henry Green), Harold Acton, Robert Byron, and Anthony Powell.*

Though some of its members, including Powell, were entirely respectable, the Eton Society of Arts was also an act of rebellion against the general philistinism of sport-loving Etonians. There were other such rebels throughout Eton's history, but few were to make so big a splash. Not surprisingly, the Society of Arts did not survive long; such groups depend upon the drive of particular individuals, and Eric Powell (about to be a Housemaster) was too much part of Eton's establishment to cherish this potentially awkward squad. They illustrate the diversity of Etonians. A.C. Benson in 1924 at the end of his life described Etonians in his diary as 'friendly, unembarrassed, fair-minded on the whole, disliking stuffy things & only unfortunate in thinking of the intellectual element as stuffy'.⁹ That is a fair description of the generality of Etonians, as indeed of the English as a race, at least until recent years.

Games continued to be a most important part of Eton life. Eton oarsmen were no longer quite so successful, partly no doubt because the climax of their season was competition at Henley against older College crews in the Ladies' Plate. In cricket, however, Eton maintained its general ascendancy – not losing to Harrow until 1939.† Houses tended to excel at cricket or rowing; some were good at neither. Success at the house level was dutifully charted in the house books. To a considerable extent boys continued to run house games themselves, oarsmen, for instance, willingly giving their time to teaching new boys to scull or row.

The Field Game was, however, *the* boys' game which continued to be wholly run by boys – except for the umpiring in house ties. A great moment for many was when the Captain of Games 'gave them their shorts' to show they were recognized members of the house side; until 1931 lesser footballers wore knickerbockers, but then shorts for all were introduced as an economy. The Field Game called for a seriousness of training and an involvement that

---

* The Eton Society of Arts figures in Henry Green's novel, *Blindness*, written when he was still at Eton. It is also described by, among others, Anthony Powell in *Infants of the Spring*.

† Attendance at Lord's fell, however, perhaps because there were too many draws. Eton did win the Ladies' Plate in 1921.

was not repeated in the Lent Half when Etonians competed against other schools in a variety of games. Rugger tended to be more popular at this time than soccer, but Etonians fairly contentedly lost at either. The same could be said of athletics, boxing, and fencing. Fives and rackets were played more seriously and successfully, but the overall effect was amateur. Possibly the Etonian attitude was insulting to other schools which arranged their games more professionally, but as Oliver Van Oss, a newly appointed non-Etonian beak, wrote, 'A Lent Half in which games are played almost exclusively for enjoyment has always seemed to be one of Eton's most precious liberal institutions'.[10] Etonian nonchalance also appealed to the occasional outsider, as for instance to a Stowe master. Arriving with a junior rugger team, and finding no one at the rendezvous, he accosted a 15-year-old in the street, who thereupon made all the arrangements for lunch in different houses and organized a team which, not unnaturally, lost heavily.[11] This seemed to show a perfect attitude to games, but Mr Heckstall-Smith was lucky: not every young Etonian would have been so resourceful.

All games were reported in the *Chronicle*, but it might seem to the outsider that the activities of the Eton College Hunt claimed disproportionate space. That would, however, be wrong, for they still attracted large fields, over one hundred boys regularly. Master and whippers-in were Etonians, groomed for futures as Masters of Foxhounds; and few boys had more responsibility, since they were in charge not only of their hounds but of Etonians away from Eton in an increasingly unfriendly environment. Accounts of their hunts are meticulously written up by each Master, ending with the prayer, '*Floreant canes Etonenses*' – though one Master reminds readers that they were not always the best scholars among Etonians with his subscription, '*Floreat Canes Etonensis*'.

As a consequence of the War, the Corps remained more or less obligatory, though a greater light-heartedness entered the ranks. Its uniform changed from grey to mulberry when H.K. Marsden, the Quartermaster, bought up a cheap lot of cloth. Field days and camp were the most important activities, when drinking and smoking seem to have been prevalent. An intriguing picture of the feeding of Etonians emerges from a note circulated by Marsden, after the cancellation of some field days; houses could buy ginger beer at 9/- a gallon, ham sandwiches at 35/- a gross, and 8-lb. slabs

of chocolate at £1 each; buns and rock cakes were on offer free –
these would no doubt have served the Corps as ammunition had
the field days occurred. Incidentally, boys were amply but not
wisely fed – in 1937 a comparison of Eton boys and Durham boys
of the same age showed the Etonians on average 3½ inches taller and
18 pounds heavier, largely due to greater length of leg – but the
Etonians did show signs of dental decay.

In 1919, Scout troops were formed for the younger boys.
Etonians had been active in the Scout movement from the start,
and Eton was the first school to organize its own Scouting. It
became popular, and there were soon some 250 members. The era
of Eton Scouting was only to last some thirty years, but during
that period Eton supplied a disproportionate number of Senior
Scouts.

It might seem that boys hardly had time for so many activities,
but it should be remembered that the older boys had long hours
out of school. In particular, unless they had fallen foul of their
Tutors, they could count on being free between 12.00 and
1.45 p.m. (though Science specialists had practicals on Tuesdays)
and games might well be played After Twelve as well as in the
afternoon. Lower boys at that time were in Pupil Room, preparing
their classical construes, and writing verses or proses under
supervision. With the commitment to games that was expected of
them, and with fagging, they led very full lives.

An attractive feature that emerges from accounts of Eton is the
respect and affection commanded by certain 'characters' met by
boys in their sporting and social lives. On the river, for example, all
knew Alf Claret who ran the boathouse (and he more surprisingly
knew all of them and their predecessors), or Froggie, the most
picturesque of his watermen. Eton was then, and has remained,
fortunate in the excellent servants whom it attracted, and who
often stayed at their posts for fifty years. Such a one was Mat
Wright, the much-liked cricket professional, who served along
with George Hirst. Boys could still buy food from a Joby, but the
School Stores ran the most popular eating places. Tom Bubb and
Jack Elkins at the Fives courts influenced boys' manners for the
better by the courtesy they showed – it was no accident that this
store became known as Jack's. Then there were the Misses
Dempster, intellectual ladies of high religious principles, who
talked of the importance of landscapes permeated with spires.[12]

They were the physiotherapists: their brother unfortunately left Eton because the authorities pettily refused to let him sign the tickets that boys used when going out after lock-up.* One must not assume that the College was always a considerate employer.

Nevertheless it was the Masters who made most impact on boys, and there were some very odd men around, by no means all savoury. Many boys – some not well-disposed to the School – would say that they were never taught by a dull or insignificant man. One who achieved almost legendary status, was the mathematician H.K. Marsden, known as Bloody Bill. A man of quite exceptional ability, he had been in College under Alington at the same time as R.A. Knox, and he figures presciently in the ephemeral, *The Outsider*: 'In the temporary absence of Marsden KS, who is engaged in the Tomline Examination, Mr Gaffney [the School Clerk] has the management of School Office.' During the War he is said in his spare time to have regulated troop movements – a job previously done by five men. He was to become almost an adjutant to Alington, and he undoubtedly relished the power that came with his organizational role. In 1923 he became Master-in-College, but he did not find Collegers easy to mould. He tried, but with only limited success, to influence Sixth Formers into greater use of corporal punishment. A.J. Ayer, the philosopher, in his memoirs gives some idea of the antipathy Marsden could arouse.[13] In *The Outsider* again one can read that 'The Head Master has acquitted himself from the charge of employing detectives at Eton, but Marsden KS has yet made no similar avowal'. Both in College and in his house, begun in 1930, his espionage was well known – boys would, for instance, fix hairs across their burries to see when Bill had been prying into their private correspondence. In his house, his sadism had freer play, and he used to beat boys – contrary to the regulations. Yet his house was extremely successful, not only within the School, but in terms of the contributions made to the country by his old boys; and most of the old boys regarded him with great affection. For he had from their angle at least two good characteristics – he was very generous, and he was extremely partisan, backing his boys even beyond what was

* Mr Dempster was George V's osteopath. The house ticket system was intended to ensure that boys only left their houses in the evening for approved purposes. It was never totally effective, and broke down once houses lacked the staff to check boys in and out.

reasonable. Needless to say, this did not endear him to other Masters, nor was he regarded by boys not in his house with anything other than apprehension and fear.

Sam Slater was another sadist with less to his credit. When Harold Caccia became Provost, in his inaugural speech he commended Slater as an example of how much boys owe to their Housemasters. This caused some older men to feel that there must be hope for every Housemaster. Perhaps at first his behaviour was more controlled, though he used to wrestle with boys when he went round his house after entertaining colleagues from his excellent cellar. But he took to beating his boys, with their trousers down, and for at least one member of his house the day he heard that Slater had been killed mountaineering was the happiest of his boyhood.

Other Masters were more or less successfully repressed homosexuals. Conybeare, a man of many virtues who became Lower Master, and Cattley, a kind man with a gift for the witty epigram,* would both try to kiss boys when saying goodnight: this did not endear them to their charges, who usually managed to take evasive action. One wonders why neither Head Master took action against all these abuses – but boys accepted these eccentricities as within the pale of tolerated behaviour, and did not complain: their attitude would be very different nowadays. For all the oddity found in their ranks, most Housemasters ran good houses.

It was an age when Masters were expected to be eccentric: none was more remarkable than W. Hope-Jones, Hojo to the boys. He was a man so utterly opposed to any pretence that he relished appearing unconventional or absurd. It was to Alington's credit that he made light of the occasion when Hojo was arrested for bathing in the nude, and that he permitted Hojo to continue preparing boys in his house for Confirmation when he changed from Anglican to Quaker. Yet Hojo was more than an oddity; by his sincerity and his simple goodness he won boys' hearts. Who

---

* Tom Cattley's most famous epigram referred to Mr J.C. Butterwick acquiring for twopence a First Edition of *Paradise Lost* in the School's Pound of second-hand textbooks, to which boys handed in no longer wanted books:

> O J.C.B., too penny-wise
> For the pound-foolish Pound,
> How dearly lost is Paradise,
> And oh! how cheaply found!

else would have bicycled to Henley and back before breakfast to dive (successfully) for a boy's watch which had been lost? Who else could have so effectively entertained Boy Scouts with his stentorian singing?* And was there a more imaginative teacher of Mathematics in his day? It is a sad reflection that many of his colleagues disregarded him, but the Mathematical Association recognized his gifts, and many boys who were not natural mathematicians were glad to be up to Hojo.[14]

Among the other notable teachers were George Lyttelton and Henry Marten, a man who held boys by his narrative gift – and by the simple trick of prompting and spurring boys to what he thought should be remembered facts: '"Roll up that map of Europe," who said that? Now gentlemen, quick, P. .P, P. .P, P. .P,' and the division would roar 'Pitt, Sir'. 'Ah, gentlemen, but which Pitt?'[15] One suspects that he actually achieved most by setting boys interesting essays and correcting these carefully. Lyttelton taught mostly Classics, sometimes to the top Kappa set, where the width of his interests enlivened many boys. Yet it was his teaching of English that made the greatest impact: his enthusiasm for literature was infectious, his humour so engaging, his wisdom so mature.

In the 1930s, the Head Master's division of top classical special-ists was admirably taught by Richard Martineau and Walter Hamilton, who was later Headmaster of Westminster and Rugby

* His song 'Woad' went to the tune of 'Men of Harlech'; it began:

> What's the good of wearing braces,
> Vests and pants and boots with laces,
> Spats or hats you buy in places
>   Down the Brompton Road?
> What's the use of shirts of cotton,
> Studs that always get forgotten?
> These affairs are simply rotten:
>   Better far is WOAD.
> WOAD's the stuff to show men:
> WOAD to scare your foemen:
>   Boil it to
>   A brilliant blue,
> And rub it on your back and your abdomen.
>   Ancient Briton
>   Never hit on
> Anything as good as WOAD to fit on
> Neck or knees or where you sit on,
>   Tailors, you be blowed.

and Master of Magdalene College, Cambridge. R.M.A. Bourne has
described the experience offered:

> Richard would sit behind the octagonal table, which served as a
> desk, wrapped in coat and scarf, and frequently hoarse from
> cold, pouring out knowledge, as one pupil said, 'like a demi-
> god', at considerable speed and in no very audible voice. To
> catch the pearls of wisdom and humour a boy had to listen hard.
> Walter walked about the room, banging the sleeve of his gown,
> weighted with chalk or a confiscated squash ball, on bench or
> table, burying his head in pretended agony at mistakes, rolling
> his protuberant eyes (as Socrates did) with their large whites
> until they almost disappeared, using all of an actor's gestures to
> stimulate interest. He encouraged participation very much more
> than Richard, but expected it to be at a high level. 'You mortify
> me, you make me feel positively sick', he could say in those
> lugubrious but wryly humorous tones, when a contribution
> appeared unworthy.[16]

They were not tied by any examination syllabus, for most boys in
the division would be aiming for scholarships. These boys could
read extraordinarily widely, and at other times probe very deeply
(for example when Walter Hamilton spent the Divinity periods of
one whole half on the opening fourteen verses of St John's Gospel,
developing the link betwen Greek philosophy and Christian faith).
Proceedings could be further enlivened by gifted boys who
handled their teachers with assured skill. Richard Martineau would
recall affectionately John Boughey apologizing for a piece of work
not shown up on time: 'Suffer but a little while in uncomplaining
love'. Boughey was not one of the ablest scholars and Martineau
reported pessimistically of his chances of a Cambridge award, but
'where scholarly attainments can carry a boy most of the way,
charm and a good batting average will sometimes do the rest'.[17]*
Cambridge tutors were different in those days, and Boughey won

---

* Another Martineau report on Boughey ends: 'He adds much to the good
temper of the Division, but I have had to restrict the exuberance of his taste in
waistcoats. One of Regency design so vividly suggests the orgies of Carlton
House that I have asked him not to wear it in morning school.' When Boughey
died, the *Chronicle* published his last poem, as earlier (in 1921) it had published
the last poem of another golden boy, Michael Davies, J.M. Barrie's ward, who
died tragically at Oxford.

an exhibition to Magdalene. The encouragement to learning at a higher level was to transform the attitudes of many boys. No wonder that some of them found Oxford and Cambridge pale by comparison.

Lyttelton and Hope-Jones were happily married men with large families; Henry Marten lived with his twin sister. But women did not play a large part on the Eton scene. Only one-third of Housemasters were married in 1930, though the proportion increased during the 1930s. Each house had a Dame, and there was a Matron-in-College, whose appointment was a matter for the Provost and Fellows because College was still titulary under the Provost. Miss Oughterson, who retired in 1930, and Miss George her successor had both been Dames and both were warmly regarded. Dames were seldom known outside their own kingdoms, but Miss Byron, who became Dame for Julian Lambart in 1928 and who was to serve for thirty-five years, was an exception. A distant relation of the poet, with her squat figure but elevated mind, she was to be something of a figure to all boys. Her recipe for success as a Dame: 'Look well after the little boys, but leave the big boys to run themselves, except in cases of urgent need.'[18]

By the end of the inter-war period, however, Grizel Hartley, married in 1923 to Hubert (a Housemaster from 1933), emerged as Eton's most remarkable lady, known very widely through the School. Hubert, himself, was an eccentric, but the straightest man that could be imagined; of Grizel, to whom he became engaged at Cambridge, he wrote to his old Tutor, Rayner-Wood, that 'She is quite as mad as I am, and in the same ways'. Both were indeed fearless in sailing or climbing, reckless in generosity. Her own particular characteristics were wit and kindness. From a wide knowledge of literature and a prodigious fund of anecdotes she could sustain any conversation. And her openness to the young was astonishing. She loved them all, and shared some of their sense of mischief. 'Darling, you do look tired. Have a glass of sherry. Don't tell Hubert.' Grizel herself once overheard a boy saying to another: 'That's Mrs Hartley. I believe she's awfully nice, but absolutely bats.' To all those many boys who knew her closely she was that and a good deal more.[19]

Grizel Hartley's drawing-room was one of a number where Masters would gather socially. Even if they were less rich than they had been, the Housemasters in particular still lived very comfortably and entertained frequently. Bachelors had their own dinner parties, in addition, often distinguished by the excellence of the wine served.* Such occasions did not necessarily interfere with the job of looking after the boys, for Masters would be sent round the house to talk to boys in their rooms. This was a useful education for young men, as well as teaching the boys social ease. The youngest bachelors lived in colonies, and it was normal for a group of three to employ two or three staff.

With no common-room life, but with many intersecting social circles, Masters could develop groups of friends to their taste, who might be bound together by, for example, a shared subject, or interest in the Arts or the river. About one-third were still Old Etonians, but it would be wrong to assume any great homogeneity on the staff. They tended to drive stylish cars incompetently. They were mostly capable of performing at some sport with distinction. Many were academically far above the level at which they were teaching. If there was a common characteristic, it was the ability to work long hours.

This did not leave much time for life outside Eton – for example, doing anything to relieve the slump of the inter-war years. Robert Birley, a young Master at the time, however, helped to organize Occupational Centres to relieve unemployment in Slough. Monty James said, 'This is just the sort of thing that needs to be done', and gave a cheque for £50.[20] Boys contributed through house collections. In 1932, the College cancelled its Founder's Day Feast and gave the money saved; Founder's Feasts were not resumed thereafter, but to save the College money, not to support the unemployed. Mrs Alington certainly had Socialist sympathies, but the majority of the Eton community were unwilling to be involved. The Eton Mission, it was felt, was an adequate response to the social needs of the time. Some boys did indeed become more aware of harsher realities there. For others, such as the young Frank Pakenham,† work at the Eton Manor opened eyes.[21] In 1937 a group of Old Etonians founded a Housing Association as a

* C.M. Wells was one of several connoisseurs; when he died an obituary destined for *Salmon and Trout* (he was also a skilled fly-fisherman) was submitted for approval to Andrew Gow, a Master at Eton before he became a Fellow of Trinity, Cambridge. The draft contained the words 'C.M. Wells was a great judge of claret, burgundy and port', but Gow returned it with the word 'burgundy' deleted.

† Later the Earl of Longford, a Labour Cabinet Minister.

practical expression of the need to help. Nobody could claim that Eton as a whole responded decisively to the problems of the inter-war years, but, as always in a School so large and so diverse, individuals were prepared to depart from the generally accepted line. Furthermore, Etonians still regarded politics as a suitable career; 106 MPs in 1931 and 104 in 1935 were OEs.*

In the same sort of way most Etonians between the wars were conventional Christians, with a growing number of sceptics. Chapel was entirely accepted as part of the routine of life, with quarter-hour morning Chapel on weekdays, and two slightly shortened services on Sundays; and the congregational singing, particularly of the psalms, was very splendid. Boys might irreverently enjoy simple mishaps that occurred; the Masters would derive more sophisticated amusement, for example from the prayers that Conduct Harvey would say for the guidance of the Patronage Committee when an appointment was to be made to a College living for which Harvey had applied – and if Harvey was regularly disappointed, who is to say that God did not answer his prayers? for Harvey was not an impressive man. The Conduct was in no sense a senior Chaplain, for such an individual did not exist; it was still assumed that Tutors were capable of preparing boys for Confirmation, or that they would find clergymen on the teaching staff to do the job.

From 1932 a second Conduct was appointed to be Master of the Choir School. Although it was still a day school, it was at the time firmly established – its boys well taught by Eton Masters in addition to the new Conduct. The Choir contributed to all the services, but only at Sunday evensong did it sing an anthem in full service. There were special choral services not attended by the main School on four afternoons a week. These helped to maintain musical standards, and the general level of the services, enhanced by the reading of the Provosts and in Alington's time by his preaching, was higher than it had been before.

Certainly the services did not influence Etonians directly to-wards good behaviour: we read of unruly behaviour of con-firmands after their Confirmation. Boys continued to behave as boys will do, despite the grievous sanctions that could fall on them, and the willingness of most senior boys to act against even those

* The 1935 MPs were pressed into service to replant one tree each on the playing fields after the first attack of Dutch elm disease.

who were fairly close in age. There are accounts, for example, from both sides, of the Junior Rugger XV showing their *joie de vivre* at Rowlands, the sock shop, after a match with Stowe; five were beaten by Quintin Hogg and Peter Fleming,* the unusually distinguished Captains of School and Oppidans. Michael McKenna KS was Keeper of the team and with four of the unruliest he was punished as the man responsible. He wrote home:

> The Keeper bent over in perfect tight position, and proceeded to receive 7 successive smart cuts, alas all in the same place – practice breeds perfection, you know. At the end he stood up, rubbed his bottom and went out, and continued his daily life. What the invisible cloud of witnesses observed was that the Keeper had courage and restraint; that no foolish thoughts of vengeance or bitterness were entertained against Hogg ma, but rather that a higher estimation of him was formed; and finally that he was glad to have suffered in a way for the others.[22]

Fleming too regarded the matter lightly (easier for him to do so!), but he also dealt more toughly later in the half with what were in his view altogether more serious offenders, boys in the Library of another house than his own who were receiving pornographic mail from France; 'they got what they deserved', he remarked in the Captain of the Oppidans' Book. The problem did not stop: a few years later (1929) Alington was writing to Housemasters: 'I have reason to believe that some works called the Grand Publications are circulating in the School. Paper-covered smallish books with titles of an obvious kind. Mostly translations from the French.'

Another prevalent form of crime was betting – in 1932 Alington issued a notice to the School: 'Boy bookmakers must not be surprised if they are told that they must carry on their pursuit elsewhere.'† There were also troubles with visits to the pub and the cinema. Many senior boys could not understand why the cinema should be universally forbidden, and it surely would have simplified the task of authority had Housemasters been allowed to

---

* Quintin Hogg, later Lord Hailsham, became Lord Chancellor. Peter Fleming, traveller and author. His younger brother, Ian, left before him after some trouble with girls – but he had already been twice Victor Ludorum in athletics aged 16 and 17.

† One Master, Philip Roome, also had to leave at this time because of his gambling debts.

give leave to suitable boys. Etonians varied very considerably in
their spending power, and there was little other than food, books,
or charity on which they could legally use their money; while this
concealed the shortage of funds of the poorer boys, it is not
surprising that many of the richer took to gambling or to breaking
out in other, often relatively harmless, ways.

The ultimate escapade of this period was the 1938 trip of five
boys by aeroplane to Le Touquet, of which Ludovic Kennedy has
left an account. Their well-planned excursion was to be fitted in
between two Absences on a holiday, to increase the challenge.
Dogged by misadventures, they did not have time to reach the
Casino or even a proper restaurant, and the return journey was at
first refused by French bureaucrats on the grounds that the King
and Queen were visiting Paris; but eventually the Chief of Police
gave authority, and the boys were back for 5.45 Absence literally
with seconds to spare. Their honour was satisfied, and they were
not detected.[23] Shortly afterwards another trio made the same trip.

It would seem that sex may have caused increased problems
between the Wars. There were a number of notorious Eton
homosexuals, of whom Guy Burgess was easily the most infamous.
Even though it appears that his character deterioriated markedly at
Cambridge, perhaps the seeds were sown at Eton? It is extremely
difficult to generalize since naturally much of this sort of behaviour would have occurred privately. Certainly the problem was
more evident at some times, in some houses, and even to some
boys within those houses. Cyril Connolly, a Colleger in the earlier
1920s, gives the impression that homoerotic relationships were
common, but Michael Longson, a Colleger a few years later, was
unaware of homosexuality until he was 18, and then only from
Greek literature.[24] Hallam Tennyson writes of sexual experimenta-
tion being prevalent in his house, while conceding that it was not
common in his cousin's time a very little earlier.[25]

Although it would be difficult to assert certainly that Eton was
particularly prone to homosexuality at this time, or compared to
other schools, two points can be made tentatively: first, that an
unusually large number of boys had no father; secondly, that some
who were most boastful of relationships with other boys were
rebels against conventional morality, and that rebellion was a more
powerful factor than sexual inclination. The attitudes of the staff
were certainly mixed. If a few offered boys encircling arms, that

would be as far as displays of affection would go. A comparable
number were prudish, and alarmed by even the possibility of a
platonic relationship between boys of different ages. Most Housemasters were constantly on guard against any physical sexual
activity. Lower boys were forbidden social access to other houses.
Boys were left in little doubt that any offenders would be sacked.
When Elliott became Head Master this was certainly the case, but
Alington was rather less firm in his principles. In one instance, in
1929, a small boy had been indecently assaulted by two bigger
boys at the School of Mechanics; a friend of the victim told the
Tutor who naturally took the matter to the Head Master; rather
than deal with the case himself he passed the whole problem to the
Captain of the Oppidans. The latter, writing up the story for his
successors, remarked that 'there is no reason why any boy should
ever be sacked again, since no crime could be more serious than
this'. Certainly the Captain of the Oppidans, Lewis Clive,* seems
to have been clearer-headed than his Head Master. (It is possible,
however, that the boy who revealed the truth was only prepared to
do so if the Head Master did not dismiss the offenders.) It is worth
remembering that if boys sometimes seem to have been too
frequently the agents of punishing malefactors in those days, at
least they were able to do so with more effect and less lasting
damage than if the Head Master had dealt with the problem.

Sexual knowledge grew during the inter-war years, but the
young, and indeed the Masters, were less instructed than they are
now. There was less cause for anxious introspection. Smutty
conversation about sex with either boys or girls was fairly common, but usually light-hearted; it is mentioned in the College
Annals towards the end of the 1930s, for instance, with some
disapproval – but generally in Eton one suspects that it was taken
for granted. The adult world was still officially very hostile to
homosexuality, but among the boys it was recognized that romantic friendships were natural and might not matter much. This
relaxed attitude certainly extended to nakedness: boys did have
more privacy than at other public schools, having the shelter of
their own rooms, but they were not prudes. Wilfrid Blunt recounts
in 1938 visiting Gully Mason, one of the party to Le Touquet, and
the owner of a racing greyhound, after a dinner party at the

* Lewis Clive was also Captain of the Boats. He later joined the Labour Party
and died fighting the Fascists in Spain.

Hartleys'; cleaning his teeth, stark naked, Mason was unabashed –
'Good evening, Sir; take a pew', and the conversation was sustained at least by the boy.[26]

In 1930 a notorious novel, *Decent Fellows*, was published,
written by John Heygate, the son of a former Housemaster.
Revealing something of this underworld, it caused great outrage at
Eton ('To the worm the world must appear all mud') and must
have been a considerable embarrassment to his parents. The Head
Master wrote angrily to the Fellows:

> It is suggested that three boys who were caught at a Night Club
> were flogged: it may be worth while to put it on record that no
> boys have, in fact, been caught at any Night Club, during my
> Headmastership, and that had they been so caught there would
> have been no question of their remaining in the School.

One wonders – though it is true that in 1928 two boys were sacked
for going to the Hotel de Paris at Bray on a Sunday afternoon (one
the Captain of his house, the other because he compounded his
offence by lying); to Alington's fury a distorted report appeared in
the press, and this may have given the young author of *Decent
Fellows* the idea for his episode. Sixty years on the book hardly
seems sensational – the most unattractive features are the snobbery
of the hero's middle-class parents, and the squalid and arrogant
behaviour of the Corps at camp.

An altogether more serious attack on the School is included in
Enemies of Promise by Cyril Connolly, published in 1938, but
describing College immediately after the War. His picture of early
days in College, and indeed of the period when he was not quite
yet at the top, is brutal. But the violence is matched by the
heartache of romantic friendships and by the fascination of political scheming. *Enemies of Promise* leaves no doubt of the intensity of
the life of an Eton Colleger. Furthermore, the story has, at least
superficially, a happy ending: Connolly wins the Rosebery, the
Brackenbury Scholarship at Balliol, and against substantial odds is
elected to Pop. Yet the happiness is illusory – for Connolly asserts
that in fact his literary promise was stunted by his success.
Etonians are condemned to permanent adolescence. In a spectacu-
lar misjudgement, he wrote that Alec Dunglass:

the kind of graceful, tolerant, sleepy boy who is showered with favours and crowned with all the laurels, who is liked by the Masters and admired by the boys without any apparent exertion on his part, without experiencing the ill-effects of success himself or arousing the pangs of envy in others ... [in] the eighteenth century would have become Prime Minister before he was thirty; [yet] as it was he appeared honourably ineligible for the struggle of life.[27]*

His book was distasteful to many who knew him in College, who thought his condemnation of faults in others hypocritical. Furthermore, as Anthony Powell was to remark, had he not had his late successes at Eton would he not equally have claimed that his genius was stunted by just missing the Brackenbury, by just not getting in to Pop? In fact more often than not, if a school can provide the growing boy with the self-confidence that comes with success, it will help develop the underlying talent. Eton between the Wars had learnt to provide arenas of success for an increasingly varied group of boys. *Enemies of Promise* does not establish any underlying trend of failure – and indeed what failure was there when Eric Blair (George Orwell) was only a year senior to him in College, or when Anthony Powell was an Oppidan two years younger? Robert Byron reckoned that he arrived at Oxford two years more mature than his contemporaries, above all because Eton had taught him to think for himself.

By the time *Enemies of Promise* was published, Etonians were increasingly preoccupied by war. A number had gone to fight in Spain; boys gave their sympathy and money generally to the Republican side, though not surprisingly there were a few Fascist supporters vociferous enough to be interned later when the Second World War broke out. That was seen to be coming, but with none of the eager excitement of 1914. The Corps took on a new seriousness, and the Head Master began preparing for hostilities.

If Etonians may seem to have been too much protected from the harsher realities of life between the Wars, at least the great majority led very normal happy lives. A remarkable number became sufficiently distinguished to have published memoirs or to have been the subjects of biographies – more from the 1920s than the

---

* Alec Dunglass was the future Sir Alec Douglas-Home.

1930s, but a higher proportion of those in the 1930s were to die in the Second World War. Most of these records show great warmth to Eton, even when the subjects were difficult boys; for example, Hallam Tennyson in the 1930s found Eton kind to non-conformists – no attempt was made to force him to join the Corps or to prevent him selling *Peace News* in the High Street.[28] Of Penrose Tennyson, his brother who was making a mark as a film director when he was killed, not yet 30, in the Second World War, his father (not an OE) wrote:

I do not think there are many schools where a boy would have been allowed such freedom of expression; where his disregard of discipline and convention would have met with such indulgence; and where his parents would have received year after year, such careful, understanding and sympathetic reports on their unusual son. Though he himself may have chafed at the conventions of a venerable institution, I am sure that in time he came to realise that the fault had been chiefly his own and from no other school could he have got the training for life which Eton gave him. For that and for the five years of wonderful happiness which he spent there, he was abidingly grateful.[29]*

* When he died, friends of Penrose Tennyson wished to establish a prize in his memory for a film 'treatment'. This was (rather sadly) thought to be impracticable.

CHAPTER NINE

Claude Elliott and the Second World War

WHEN THE TIME came to replace Dr Alington in 1933, the Provost and Fellows found themselves in some difficulty. Many admirable men must have been killed in the War, and the field of potential Head Masters was thin. At Eton itself, George Lyttelton was felt to be a possibility, but he was too lazy and unambitious, and he had little more gift or inclination for administration than his Uncle Edward. Two Oxford dons, Sir Walter Riddell and J.C. Masterman, were considered, but the former did not want the job – thinking that a headmaster must be a teacher, which he was not – and the latter had written a detective story in which a don has venereal disease, not a qualification for a Head Master in the eyes of the Provost. Lionel Smith, recently appointed Headmaster of Edinburgh Academy, seemed to be the ideal man, but he refused to be considered, not being particularly attracted to Eton and feeling himself bound in honour to Edinburgh. A man with charisma, he might indeed have been a notable success.

To advertise the post and interview applicants was not the Fellows' fashion, but luckily their thoughts were directed in April to a Cambridge constitutional historian and tutor at Jesus College, Claude Aurelius Elliott.* He was said to have shown gifts for administration, which would be welcome after two Head Masters so indifferent to such matters; and he was an Old Colleger. By the end of May they had decided that he was the man, and invited him

* The Hon. Jasper Ridley was probably responsible; he was a friend of Elliott's, and a most supportive Fellow throughout his term as Head Master.

at three days' notice to an interview, at which he offended no one and was to his amazement appointed: there is some advantage in having a short list of one. He was not widely known, and the educational world was astonished. He himself was even questioned by a stranger at a dinner party about this chap Elliott: there were certain odd rumours about him.[1]

He was just 45 years old when he began as Head Master. He had squeezed on to the bottom of the Election Roll in 1902, thanks to Henry Marten discerning promise in his General Paper answers, and only entered College because a boy's death created a vacancy. He had not been happy in his Oppidan house, but he enjoyed College. There was one very educational experience 'when I was in the semi-compos state which many boys get into at the age of 15–16'. The Captain of the School was sick and he decided he would not obey the substitute, and stayed seated in College Hall on the order, '*Surgite*' (Rise for grace). Unwilling to apologize, he was beaten. The next two days the same happened; on the fourth day he rose. On reflection, 'I fully realized the extent of my hubris and my idiocy'. He came to like the substitute Captain of the School, who took the trouble to talk to him after the episode, and he was grateful for this painful lesson. When he was able to specialize partially, he tried Science and, when that did not work, History; Henry Marten immediately captured his interest by giving him a number of books to read and inviting him to decide from them who wrote the Casket Letters.* Henry Marten was Vice-Provost in 1933, and he was to be Provost while Elliott was Head Master; thus he had an enormous impact on Elliott's life, which was gratefully acknowledged.[2]

He was physically active and a decent oar, but not as distinguished athletically as his predecessors had been. In the semi-finals of the School boxing during his last year at Eton, he had been knocked out by a blow which left him permanently deaf in one ear. He liked even as Head Master to wear games clothes under his enveloping cassock so that he could slip away quickly to the river or squash court. Above all he was an enthusiastic mountaineer, despite a fall in which he broke a knee-cap, which preserved him from the front line and therefore probably from death in the First War. Indeed, he became a don because it would give him sufficient

---

* These purported to be by Mary Queen of Scots, implicating her in the murder of her husband Darnley.

leisure to climb mountains. At Cambridge he administered a fund which gave grants to help undergraduates climb, with Professor Pigou, an Old Harrovian economist, and Geoffrey Young, the historian, who had briefly been an Eton Master until dismissed by Warre; it was an ideal committee, apparently, since so few undergraduates qualified that funds were always adequate: 'I would not have anyone who wrote poetry, Pigou would not have anyone who believed in God, and Geoffrey Young would not have anyone with spots.'

Here Claude reveals two of his characteristics, his anti-intellectualism and his humour. He was not a man in any case to over-value himself, but his humour was particularly self-deprecating. He was not as philistine as he sometimes represented himself – he had a taste for art and architecture. He certainly was profoundly unmusical: overhearing the choir at Jesus practising a descant, he had assumed there was a riot and tried to restore order; the School Concerts at Eton were to be well-advertised misery to him, relieved by covering his programme with drawings of the Cuillins. It was always easier to say what Elliott was against than what he was for. In religion he was probably agnostic, though comfortable enough with the *via media* of the Church of England, but he was against any display of fervour. He was supported by a loving wife; it is touching to think of Claude regularly stopping the car when they crossed the Trent *en route* to their beloved Lake District home, for them to embrace.

The approach of Elliott's headmastership was sadly marred by tragedy. Four Eton Masters, three of them close friends, fell to their death in the Alps.* Even if Slater was not universally regretted, Powell and Howson were respected Housemasters, and White-Thomson was a promising young beak. There were consequent new appointments to be made, and though Elliott did not always succeed in his choices, he showed himself, then and later, a good judge of men. Sometimes his approach to selection seems to have been elementary, but he took certain precautions which others neglected. He did not, for example, appoint Guy Burgess to the staff after making enquiries of Dennis Robertson, the Cam-

---

* Eton Masters were much drawn to mountains. In 1909 Herbert Tatham, a Housemaster, fell fatally in the Alps, as did a young Master, O'Connor, in 1930. Others such as Tom Brocklebank, who was on one of the Everest expeditions, survived.

bridge economist, and getting this reply: 'My dear Claude, I would very much prefer not to answer your letter. Yours ever, Dennis'.[3] Elliott later could say that it was a pity the Foreign Office never asked him about Burgess. An appointment that Elliott did make was of a young linguist, Bud Hill, who reported that his interview proceeded stickily; at length the Head Master enquired, 'Do you know anything about the theory of education?' – Hill, assuming the worst, 'I am afraid I don't, Sir' – Head Master, relieved, 'Oh, that's all right then.'[4] Following the mountaineering accident Elliott was to appoint a young ex-grammar-school graduate from Cambridge, Walter Hamilton, not only to teach the top Classics division with Richard Martineau, but very soon to be Master-in-College, a selection as imaginative as it was successful. He also brought in Robin Darwin to assist at the Drawing Schools.

Elliott was no doubt looking to his mountaineering friends for advice, but he did not lack for other counsel. King George V indeed recommended to him the use of the rope's end, which had been effective in keeping order at Osborne. Claude's own son Nicholas was a boy in the School, and must have helped considerably – not least, as he relates, by preventing Claude saying in his address to leaving boys, 'while you have been at Eton you will have learned how to handle boys; in future you will have to learn how to handle men'.[5] Two of his first Captains of the Oppidans were consulted and gave good advice. David Bury reported in the Captain of the Oppidans' Book that 'the new Head Master was extraordinarily thorough, giving his whole attention to the smallest question', and Rex Fripp wrote that he was a contrast to 'Dr Alington [who] in his last few years had been rather inclined to skim over the surface and hedge whenever the occasion permitted'. In return the boys lobbied the Head Master to restore the sale of beer in Tap, and eventually, in 1938, this happened.

Elliott did indeed have more trouble with the staff than with the boys. Some of the younger men appointed by Alington derided him as dull; he was known to them as 'Muttonhead' and then 'Mutton' with a long, slow stress of the first syllable. The boys, who also imitated his very distinctive intonation, on the other hand knew him as Claude. An epigram of the witty but idle Housemaster, Tuppy Headlam, had wide currency among Masters: 'I have served under four Head Masters; Warre was a greater man than I am, Lyttelton was a better man, Alington was a cleverer man; and

Elliott is a deafer man than I am'. H.K. Marsden was typical of some of the resentful older men; he had been two Elections senior to Claude in College, and attached to Alington; he despised Claude – not that that prevented him giving advice – but eventually he was won round by Claude's abundant common sense and charm. Others, of course, were always loyal, and the Lower Master, Conybeare, was a congenial spirit.

Though it must have cost him some prestige with the staff, Elliott wisely decided to do very little teaching. He knew that he was not good at it, and in any case he could not take on the traditional task of teaching the top Classics. Instead he concentrated on administration and soon, when Mr Bendell became School Clerk, he took on a full-time secretary. There was work to be done in three fields: order had to be brought into the appointment of Housemasters, there was need to improve the accommodation and feeding of boys, and the financial situation was unsound. Yet even on his first day as Head Master there was a problem to which he undoubtedly took the right attitude. The River Master escorted him to the Brocas, where there was the usual large number of courting couples in the grass: would he not get them turned off? 'I refused – for several reasons, and not least because I did not think that the sight really did boys any harm. I noticed that when we were there boys took not the smallest notice of them.'[6]*

Alington had exercised no proper control over the selection of Housemasters – men were encouraged to start collecting house lists, when there would not in fact be buildings for them to occupy. One of the new Housemasters, Lionel Fortescue, who had replaced Slater, turned out to be quite unsuitable, and at the end of the year he was happily removed to concentrate on gardening for which he had much more talent. Even so, Elliott had to disappoint four Masters who had been promised houses, and they received financial compensation from the School Fund throughout the years when they would have held houses. Later when an equilibrium had been established between Housemasters and buildings, he perceived that by the fifteen-year tenure established by Alington, men were starting and finishing too young, and he increased

---

* It must not be assumed that courting couples ran no dangers; Hubert Hartley bicycled straight over one pair when coaching a boat in a race.

the life of houses to sixteen years, which would over the years push back the tenure.

Elliott was also faced early in his career with a memorandum from twenty-five parents about boarding conditions in the houses.* Housemasters ran their houses for profit, and expenditure under the control of the Housemaster varied considerably, with the provision of food and coal for fires much more liberal in some houses than others; generally speaking bachelors were the more generous, but the Hartleys were an outstanding exception. The coal problem was solved by an edict that after a certain date all boys could have fires every day. Feeding was more difficult, Elliott's suggestion was that Housemasters should be allocated a budget for food from the Bursary, which there would be no gain from underspending, with a corresponding reduction in the amount that Housemasters retained from the total fees paid. This is approximately the system now operated, but it seemed an intolerable reduction of freedom to Housemasters in the 1930s, and the Head Master accepted that the existing system must continue for the time being.

The parents also complained about the sanitary conditions in some houses. Investigations† revealed some failures to reach even the not very demanding standards of the day: for houses accommodating forty-two boys, four bathrooms or showers were expected and six or perhaps seven lavatories; there was also a general shortage of hand basins. This study led to some piecemeal improvements; but Elliott had already perceived the need to start renovating Eton's plant, and a ten-year plan was initiated, including the replacement of one boys' house. Carter House on the corner of Keate's Lane was felt to be the worst, but eventually Coleridge House, almost opposite it, was selected for demolition, since that would allow improvement of its neighbour, Hawtrey House, also. The problem then arose: where should the new building be? The College still did not have control over all the

---

* The memorandum argued that the School should be reduced in numbers; this would have been financially quite impossible without a big increase in fees; and many parents with sons entered for the School would have had to be disappointed.

† The Eton word for lavatories was rears. Elliott enjoyed announcing in Chambers that he had appointed a committee of Masters to sit on the rears.

central Eton land,* and in the end the new house required the demolition of an existing Assistant Master's residence, Mustians.

Financing the building was also a difficulty, but this was merely one aspect of a larger problem, the continuing deficit on the College Account. The School Fund operated with a small surplus, but overall the combined College and School Account was still in deficit, not of alarming size, but worryingly persistent. How could a boarding house be afforded, when the rent that could be charged to a Housemaster would inevitably mean only a low return? The Fellows appointed a committee with a Master, Harry Babington Smith, as Secretary, who seems to have played an influential part, and this produced a range of measures designed to restore the balance. The options eventually selected were a rise in the School fee of £15 to £245 p.a., which would not be mandatory for boys already in the School, and reductions in Masters' salaries amounting to roughly 3% overall. These cuts were traumatic, but were justified by the argument that the increments of 1920 were granted temporarily to cope with post-war inflation and prices had fallen since then. It was true that even after the salary cuts Masters were better off in real terms than they had been in 1920, but naturally not many Masters could achieve so dispassionate a view. The Head Master who had been appointed with a salary of £3,860, but more generous allowances than his predecessors, accepted a reduction to £3,730. The great majority of parents paid the extra fee, and a larger increase with more help for the less wealthy would doubtless have been possible.

These measures all affected the School Fund rather than the College. Indeed the College's finances were about to be further damaged by the 1936 Tithe Act, abolishing tithes, for the College had been, through its rural patronage, a net recipient of tithes; compensation was paid, but the College is left with the responsibility to maintain the chancels of numerous churches and no corresponding income. No major economy was possible with College expenditure, but at least the possibility of a Quincentenary Appeal to raise funds was mooted. Meanwhile it was necessary to bring about a transfer of some £9,000 a year from School to College, and this was effected by having the School Fund (which in 1929 had assumed responsibility for Masters' pensions) take on some further

---

* The final freehold of a boys' house to pass to the College was Warre House, in 1944 when George Lyttelton retired as Housemaster.

expenses, for example part of the cost of the Bursary, Lower Chapel, and some of the ancient buildings; the College was to receive a 4% return on capital provided by the College, and quite properly the School began to contribute to depreciation by the establishment of a Sinking Fund.

The College was still, of course, bearing the cost of the seventy King's Scholars, who paid at the most £150 p.a., and could be remitted all fees (about one-quarter were). The College also provided the free use of College Chapel. Eton was no doubt better placed than almost every other school, but it was not so rich as was popularly supposed – the College's income was only just over £40,000 – about £1m. in 1993. The depredations of the pre-reform Fellows and the extravagance of Dr Warre's time were much to blame, but the College suffered because many of its assets earned no income (like College Library) or were in low-yielding agricultural estates; in the 1930s the Chalcots estate was potentially valuable, but its possibilities could only be realized when long leases started to fall in from the 1940s. Even after the 1935 measures, the College continued to have to watch its pennies anxiously. For example, when the laundry run by the Clewer House of Mercy increased its charges by £65 for washing College sheets, it was thought necessary to recoup five shillings a half from each King's Scholar. The one substantial improvement in amenities of this time, the laying out of an athletics track, was financed by the profits of the School Stores, not by the School or College.

Elliott did not neglect educational matters, though his only distinct personal preference was in favour of compulsory Physical Training being restored to the curriculum. With typical caution he commissioned an inspection by the Board of Education before introducing any change, and the inspectors' Report became available in mid-1936. Its general tenor was friendly: the inspectors had been impressed by the vigorous life of the School and the hard work of the Masters. In every department there were good teachers – proportionately most in Classics, fewest in Science; History, which attracted 45% of the specialists, was evidently the most successful department, but Modern Languages under the effective leadership of Charles Gladstone were improving rapidly; German singing was praised. The main failure was to provide enough time for Science, and the Science course was not organized to make effective use of that time. Etonians took School Certificate later than boys in most other independent schools, and that in itself limited the possibilities for specialist Science and Maths,* so that there were many fewer Science specialists than in comparable schools; yet the large numbers in the Scientific and Natural History Societies show that Etonians had as great intrinsic interest in Science as others. At the same time the results in Classics did not seem to the inspectors to justify the time devoted to the subject – they were worried by the overlap between work done in School and in Pupil Room, and they thought verses were not a useful exercise for many weaker boys, who also could not cope with some of the harder set books. There were many other detailed criticisms relating to individual subjects, some so harsh that it was thought proper to black out parts of the Report before it was issued to Masters; this task, entrusted to the Science Department, was performed with an efficiency which dismayed those Classical Masters who tried in vain to decipher what had been written about their scientific colleagues.

Reforms were considered in committees, and by 1937 modest changes were ready in the Lower School; the main ones were that PT was introduced with some reduction of classical work – Kappa boys were allowed to give up Latin verses – and the teaching of Science in E Block was put wholly in the hands of the Scientists. The following year a little more Science was added in D. In C Block boys could start German or take more Science. Older boys were allowed to take the School Certificate from C, others would take it in B, by which time they would be equipped to pass in German or Science. The effect was to widen the curriculum overall, particularly as provision was made for most specialists to continue Science for two halves after School Certificate. More general courses were also introduced for boys who did not wish to specialize.

The continued growth of the School had already compelled the Head Master to add slightly to the staff, and these changes caused further readjustment with a temporary increase in staff numbers. This was catered for by building more houses for married Masters and a new block of schoolrooms which replaced the outdated laboratories on the corner of Keate's Lane. These and other buildings of the time reflected the current architectural taste for

* The Mathematical Department surprisingly had the highest proportion of OEs (eleven out of sixteen), and had many men with First Class Honours.

asbestos, which has since had to be expensively removed since the risk it conveys to health is now thought to outweigh acoustic and fire control benefits.

Before these buildings were completed, on 12 June 1936, the Provost died. With his gift for friendship with boys as well as adults he was widely honoured and deeply mourned. He had by his own scholarship helped to set a standard of learning at Eton, and he was a pattern of service to the College that he so much loved. The new schoolrooms were naturally named Montague James Schools in his memory.

It seems that it was almost by chance that the Fellows discovered that Lord Hugh Cecil might like to be Provost and put his name to the Old Harrovian Prime Minister, Stanley Baldwin, who nominated him for appointment by King Edward VIII. He was the youngest son of the Prime Minister Salisbury, known to his family as Linky, perhaps because his appearance suggested the missing link between man and ape – and this name reached the School through a great-nephew and was adopted by Masters and boys as a nickname. Born in 1869, he had spent only two years at Eton, and had not enjoyed his time there, partly because he had not been to any school previously and had been treated very much as a young adult at home – a course of education that proved unhappy for his older brothers also.* At least his exceptional intelligence was recognized, and he in due course obtained a First in History at Oxford and became a Fellow of Hertford College. He was elected MP in 1895, was defeated in 1906, but from 1910 had served continuously as Member for the University of Oxford, writing an admired short book, *Conservatism*, in 1912. During the War he had joined the Royal Flying Corps and courageously learned to fly.[7]

He had always been a back-bencher, espousing causes, sometimes admirable, sometimes silly, but never with moderation. The Provostship of Eton was the first job requiring any sort of responsibility that he had held. He cared greatly for justice and the liberty of the individual and was wholly opposed to the Fascist dictators. He had an obsessive interest in religious questions and had held traditional church principles all his life; thus his intemperate opposition to the law allowing marriage to a deceased wife's

* His Tutor, Marindin, was still alive and was a guest at his installation as Provost.

sister. His views on the sanctity of marriage, like the intrepidity with which he first rode to hounds, were unhampered by experience.* With him logic usually came before pragmatism. As qualifications to be Provost of Eton he could plead fondness for youth and freedom from any sort of boring conventionality, but against this was an eccentricity that was certainly vexatious, if not perverse.

For Claude Elliott, who had enjoyed a happy relationship with Provost James, Lord Hugh Cecil was an alarming additional problem. Often charming in conversation and personally kind, he was nevertheless frequently at odds with the Head Master, who must have come to dread the letters either typed or scrawled in a very large pencilled hand on small notepaper (a reflection no doubt of the Provost's poor eyesight). On his very first morning, in the Antechapel, he remarked to Elliott that he regarded the Head Master as the Mayor of the Palace† who had stolen the Provost's powers, and that he intended to do all he could to recover them. Indeed so troubled were early relations that Elliott soon wrote to suggest that one or other of them should resign; but the Provost was disarming – he told Elliott that he considered controversy, particularly if acrimonious, the most desirable occupation for a gentleman.[8] In some cases it is hard to tell whether he was maintaining the power of the Provost or indulging in his favourite occupation.

An early dispute occurred over the Mackennal statue of the Offering of Youth, which had been housed in the entrance to the Provost's Lodge. Provost and Head Master agreed in disliking it, but the Head Master was unhappy when it was placed in the gallery between School Hall and School Library; he felt tall boys in a press to get out of School Hall might lose their eyes on its outstretched fingers. He expressed his fears to the Provost, who replied:

My dear Head Master,
    Thank you for your letter which I admire for its humane anxiety about the safety of the boys. But I must say that your

* He told the boys once: 'Always remember that the commandment against adultery is placed between those against murder and stealing'.
    † The Merovingian Kings were left as figureheads, their power usurped by the Mayors of the Palace.

fears, amiable as they are, seem to me excessive and even fantastic. I have, therefore, no difficulty in taking the full responsibility – if there be any responsibility – of deciding that this unpopular statue must for the present remain where it is.[9]

The Head Master, however, was responsible for boys' health – perhaps over-anxious about it. Eventually a compromise was reached by the Fellows: the statue was placed in a corner of the lobby of School Hall, where its arms indicated the way down to the lavatories.

The Provost was certainly in charge in Chapel, and he introduced some improvements – loudspeakers were installed, and the services were shortened. He was ahead of his time in the particular importance he attached to the Eucharist. 'Nothing in the world, I believe, matters so much in the spiritual life as to acquire the habit of frequent Communion in youth': so the morning service on Sunday became Ante-Communion for all, to be followed by voluntary Communion. But the boys were still required for Sunday Private, and thus preferred to attend Communion, in good numbers, before breakfast rather than the Provost's service. He had no time for clergy who felt that they knew better than Archbishop Cranmer: 'I attach great importance to authority. It is I think very edifying to say the prayers which are ordered by the authority of the church rather than to seek to please oneself.' The Provost was also keen to protect congregational singing from the inroads of the Choir – in consulting the Captains of the Oppidans and of the School he wrote that he was anxious 'to protect the unmusical majority against the more refined, but rather oppressive demands of the musical minority'. His own part in the services was remarkable – for example, the explanations that would precede his reading of the lesson. Richard Martineau described them in his obituary of Cecil:

> Of rival interpretations the oddest would be preferred. Then in a pitying tone the learned would be dismissed, and the Provost would draw on the riches of his imagination; 'The learned used to be puzzled, because the narrative of the Ascension seemed to postulate a local heaven above the visible sky; but to us the wonderful new discovery of the fourth dimension has made all easy.' He might give out notices, but they would not be

commonplace. Once he meant to announce that the Nunc Dimittis would be chanted after the evening service on Sundays, but by mistake he said 'the Narcissus'. The boys were audibly amused but not more audibly than the Provost. Latterly he wore at the lectern a green and white eye-shade, such as was then in fashion at Wimbledon.

His sermons invariably began: 'I speak as a layman to laymen without the authority of the priesthood', and they went on to be very authoritative indeed.[10]

The Provost thought that he also had powers over Lower Chapel. In May 1937 at the time of the Coronation he tried to prevent the substitution of special lessons authorized by the Archbishops for the canonical lessons. Then in November he was critical of the services in Lower Chapel. On each occasion, the Head Master had great difficulty in dissuading the Lower Master from resigning. On the second occasion Elliott took Conybeare to see the Provost: 'Both lost their tempers. The Provost trembled violently all over, as he did when he got very angry, and Cony strode up and down declaring he was going to resign at once.' Eventually the Head Master persuaded the Provost to agree that the Lower Master was like the incumbent of a parish, and could do anything that an incumbent could legally do. As a result of the conflict the Provost's opinion of Conybeare rose, and after his death the Provost wrote that 'I always found him one of the pleasantest people to deal with when I was at Eton. He seemed thoroughly efficient, with a mind of his own.'[11]

The Provost certainly enjoyed entertaining both Masters and boys. He himself wore knee-breeches; the Masters were required to wear white ties and tails; the boys only needed dinner jackets. The conversation, the food, the wine were of the richest; his butler, Tucker, clearly had orders never to leave a glass empty. One of Hubert Hartley's boys said, 'Tucker is a lovely man, when you say no thank you, he fills your glass; and when you put your hand across it, he pours through your fingers.'[12]

The approach of war led to increasing conflict between Provost and Head Master. Both were agreed that the School should not move, for that would be a concession to Hitler. Also it would be difficult to move the School and subsequently reassemble it at Eton. The Provost held the view that what mattered was boys' immortal souls, and that their bodies did not need to be protected. (In much the same spirit he had been against conscription, and tolerant of conscientious objectors, since he felt there was greater virtue in a volunteer sacrificing his life in battle than a conscript.) Now he opposed precautions against air raids. With greater realism the Head Master felt that parents would expect all reasonable precautions to be taken to preserve their sons' lives.

The Head Master had already received intimations of war, some of them bizarre, in 1937. Two Old Etonians, Field Marshals Lords Cavan and Chetwode, came down to see him, alarmed that the mulberry uniforms of the Corps would look unduly conspicuous if the Germans invaded; to this the Head Master turned a Nelsonian eye.[13]* Then there was a sinister request to bring two German educationalists to see Eton, received from Prince Bismarck, in charge at the German Embassy when Ribbentrop was on leave. (The Head Master had already politely turned down Ribbentrop's application to send his son to the School.) The Head Master arranged a lunch party with Charles Gladstone as another guest – so that the grandsons of the great statesmen should meet. But the educationalists proved to be no such thing – with guns visible under their coats; when Mrs Elliott remarked to one that she understood he was interested in education, he indignantly exclaimed, 'No! I am of the Fuhrer's bodyguard'. After lunch Charles Gladstone took them on a difficult tour in which their interest proved to be more in the Head Master's politics. Possibly the thugs believed that the Head Master might prove pro-Nazi, and that he could bend boys' minds to his thoughts – but, as Elliott observed, 'anyone who had the slightest knowledge of English schools or boys would know how completely ridiculous that idea was'. It is fair to say that the episode was profoundly embarrassing for Prince Bismarck.[14]

Now in 1938 the Head Master began to establish ARP precautions. The Home Office advised disbanding the School in the event of war, but Elliott felt that not all boys would be able to go home to a place of greater safety and that there must be a measure of protection available at Eton. He appointed ARP Masters, and began to organize for war. Masters behaved badly at the lectures

---

* The mulberry uniforms were abolished in the War, when the Corps received battledress as part of the Home Guard.

laid on for them – 'Claude used to look sideways at us with a glint of concentrated annoyance'.[15]

However tedious some Masters found the preparations to be, nevertheless in the last days of the summer holidays, during the Munich crisis, heroic efforts were made by Masters and boys to make houses reasonably secure with sandbags and shutters against sudden air attack. When the boys returned on 26 September, they were instructed in dealing with incendiary bombs, and so on. One precaution remained incomplete; Eton town was issued with only 3,500 gas-masks. These were assembled in School Hall by Masters, but there were not enough for town and gown. Elliott therefore decided that the town should have the gas-masks, and more than half the boys were allowed to go home. Some of those who stayed at Eton were at Hendon to greet Mr Chamberlain, and the *Chronicle* hailed the Munich agreement, though many boys were politically aware enough to regret it. The episode demonstrated that some parents would be anxious to take away their sons in the event of war, but by no means all; and at this time the Home Office altered its position about the security of the Eton neighbourhood – they began to arrange for children from London to be evacuated to the area.

Elliott drew the conclusion that the future of the School would depend upon inducing as many parents as possible to leave their sons in the School if war came. 'Without doubt the better the protection available the more boys will stay ... We have a moral responsibility to do our utmost within reason to ensure their safety.' Lord Hugh Cecil, however, drew different conclusions from the Munich crisis: 'I do not think a war in the next few years at all likely' – the Germans had gained so much without war simply by its threat; if there were to be a war, Eton would only be bombed by accident or oversight; it was not practical to take precautions against remote dangers, and the College's financial embarrassment added to the impracticality; Eton's job was education – the State had responsibility for protection; and if Eton expressed fear, that fear would prove infectious.

The conflict between Provost and Head Master came to a head at the meeting of the Provost and Fellows on 21 February 1939 when the question was whether air raid shelters should be built. Only Lord Halifax, the Foreign Secretary, was absent, but he had already reported that the Home Secretary's view was that Eton

College should take precautions on a reasonable scale at their own expense. The Head Master was present, and all the Fellows expressed opinions. In the end eight voted for the provision of shelters, only the Provost and Lord Rayleigh, the scientist, voted against – with Dr Stewart in favour of the shelters, but preferring to move the School. The cost of the shelters would be met by a charge on School bills. The Provost then pointed out that in his reading of the Statutes, the Head Master did not have authority over air raid precautions, and that therefore the Governing Body must give special permission for him to act. Instead the Fellows preferred to set up a Committee of the Vice-Provost, Mr Ridley, the Head Master and two Assistant Masters to carry out the work, and this began its operations on 1 March.

The Provost was deeply wounded by the rebuff to his authority, and he wrote to the Fellows accusing them of disloyalty. It was for him to interpret the Statutes and see that they were obeyed. He was the Chief Executive Officer of the College. The Head Master was charged with the general discipline and superintending the instruction of the boys; evidently his duties did not include the building of shelters. 'In so far as the Fellows did not accept that interpretation, I admonish them that they acted wrongly.' Though the Provost was careful to exclude the Vice-Provost from his criticism, he noted sadly that 'Some of the Fellows are disposed to render to the opinions of the Head Master a loyal deference which they do not seem to extend to the opinions of the Provost.' As for the Head Master, 'I have a great respect for the Head Master, though I think he is sometimes a good deal less wise when he strays beyond [the] duties [of his office]'. The Fellows wrote back protesting their loyalty, but often disagreeing with the Provost's interpretation – their oaths had been taken to serve the good of the College, and they felt no doubt that this demanded the shelters. Overwhelmingly, indeed, both the parents and the staff sided with the Head Master.*

The shelters were not easy to build for the high water table at Eton prevented them being sunk into the ground. Nevertheless, more or less adequate arrangements had been made by the summer of 1939. Masters were recalled early to finish filling sandbags, and the School could open as planned despite the War. The Provost

* The Provost had no shelter prepared for himself. When asked what he would do if a bomb fell, he replied, 'I would ring for Tucker'.

wrote generously on behalf of the Fellows to thank Masters for their heroic efforts. Though the shelters never in fact saved a life, their justification was that almost a full complement of boys returned. It was not as easy to join up as it had been in 1914, and boys who tried to enlist before they were summoned found themselves rebuffed. Comparatively few Masters left at once, since teaching was a 'reserved occcupation', and Elliott wanted to find competent substitutes before letting Masters go;* during the so-called phoney war, therefore, the life of the School continued with amazing normality. Long Leave was abandoned and Trials were dropped in the Lent Half. Boys were expected to carry gas-masks and the wearing of top hats in the centre of Eton was consequently stopped, and not resumed even when it was realized that the respirators would soon disappear or become useless if boys had to carry them every day. There were anxieties about finance; with higher taxes a number of parents could not afford the fees, but the generosity of Lord Camrose who had sent his sons to Eton enabled new bursaries to be established which helped some in difficulties.

Then in the Summer Half of 1940 the situation was entirely transformed by Hitler's invasion of Holland and Belgium. Even before the Local Defence Volunteers (the LDV, the future Home Guard) was formed, Etonians were licensed to patrol the area of Eton and shoot Germans. In due course, the Eton contingent of the Home Guard became one of the strongest in the country, containing members of the Corps over 17 years old, members of the Eton staff, and a platoon from the town. It was also better equipped – having the rifles of the Corps, and one original bren-gun from Czechoslovakia. It therefore was able to mount successful Weapons Training courses for LDVs from all over South Buckinghamshire – and by special request, for the local police. Boy instructors under Bud Hill's command won a reputation for tact and efficiency.[16]

Corps patrols were also mounted, but their only action occurred when a light aeroplace landed at the end of Agar's Plough, reported to contain two men, 'one dressed as a British officer and the other as a spy'. The officer proved to be Gubby Allen, the Old Etonian

---

* The replacements varied from excellent teachers, such as G.B. Smith, formerly Headmaster of Sedbergh, to exotics like the Baron Marochetti who had to go in the middle of the half.

who had recently captained England at cricket, who thought he could make use of the familiar playing fields to visit his mother in Datchet. After this, the playing fields were skilfully protected by posts which prevented landing but allowed games to continue. The only shots that the Corps fired were in error, but luckily with no fatality.[17] (The boys in general proved more sensible than Masters; towards the end of the War, Claude Elliott came on a Housemaster patrolling his garden with a loaded revolver – the Library were reassuring: 'It's all right, Sir, one of us unloads it every evening during Prayers'.)[18]

During the holidays, boy volunteers and Masters continued to guard Eton. Then in September bombing raids began. Every night until November, and often thereafter, London was attacked, with the bombers sometimes approaching over Eton up the Thames. The shelters came into use. They were, however, too crowded for houses to sleep in them, and a compromise had to be evolved: boys whose parents wished used the shelters; others normally remained in their houses, but each top storey was left clear. Windsor Castle relayed information to the Head Master when an attack on the Windsor area was thought imminent, and only on such ocasions were houses roused to take refuge in their shelters. A posse of boys to give alarms (later replaced by electric alarm bells) and to keep watch against incendiary bombs and fires, with a Master in charge, was posted every evening. One night in November a carpet of incendiaries was dropped all over Eton without a red alert being received. Most were successfully extinguished; one boy woke to find a bomb on his bed, but he was able to throw it out of the window without its doing any harm. Two bombs, lodged in roof spaces, caused more persistent fires, and one Master's car was destroyed.

Then on 4 December, two high explosive bombs were dropped on the middle of Eton. One fell on the centre of Savile House, destroying the dining-room where the Leys would have been having dinner had not Dr Ley detained his wife to share a joke in *Punch*. A boy on duty in the Corps Orderly Room across the Slough Road also had a miraculous escape when the heavy window above him was blown out.

The Head Master was hosting a fork supper that night, as he often did during the War, and the company gave thanks for the preservation of friends. Relief was a little premature for as guests dispersed a smell of gas was detected in School Yard, and soon a hole was found in the paving under the colonnade by the Head Master's schoolroom. The second bomb had been forgotten. College was evacuated. The next day bomb disposal experts came and found they could do nothing. The Provost prodded the bomb with his umbrella, repeating 'It's a dud'; Hope-Jones offered to carry it to the Fellows' Pond for disposal; Mr Bendell cleared essential documents from School Office. Then in the evening the bomb exploded, destroying the Head Master's schoolroom and part of Upper School, and removing the windows on the north side of Chapel together with the east window.* Remarkably, Lower School stood firm – a tribute to its fifteenth-century builders. The destruction of glass was said by some to be the best deed for which Hitler was responsible, and a few Masters ground fragments of it under their heels to ensure that nothing could ever be replaced. The Founder's Day Service the next morning was chilly, but the congregation knew that they had much cause to be thankful. The *Chronicle* only published its account of the bombing at the beginning of the next half, unusually slow by its standards, but the Founder's Day number was already at the printer – it was a special 500th anniversary number, including a cheery article by the Provost recommending that the School should return to wearing blue coats.[19]

There was another attack of incendiary bombs during the April holidays of 1941, and again the damage was contained by the stirrup-pump parties. The Provost, newly promoted Lord Quickswood in the New Year Honours by Churchill, whose best man he had been, wrote sharply to the Governor of Windsor Castle, blaming the anti-aircraft guns around the Castle for Eton's misfortunes: the German planes only dropped their bombs in his view because they were being shot at, and so it would be better if the Castle's AA protection were kept quiet. There was some truth in this contention, but naturally it hardly commended itself to the military men.

Thus ended the period in which the War made most physical impact upon Eton life. It was a difficult and fatiguing period for the boys, but at least those who had night duty were excused early

---

* The Provost immediately placed an order for stone with which to repair Upper School in due course.

school. For Masters there was no such relief, and by the end of 1940 they were woefully tired. Remarkably the 1940 scholarship season, with twenty awards won at Oxford and Cambridge, turned out to be the best since 1923; and School Certificate failures were fewer than normal.

For the rest of the War Home Guard, ARP, and Fire Service duties continued for Masters and older boys, as did the First Aid Post established by Mrs Elliott for wives. For boys there was voluntary work in factories and on farms, both in term-time and in holidays; and in the College records there are a number of letters of warm praise for what the boys achieved. Particularly notable was the contract secured by Cecil Mayes in charge of the School of Mechanics for munition parts to be made there. John Herbert, the most distinguished Mathematics Master, somehow found time to work on the engineering problems of the floating harbours needed for the invasion of Normandy. The reality of war continued to be brought before the School community in weekly intercession services, when lists of OE casualties were read – for the adults a reminder of lost friends and promise destroyed, for the boys an indication of what soon faced them.

By the end of 1940, more Masters had been called up; not all were replaced. The numbers in the School inevitably fell, and it was possible to reduce the size of the staff. The School Fund remained therefore more or less in balance. School fees and Masters' salaries were frozen in spite of rising prices. The biggest problems were suffered by Housemasters who received diminished boarding fees from fewer boys with no change in overheads. One helpful decision made in 1940 was to close a boys' house. One of the less successful Housemasters nearing the end of his time was induced to give up early, and as a result the worst premises were vacated. These were requisitioned by the Navy and used to house women in the WRNS. Even so, Housemasters were no longer so keen to maintain their independence, and in 1944 a scheme was introduced, initially voluntary, by which Housemasters would receive a salary and would run their houses on a budget for which they would be responsible to a House Fund Committee. This change was in fact the second major salary change of the War for earlier, arising from a pre-war committee, another distinctive feature of Eton had vanished: it was agreed that all Masters should be on the same salary scale, and that there should be no extra payment for extra pupils. This at least ensured that the financial hardships of the War period were equally shared.

There were naturally other problems for Housemasters besides their diminished profits. Boys had to be fed and houses heated. Somehow adequate standards were kept; nobody proved more resourceful than Miss Iredale-Smith, the Matron-in-College.* One change resulting from the War actually improved boys' health: with daylight saving all the year round, early school was suspended in the early part of the Lent Half; traditionalists thought this would soften boys, but statistics showed that they benefited. It was the first small breach in the ancient institution of early school.

In 1942 there was an almost farcical interlude in the horrors of war. MGM revived a plan that had been mooted in 1939, and apparently dropped – to produce a film called *A Yank at Eton*. In 1939 the College had been prepared to co-operate with this production, allowing some location shooting, but they were worried that in the context of war it would present an unwelcome picture of Eton. There was, however, no way of stopping the film. Luckily the American critics regarded it with contempt, and thought that Eton hardly deserved this film – as one of its characters said of Eton, 'they have been through an awful lot'. All that can be said is that the naive representation of the School and the banal story gave almost unalloyed pleasure to the boys when it was shown at Eton.

The sparring match between the Provost and Head Master continued, for the Head Master a war on a second front. As a consequence he would not always tell the Provost what he should have told him – and he was subsequently ready to admit that he was at fault. One example will suffice. Elliott cancelled the Fourth of June Procession of Boats in 1940 without alerting the Provost. The Provost's rebuke was more temperate and more justified than usual:

My dear H.M.,
    Jealousy for my office makes me feel bound to say that you

* The determination of this diminutive but redoubtable lady to maintain the standard of feeding in College created its own myth; on one occasion boys were excused Chapel to conceal the illicit rice store when word reached her of an inspector's visit, and she was popularly supposed to own a chicken farm in Wales. She lived to 96, and her obituary in *The Times* was written by Douglas Hurd, then Home Secretary.

ought not to have cancelled the procession of boats &
announced it to the Press without consulting me. Of course
'wartime' covers very much. But it would have been quite easy
to ask me or send the Capt. of the Oppidans to see me. It was
really very disrespectful to act as you did.

Yrs, HC[20]

On other occasions sympathy must be with the Head Master. In
1943 Kenneth Wickham, a Housemaster, married a lady who was,
before he met her, an innocent divorced party. In the Provost's
view he had committed adultery and was therefore unfit to be a
Housemaster. The Head Master was naturally keen to keep a good
man. Quickswood permitted this, as being in the Head Master's
province, but made it clear that he considered Elliott was condon-
ing adultery. Unfortunately Wickham, a devout Christian, wrote
to Quickswood to ask leave to receive Communion: this was the
Provost's province, and Quickswood wrote to forbid Communion
and to tell Wickham that he ought to resign his house. Elliott
found himself with a problem that he could only resolve some
years later, when a new Provost was prepared to drop the interdict.
By then Quickswood himself had concluded that persons who
remarry in good faith should not be excluded from Holy
Communion.[21]

The culminating row came on the first Sunday in July 1944. Eton
was by then threatened by doodle-bugs, the V1 rockets. Nobody
could tell where exactly they were going to fall; and when there
was an alarm that one was coming in the general direction of Eton
during the morning service, Elliott decided that the boys should
leave Chapel and disperse. The Provost was in charge of the Choir,
and decided that they should stay and continue the service. The
Provost then wrote a letter to the *Chronicle* justifying his action,
which the editors showed to the Head Master. The Head Master
told them not to print it, fearful of the effect on public opinion if
the press learned that Etonians had been told to disperse, leaving
the Choirboys: it could so readily be turned against the School.
Luckily Halifax and Ridley sided with the Head Master. So
Quickswood wrote more in sorrow than anger:

My dear Head Master,
    I am afraid I must not refrain from telling you that you have

acted with serious impropriety. You have no right whatever to interfere with my letters to the Chronicle without my previous consent. But I know that you are quite excusably suffering under severe strain, and therefore will say no more . . .

I am very familiar with the reactions of public opinion, and I know that they are often foolish, but I also know that they are always very ephemeral, and that it is therefore unnecessary to pay great attention to them. A fortnight after the war, or even after the cessation of these bombs, nobody will take the slightest interest in the subject which now fills your mind.

I remain,
    Yours sincerely,
      Quickswood

Nevertheless Elliott expected more warfare when he found the Provost waiting for him on his way to Chapel. But Quickswood trotted towards him saying, 'You must always remember that I was one of a very large family and we were taught to say exactly what we liked to one another and never to mind what any of the others said to us. So you must never mind anything that I say or write to you.' As Elliott commented later – how could one be angry after that?[22]

Anyway, the Provost knew that he was going to retire in November, and at the next meeting of the Provost and Fellows he told them of his intention. And he allowed the suspension of almost all services during the rest of the half while the doodle-bug attacks continued. The Provost had always tried to shame Bishops into retirement at the age of 75, and he decided that he was in the same position. He was indeed the first modern Provost to retire on his feet. He decided to address the School after morning Chapel from the Chapel steps – as he said 'in a tone of persiflage'. The speech was not recorded, but a few sentences were quoted so often as to carry almost scriptural authority: 'I dare say that at fifteen the prospect of having nothing to do is alluring. I can assure you that at seventy-five it is irresistible . . . In these last weeks people whom I have met have addressed me in sympathetic tones, as though a death were imminent. But I have not been sure whether I was cast for the part of the corpse or the chief mourner – the corpse, I hope, for its position is more reposeful.' Then he ended: 'And so I go in lieu of paradise to Bournemouth.' Beneath the persiflage he was deeply moved. When his health was proposed at his last meal in College Hall, he rushed away in tears.[23]

He only returned once to Eton, and that was to the funeral of his successor, Henry Marten. Before the service, Elliott went into the drawing-room of the Provost's Lodge and saw Quickswood sitting by himself. He went up to him and started, 'Hello, Provost – but I suppose I must not call you that now'. 'No,' he replied, 'Now you must call me Linky.' And the two antagonists exchanged affectionate letters until his death.[24]

The first of these letters to 'My dear Claude' written immediately after the funeral, survives: 'I thought the Trumpet Music at the end of the funeral quite magnificent. But why Revelations for the lesson? I definitely sense Henry is not dwelling in a new heaven or a new earth.'[25] Indeed, we must hope not, for Henry Marten, admirable as he was, was not one to relish anything new. Yet he was a clear choice for Provost, and the qualification that he always possessed – great and devoted love of Eton – was enhanced during the War by his role as Tutor in constitutional history to the royal princesses – for which he was knighted by the King in 1945. If he was not the man to think radically about the problems of Eton, at least he was universally regarded with respect and affection, and his relations with Elliott were always good.

By Michaelmas 1944 numbers in the School were rising strongly again, and at least the younger boys could look forward to peace before they left. Then on 7 May 1945, VE day was celebrated with a bonfire on Fellows' Eyot. There was some of the unbridled expression of joy that marked the notable occasions of the Boer War, but there was a disturbing element too. Suddenly the crowd began to call out for two or three unpopular boys – one a boy in Pop who was thought to have beaten unreasonably. Nothing came of this, but it was an ugly demonstration of mob psychology. It is always the case that boys, delightful as individuals, may be reluctant to show their better nature in the company of their contemporaries – hence, for instance, the ragging of weak Masters. VE day saw an extreme expression of collective ill-nature, and many boys reflecting later were worried by this departure from the tolerance on which Etonians prided themselves.[26]

In the summer holidays the War at last ended. Etonian casualties were not so numerous as in the First War, 748 out of nearly 5,000 combatants. Nevertheless, as the casualty rate in the nation was considerably lower, the Etonian death rate was relatively higher than in the First War, at about twice the national average. This is because Etonians wanted to be in the fighting arms, mostly in the army. Etonians won 5 VCs, 3 GCs and 3 GMs; 254 won DSOs (of whom 26 had one or two bars); 355 won MCs (34 with one or two bars) and 1 an MM; 61 won DFCs (4 with bars) and 10 AFCs; 43 won DSCs (2 with one or two bars); and 119 won foreign decorations; there were many other awards gained not for gallantry. These numbers may seem low by comparison with those in the First War, but awards were more sparingly given. One startling small record: six successive occupants of a room in Headlam's between them won 2 VCs and 4 MCs.[27] Etonians certainly did not fail to serve their country. Eight Old Choristers are commemorated with the Old Etonians; four officers, four sergeants; this suggests that they had been given a good start by their early education. Five Masters died, and one boy in the School, Drew KS who had been evacuated to America, but insisted on returning – sadly his boat was torpedoed, but survivors paid tribute to his courage in helping others in the water.[28]

The record of the First World War was duplicated, not just in gallantry. Old Etonians had gathered for Fourth of June dinners in improbable places – including three held in Brixton Gaol under the Defence of the Realm regulations – and they would send back suitable messages.* Perhaps the only difference was that David and Jonathan relationships had now become much less common.

The end of the War certainly did not end wartime austerity; indeed the hard winter of 1947 made the boys colder than at any time previously – and the *Chronicle* was suspended, as never happened during the War. For the boys at least there was consolation in the worst floods since 1894, which caused them to be sent home. The problems about Eton's buildings and finance which were beginning to be addressed before the War were increased by the War years. Furthermore, Eton was now operating in a more difficult political environment. This, however, should not be exaggerated. Mr Attlee had several Etonians in his Cabinets; his cousin had been School Doctor for many years, and he was

---

* Elliott was fiercely criticized by Crookshank, an OE Minister, for allowing the *Chronicle* to publish the telegrams from Brixton, but he stood firm. The men had not been accused of treachery, only detained. And if they were traitors, how could Crookshank as Postmaster-General have allowed their telegrams to be sent?

very willing to come and talk at Eton. Other Labour politicians visited, and the Head Master was able to establish good personal relations with them. Ernest Bevin, for instance, gave a First Hundred Lecture. He charmed the boys, and was charmed; as he was escorted back to the Head Master's house, he stopped, waved his arms at the boys and the buildings around him; 'We must never change any of this', he said.[29]

Nevertheless, it was not an easy economic climate in which to rebuild. With very high rates of income tax, fees could not easily be raised, but prices had risen and continued to rise so that by 1949 they were nearly double what they had been when Elliott became Head Master. Salaries of all Masters had fallen in real terms, and some improvement was necessary if Masters (who did appreciate the difficulties of the time) were to be kept reasonably content.

The pre-war Masters' Representative retired in 1940; Richard Martineau and Walter Hamilton were able to drive to Cambridge and persuade Keynes to serve. Despite being incredibly busy he managed to contribute a great deal to the College. In particular he persuaded his colleagues that the College assets could be more actively managed. In 1943 he wrote a long paper on the Chalcots estate in which he envisaged parts being sold. He did not foresee the rise in London property values, but he realized that housing property would become more difficult to manage with legislation adversely affecting the property-owner; and he was keen that Eton should obtain a greater spread of investments. Although the College was still limited by law in what could be held as assets – only trustee securities could be held until 1954 – the College began to review its portfolio more purposefully. Keynes' early death in 1946 was a serious blow.

Apart from the improvements which came as leases fell in at Chalcots, and with better management, the College's capital account was helped by a number of memorial donations. Many of these were gifts of objects rather than of money, but there was a fairly steady stream of donations to help bursaries. Then at the end of 1946, Fellows heard that Gaspard Farrer had executed a Declaration of Trust in favour of the College which in its munificence exceeded anything since the Founder's initial gifts.* The £200,000 (about £2½m. today) was to be used to improve the buildings adjoining the churchyard and these should, when neces-

* Farrer was a bachelor banker at Barings. He had been in Warre's house.

sary, be rebuilt on new sites. The capital was invested with Barings, and Arthur Villiers, who had done so much for the people of East London through the Eton Manor Clubs, was now as Senior Trustee to use his investment expertise to Eton's very great gain.

Thus there were some grounds for optimism, along with many problems. The College began to survey the state of its ancient buildings and to plan improvements. Licences could not be obtained at once to build new structures, but some of the war damage was made good. The delay in practice proved to be no great loss, since the Farrer Trust at least grew more rapidly than building costs.

The current account problems were more serious. Fees were raised by £35 to £280 p.a. in 1946, and a scheme was introduced for prepayment of fees which proved advantageous to the School as well as to parents, who preferred to pay from capital rather than to try to meet fees from their heavily taxed income. A small improvement in Masters' pay was made possible. By 1947 further increases in fees (to £318 p.a.) and salaries were necessary. For Masters there were small increases at the top and bottom of the scale, where it looked least competitive. But the top salary for non-Housemasters was £1,180 p.a., only about £15,000 in modern terms, a very substantial decline from the beginning of the century. Some reduction was made in the rent and rate charges Masters paid for housing, and there was an improvement in pensions in recognition that Housemasters had not been able to save lately as they had earlier. Masters might now reclaim out-of-pocket expenses, but it was to be a few years before this was felt to be quite professional conduct at Eton. These new arrangements meant that the College was accepting lower rents in order to help the School Fund – a small step reversing the pre-war tendency for the School to have to accept expenses of the College. Housemasters were certainly still well off by the standards of the teaching profession generally, but the House Fund exceeded its estimates and reductions of salary were imposed on Housemasters who were felt to be unduly extravagant. This caused more friction than could occur under the old system. Previously, if a Housemaster managed badly, his profit was less and the School did not even know; but now Housemasters felt that they were being fined by the School.

A committee to bring about economies in 1948 was able to produce nothing much more than the final abolition of the top hat.

Yet parents felt that the Eton education gave value for money; by the end of Elliott's time as Head Master, numbers were more or less back to their inter-war peak. The boys' house which was closed in the War reopened in September 1946.

One small source of extra boys was provided by the Fleming Scheme by which Counties sent boys out of the Maintained Sector to independent schools. The Fleming Committee was convened as a response to the anxieties of many independent schools about falling numbers (as a result of the low birth-rate of the 1930s). Eton, less affected, played little part, but did agree to keep open a number of places – not all of which were occupied, as few Counties were prepared to bear their share of expenditure. Nevertheless, beginning in 1948, a number of boys arrived – initially from Dorset, where the College was a landowner, and then from Hertfordshire, where the Director of Education favoured Eton, Winchester, and Rugby. Earlier, at the expense of Julian Lambart, a Housemaster, and of the College, an ex-chorister went to Lambart's. These boys proved welcome additions to the School.

In the summer of 1948, Elliott's term as Head Master expired, but the Provost and Fellows knew that they wanted Robert Birley to succeed him, and Birley was working in the Control Commission in Germany for one more year. They therefore asked Elliott to stay an extra year. In November, Birley was appointed. Then on 11 December, after presiding at a meeting of the Provost and Fellows, Henry Marten died. He had been a wise, good, and happy man. The honours he had earned over a lifetime as a schoolmaster came to him late in life, but they gave him great satisfaction. During his long time as Vice-Provost he had accepted change, but tried always to see that Eton remained true to its history. His years as Provost saw signs of a new resurgence. It was a particular pleasure to him to have presided at Eton in 1947, when Eton's Quincentenary was belatedly acknowledged by an Exhibition intended to reflect some of its history.*

The Fellows were clear that when Claude Elliott retired in the summer of 1949, he should succeed to the Provostship as so many Head Masters had done. Mr Attlee, when told of their wishes, said, 'So be it; but I would have given them a better man'. It has been

---

* In 1948 he also enjoyed holding a Court Leet, appropriate to the feudal tenure of land still prevailing at Eton; the *Chronicle* carried a notable report by S. Barrington-Ward, later Bishop of Coventry.

said that he was thinking of Lord Ismay. Whether he would have been a better Provost than Elliott is impossible to say, but Elliott was to achieve a great deal as head of the College.

Certainly he had served Eton well as Head Master. Perhaps he lacked the vision to be a great Head Master, and he was not one to mould boys – indeed it would not have been to him a remotely desirable objective. Boys imitated him saying, 'I distrust enthusiasm of every kind'; perhaps he never said it, but nevertheless boys *thought* that he said it, and that is significant.*

He himself believed that a Head Master made his greatest impact by the men he appointed, rather than directly. He took this part of his work very seriously, welcomed back the better Masters who had been away to the War, and found new ones to maintain the standard despite the drop in salaries. Improved results were a consequence, and Elliott has seldom been given the credit he deserved.†

During the War he had shown a true quality of leadership. His steadfastness helped to keep staff and boys calm in circumstances which were often difficult. H.K. Marsden wrote to Claude, when Birley's succession was announced, to apologize for his early churlishness, and paid tribute to his headmastership.

> You will go down to the histories of Eton as yet unwritten, as an able administrator: but the finer points will get no mention, & though many of us loved & admired CAA [Alington], the difference has been that everyone has trusted you, whether they agreed or not – & that was not always the case with CAA.[30]

There was also something special to Claude Elliott which Marsden perceived:

> There are small & trifling concessions, winkings of the eye, & the like which have shown you still to have the spirit of the boy & to hold fast to the memories of youth. The boys don't know it, & take it all for their right: but so many privileges & joys

* He could hardly have said 'enthusiasm of *every* kind', since he was certainly enthusiastic about wine as well as mountains.

† On average Etonians won fifteen awards a year at Oxford and Cambridge in Alington's last three years; in Elliott's they won over nineteen. In 1944-5 there were twenty-eight awards, with many won by Oppidans, and in subjects other than Classics.

might have gone west in the austerity of the war & its aftermath that we owe you a lot for keeping the Eton of the past as far as possible unsullied.

At the end of his last Summer Half as Head Master, Claude, who had presided over the Essay Society after Robert Birley went to Charterhouse as Headmaster in 1935, read a paper on mountaineering. He recalled how he had been trapped under an avalanche: 'And all the time I kept saying to myself, "what a bloody fool I am! what a bloody fool I am!" And the truth of the matter is I *was* a bloody fool.' Neither Claude's predecessor nor his successor would have recounted anything of this sort to boys; it is a measure of his humanity as well as of his humility that he should do so, and it helps to explain why the respect he enjoyed from boys for his firmness and fairness should have been warmed by a glow of affection.

CHAPTER TEN

Reconstruction

IN SEPTEMBER 1949 the School resumed with the newly promoted Provost and a new Head Master. Robert Birley was just 46. He had been educated at Rugby where his intellectual development was curiously one-sided – he was forced into premature specialization on the modern side, and, failing in Latin, never actually obtained School Certificate; but his ability as an historian was certainly stimulated, and he became Brackenbury Scholar at Balliol along-side Cyril Connolly in 1922. Balliol influenced him even more profoundly, and he emerged with a First in History and a conviction of the importance of public service as well as of scholarship. It had been his intention to stay a fourth year at Oxford to read PPE, but that course was not proving a success, when he was offered a post as a temporary Master at Eton in January 1926. Luckily Henry Marten spotted that he was an historian of unusual merit, and he was soon given a permanent post which he found so enjoyable that he turned down the chance to become a don at Christ Church. Under the tutelage of M.R. James, he discovered the riches of College Library, which converted him into a life-long bibliophile; and he interested himself in local government. A large shambling man with immense presence, he proved so outstanding a teacher and Tutor that at least two senior Masters (Gladstone and Powell) thought that he might be the man to succeed Alington. By then he had married his beautiful wife, Elinor, but he was still only just 30 when Alington left, and that was too early. Instead in 1935 he was appointed Headmaster of

Charterhouse, where he quickly gained a considerable reputation. He took an active part on the Fleming Committee, and was anxious to open the independent schools to boys who could gain from what they offered. Then in 1947 he was asked by the Labour government to become Educational Adviser in the British Zone of Germany, and in just over two years he made a great reputation by the creative and influential work that he achieved there.

It was not surprising then that the Provost and Fellows were keen to appoint Birley, and he for his part wanted to be Head Master of Eton, both for his love of Eton and because he felt it would give give him a position from which to influence British educational policy. He was even prepared to accept the same salary as Elliott,* with a reduction in the size (and expense) of the Head Master's house, thus releasing rooms for an expanding bursary (necessitated by the centralization of the administration of boys' houses). Mrs Birley had a Scottish thriftiness, and both would have felt it wrong in the post-war period to live more extravagantly than was absolutely necessary. This led to guests being welcomed at one end of Dr Warre's large drawing-room, and then being conducted round the shelves of P.G. Wodehouse first editions to dine at the other end; the amenities of the house were reduced, and the Birleys, though always hospitable, lived in a lesser style than any of their predecessors or successors.†

Birley returned to Eton with the reputation of being left-wing, and became widely known as Red Robert – though not among the Eton staff. It was true that the Fleming Committee was regarded as favouring social engineering, and that he had been picked for an important job by a Labour government. But the myth of Red Robert hardly corresponded with the reality. It is said to have been encouraged by a visitor spotting a portrait of Brahms in Birley's German office, and reporting this to be of Karl Marx – a good story, but not influential when he arrived at Eton.[1] The myth was in any case unfortunate since he was regarded with unjustified suspicion by many Old Etonians and even some of the Governing

---

* At his interview he was shown a piece of paper by Henry Marten with three salaries on it – but the two largest had been crossed out: the Fellows indeed had previously agreed to offer no increase.

† Some parents did not easily adjust to the new standards. 'Is it right,' one asked, 'that when I visited my son's Head Master, the door should be opened by a young woman in a jumper several sizes too small for her?'

Body as one who might wish to change the character of Eton radically. In fact he was very much a nineteenth-century liberal, with a passionate belief in academic freedom, matched by an equal conviction of the responsibility that this implied. A favourite theme of early addresses at Eton was the failure of German universities to resist the rise of Hitler; and he was as zealous as Dr Warre that Etonians should play a major part in the governance of Britain.*

It was the Provost's responsibility to bring-about the physical reconstruction of Eton, and the Governing Body controlled the available finance; the Head Master on the other hand had to articulate the needs of the School. In general they worked well together, though Elliott was occasionally sensitive to possible damage that Birley's reputation might cause to the College's efforts to raise funds. The most unfortunate episode was a visit to Eton in March 1951 made by Mr de Valera, the Irish leader. Fenner Brockway, the MP for Eton and Slough, had induced the Birleys to give him lunch on what was supposedly an entirely private visit made out of academic interest by de Valera as Chancellor of Dublin National University. In fact de Valera was going to address a meeting in Slough against the partition of Ulster, and his visit was a political event which was leaked to the press. It was naive of Birley not to realize the potential for harm, and it fell to Elliott to pacify Old Etonians whose relatives had suffered in the Irish troubles or who resented the Irish stance during the War. Elliott was able to stress that the visit was in no way official, and that de Valera had met no boys; but the Head Master's reputation undoubtedly suffered. For Birley, who was already deeply suspicious of the press, this was a painful experience which confirmed his distrust almost to the point of paranoia.[2]

In general, it was an advantage in this matter, as in the rebuilding programme, that Elliott had been Head Master. He knew the problems of the post, and his handling of Birley was quite different from Quickswood's of himself. He also knew the shortcomings of the Eton fabric, and had stirred the Fellows into slow action in the 1930s. Now he and Birley were able to set in motion a radical transformation of the buildings of the School and College. Already

---

* He was irritated by 'Red Robert': when he was Head Master he said that he had always voted Conservative.

under Marten there had been a first approach to repairing war damage. Compensation, ultimately £90,000, was negotiated and first thoughts had been given to the restoration of Upper School and College Chapel. Also the Farrer Trustees had begun investigation of the area around the churchyard.

Nevertheless Elliott realized that extra funding would be necessary and the Provost and Fellows decided to launch an appeal for £1m. (about £13m. today). A convincing case was presented. The College's income was only £38,000, barely adequate to meet running costs. School fees had risen by 27% since before the War, but costs had increased by more, despite a continuous pressure for economy, and it was argued that further increases in fees were not feasible, at least without discouraging Eton's traditional parents. An attractive programme of works was presented. The repair of the ancient buildings would require nearly £100,000 in addition to the allowance for war damage. The Farrer Trust would in practice provide two new boys' houses as part of its programme, but two further new houses were required and would together cost £200,000. Enlargement and alteration of five others, partly in the interests of economy, would require a further £200,000; and a further £200,000 was budgeted for the modernization of the other fifteen; the interests of domestic staff were as important as the boys'. The Head Master was very anxious to improve the provision for Science teaching, and the Science Schools were too small and antiquated, as well as inconveniently split between two sites. A sum of £100,000 would be required for alterations and new building. Finally swimming in the Thames was becoming more of a health hazard, and had had to be stopped at various times; the idea of purifying the Cuckoo Weir backwater was found not to be practical. So £60,000 was required for a new pool. The overall Appeal sum was rounded up to the full £1 million.

The Appeal was well conducted. The OEA co-operated; a powerful Appeal Committee was appointed under the chairmanship of Arthur Villiers; conveners for almost all houses were chosen to approach fellow members of their houses. The press, notably *The Times* and *Country Life*, were helpful. Nearly half the Old Etonians approached gave, and £400,000 was quickly raised. There were problems in relying largely on OEs. They felt that Eton might lose its independence under a Labour government; some of them (with some reason) distrusted the managerial record of the Provost and Fellows; and many were worried whether their own sons would continue to be able to go to Eton, which they felt would be changing under the influence of the Head Master. In fact 60% of Etonians were sons of OEs at that time, and the Head Master claimed that this reflected the advantage of the house list system of entry. OEs had personal contacts with future House-masters, and knew that it was important to register sons early. Birley did appoint two OE Masters to give advice as a public relations exercise, and continued to be sensitive to this problem, discussing it with the Fellows in 1952, for instance, when a number of OEs' sons could not be found places after the Common Entrance Examination.

Not all the money came from Old Etonians: King's College gave £5,000, the Pilgrim Trust gave £21,000 specifically for College Chapel, the Dulverton Trust gave £20,000 for the Cloisters, and the Industrial Fund for the Advancement of Scientific Education in Schools gave £32,000 for new Science Schools. The Appeal Fund was well looked after. It could not be spent as it came in because of the post-war restrictions on building, which were at first very severe, and it, like the Farrer Trust money, was skilfully invested. Both Appeal Fund and Farrer Trust were administered by Barings; and it was from 1951 that Barings became the College's Investment Managers. Thus though the Appeal Fund only reached some £800,000 the programme aimed for could be largely financed.

During the 1950s the College's finances were also to receive help from leases at Chalcots falling in. The decision was quickly made to renew most of these at substantial premiums but low rents, but there were also sales of outlying parts of the estate. Altogether more than the originally planned £¼m. was taken to use for the building programme. By 1962 the decision had been reached to enter into a comprehensive redevelopment of the central area in partnership with Mr Max Rayne of London Merchant Securities. Furthermore the College also decided to sell most of its agricultural property. It is true that the College's income-earning assets were reduced in so far as the proceeds from these sales were spent on rebuilding, but the College did acquire a portfolio of stocks and shares, which raised its income above 1950 levels. What the College would not sell is also of interest: it refused an offer of £1m. for a very long lease of the entire Chalcots property, and it refused to sell the Gutenberg Bible that had been given to College Library in the early nineteenth century. Also the College refused a large bribe to take a boy not qualified for entry.

The restoration of the historic buildings had the highest priority, and in any case was all that was permitted under the post-war restrictions on building. Upper School was restored as it had been, using so far as possible the original materials which had been salvaged. Savile House, which Warre had found too small and wanted to enlarge, was turned into three houses but retained very much its old exterior. College Chapel was to represent a greater problem, with its stonework decaying as well as its bomb-blasted windows.

In February 1949 Lord Crawford and Balcarres formed a small committee with the Dean of York (Dr Milner-White) and Sir Kenneth Clark to advise on a new east window, which was correctly seen to be the essential first step. The Committee was divided: Lord Crawford had become enthusiastic about the glass of Miss Evie Hone, which he had travelled to Ireland at the instigation of Sir Jasper Ridley to study, and he had qualified support from Sir Kenneth Clark; but the Dean of York was wholly opposed – he thought the Celtic School of stained glass artists did violence to the architecture of buildings in which their works were inserted, and he argued that the Perpendicular style needed a good deal of clear light. The Dean also opposed Miss Hone's suggested subject, the Ascension, arguing that stained glass could not represent movement. He did not however produce a convincing alternative artist, and the opinion of Masters when sought was for Miss Hone. After an acrimonious meeting in June 1949, the Provost and Fellows invited Miss Hone to submit cartoons. In October they considered four drawings, and in November they commissioned her to make an east window showing the Last Supper and the Crucifixion, with the giant figures of Melchizedek and of Abraham about to sacrifice Isaac, and with many Christian symbols filling the tracery. This was a brave decision: the Dean of York had his supporters, and when the cartoons were displayed in the summer of 1950 the Provost had a number of angry letters to answer, and more seriously the College's architects, Messrs. Seeley and Paget, resigned. Certainly it was as well that the Ascension was not the chosen subject, not perhaps for the reasons that the Dean suggested, but because fewer nowadays believe in the Ascension as an historical event. The Dean was correct in his desire to respect the architecture, in that Christ's arms, broken by the uprights of the window, are probably the weakest feature of Miss Hone's composition. Yet the composition as a whole is as successful as its colour is blazing. Sir Kenneth Clark told Robert Birley: 'Either you have something which is architecturally right and dead, or architecturally wrong and alive.'[3] Most visitors will agree with Pevsner's judgement that 'the East Window is a triumph for the Eton authorities'.[4] Unfortunately it is wholly alien in spirit to the Burne-Jones tapestries below it, which are in any case hardly now to be discerned in daylight: admirers of the tapestries have to visit the Chapel after dark.

Miss Hone was also commissioned to produce the two flanking windows, but she had only begun work on her cartoons when early in 1955 she died in middle age. Once more the College made a successful decision. Oliver Van Oss, the Master most widely cultured in the arts, suggested that John Piper should be commissioned. In March 1956 the Provost and Fellows agreed to look at Piper's work, and in June they asked him to submit designs for two windows. By then the College was committed to grisaille glass decorated with the coats of arms of distinguished men from Eton's history in the west half of the Chapel, a second-best decision dictated by the need for economy, but one which does no violence to the Chapel. It would have been wiser to have asked Piper at once to provide the eight remaining windows. At any rate he did not react quickly to his commission and his ideas only began to flow when he started to think of a common design for all eight. Various suggestions were made: 'Sacred love and profane love', 'a cloud of witnesses' and when the Provost and Fellows were beginning to entertain doubts about their decision, in February 1958 they were offered a choice between Christian symbols, and miracles and parables, and preferred the latter. The windows, executed by Patrick Reyntiens, were completed in the next five years, carefully graduated in colour from the dark hues necessary to avoid throwing excessive light on to the inside of the east window to the lighter shades harmonizing with the grisaille glass. In February 1964, the Fellows made up for any earlier hesitation by expressing their great appreciation of the completed set, and indeed they were right to do so. It is possible to criticize in detail, but the overall effect is very fine. Robert Birley had quickly formed a close relationship with John Piper, and the final result owes much to his enthusiasm.* He remarked in jest to Claude Elliott that now Claude would perhaps be rewarded for his imaginative patronage by election to the Vice-Presidency of the Modern Art Society: it was apparent from the look in his eye that for an awful moment Claude believed him.[5]

A consequence of the choice of Evie Hone to create the East Window was that the College needed a new consultant architect. Professor (later Sir William) Holford was chosen.† He had already done some work for the OE Trust on the War Memorial in the colonnade under Upper School and for the Farrer Trust around the churchyard. His architectural merits are not likely to be commended by historians, but he was a thoroughly professional man though slow, and Claude Elliott found it easy to work with him. It fell to him to supervise the construction of the windows in College Chapel, and he was reponsible in 1952 for the renovation of the north-west stairs to the Antechapel when death-watch beetles were found in its roof. The staircase was restored, paid for by a legacy from Vice-Provost Conybeare who died that year. The concrete coffered roof has mercifully now been concealed.

In June 1956 a much more extensive infestation was discovered in the main roof – cleaners had for some time been sweeping up the corpses of dead beetles. The Provost insisted on having a thorough investigation, and the situation proved far worse than anyone imagined. The oak roof dating from 1699 (gothicized in the 1840s) was crumbling throughout: no two-foot length was free of infestation. It was evidently necessary to replace the entire roof. It is likely that the Founder intended a stone roof (because the Chapel has buttresses and vaulting shafts inside), but it was not considered possible in the twentieth century to construct so wide a vault in stone. So the Fellows found themselves choosing between res-

---

* Birley was particularly eager that the scenes should mean something to boys; he and Piper rejected the idea of angels – after all neither really believed in angels and so could not expect the boys to do so. On the other hand he thought the depiction of the Feeding of the Five Thousand very fine: both miracles on the north side, and parables on the south, show the imperfect scene below the heavy transom and the Christian transformation above; in this particular window grasping hands try to get at the loaves and fishes, but above the baskets overflow, with the message to boys that real generosity means giving so that there is likely to be too much.

† Later still Lord Holford. His best-known work was the buildings and space around St Paul's Cathedral.

toration of a wooden roof and constructing a simulated stone roof. 'Why', a Fellow asked, 'should we set out to provide fodder for these insects?'[6] So a simplified fan vaulting of stone ribs with plaster panel infilling was selected, suspended from steel trusses below a light aluminium roof. Stone bosses designed by Nigel Wykes, a Housemaster, were placed at the eight apexes of the ribs. It was a notable and innovative practical solution of a very difficult problem, and one which could be financed by the College (with the help of a further £15,000 from the Pilgrim Trust). It quickly established itself as part of the original structure: one of the cleaners employed to sweep up before the boys returned was heard to remark, 'Come up lovely, hasn't it, mate? Christ, you don't get workmanship like that nowadays!'[7] When the external stonework had been all renovated and the wall-paintings cleaned, the Chapel looked finer than at any time, at least since the Reformation. In September 1959 the boys, who had been attending chapel in the parish church, were able to return for worship, and Parry's anthem could sound again, 'I was glad when they said unto me, we will go into the house of the Lord . . .'.

Meanwhile work continued on the other historic buildings. All in turn were tackled, many with results that were real revelations – for example the College Library. The process was not perhaps completed until, 550 years after the Foundation, School Yard was relaid. But that so much was done so quickly was greatly to the credit of the Governing Body, and Eton showed more urgency in this expensive but necessary task than most of the Colleges of Oxford and Cambridge.

The need to renew the fabric of the ancient buildings may have seemed to direct energies from the very necessary modernization of the School's plant, but a start was made on this as soon as possible. One of the first tasks to be tackled was the construction of a new swimming-pool. It was the time when poliomyelitis was almost an epidemic in the country and Eton was affected. In a sad Summer Half in 1952 one boy died (and another died playing cricket), and the river was suspected as a possible source of infection. A handsome new pool was constructed, of an irregular design drawn on the back of an envelope by Oliver Van Oss.* Swimming was seen as recreation, not as a competitive sport, and

* Architect David Hodges, a former KS. He was responsible for the actual design, but the brief given him was Van Oss's work.

the intention was to recapture the picturesque charm of a Thames backwater; the curved outline did not add to the expense of the pool, though many supposed that this unique design must be more costly. The Summer Half in those days ran until the end of July, but critics also argued more justifiably that it was extravagant for what was, at best, an eight-week season of swimming, and that season has been further shortened by the earlier end to the half. In 1979, Eton acquired an indoor pool to match the facilities of other schools. The outdoor pool still offers an altogether more attractive experience of swimming, but it is now largely irrelevant to the needs of the School.

The swimming-pool was built in 1956, and at the same time Birley was negotiating with the Industrial Fund for the Advancement of Science Education for a grant towards new Science Schools. The Fund required that schools they helped had 10% of their pupils Maths and Science specialists, which Eton lacked. The College helped by offering to put up a substantial sum itself, but nevertheless it is a tribute to Birley's powers of persuasion that the Industrial Fund was willing to contribute. There was not enough capital available even so to build a big enough new block to accommodate all three sciences, and a compromise plan had to be adopted in which Physics continued to be taught in a reconstructed Boyle Schools, whereas Chemistry and Biology were housed across the road in an enlarged Queen's Schools. Only twenty-five years later could Queen's Schools be extended to house all the scientists, and Boyle Schools, appropriately renamed Birley Schools, were converted for the linguists, with language laboratories where once Etonian physicists experimented.

The main task, however, was to tackle the boarding houses. Many of these offered accommodation well below even wartime standards. Bud Hill moved into Corner House in 1952, and found it little better than his cousin Matthew Hill had found Gulliver's in 1906:

The Corner House was an amazing building. It had been in use as a boys' house since at least as early as 1596 . . . The boys' side consisted mostly of Victorian additions built on by various occupants . . . at their own expense to house more pupils . . . The boys' lavatories were covered by a sloping roof with a permanent gap of about a foot between it and the wall so as to form the sole means of lighting and ventilation; the ventilation was infinitely more powerful than the lighting. The interior walls were constantly wet since there was no heating of any type and the sun never penetrated this dingy abode . . .

A narrow staircase with uneven wooden treads worn shiny, smooth and razor-edged by generations of boys led up to three boys' passages. There was little uniformity about either the passages or the boys' rooms. In parts the passages were broad; in other places they were so narrow that two people could pass only by turning sideways. There were constant changes of level so that it was impossible to wheel round the crockery and cutlery for boys' teas on a trolley . . .

Primitive cooking in the passages and forty-one coal fires in boys' rooms were liberal sources of dirt and dust and very little decoration had been done in the house for twenty years or more. The result was that the lime green paint had either worn off completely or else was covered with a sticky brown film like badly applied varnish. The appearance of the boys' side was mournful to a degree; in fact taken as a whole it looked like a slum tenement, with two dingy bathrooms with concrete floors at the end of the bottom and middle passages for the use of forty-one boys.[8]

Environmental health officers would have found ample excuse to close half the houses. In Evans's, for example, the same room contained the boiler, the gas-rings for cooking and the racks holding the football boots; it had no external ventilation, which made it an attractive place for boys to linger in winter.* Some of the boys' rooms had real charm, and the boys themselves tolerated cramped quarters early on in the expectation of better before they left. The domestic staff on the other hand were worse housed, without the adaptability of youth and with expectations much greater than they were in Victorian days. Housemasters saw their conditions as intolerable, and of course realized that their Dames must be able to recruit servants.

Consequently, rebuilding placed much more emphasis on the requirements of the staff, and at the same time it was realized that the houses should be as large as possible to spread domestic labour

---

* Standards had risen: this same room had a further use in Miss Evans's time, for boys to take baths in their tubs.

costs. In 1950 a committee of Masters and Fellows was appointed
to oversee rebuilding, and it saw at once that numbers should rise
to roughly fifty per house, though perhaps there would eventually
be a closure of a boys' house. Professor Holford carried out a full
structural survey of the School, and houses were divided into those
which could be improved with the boys in occupation, and those
from which boys would have to be decanted. That in turn would
require at least one spare house, and here the Farrer Trust was able
to help.

If there was to be an improvement in the area around the
churchyard as Farrer wished, the two boys' houses south of the
Chapel would have to be removed or at least rebuilt; so the
Trustees could legitimately pay for a Farrer House, begun in 1956
in the rather derelict park of Warre House, as part of the main
object of the Trust. With ample funds for its purposes it built with
a lavish attention to detail, but distinctly qualified architectural
success.* As a curious reflection of the Cold War, the house
contains what was seen as an appropriate air-raid shelter for an
atomic age. When it was finished in 1959 the Farrer Trust still had
funds to build another house, which was very properly called
Villiers House to commemorate the enormous services of Arthur
Villiers. Even though the new building just beyond Farrer House
was unkindly compared to a sanatorium facing a prison, most
critics regard it as a more successful structure.[9] Its completion in
1962 allowed the eventual elimination of Corner House, smaller
accommodation being retained on the site just for Masters. It also
permitted the further rebuilding of boys' houses to go ahead apace.
As part of the Farrer Trust's scheme, the boys in Baldwin's Bec
were decanted, and that was rebuilt behind its expensively retained, but lowered, façade. Other houses needed equally drastic
treatment, whereas some had little more than improved domestic
quarters and central heating.† In another special operation, which
married the restoration of the historic buildings to the meeting of
modern requirements, the young Collegers were given new quar-

* Gaspard Farrer had been a friend of Lutyens who had built for him The
Salutation in Sandwich and 7 St James's Square: the expensive materials but not
the quality of the architecture are reminiscent of Lutyens.

† There was a bizarre idea considered by the Provost and Fellows in the middle
of the 1960s to build two vertical houses, saving valuable space; luckily the more
practical counsels of the Masters prevailed.

ters; Chamber with its stalls was replaced by small rooms, and floor levels were raised to give boys a proper outlook.* The whole programme was eventually completed at the end of the 1970s: the reduction by one in the number of houses took place, and thus ultimately Carter House and Hodgson House could also be changed from boys' houses to alternative uses.

Although a second round of renovations has had to be started, nobody at Eton would now question the value of what was achieved in practical, if seldom in aesthetic terms for the School; and Eton has survived inspection by fire officers, by environmental health officers, and by teams from the Social Services, while somehow meeting the requirements of conservation and planning officers. Oddly boys are so conservative that they did not always welcome the changes. The idiosyncrasies of buildings were lost, and central heating lacked the appeal of an open fire, especially if a fag was available to light it. The new houses, which involved boys in more walking, were particularly unpopular at first, but they came to be accepted once those who knew the old had left.

Perhaps the renovations disappointed the hope for eventual economy, which was much stressed in the Eton Appeal documents, and which was always and indeed excessively in Claude Elliott's mind. Long before the rebuilding was complete he had retired. He had become Sir Claude Elliott in 1958, knighted 'for services to education' – an irony considering that few headmasters have been more determinedly not educationalists. His last two years at Eton were saddened by a stroke which incapacitated his wife, and at the end of 1964 he left, settling eventually as a widower at Buttermere. The financial and structural regeneration of Eton meant that he was an exceptionally busy Provost, and his administrative ability was fully deployed.† As Head Master he had preserved Eton in a very difficult period; as Provost he brought about a transformation. He died in 1973 aged 85, and there was by his own wish no memorial service. He was indeed a modest and private man to the end, but many who felt his charm and experienced his kindness were sorry for this decision, and the College could not formally express its very great debt.

* For a brief period during the rebuilding it was possible to see Long Chamber as it had once been.

† His gifts were also of great importance when he was President of the Alpine Club at the time of the successful expedition to climb Everest in 1952.

CHAPTER ELEVEN

Robert Birley

THE HEAD MASTER knew the building programme was necessary, and at least the renovation of the Chapel was close to his heart, but he cared more for academic matters, holding strong views on two of the issues of the time. The first of these confronted him on arrival, the introduction of the General Certificate Examination at O and A levels in 1951. A level was the particular problem. Birley foresaw that A levels might become almost obligatory, at least for boys with University aspirations, and he wished to avoid the loss of freedom which Eton enjoyed, both in the allocation of time and in the choice within courses which was permitted by the Grand July Examination. A level pressures would drive out some of the non-examined subjects, and limit the breadth of the Eton education. In individual subjects the prescribed syllabus would dominate, and thus, for example in History, boys might not be able to continue the study of a 'big' author – say Macaulay – because of the risk that there would only be one A level question on the Glorious Revolution. Immediately he feared that boys would lose the chance of State scholarships if they did not do A level, and wanted the College to consider varying the Trust deeds of existing leaving scholarships so that they could be used as State scholarships. In practice scientists soon switched to A levels with little disadvantage and did win State scholarships. A related problem was that it would be desirable to give boys more time before A level than was normal under Eton's existing arrangements, and thus boys would somehow have to come to O level earlier; how was this to be managed without premature specialization? Birley's answer was to start boys higher up the School; Third Form was quickly abolished, and older entrants had to pass into a form above Lower Fourth to be acceptable. This effective raising of the standard of entrance was possible with the large number of applicants wishing to come to the School.

Later some Colleges of Oxford and Cambridge were wanting their candidates to achieve two A levels before taking College Entrance examinations, and Etonians were often too old even after the changes to stay willingly beyond A level. In spite of this difficulty, over eighty Etonians annually obtained places at Oxford and Cambridge, an indication of Birley's success in persuading Colleges to take into consideration Eton's arrangements. Other Universities were beginning to require three A levels, and Etonians on the Arts side were disadvantaged – often having to offer subjects like English or Economics done in the very limited Extra Studies time. Birley strongly approved of the growth of other Universities, and wanted to encourage Etonians to go to them. It was therefore an unfortunate weakness that Eton lacked, even at the end of Birley's reign, a professional approach to taking A levels.

If Birley resisted the coming of A levels, he was ahead of his time in being aware of the problem of 'two cultures'. Although he was as ignorant of Maths and Science as Alington had been, he did at least realize that a one-sided education was wrong. The arrangements for those specializing in Maths and Science – and with Birley's encouragement their numbers more than doubled in his time – were admirably balanced. They were required to do four periods of History, and two of Divinity, as well as three periods of Extra Studies, along with seventeen periods allotted to two Sciences and Maths. It was less easy to argue that Arts specialists were kept abreast of Science. In a characteristic, but not wholly successful, exercise Birley himself tried to teach historians the History of Science, with Dr Goodier, Head of Science who was appointed from outside in 1955, performing some of the relevant experiments. At least all boys on the Arts side had to take an Extra Study, where the substantial choice did include practical subjects and ones with a slight basis of numeracy such as Economics. Also the great majority of Etonians did obtain one Science at O level.

When HM Inspectors revisited the School in 1955 they observed the individual features of the Eton curriculum, and they sided with the Head Master. They liked the modern general division (largely based on Geography) which had been added to the classical general division. They thought the arrangements for Science much improved, and were only somewhat critical of the late start of boys wanting to study German. Their view that 'it is most important that Eton should, as far as possible, control its own destiny in deciding the nature and standard of its Specialist work' was what Robert Birley wished them to say.[1]

The Report was so extraordinarily complimentary (except about the boarding conditions) that Eton Masters themselves put it down to the excellence with which Inspectors had been wined and dined; nevertheless it is a tribute to the strength of the staff appointed by Elliott and to the improvements that resulted after the first inspection, which were certainly carried forward by Birley.

The Head Master set a good example; he loved imparting knowledge and taught a heavy programme. His lectures – for so they were – were discursive and leapt across the centuries to find contemporary relevance; they were lit by his moral commitment and enthusiasm: 'And, you know, it is an extraordinary thing . . .', 'Had he lived, he would have been quite one of the most important men of the Middle Ages . . .'. Boys imitated and sometimes mocked, but they remembered. There were seldom opportunities for them to interrupt the flow, but when they wrote essays, their work was corrected with a care that sometimes flattered their aspirations, Birley's comments running on for as long as the original essay. Nor did the Head Master shirk hard tasks. He would deliver Divinity lectures to the complete C Block, but in that his capability did not match his courage; partly because he was so often unpunctual, boys misbehaved and the curator of the Music Schools, where the lectures were held, remarked that he had 'gathered up that many sweet papers it was like the Feeding of the Five Thousand'; Masters had to be brought in to sit with the boys to exercise control.

All this teaching based on wide reading had its cost. Other tasks suffered – for instance replies to letters, which might be six hand-written pages or which might never be made at all. Knowing his own weakness at administration, he created a new deputy for himself, given the title Chairman of Committees, to handle matters concerned with the School Fund, House Fund, and Finance

Committees – the last becoming the co-ordinating Committee of Masters and Bursars reporting to the Provost and Fellows. Neither Birley nor the Finance Committee was adequately aware of the financial worries of Masters. The Provost and Fellows were determined to keep the level of fees down, and this left no room for restoring Masters' salaries to pre-war values. Some increases had to be granted to keep Eton salaries competitive with those of other schools, but the teaching profession as a whole suffered relative decline, and Eton Masters did not escape.* Also Birley was severely constrained by the Fellows when he wished to appoint extra Masters needed by the shift to earlier specialization.

There were other non-financial limitations on Birley's appointments. The tutorial system still required large numbers of Classical Masters for Pupil Room work, and it was only at the end of Birley's time that the first English and Geography Masters could be introduced; until then the Classical Masters had to teach these subjects as well as Divinity and their Latin and Greek. Also, the Head Master was not really good at appointing – at interviews he talked too much himself. The turnover of young men was rapid, and some who were billed by Birley as 'extraordinarily interesting' either failed to justify his hopes or took themselves off to a more glamorous or financially rewarding life. New Masters had very seldom been trained as teachers, and little instruction was given to beginners once at Eton; the Head of the Maths Department, for instance, advised knowing thoroughly what to teach the first day, and consolingly remarked that those who did not last at Eton frequently did well in other walks of life – advice which was of limited value. The real training came from the time-honoured testing by boys of new Masters' control.

The Masters that Birley inherited were of generally high quality; quite a number were promoted to headmasterships elsewhere. This was partly possible because many more Masters were married, and thus apt for promotion, than before the War. Housemasters mostly contrived a sort of bigamy – wedded to their boys during the half and to their families in the holidays. The increasing numbers of women on the campus probably made for a less exotic atmosphere than twenty-five years previously. Also the propor-

---

* Before an increase in 1958, Eton Masters' salaries in the first years, and their maximum salary, were substantially below those of Rugby.

tion of non-Etonian Masters tended to rise, and some of the newcomers were more critical of the mystique of Eton.

Most Housemasters had, of course, been teaching at Eton before the War, but their style and the traditions of their houses could vary greatly. A glimpse of an almost nineteenth-century eccentricity is to be obtained in Jonathan Franklin's delightful and popular *Two Owls at Eton*. Generally speaking, the trend was for houses to become more relaxed. Exercise was still compulsory for almost all the younger boys, and house games were still regarded as very important. Fagging remained, but 'Boy!' calls were being questioned by some. Beating in general declined, and by 1960 the majority of boys in most houses passed through their Eton careers without suffering. House books suggest that almost all Captains of houses thought corporal punishment a necessary sanction, but they record that they beat perhaps three times in a half. There were, however, some successful houses where more authoritarian regimes still existed, and in such cases this would have been with the approval of the Housemaster.

Even in such houses, where the lower boys might be thoroughly regulated, the older boys could behave badly – for example, covertly smoking or drinking. During and after the War high prices discouraged such misbehaviour,* but by the 1950s older boys were beginning to have more spare funds, and Housemasters needed the usual vigilance. Yet Williams's, the most evidently unsuccessful house, was not as barbarous as P. Williams's at the beginning of the century. Birley waited until there was more than casual evidence of the indiscipline and disrespect of the older boys† before removing the Housemaster – an action so sensitively handled that Watkin Williams seems to have convinced himself that he was retiring just because he had become overstrained.

House books showed a growing tendency to dwell on personalities, which was to lead to their general suppression in the following years. Accounts of house matches grew shorter, but in some cases character studies were provided regularly, not just of boys leaving but of the entire house. These often showed insight, for boys

* At the end of the War, the basic rate of income tax had been 50%, and the real price of spirits was more than double what it is now.

† Williams's Library had the misfortune when smoking on the roof of their house to be spotted from the roof of College Chapel.

certainly had great opportunities to study each other's characters, but were objectionable when harsh – and they could be very harsh: 'X is wholly devious, but he is a coward and can be controlled by the threat of punishment' or 'Y has no friends in the house, and it is hardly surprising': not fun for X or Y to read, even if the book did not come into his hands until a year or two later. Nor can one commend patronizing analyses of the Housemaster, which might verge on the disloyal, or of the Dame, which demonstrated that Etonians were not always chivalrous.

The Dames' lives were indeed becoming more taxing. The relationship with boys has always been problematic, and now they faced increasing difficulties in obtaining staff. It was normally still possible to get high-grade boys' maids, who would cherish their charges and influence them to considerate behaviour. Resident kitchen and cleaning staff, however, had higher expectations of accommodation and salary than could be met, and Dames found themselves relying on a succession of foreigners often of uncertain temperament. Furthermore many were worried by their accounting problems: they knew they must somehow keep their Housemasters within the flexible limits of the House Fund Committee. The School authorities began to explore the possibility of central cooking, but there was a very strong desire to preserve traditional catering. When one Housemaster tried providing high tea instead of messing, he found himself 'invested with a mantle of moral turpitude';[2] Robert Birley received so many complaints that he had to ask for the experiment to be discontinued.

A great emergency for harassed and underpaid Dames occurred when the Asiatic flu epidemic struck Eton in October 1957. Most houses had half their boys in bed at the worst moment, and Eton's small sanatorium was of no real help. At least the Dames and domestic staff were granted a small extension of Long Leave. The health of boys was less good than it is today; diet was less satisfactory and the boys more spotty. Measurements in 1957 showed that Etonians had not grown bigger since 1937, though their contemporaries had caught up. Boys did, however, benefit from the introduction of central heating; to the Provost's dismay sickness declined in what he regarded as mollycoddled houses.

Outside the houses, boys' behaviour showed some of the same patterns as were evident in the country generally. There was a gradual decline in public manners, and, most obviously, boys' language deteriorated.* Illicit smoking and drinking parties occurred more frequently than in the previous decade. Pop could still normally be relied on to deal with troublesome groups of younger boys – often athletes rather above their station like the self-styled 'Junior Joint' of 1957; and they were still prepared to check dress and public behaviour. But Birley seems to have had more trouble than Elliott with irresponsible behaviour by Pop itself, and towards the end of his time senior boys were beginning to abdicate from the duties that were expected of them. Some boys questioned whether it could be right for boys to be placed so much over their fellows, and felt that the exercise of boys' authority was fascist; they were anxious to be liked rather than respected. It is clear that some of the attitudes associated with the 1960s were developing at Eton by the end of the 1950s.

Not surprisingly Birley fought against this trend. More than once Pop was 'reformed', when the President could be persuaded that he would be wise to make changes rather than see it lose some of its privileges or conceivably even its existence. Such reforms normally followed a scandal in which one or two members of Pop had to leave the School early; they might involve changes in the mode of election or in the numbers of Pop; but it cannot be said that an outsider could detect any lasting improvements. Birley was realistic enough to perceive that it would not be easy to create a body of prefects, chosen by himself, to fill the vacuum of authority if Pop were to go. So Pop continued through its 150th anniversary – celebrated in October 1961 by a dinner attended by 750 former members (of 1,300 living) in an appropriately less pretentious fashion than the Centenary junketing.†

Birley also reformed Sixth Form, here making considerably greater differences. In 1958, in an effort to encourage intellectual competition in the School, he decided that promotion to Sixth Form should not be by seniority only, but that all boys must have a number of distinctions in Trials. Furthermore, the Captain of the Oppidans was to be chosen by himself from the members of Sixth Form. College Sixth Form was less affected, but again distinctions in Trials were to influence the order established before Collegers

---

* Luxmoore at the beginning of the century wanted to put one of Benson's boys in the Bill for saying 'Blast!' on the football field. By the 1960s umpires were having to send off boys for much worse profanities.

† Even more applied to attend, but space was limited.

took their O levels; this brought considerable incidental benefit by reducing the excessive competitive pressure experienced by Collegers when all their subsequent careers depended upon that one Trials order. Making Sixth Form more of an intellectual élite did not in practice increase its power or prestige; it became younger, and contained fewer house Captains. Since that date, however, further reforms have been made in the same direction, which have led to the inclusion of more of the cleverest boys in Sixth Form, now officially renamed Sixth Form Select to accommodate the national use of Sixth Form as a term for all specialists. There are still normally ten Collegers and ten Oppidans, though the case for including more Oppidans is growing.

Along with the changes in selection of Sixth Form, an experiment was made of giving boys marks for work in school to count as well as Trials in determining school order. Masters did not reckon this approach to continuous assessment was worth the trouble it caused, and it did not apparently provide extra incentives for the boys. Most Masters were dissatisfied with the standard and attitude of the weaker boys, though they may have underestimated the amount of work that Eton extracted from them. There were still only twenty-five schools for almost all, but there were five long sessions of Pupil Room for lower boys, and three periods of Private Business (one of them on Sundays) for others, and Extra Works intended to occupy each evening except Saturdays. And the days were long even if they were leisurely.

Boys had as ever plenty of time to carry forward their social lives, but the School Stores Sock Shops were not so prosperous as they had been before the War. Spending power, even if it grew in the 1950s, was less in real terms, and there were growing attractions for teenagers' money in the shops of Windsor. Tap remained the most prestigious club for older boys. When Mrs Hobbs, who with her husband had run Tap with great success for many years, retired, its position was found to be anomalous – selling beer to under-age consumers without a proper licence. A club licence was secured, and Tap came within the control of School Stores, but even it, to the boys' surprise, made little financial profit. Its value, however, was considerable, and it began to be imitated in other boarding schools.

Eton still offered a gratifying range of out-of-school activities. Perhaps the Debating Society deserves special mention, achieving at the end of the 1950s a higher than usual standard culminating with success in the 1964 and 1965 *Observer* Mace Competitions. It had the useful advantage of bringing the Collegers more into contact with a cross-section of Oppidans at a time when there were a number of unusually able boys in College. The average attendance was over one hundred.

Robert Birley was much keener to encourage music and the arts than his predecessor. Sydney Watson, precentor from 1946 to the end of 1955, was not so exceptional an organist as Henry Ley, but he raised the general standard of music in the School. Some of the best concerts put on were held in the Birleys' drawing-room with mixed bands of Masters and boys, and Birley himself was suffered to take a very small part in Leopold Mozart's Toy Symphony.

Arrangements for teaching Art in schooltime remained inconvenient, but good work was done on half-holiday afternoons, perhaps particularly in ceramics. Wilfrid Blunt, who in his memoirs disparaged Elliott, was more warmly inclined to Birley, but as he himself admitted, he was not really one to encourage boys to experiment in art; his own skill was in flower-painting and in calligraphy, and he was a fine singer. As with music, there were good performers, but the provision for art was some way below what it is today.

The number of plays increased considerably. Some houses put on plays in their dining-rooms, in the gym, or under some other difficult conditions; and annual School plays were mounted in School Hall, where at least actors learned to project their voices in that cavernous building – and a number went on to professional careers on the stage. The Shakespeare Society and the Play Reading Society remained important. Boys also had the chance to make films, one of which won an award. In 1956 a relaxation was permitted in the traditional Eton Sunday – boys were permitted to play games on Sundays, but not competitively. Yet music continued to be played on Sundays, and the School of Mechanics and Drawing Schools were active.

As for games, the competitive instincts of Etonian soccer players were gaining ground, with the first overseas tours by Eton XIs. In most games, however, the School had only mixed success, with Eton on fairly equal terms with Harrow at Lord's. These were still two-day games, but attendance figures continued to fall from 20,000 a match immediately after the War, to 10,000 at the end of

Birley's time. On the river, Eton won the Ladies' Plate in 1960,* but there was some feeling that Eton should be competing against other schools in the newly established Princess Elizabeth Cup, in which the 2nd VIII was entered.

The Captain of Boats remained very much master of all that occurred on the river. He still had the ability to fire the Master coaching the VIII, and during this time did indeed do so. Internal rowing events were organized by the boys, under conditions on the river which were getting more difficult as the Thames became congested by pleasure boats. A new boathouse, one of Eton's better new buildings,† was constructed at Boveney with the help of a legacy from Mr G.M. Andrews, and from 1960 most races were organized on the reach below Queen's Eyot.

Beagling was another sport operating under increasing difficulties as new areas were built up around Eton, and new roads – including most valuably a new Eton bypass – were constructed. Masters of the beagles have had unusually responsible jobs handling relations with adults as well as controlling boys and their hounds, but they have been driven further and further afield to hunt, and they have been able to attract diminishing numbers of boy supporters.

The Corps underwent a considerable change too with the end of National Service. It had never been strictly compulsory at Eton, but the very great majority of boys had joined, largely to help themselves gain commissions in the army, and some Housemasters more or less forced boys to join the Corps or the Scouts. The Scouts came to an end in the early 1950s from lack of support, and from 1957 the Corps changed its character, recruiting little more than half the specialists. More interesting courses were devised for the members, and there were some exciting camps, particularly in Norway. The reformed Corps was a success, with some candidates actually turned down. A Corps band was revived after many years.

The end of National Service gave an opportunity for boys to undertake rewarding trips after leaving School. Robert Birley was an enthusiastic supporter of Voluntary Service Overseas, which at that time recruited 18-year-olds, and was even able to persuade the

* This was the final occasion on which the Eton VIII rowed with fixed pins, handicapping themselves against other crews; it was the last hurrah of the classical style of Eton rowing deriving from Warre and de Havilland.

† Architect, Michael Pattrick.

College to give small financial backing. Some such expeditions to
the Third World produced remarkable results, with young Old
Etonians achieving positions of surprising influence, and one or
two led to appeals for help from the School. The continuing
obligation to finance the Eton Mission began to appear something
of an obstacle to Eton's charitable efforts spreading their wings.
Yet Robert Birley remained a strong supporter of the Mission. In
his last few years as Head Master it was particularly dynamic, and
Etonians who visited could see how the young danced in a
different style from their own, and could mingle with ton-up
motor-cyclists, but it was not possible for them to participate in
any useful practical way. Influenced by Robert, but also doubtless
by Arthur Villiers, who supported the Mission as well as the Eton
Manor Club, the College actually gave £15,000 for necessary work
on the church, although it had always been a School rather than a
College enterprise, a group of Masters rather than the College
appointing to the living. This exercise of persuasion was remarkable considering the generally tight-fisted attitude of the Provost
and Fellows.

Robert Birley was devoutly Christian and certainly cared passionately about the Chapel services as well as the actual building.
He even encouraged senior boys to attend the weekday evensongs
sung by the Choir, and they could obtain leave off one school a
half to do so. Masters claimed that boys would take sanctuary
when a construe was to be tested, but their opposition made no
impact on the Head Master who argued that it was necessary to
make a statement of values to the boys. A rather more significant
change was brought about by Birley early on, the appointment of a
Senior Chaplain. He had to explain how a Senior Chaplain could
have a proper role at Eton although the control of the official
services remained with the Provost and the Conduct whom he
appointed. The Senior Chaplain would have responsibility for
voluntary worship, for preparation for Confirmation, for Divinity
teaching, and he would deal with any pastoral work beyond what
Housemasters could handle. Some of Birley's lengthy hand-
written letters on the subject survive, and throw light on the
relationship between College and School at this time, which he
defended as complementary and not a source of conflict. Happily
Birley found an excellent man for the new post, Ralph Sadleir – a
man so special that the School collectively gave him a generous

leaving present on his retirement, unprecedented for any but a Head Master.

Just before Birley left, he told a Masters' meeting that he had always favoured making Chapel voluntary, at least in part (and indeed he had done so successfully at Charterhouse). The implication was that only the Provost had stood in his way. Yet such was Birley's prestige when he came, it seems inconceivable that he could not have achieved some change. Arguably voluntary Chapels might have been more successful at this time when most boys were more devout than they were to be later. The clergy preferred voluntary Chapels, feeling their congregations would be more receptive, but other Masters were mostly opposed, either because they welcomed the occupation of large numbers of boys with little effort from themselves, or because they feared that boys would more question the value that the School attached to religious worship once it lost its priority over all other activities.

For many Masters this meeting threw even further doubt on Birley's commitment to liberal causes; perhaps he was almost as conservative as Elliott. Towards the end of his reign a group of Housemasters felt obliged to complain to Lord John Hope, the Masters' Representative on the Governing Body, about Birley's unapproachability. Letters went unanswered, and even personal meetings were unrewarding unless the subject happened to chime with Birley's interests. Birley was unaware of the problem when it was brought to his notice. More seriously, a group of parents questioned the value they were getting for their money – the place was scruffy, and the preparation of boys for A level was inadequate. Some Housemasters led by Bud Hill agreed with them and took the matter to Lord John Hope. Birley was furious:[3] he was the proper channel for such complaints. Yet it was difficult for the Housemasters, when they saw the Head Master himself as the cause of the problem which they wished to raise.

Criticism of Eton was also mounting externally. This was the time when the movement for comprehensive education was growing in the country, and indeed it enjoyed the support of the Old Etonian Sir Edward Boyle when he was the Conservative Education Minister.* Eton was selective both socially and academically,

* Sir Edward Boyle had been Captain of the Oppidans, and was even then recognized to be remarkable. A boy wrote in a Sunday Question, 'the three best memories I know are Lord Macaulay, Mr Martineau and E. Boyle at Routh's'.

and became the particular butt of educational reformers. There had
over the years been plenty of attacks on the way Eton had been
run, but now there were threats to its very existence. Birley argued
somewhat disingenuously that Eton was comprehensive; there
were Etonians who would not have passed an 11-plus exam for a
grammar school, and there were boys from almost every income
bracket. For a time it was the fashion to mock the School as
'Slough Comprehensive'.

In fact the only real social dilution was the Hertfordshire
Scholars originating from the Fleming Report. These did contribute to the School academically and socially. A book by David
Benedictus, *The Fourth of June*, a counterpart of the earlier *Decent
Fellows* with an alluring dust-jacket, was built around a sadistic
beating of one of these boys. A beating such as was described could
have occurred, but not to a Hertfordshire boy. Brendan Lehane
published a non-fictional account of his time at Eton in which he
does explain the difficulties that he faced – not least at home:
'None of the bruises were physical, all on the sensitivity, of which
I had a normal adolescent surfeit.' He mentions one boy in a
temper saying 'Why don't you go back to your grammar school?';
but if that was the unkindest cut, he had a sheltered life.[4] His main
complaint against Eton was that he could not specialize in English,
and found himself forced into Classics. He became house Captain,
and other Hertfordshire boys were in Pop. Few were outstanding-
ly able, because Winchester always chose the academically bright-
est – whereas Rugby and Eton selected on more general grounds.
Only once in Birley's time was there a conflict, and that gave him
pleasure and amusement. Eton wanted the cleverest boy, so did
Winchester; the Director of Education said that the boy must
choose, and 'Eton, of course' was his reply.

There was also an attempt to attract grammar school boys to
take the Eton Scholarship, and there was a slight relaxation of the
dominance of Classics in the College Examination. This, however,
failed as hardly any candidates came forward. The Provost and
Fellows still nominally controlled the Election to College – and
indeed tampered with the list put forward by the Masters examining – and the Provost and Vice-Provost interviewed. Elliott
particularly distrusted the value of the French results, supposing
that if a boy shone at French, his father had either married a French
wife or had a French mistress. When a boy from a Welsh grammar

school applied, he was totally puzzled by the Provost, who had not been forewarned, asking whether he had a French nanny. Widening the entrance to College was a failure. It is once again surprising that Birley accepted his lack of control of this most important part of the entry to the School. Indeed he rather enjoyed proposing something slightly different from what he really wanted, to allow the Provost and Vice-Provost to make the change he desired – it appealed to his delight in political manoeuvre.

The College ran into more serious difficulties in 1961 over the selection of King's Scholars. The Statutes had allowed exclusion at the Provost's discretion. In 1939 a boy from the Levant aged 12 was excluded because he was so extraordinarily mature: it was distinctly awkward explaining that there would be no point his trying again next year. In 1944 the Statutes were revised in a way which would have avoided this problem – candidates had to be the sons of British-born fathers. This was likely to exclude the sons of European immigrants, who might be Jewish. At the end of the 1950s technical changes were made to mitigate the inconvenience of College having to be exactly seventy in number, and at the same time the wording of the Statute was altered to account for changes in the nationality law. This revision attracted public attention. The effect was again to exclude the sons of immigrants, and it was attacked as anti-Semitic. Curiously it certainly had excluded several non-Jewish boys, one the son of an Old Etonian Irish baronet, and it did not operate against members of the Empire who were at that time British citizens; and of course there were English Jews in College. Professor Ayer led the attack, pointing out that he himself would have been excluded from College since his father was Swiss. Another even more exalted Old Colleger, the Prime Minister Harold Macmillan, joined in. The Fellows, who included the much liked and respected Lord Cohen, decided that there was no course but to abandon the nationality clause altogether. They had been inept rather than ill-intentioned, but they had lost face.*

Despite the few exceptional boys from the State system, the overall composition of the School remained very much unchanged at the end of Birley's time. The count of peers' sons had fallen a little in 1960 compared with 1930; there were forty-nine sons of

---

* Winchester had the same Statute, but escaped attack because they, more prudently, had also a clause to permit the Warden to override the bar in special cases.

peers and one baronet (as against sixty-four and ten). There were three royal princes and the heir to the throne of Nepal. Altogether 60% were sons of Old Etonians. The parents of many boys still considered 'University' to mean the Oxford or Cambridge Colleges that they had attended, and in 1962 eighty-six boys managed to gain places. Only fourteen went to other Universities. By 1962 Eton had recently acquired a Careers Master, and his statistics for that year suggested tentatively that about one-fifth of Etonians were headed for commerce and industry, with another 5% intending to be engineers. This was more than the public school average, but Etonians were not as hostile to the profit motive as their contemporaries were reputed to be. Those going into the Services, often only for a Short Service Commission, numbered 15%, again a high figure. Conspicuously few Etonians became scientists or doctors; the expansion of Science at Eton in Birley's time had not made that large a change.

The story of Eton over the fourteen years of his headmastership is one of continuity with limited evolution. It was a period of moderate academic success. The O and A level statistics were above the national average, but at A level not conspicuously so. This could be said to indicate a healthy disregard for examination results, and a care for wider education; and even at the end of Birley's time most boys specialized late. Awards at Oxford and Cambridge continued at about fifteen a year, not quite matching the best years of the 1940s, but probably competition had increased and Etonians handicapped themselves by not trying a sufficient range of Colleges. Although the number of Classics specialists had fallen to only twelve or so a year, about a third of the awards were classical. Maths and Science now accounted for another third, from about sixty specialists a year. Some ninety historians were responsible for another third; the History Department attracted very clever boys, but also looked after some of the least able who did not all continue to A level. There was usually a Modern Languages award too – about fifty specialists a year were modern linguists.

It was a worry to Masters that many of the Etonians who gained awards, or entrance, did not achieve the academic success at University that their strength at entry suggested. Arguably Etonians were not really fired with intellectual interest, or were too much spoon-fed by their Masters. On the other hand Etonians at

39. H.K. Marsden, 'Bloody Bill', between W.W. Williams, 'Fishy', and Conduct Harvey. The drawing, believed to be by Robin McEwen, was retrieved from the floor of the Drawing Schools by Wilfrid Blunt.

40. Geoffrey Nickson is conducting Pupil Room in the 1930s. It will be noticed that he might also have been a successful pavement artist. The photograph was taken by his pupil, Peter Opie, for Opie's book *I Want To Be A Success*.

41. Jack's Sock Shop

42. Montague James OM

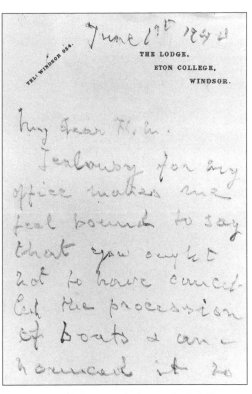

44. Letter from Lord Hugh Cecil to
Claude Elliott, 1940

43. Lord Hugh Cecil, later Lord
Quickswood

45. The Precentor, Henry Ley, acting as a casualty for First Aid practice at the beginning of the Second World War

46. It might have been real – his bombed house.

47. Fagging. A 'Boy!' call

48. Fagging. Has the bed been well made?

49. College Chapel before the installation of the Burne-Jones tapestry

50. Boys at prayer in College Chapel. To accommodate all the boys it was necessary to use the 'knife-boards', uncomfortable seats flanking the aisle.

51. College Chapel today

52. Sir Henry Marten knighted by King George VI in 1945. The Choir lining the steps are the Etonians from Lower Chapel rather than the boys of the Choir School.

53. A drawing of Julian Lambart by Humphrey Lyttelton, son of George Lyttelton.
Lambart would seem to have been the quintessential beak, and was indeed pernickety
about small matters. But he was wiser about big issues; and he once remarked that
he counted himself lucky to have been paid to do a job that he would gladly have
done for love.

54. Robert Birley at his last Fourth of June Absence, 1963

55. Anthony Chenevix-Trench with Oliver Van Oss (centre) and Julian Lambart (right). He gave up wearing a cassock, and his successors followed his example.

56. Lord Caccia accompanying Queen Elizabeth, the Queen Mother. Behind them Michael McCrum and Lady Caccia

57. The Procession of Boats after the abolition of the night-time procession

58. 1967. The VIII, on their way to victory in the World Junior Championships, win the Princess Elizabeth Cup at Henley Regatta from Tabor Academy, USA.

59. Michael McCrum

60. Eric Anderson

61. The School Orchestra rehearsing Arutiunian's Trumpet Concerto in School Hall. The other works for performance in December 1993 were Lutoslawski's Preludes & Fugue and Shostakovich's First Symphony.

62. A scene from *West Side Story* in the Farrer Theatre, 1992

63. The Boys say farewell to Lord Charteris, Fourth of June, 1991. In a spontaneous gesture they threw flowers at his feet.

University complained that they were not stretched on arrival – that University offered less good teaching and little socially that they had not tasted at school. Certainly they tended to do better if they changed their subject. In the long run the Universities were clearly more likely to find the fault in the Etonians rather than in themselves, so that even Eton's apparent success at getting boys into Oxford and Cambridge may have been creating difficulties for future Etonians.

Robert Birley was a man of vision, and he would occasionally remark that his ideal Old Etonian would be director of the Atomic Energy Authority and churchwarden of his local church, following the second lesson in his Greek Testament. This is a picture of the pursuit of balanced excellence in which he believed. Many Etonians of his time have done well in later life, but it does not appear that they have achieved the wide distinction of earlier generations. They have operated in a more difficult environment – more competitive and more hostile. Perhaps they could not achieve the self-confidence of their predecessors, or were not fired with the same ambition. Etonians of the later Birley years were probably more critical of the education they received, accepting some of the routine, but often unjustified, condemnation of Eton as out of touch with modern reality. Should this be held against the Head Master? Certainly boys had more contact with Birley than with Elliott, because of his teaching and preaching. A few knew him well – interesting boys who perhaps had unsympathetic House-masters, and whom he delighted to help. Most boys, however, did not feel that he knew them, and Birley's influence on the School operated through the Masters.

For them he was in every way a big man, despite occasional blatant faults such as displays of vanity. He knew what were major matters and what was ultimately trivial, and he had a sense of fun which helped him to communicate that education was an exciting business. Masters knew too that at the end of a long day he would take himself off to College Library to research in the small hours, thus establishing the priority of academic matters. Furthermore, he rose to the occasional emergency, for instance at the time of the polio epidemic, or again towards the end of his headmastership when Eton boys were molested along with those at many other schools in the Thames Valley by a compulsive pervert called Andrews. He would climb into boys' rooms, but somehow kept eluding capture though sighted and pursued. He was eventually caught in a house pupil room by a senior boy, Jonathan Aitken, but evidence of assault was hard to obtain, and only after he was trapped at another school could he be locked up for a number of years.* This troublesome and time-consuming episode aroused in Birley the fire of battle.

Birley's greatness was also apparent in the manner of his departure. He was due to retire in 1964, but at the end of 1962 he announced that he was accepting the post of visiting Professor of Education at Witwatersrand University. He felt the urge to make some stand against the increasingly authoritarian and racist regime in South Africa, and he and his wife were to do much to keep liberal values and political decency alive there. The courage of this move, when he was reaching 60, greatly impressed Masters and boys. In the summer of 1963, the School bade him farewell. There were the customary presents, and speeches – the Captain of the School so generous in his tribute that 'I could hardly recognize myself' – and a three-minute ovation from the boys. In College Hall the Masters were entertained to dinner, but it struck many as remarkable that two Masters, Richard Martineau and Giles St Aubyn, were the hosts rather than the ever-economical Provost and Fellows.

Robert Birley, unlike his predecessors, was neither so successful nor so influential at Eton as he was in his jobs immediately before or after. Even during his Eton period he probably gained more unqualified admiration at the Headmasters' Conference than he did at Chambers. Yet many Masters believed, partly because of the importance of his work before and after, that he was the greatest man to be Head Master, even though he was not the greatest Head Master. His knighthood was fully earned. Even to the end of his long life, in 1982, he continued to show his wisdom. In his last letter to the Provost in 1980 he stressed the importance of choosing a new Head Master who would care for general education and not be hidebound by examinations.

* When Aitken became a Minister thirty years on, he received a congratulatory letter from Andrews.

CHAPTER TWELVE

Upheaval

ONLY TWO CANDIDATES were seriously considered to succeed Robert Birley: Anthony Chenevix-Trench and Brian Young. Trench, an Old Salopian and a good classical scholar, could have been a don, but had preferred to teach at Shrewsbury; from there he had become Headmaster of Bradfield, which had gained reputation in his charge; and he had made some name on a wider stage by his membership of the Robbins Committee on Higher Education. Brian Young was an Old Colleger, had returned to Eton as a Classics Master after the War, and in 1952 had become Headmaster of Charterhouse when he was only 30. He was very much the choice of the Provost and Vice-Provost, but the opinion of the majority of Masters, fed through the Masters' Representative, was that he would be too much in Birley's image, and that Eton's need was for change and a relaxation of style – which it was felt Trench was more likely to provide. Most of the Fellows were swayed by this opinion, though Elliott was not, and consequently Chenevix-Trench was appointed. Subsequent events suggested that the wrong choice had been made, but Brian Young was lucky. It was a difficult time to be Head Master and he was spared the problems of the 1960s at Eton. His considerable capacity, which no one at Eton had doubted, found a useful new field, when he was appointed Director-General of the Independent Broadcasting Authority.

Tony Chenevix-Trench, who was aged 44, had an excellent wife Elizabeth (and a young family), but he was also considerably handicapped. He had been a prisoner of war of the Japanese on the Burma Railway, and had shown stoic courage and leadership; but his health had been permanently damaged. He was a small man, and his physique was not up to a demanding job. More seriously, he doubted his own ability to handle a school twice the size of Bradfield. There he had known practically every boy: even at interview he wondered whether he could communicate with Etonians through a layer of 'twenty-five robber barons' (the Housemasters). Thus, before he arrived at Eton he was already questioning the wisdom of his move. As the pressures mounted on him he turned to alcohol for relief and, because of his damaged constitution, he was easily affected by it. Another problem may also have been a legacy of his war-time experiences: he regarded corporal punishment not as the last resort, but almost as the first resort in punishing boys; and though many boys still accepted this, adults on the whole did not. Masters, certainly, and the Fellows should have been aware of this propensity to beat, for some warning was given by the Chairman of the Bradfield Governors. Trench had been asked at interview for his views on corporal punishment: 'It can be useful', he said – not quite the whole truth.*

Yet Trench had also great virtues as a schoolmaster. He was a man of instinctive warmth and sympathy, who responded to boys as individuals. He was most approachable, and could even achieve rapport with the media – always enjoying a more favourable press than Birley. He had a genuine love for Eton and a vision of what he wanted to do for it: 'It is a great eighteenth-century institution, and I want to bring it into the twentieth century.'

Because of his contract with Bradfield, he did not take up office at Eton until January 1964, and in Michaelmas 1963, Oliver Van Oss, by then Lower Master, acted as Head Master. At once there was change and relaxation which may have increased the task facing Trench. The values and the arrangements that had prevailed were called into question. Very possibly the Provost and Fellows should have appointed Van Oss instead of Trench for a limited spell of seven years; although colleagues regarded him as not quite trustworthy, he was a big enough man to unleash change and to

---

* At a dinner in the summer of 1963, Lord Cohen remarked that the Fellows had chosen the smallest Head Master since Dr Keate. 'I hope he does not resemble Dr Keate in other ways', he said. 'Oh but he does', he was told.

ride it. As things were, he started a process which Trench could not entirely control.

A glance at the *Chronicle* shows the new direction. Under Birley serious discussion in its pages of educational issues at Eton was not really possible because Birley knew that it would be taken up and distorted by the national press. Consequently editors had to aim for a light but insubstantial style. Now under Van Oss the *Chronicle* was to examine most aspects of Eton life in a critical but reasonably charitable vein, with predictable media attention.* This further encouraged the expectation of change to come.

The new Head Master's initial moves were all sensible: he approved a scheme for social service in the local community which had been prepared in the autumn by two young Masters, Peter Pilkington and Roger Thompson. This overdue provision was popular with the boys and soon one hundred volunteers were at work on programmes, some of which have endured for thirty years and have been of lasting value both to the community and to Etonians. Sunday Chapel was relaxed, so that only one service, rather than two, was compulsory each week. On what were called A and B Sundays, a compulsory mainly congregational service was retained in the morning and afternoon respectively, with a voluntary largely choral service in the evening and morning; and on C Sundays boys could attend either Holy Communion in the morning, or a sermon bracketed by hymns and a few prayers in the evening, and indeed some boys initially attended both. Furthermore the Head Master appointed a committee under Christopher Gowan to review the curriculum fundamentally.

In the summer of 1964, Provost Elliott announced his retirement to take effect in December. The Fellows had already discussed privately what sort of Provost they should request, and had decided that, with public opinion questioning independent education, they should seek a political rather than an academic figure to head the College. They also believed that there was need for greater business expertise than some academics possessed – though not Elliott. They were confident that the job could not be done by a non-resident (Winchester has a non-resident Warden). They therefore produced a new specification for the Provost: he should live at Eton, and regard Eton as his primary job, but he should be

* In Lent 1965, the Editors of the *Chronicle* reported that their first six issues had all been taken up by London newspapers.

allowed to hold other part-time appointments and should have a licence to be absent for short periods during the half. It was with this new pattern in mind, which has been adhered to subsequently, that the Fellows considered candidates for Provost. They had heard that Harold Macmillan (no longer Prime Minister, but almost the same age as Sir Claude Elliott) would like to be asked but decided that they wanted Sir Harold Caccia, formerly Permanent Under Secretary of State at the Foreign Office, who was nearing the completion of his time as Ambassador in Washington.* At the same time Oliver Van Oss went to Charterhouse to be Headmaster, and Fred Coleridge, an impressive Housemaster, became Lower Master. So except for Vice-Provost Lambart (who had to act as Provost for one half), there was really a new team.

The new Provost, now Lord Caccia, brought a complete change of style. A sharp and active man, who still followed his service briskly to the net, he thought that the time had come for considerable reforms at Eton. His installation on 1 May 1965 marked the intermediate point that Eton had reached: the service in College Chapel had traditional Latin words, but the speeches of welcome in School Yard were for the first time delivered in English. It was quickly plain that the Provost's influence would be directed against the retention of what he thought to be outmoded ways.

In one respect he was fortunate – the prudent management of the Elliott years had considerably improved the financial position of the College. Although the redevelopment of the Chalcots estate was still beset with political difficulties, which had been increased by the election of a Labour government in 1964 (this time with only one Old Etonian Cabinet Minister), capital was being released. Building costs were rising rapidly, but it became clear that the rebuilding programme would be managed. Then in February 1965 the Farrer Trustees told the Fellows that they still had enough money to set up a maintenance fund for what they had already built and to undertake another project, which they wished to be something of a luxury. This maintenance fund improved the School's income account, and the prospect of looking for something to spend on instead of looking for funds inevitably changed the perspective of the Governing Body.

* Strictly the appointment was made by the Queen on the advice of Sir Alec Douglas-Home.

Certainly the Provost was immediately able to show a more generous disposition in his reaction to the proposals of the Curriculum Committee. It had made far-reaching recommendations which were profoundly significant, and which ended the dominance of the classical tradition at Eton. The priorities set were to provide boys with a more thorough preparation for A levels; to spread the academic pressure on boys, which had tended to be concentrated in their third and fifth years; and yet to delay as far as possible the choice of specialist subject – one of the principles of Eton education which almost everyone wished to retain. Inevitably the Committee was drawn into related issues, so that more was involved than appeared on the surface, and Masters were divided almost as fiercely as they had been over the tutorial question.

After months of argument, the Committee produced two agreed papers, one setting out the arrangements for two A level years, the other for two O level years. Each boy (with just a few exceptions initially) would take three A levels, with seven periods allotted to each, as well as a General Study and Divinity. This permitted great flexibility – boys did not have to be just classical specialists or modern linguists or scientists, they could combine Classics for example with a modern language, or Maths with History and Geography.* The O level years caused greater problems, but it was agreed that four O levels should be taken at the end of the first of them: Latin, French, English Language, and (except for the weakest) Mathematics. This allowed a complex choice of subjects for the second O level year, with a large block of hours available for those wanting to start a new language, with some choice among the Sciences, with English Literature, Geography, French, Latin, and Greek competing, and with Maths and History compulsory; boys had to take seven subjects and Divinity. Up to thirty periods were required.

This meant a new timetable with all boys working After Twelve, when hitherto only lower boys and those believed by their Tutors to be slack had been occupied in Pupil Room. Conservatives could see that the tutorial system was weakened: indeed the Head Master had already made Sunday Private Business voluntary – which more

---

* There were said to be 177 different specialist programmes available. Boys' subjects were indicated in the School List by initials in front of their names – for example 'whg' indicated Maths with Statistics, History and Geography. Care was taken to ensure that no unfortunate combinations of letters occurred.

or less terminated it, for boys would not willingly attend for one Tutor if their colleagues were free. Although all boys retained a Classical Tutor until O level was complete, Classicists could foresee that in the long run the number of other Masters would inevitably increase to staff the new subjects and that their import-ance would shrink. Furthermore they had now lost their command over the ablest boys up to O level – it would be far easier for such boys to give up Classics, though there certainly remained pressure for boys learning Greek to continue it to O level.

The publication of the reports provoked fierce reaction from die-hards. The Head Master had never quite gripped the complex-ities of the issues involved or the subtleties of what in Eton is called an Abracadabra – a sort of universal timetable where groups of hours, labelled shall we say 'abcd' or 'efgh', are allocated to different subjects in different blocks of the school. He also tended to agree with whoever last spoke to him, and for a time it seemed that all the efforts of the Committee had been lost. In the Easter holidays of 1965, however, his resolution strengthened, and when the Fellows met for the first time under Lord Caccia, he told them at dinner the evening before, 'This is what we want to do'. Gowan and Coleridge were invited in after dinner, which was as well since the Head Master was tired and muddled, and needed Gowan to elucidate matters. The Provost at once saw that at least temporarily there must be an increase of Masters to teach the new A level subjects, and the Fellows amazingly agreed that there could be up to twelve new Masters on the understanding (never quite fulfilled) that Classical Masters would not be replaced when they retired. Indeed, Provost and Fellows were all enthusiastic, reckoning (rightly) that they were bringing Eton up with the times. The reaction was very different from Elliott's reign, when Birley had the utmost difficulty in appointing even one specialist English or Geography teacher.

Immediately results improved – they could hardly do otherwise. Taking some O levels early produced no adverse results, and very many more boys achieved three A levels with better grades. The tally of Oxford and Cambridge scholarships benefited also – the first award in Economics was won in 1963, in English in 1966, and in Geography in 1967 – and many more Oppidans were successful. Not all was accomplished in this first sweep – for example, many boys were still taking O level in December and thus had only five halves for A level work; but the framework was created, which enabled Eton to get continuously improving examination results without the excessive specialization of some other schools. By the end of the decade every Etonian was to have two years' A level work, even if this meant curtailment of the time before O level.

The new Provost had also to react to the Farrer Trust's offer. Some schemes were already afoot. Even before he arrived the Fellows had been impressed by the arguments of Geoffrey Agnew, John Carter, and Noel Blakiston* that the College should do something for its collections. There was also a plan for a rowing trench, which originated with a proposal by the Amateur Rowing Association that it should build an Olympic course for regattas on College land at Dorney.† The College was not keen on this, but the rowing Masters revived the plan, to be financed to some extent by gravel extraction, for an Eton course which could be leased to the ARA; conditions on the river were getting more difficult; indeed, in 1968 a boy was drowned when his boat was swamped by a river launch – the first fatality since 1882.‡ This plan, however, looked financially speculative – particularly as the ARA had no real funds to contribute.

Among other proposals the building of a theatre stood out. Etonian drama was flourishing, and more house plays were being mounted. Eventually the Fellows decided to build a theatre, if possible with a picture gallery. This occasioned a further wrangle among the Masters, with the theatrical lobby wanting a theatre in the round; while the Head Master and probably the Provost wanted a building which could be used for other purposes as well. The Head Master did not handle the meeting of Masters at all well – he was somewhat the worse for drink and some Masters abused him. That, however, did not prevent a fairly satisfactory outcome. The new theatre, designed by A.M. Gear, looks handsome inside, though its exterior is unappealing, and it serves its many purposes very well. A concession to the theatre lobby – the provision of a

---

* They were three Old Etonians distinguished as art dealer, bibliophile, and archivist, who gave the College helpful advice in their own fields.

† The College had bought the land on environmental grounds to curb the expansion of a ribbon development along the river bank, called Dorney Reach. Ironically the inhabitants of Dorney Reach were the most vigorous in condemning Eton's recent plans for a rowing lake – on environmental grounds.

‡ He was a Hertfordshire Scholar, and this made his death all the sadder. Nobody could be blamed for what was a complete accident.

thrust stage and some movable seats, to give a semblance of an open stage as well as a proscenium – increased the cost, and consequently there could be no picture gallery.

Another problem to face the Governing Body almost at once was the need to improve pay and pensions. In May 1965 salaries were increased by 12½%, which moved Eton salaries a little ahead of rival schools. Pensions were a greater difficulty: before 1952 Masters had a non-contributory pension one-third of final salary after full service, and those appointed after that joined a contributory Eton scheme which provided a pension of one half of final salary. Because of inflation and the substantial fall in real salaries since pre-war times, these sums were inadequate – especially for married men who commuted their pensions into joint annuities. The Finance Committee recommended an *ex gratia* increase be paid to those who had already retired, and decided that Masters should in future have the option of joining the State scheme which offered pensions of two-thirds of final salary, but only after forty years' service – a total which Eton Masters could not reach. Still the switch, which was keenly supported by the Head Master, did give Masters greater protection against political threats to Eton and against inflation. For those in the non-contributory scheme they recommended an immediate increase from £800 to £950 p.a., which raised the level very slightly above one-third of the new final salary of £2,700.

This improvement, however, only awakened older Masters to the inadequacy of their pensions. All the Housemasters felt that they deserved a supplementary pension – they were no longer able to save as their predecessors had done. They approached the Masters' Representative direct, and Lord John Hope, now in the Upper House as Lord Glendevon after his ministerial service, was convinced of the justice of their case. After a fierce struggle he persuaded the Fellows to appoint a Special Committee which did at the end of 1967 produce results acceptable to Masters. In addition the Committee recommended retirement at 64, a change which would benefit those in the State scheme. This change was made with singularly little consideration of the side-effects and against the advice of the Head Master; he was, however, able to secure a provision that Masters could be retired at 60 with some compensation. A more sensible further provision, which took account of the fact that many good Masters in the expanding staff would not become Housemasters, allowed ex-Housemasters and others such as Heads of Department who had contributed valuably to the School to reach a higher final salary, and thus gain a higher pension. This last provision has endured, but the age of retirement has reverted to 60.

A curious feature of the times was that the Finance Committee, which included former Housemasters, a serving Housemaster, and a future Housemaster was more cautious than in the end the Fellows proved to be. In practice at this time the Finance Committee was always anxious not to be self-serving, and some Masters thought it should fight harder for their interests. On the other hand, its recommendations were almost always accepted by the Fellows, which meant that the financial management of the School (as opposed to the College) was influenced by Masters, with considerable advantage.

Other controversies were dividing the community at this time. In the half before Caccia was installed as Provost, the Vice-Provost, Lambart, drew the Fellows' attention to a serious situation at the Choir School. Numbers were down from the twenty-eight aimed at to only twenty-one, barely enough to sing in Chapel, and the condition of the Brewhouse where the choristers were taught needed urgent attention. The value of a Choir School education was being questioned, and parents wondered whether chorister children would enter an educational dead end.* The Vice-Provost felt there were four possible courses: to do the minimum work on the Brewhouse; to make structural changes and try to continue with twenty-eight day boys; to aim at expanding the Choir to thirty-five or forty boys, with a few boarders, in a different building; or to develop a fee-paying prep school such as supplies the Choir to St George's Chapel in Windsor. This was the course favoured by the Head Master, who felt that such a prep school could be a vehicle for preparing a wider entry to Eton. The last two courses would be extremely expensive, and the new Provost thought that he should at least talk to the Dean of Windsor about the possibility of combining Choir Schools – not quite the same as the arrangement which had prevailed until the 1870s when Choirs did double duty. There was also a problem getting enough lay clerks to provide the men's voices; Eton Music Masters were

---

* Old choristers are loyal to their school; their subsequent careers, and the reminiscences published in 1993, suggest that they were in fact well educated.

being recruited to sing services as well as to teach. A link with St George's, however, did not seem possible, and in June 1965 the Fellows decided to make a success of a day Choir School. A temporary building was put up; three bursaries a year were to be awarded for choristers to go on to Eton. A new headmaster had some success with this policy, raising the numbers to thirty-eight.

During these discussions, however, it became clear that many at Eton did not value the cathedral-type services put on by the Choir. The clergy thought the Choir should only be an aid to congregational worship. There was no merit in an archaic institution. The clergy were indeed experiencing much greater difficulties in the more liberal atmosphere, with the value of collective worship more freely questioned in discussion and in the *Chronicle*. The Head Master sympathized with the wish to experiment in Chapel, and sided with the clergy – at about this time for instance a nave altar was introduced for Communion services, with chairs rather than pews at the east end.* It was left to the Precentor, Kenneth Malcolmson, who had himself enjoyed the choral services as a boy at Eton and been led to a career as cathedral organist, to defend the Choir.

By the summer of 1967 when the Fellows appraised their 1965 decision, the Choir School was still causing anxiety. Both running costs and the capital costs of a new building were well above the original expectation. Even the expanded School was felt to be too small. The Fellows, faced with the end of the permission to have a temporary building, decided in March 1968 to close the School in summer 1969. Again they tested the possibility of a merger with St George's – but St George's, with its regular choral services, did not believe that its requirements could coexist with Eton's; the administrative difficulties would also have been immense. The Fellows agreed that the money saved from the Choir School should be used to further music at Eton, and the three annual awards available for the choristers would now be open to a wide field – with the prospect of more Music Scholarships to be awarded in the future, once obligations to the boys of the Choir School were met.

There were Masters who felt passionately that the Founder's wishes had been betrayed. It was true that the Fellows had no statutory obligation to run a Choir School, but they had permis-

---

* The Head Master was devout, and the Provost allowed him more discretion in Chapel than any of his predecessors would have done.

sion to do so, and the Founder had certainly established a choir initially. Furthermore, the Choir School educated freely boys who could (but did not always) come from very poor backgrounds. Many Masters were worried, but believed that the new arrangements might work at least to the musical advantage of Eton. And so it has turned out.*

In practice the Choir School closed in the summer of 1968, because parents naturally wanted to re-establish their sons elsewhere rather than wait to the last moment. The College made grants to pay for all who did not get awards elsewhere, and a number of boys were placed at Eton itself. A new voluntary choir of boys was recruited – a group of some ninety singers with a smaller select group to aim at a higher standard. The voluntary choral services on Sundays naturally ended, but one good congregational service with anthems each Sunday could be continued, and a basis was established which could be steadily improved.†

Nor was the Choir School the only institution dropped at this time. A change of Missioner in Hackney Wick ended the lively clubs, substituting a devout and quiet style which did not easily appeal to the Etonians who visited. Etonians wished to give to causes of their choice, rather than to one that their ancestors had chosen, and they saw their contributions to the Mission more as a levy than an act of charity. There was increasing affluence in East London. Arthur Villiers was winding up the Eton Manor Clubs at the same time: the coming of motor cars and television had reduced the need for the provision of leisure facilities; the days of social clubs, he said, had gone. Consequently the Eton Mission gave the buildings to the London Diocese with a small endowment fund which had been built up. In theory the Mission became the parish of St Mary of Eton, but the old links did not die completely. Not all sources of finance at Eton dried up, and it is still possible to help the parish. Sadly the prospect of better times proved illusory, and in the 1980s deprivation and violence have returned to an area where so much good had been done in the name of Eton.

Meanwhile at Eton a new institution was set up with its first

---

* The Brewhouse, where the Choir had been taught, became the Exhibition Gallery.

† At this time Music Masters (and Art Masters) were brought on to the same salary scale as other Masters, though they did come to an earlier plateau – which was intended to encourage them to move to other posts by middle age.

open meeting in May 1969 – Eton Action, which was to be a sort of holding company for Eton's charitable activities. It was not possible by modern charity law to give the boys as much control on paper as they had been permitted eighty years earlier when the Mission was founded, but in practice they decided what causes to support. Eton Action has run numerous fund-raising projects, notably sponsoring an annual Fair which has been very popular in the locality. It does support Eton Social Services and the Eton-Dorney Project (a conference centre and holiday home in Dorney); but inevitably there is not the close involvement that was possible for Etonians in the best days of the Eton Mission.*

Other controversial initiatives did not come to complete fruition. One such surfaced at the end of 1965, and it seems clear that the Provost was responsible. Eton should give up school dress. He himself regarded formal dress as stuffy,† but more importantly he recognized that Eton's anachronistic clothes were perceived by the external world, however wrongly, as evidence of Eton's conservatism. The Head Master may have felt that a change was desirable, but in any case was disposed to accept the wishes of his reforming Provost. A meeting of Masters was convened in December to discuss school dress, and for Trench it went disastrously wrong. There were men who spoke for change, but they were divided: some argued that Eton dress had followed smart fashion until the late nineteenth century and that what was now needed, therefore, was for the School to go into dark suits, and others said that if there were to be change, it must be the abolition of any uniform whatsoever – boys were admittedly hostile to school dress, but they would be more hostile to the imposition of a new uniform. These voices, however, were a small minority – and rather to the Head Master's surprise, mainly drawn from the supposedly tradition-bound Old Etonian Masters. Overwhelmingly others spoke for retention. One of the most pervasive traits of Eton Masters is a dislike of having their minds made up for them. Now they pointed out that tail coats were classless in their total absence of distinguishing marks, that they were economical, hard wearing, and no

---

* Eton Action's first campaign, on behalf of the housing charity Shelter, raised nearly £5,000 – about £50,000 in 1990s money.

† Some lucky Masters much enjoyed overhearing Harold Macmillan rebuking Harold Caccia for wearing brown shoes with a grey suit.

more extravagant than any other uniform. Whatever the uniform, boys would not wear it in the holidays – simply because it would carry the stigma of school uniform. In despair the Head Master turned to an American Master at Eton on exchange: Trench had not noticed that he wore tails not only on Sundays as some traditionalists habitually did, but on weekdays also. 'You must think our dress absurd', said the Head Master. 'Oh, no. I like my cutaway', replied Dr Clerke. In January 1966 the Head Master had to report to the Fellows that change was not practicable then. His own views had altered, he said; and he told them that the Hertfordshire boys unanimously favoured school dress.

One valuable and overdue change, however, did occur on which there could be general agreement: Eton jackets were abolished for the smaller boys. Late-developing boys often worry about their stature, and the different dress added to their disquiet. It was announced that everyone would wear tails from September 1967, and new boys, however small, were at once admitted in tails. This was in fact the second change to deal with a possible sense of inferiority – for Robert Birley had abolished the wearing of caps with change clothes, which used to be compulsory for all but Sixth Form, and which made the older non-athletic boy visible by the obligation to wear the so-called 'scug cap' that was uniform for younger boys. Both these changes were most desirable, but they did not deal with the problem of the external image of school dress.

In 1969 the Fellows returned to the attack, this time arguing that Eton must cut its costs in the face of inflation, and that school dress must be abandoned for the sake of economy. A committee of Masters did accept that Eton's clothes were more expensive for the new parent than other schools', but a more prudent confidential approach by the Head Master to Housemasters alone revealed that all but two (who were against any uniform) wished to preserve school dress, and that they were unanimous that change at that time was wholly unwise: Eton had seen so many changes, and particular odium would attach to a new Head Master, soon to take office, if he were associated unfairly with an unpopular reform. This view was accepted, and since then the school dress issue has been quiescent. Boys have indeed been asked for their opinions, but have shown that they would rather retain their distinctive uniform than change to another uniform; there is no reason to think that the boys of the 1960s would have reacted any differently had they been offered the chance to express more than hostility to uniform in general.

Another partially resisted pressure for change was over the arrangements for winter games. The appeal of soccer, very much more popular than rugger, was growing, and the experts felt, with some justice, that their season in the Lent Half was too short, and that they had to play schools which had built up teams over the autumn. Some wished soccer to become the School's main game, replacing the Field Game even as the main inter-house game. The rugger players were also dissatisfied with the existing arrangements, since they also played other schools at a disadvantage; but rugger was not a feasible house game since Eton houses are too small to produce 15-a-side teams. There was also comment in the *Chronicle* that the Field Game was responsible for the absence of school spirit at Eton, because it was not an inter-school game, and Etonians therefore were never habituated to cheering for an Eton team; this was not, of course, quite true since Etonians did support the XI at Lord's and the VIII at Henley, though not with the zeal of their opponents. It was odd that the *Chronicle* should support school spirit, regarded as a typical public school value, just when rebellion against traditional institutions was gathering pace. It was also odd that boys should have become more competitive on the school level at this time, and not entirely because of the influence of the Masters coaching them.

The Head Master handled this issue well. A committee of Masters was appointed which reported in 1967, giving a full analysis of the problems and requirements of X boys, the most expert 10%, Y boys, the 80% of adequate performers, and the Z boys' to whom games were misery. They recommended more indulgence to these, both by the encouragement of non-games activities, which should be allowed to count as Times,* at least in part, and by setting up Minor Sports Days to give all a chance to develop enthusiasm for the variety of other sports available. The committee was united in rejecting the course of action which was eventually implemented, a switch of activities between the Lent and Michaelmas Halves, and a majority favoured the abandonment of the Field Game. A poll of boys, however, revealed that a small majority preferred to keep the Field Game as the main game

---

* This proposal encouraged the reckoning of a visit to the School of Mechanics, for example, as an acceptable Time, or exercise, once or twice a week.

(mostly Y boys). So the only change made was to start soccer and rugger in the last few weeks of the Michaelmas Half. Yet by the summer of 1970 opinion had swung enough for those wanting change to be a majority; only Housemasters still tended to support the Field Game. It was then easy for a new Head Master to change the arrangements in 1971. The Field Game has clung on, perhaps under increasing difficulties, operating for a limited season of the Lent Half. Some still resent it as a diversion from better-known games – others remain grateful for a game which the boys themselves can largely run and which is free from pressures to compete with other schools.

The Games Committee's report stated : 'It may be regretted, but it cannot be denied that ... games in schools have tended to become professionalised'. No doubt the media were to blame. Even the Field Game was affected, with some houses kicking for touch (as in rugger), which was within the laws but against the spirit of the game. This professionalism could nevertheless bring valuable results. The most notable sporting achievement of Trench's time was the VIII's triumphs of 1967. After winning the Princess Elizabeth Cup for schools at Henley, the VIII represented the United Kingdom in the World Junior Championships in West Germany. The Americans scoffed at the relaxed approach of the 'long-haired Limeys', but the Etonians were victorious. The next year the East Germans, absent in 1967, were far more powerful, but Eton won the Silver Medal; and in 1969 an Eton IV won a Silver Medal.

It was characteristic of Tony Trench that he should have encouraged Eton to compete overseas, and a break with the negative attitude that Birley had shown to similar suggestions. It was a great strength that any Master with a good idea could hope to get it adopted in a way that had not happened before, and the School was full of men with ideas for change. Thus in 1968 there was an Arts Week to lay before boys some of the more ex-perimental work in the visual arts. From 1964 Music Circle Concerts were introduced by Inniss Allen to enable boys to perform chamber music in a less daunting atmosphere than the School Concert; and these continue vigorously to this day. Two industrial conferences were held, with the enthusiastic support of the Provost, which were designed to awake Etonians to the challenge of industry; once again these were warmly received, and have been continued with only small variation. It was also possible for a Head of General Studies in 1967 to introduce Eton wives to the schoolroom, an innovation as obvious as it was overdue, considering the extra expertise that some wives have been able to bring. And with the completion of the Farrer Theatre, which opened in 1968, there was an explosion of theatrical activity.

There were many new beginnings, but at least one end – to the fireworks on the Fourth of June. The celebrations of that day had always been viewed with apprehension at Eton. It was a very long day to be spent leisurely seeing the exhibitions, watching cricket, drinking with Housemasters, picnicking, parents talking to parents – sons sometimes impatient or pursuing decorative girl-friends. At either end of the day there were picturesque ceremonials, one the enjoyable survival of Speeches by Sixth Form, the other the romantic Procession of Boats immediately after dark, followed by fireworks. In the long preliminary wait much alcohol was consumed. And then there could be an anti-climax, for Fellows' Eyot is not a natural arena – only those on the river bank could see action on the river. Large crowds, reinforced towards the evening by young Old Etonians and others coming down after work, would grow disorderly. Attempts to control the crowds by tickets hardly worked. Claude Elliott used to fortify himself against the approach of the Fourth by remembering that 'it's one day nearer to the fifth of June'. In Robert Birley's time, in 1958, there was nearly a disaster when four cadets from Sandhurst, two of them OEs, thought it would be a merry jape to explode gun-cotton in the river opposite the enclosure for distinguished guests – drenching them all; the explosive drifted in a strong current under the raft where oarsmen disembarked, and would have caused considerable harm had it been detonated.* Then in 1966, Provost and Head Master, shocked by the bad behaviour of the crowd, thought to number about 7,500 with many interlopers, determined to end the evening festivity. From 1967, the Procession of Boats was moved to 6.30 p.m., losing much of its effect, after which boys could take supper with their parents – or parents could simply melt away. Boys accepted this decision with some regret but at least understanding, while on the Masters' side there was considerable relief.

There had always been a few boys in disciplinary trouble after

* The wiring was faulty. Birley showed great determination in pursuing the miscreants.

the Fourth, but it was the behaviour above all of young adults that caused the curtailment of celebrations. Generally in the 1960s it was the behaviour of the boys themselves that was to create problems for the School, along with almost every other educational institution. Adolescence is an age of experiment, and in the 1960s boys were suddenly presented with two largely new areas of exploration, drugs and girls. The first was to be a continual worry from 1966, when steps had to be taken to educate Masters in diagnosis and attempts were first made to warn boys of the risks they were running. The change in attitude of teenage girls who had previously been restrained from early sexual adventure, and who had tended to be more interested in any case in older males, was perhaps of greater significance. Thus sexually active boys were less frustrated than they had been previously. One benefit was that from this time Housemasters had less anxiety about homosexuality among their boys; it did not disappear completely, but became very rare. Indeed Etonians have developed an almost excessive horror of homosexuality over the years, for instance even shunning shops where an attendant is rumoured to be homosexual, and becoming as prudish among other males as Victorian maidens. On the other hand, Housemasters had more trouble from girls and from the behaviour that they induced in boys; often they met the excuse familiar since Adam, 'The woman ... she gave me of the tree' – fruit which might be cigarettes, drink or even drugs.

At this time too there was the social revolution associated with the growth of pop culture. Fashion, which had percolated down through society, now moved in the other direction. Boys were determined to look and sound as much like their contemporaries as possible. Scruffiness and long hair became appealing, and senior boys were no longer willing to check the appearance of their juniors – even though members of Pop themselves retained a certain elegance. Masters were drawn into an uphill struggle to maintain dress regulations – which had hitherto not been needed. Once Masters began to intervene, any hope of senior boys regarding this as a matter for their discipline disappeared. By 1968, the Fellows were pressing the Head Master to improve boys' appearance.

The 1960s were also a time to question any authoritarian decision. School rules needed to be justified to young Etonian rebels – who were almost as likely to display posters of Che

Guevara as of curvaceous models in their rooms. Difficult boys would describe other difficult boys as 'sincere', meaning that they paid no lip-service to convention and quite frankly behaved badly. Such boys were very much a minority, and for the great majority school life was not so very different from that of their fathers. Games were still to be contested; work was even of increased importance as boys met greater competition for university places. In the mid-1960s, in a *Chronicle* poll, 80% of Etonians described themselves as happy or very happy at Eton – and the figure would not have been very different at the end of the decade. Yet even a small group of bad boys has a corrosive effect out of proportion to its numbers in a house, and it was unquestionably more of a struggle for Housemasters to maintain proper values in their houses than had formerly been the case.

The more troublesome behaviour of boys inevitably meant more work for the Head Master. The pastoral side of the schoolmaster's life was what he felt particularly called to, and he did have insight into boys' behaviour. He endeavoured to fit the punishment to the boy – which is probably a better policy than fitting the punishment to the crime. He could forgive boys if leniency was likely to be rewarded; but very often – even with boys in their last year – he would beat offenders; he felt that boys accepted beating if it was 'done with love'. Routine offences of Etonians are dealt with in the Head Master's and Lower Master's Bills, and are recorded in books open to Masters; more serious matters such as stealing or sexual misdemeanours are noted in confidential books. Trench dealt with more cases outside the Bill than others, and yet even the Bill Book reveals much more resort to beating than had been customary for many years. In the Lent Half, 1966, when Trench reported to the Fellows that the discipline of the School had been particularly good, eight boys in the Upper School had either been beaten (caned) or flogged (birched); under Birley three or four cases would have been normal, for such offences as cheating in Trials or climbing out of a house at night. In other halves the comparison would have been much more unfavourable – and on top of that were the private beatings. These were generally not approved by boys – Chenevix-Trench himself had written a Roman History text in which the Emperor Nero was commended for ceasing to deal with offenders *intra cubicula*, in his private chambers; should he not follow Nero? There was also a tendency to overdo punishment – 'a good thing the N.S.P.C.C. do not know anything about it', he remarked once. Against this, more boys would perhaps have been sacked under a different regime – and with the onset of drugs the numbers dismissed did in any case rise.

Certainly many boys, including some habitual offenders, liked Chummy, as he was known to Masters and boys. He was very ready to be friendly to all, and an extending arm would embrace anybody with whom he was conversing. A Captain of the Oppidans reported:

> He is very affable and tells one everything (FAR more than he should by any standards!) He will support you against a beak in any circumstances, providing one clears the ground first ... He will say to you when some house beak complains later: 'Dear old ... (Christian name) he's got a very low flashpoint.' His reputation, which is bad, is wholly undeserved and should be erased at the earliest opportunity. It springs from two sources, both of which are quite innocent – 1: he is very pally, and 'dear' and 'darling' have become a habit with him. 2: he beats in his house, which is under certain circumstances fair enough.

The next Captain of Oppidans, however, simply remarked that he found Chummy physically repellent.

Chenevix-Trench was opposed to beating by boys, though he was quite happy if Housemasters beat. The boys of their own accord were turning increasingly against corporal punishment, and the Head Master's reputation encouraged this. In 1965 a motion disapproving corporal punishment was only lost 78–72, a result which surprised the boys themselves.[1] By 1970 beating in houses had become so rare that it caused anxiety to the senior boys: indeed once it had ceased to be generally accepted it was plainly better dropped, and in 1971 it was formally stopped.

The Head Master's use of corporal punishment caused anxiety to Masters who often disapproved on principle, and who feared a scandal. They were also embarrassed by the Head Master's drinking, which the boys apparently took for granted and forgave readily; his breath often smelt of alcohol in Chambers, and on one occasion he had evidently fortified himself before preaching at evensong. On other occasions his exhaustion was interpreted as drunkenness; his wise and loyal Lower Master at this time, Martin

Forrest, relates one occasion when he displayed the symptoms without having touched a drop of drink.

A more damaging problem in the long run was Trench's desire to please everyone. Contrary and incompatible assurances would be given to different Masters. Unpleasant decisions, such as have to be faced by any headmaster, were fudged. The position of the Head Master accordingly became an issue: feelings were relayed back to the new Masters' Representative, Sir Michael Cary. In the summer of 1968 there was some trouble in one particular house, which came to the notice of the Provost and Fellows. The Head Master did not dismiss the Housemaster concerned, but honourably wrote to the Provost offering his own resignation as the man ultimately responsible. This was refused, but after more parents' feelings had become known, the Head Master was urged to replace the Housemaster; the matter was not well handled and further damaged Trench's standing with both Fellows and Masters. In 1969, it became clear that parents generally were becoming disquieted. In 1969 and 1970 the School was not full – the actual dip in numbers was small, but with the rebuilding, extra beds were available. This was principally caused by bad planning – Housemasters should have been told much earlier to promise more places than they did – but the reputation of the Head Master was a contributory factor.

The Provost at least had been aware for some time of the Head Master's problems; the Vice-Provost, by now Coleridge, from his time as Lower Master must have realized that all was not well even earlier. Whether a firmer line from above in, say, 1966 would have helped Chenevix-Trench is impossible to say. In the event in Lent 1969 the Fellows had to decide whether the Head Master must go. They, too, had picked up rumours from parents. They were aware of his administrative weakness and his vacillation; they realized that he was physically not up to the job – and indeed his health, mental and physical, was an anxiety. Fellows who had helped appoint Chenevix-Trench were perhaps more reluctant to admit that a wrong choice had been made, and were more inclined to attribute the Head Master's problems to Housemasters. Really, however, the only question was one of timing. Sir Michael Cary carried out a poll of Housemasters. A decision was made to let the Head Master go after a decent interval: the summer of 1970 was agreed. The Provost handled the dismissal well, and Trench, who was basically a humble man, accepted it with dignity and without surprise. Indeed, once he knew he was going, he was less anxious to please and found decisions easier. The press continued to be favourable to him, and when his departure became public, the Head Master was represented as a reformer defeated by the forces of conservatism.* *Private Eye* had carried an article entitled 'Jolly Beating Weather', but there was nothing worse.

The judgement that Trench's desire to reform had been defeated could hardly have been wider of the mark. The most valuable changes of the period originated with Masters, but Trench was remarkably open to ideas, and the School was fundamentally in a stronger position in 1970 than it had been in 1963. Some evidence to support this came from the visitations under the Newsom Committee, appointed by the Labour government in December 1965 to advise on integrating the public schools with the State system. Eton was visited by three of the Commissioners in November 1966, but not those most hostile to independent education. They were charmed and impressed. Professor Vaizey, before he departed, described Eton as 'the only good school I have ever seen'. In a more sophisticated judgement which must particularly have pleased Tony Trench he remarked, 'Eton seems to me to have made an effortless leap from the eighteenth to the twentieth century without going through all that Arnold rubbish'. Before the Commissioners left they suggested that the College Examination should be altered along the lines on which it was actually developing† – to be open to as wide a field as possible, not just those classically trained at preparatory schools; that each house might contain, along with thirty fee-payers, ten Oppidan Scholars, and ten boys with a boarding need paid for by the State. The Eton community felt that they could live with this. In the summer of 1967 Dr Royston Lambert, who was leading a research team on behalf of the Commission, was also impressed. Eton was the last school he visited, and he thought it utterly different. 'The boy has a prominence that makes him the centre of attraction of the whole system.' He recognized that Etonians seemed to erect a protective wall, perhaps as a consequence of being too much in the public eye,

---

* Chenevix-Trench's expert handling of the media extended beyond the press. In 1965 there had been a slightly artificial but favourable film about Eton on BBC Television. ITV carried a broadcast of a Sunday Service, as did BBC radio.

† In 1968, Latin became an optional paper in the Scholarship.

but the freedom of Eton (even for girls to be around) appealed to
him. In the sociologists' jargon he described Eton as less *total* than
any other school, except Dartington Hall.[2]

In fact the Newsom Commission was effectively shelved by the
Government who were not keen on any scheme that would cost
money. The Provost, who had been on the Governing Bodies
Association and Head Masters' Conference Committee which
considered the response to be made by the independent schools,
began from 1968 to direct Fellows' attention to a possible loss of
charitable status rather than to a fundamental change to Eton
itself. Eton, the most obvious target of abolitionists, had survived
critical examination well, and that must be to the Head Master's
credit.

The average annual number of academic awards in the second
half of the 1960s was 30% higher than in the first half; A level
results were continually improving, and Etonians were increasingly finding places in Universities other than Oxford or Cambridge.
The non-academic life of the School flourished, and musical and
theatrical standards in particular were rising remarkably. There
were also some notable sporting achievements: in 1970 Eton
cricketers had fine victories over Winchester and Harrow, and the
tennis team won the Youll Cup for schools for the first time since
the 1940s. Social life was probably more good-tempered too,
partly thanks to the Head Master. Leave regulations had been
eased, and senior boys could obtain permission, for example, to
visit London for concerts. If this leave was sometimes abused and
discipline suffered, there was a gain from boys feeling less corral-
led. Within houses, too, a friendlier tone prevailed, as the use of
Christian names spread even between fags and fagmasters and as all
types of punishment became rarer – with only a limited loss of
good order.

Nobody could say that Trench's headmastership was a tragedy
for Eton. It was, however, something of a tragedy for him and for
his much-loved wife Elizabeth. To her Eton owes the Society she
started for the ladies of Eton, called the Jane Shore Society – most
inappropriately considering that the members were ladies of
unimpeachable rectitude and Jane Shore was the prostitute reputed
to have saved Eton by her advocacy with King Edward IV. She and
Tony together had great sympathy for those in misfortune, and by
ill chance there were more personal disasters in this period than at

other times at Eton.

Certainly there was no feeling of ill-will when they left, no doubt partly because they did not fight against their fate. The Head Master was given two years' salary, and retained the right to favourable terms for his sons to come to Eton. The Fellows dined him out at Brooks's. And there were the usual presents. After a year quietly spent at their Hampshire cottage, he became Head-master of Fettes, where he recaptured some of the success he had enjoyed at Bradfield, and there sadly he died just before his time for retirement.

CHAPTER THIRTEEN

Innovation and Consolidation

THE PROVOST AND Fellows were naturally eager to avoid another embarrassment in choosing the next Head Master. They had plenty of time to make enquiries and were sure that the man they wanted was Michael McCrum, Headmaster of Tonbridge; but not so confident that he would accept, they had several good candidates in reserve. In fact they were persuasive enough to secure McCrum, a man of ample experience who would be 46 when he took office. He had taken the Eton Scholarship unsuccessfully – which he later felt gave him the detachment to rule Eton. Instead he obtained scholarships at Sherborne and at Corpus Christi College, Cambridge. After service in the Navy and a distinguished undergraduate career reading Classics, he taught for a time at Rugby, where he met his admirable wife Christine, his Headmaster's daughter. He returned to Corpus as Tutor, and then Senior Tutor – an experience which was useful as a preparation for Eton, the Senior Tutor's relationship to the Master of a Cambridge College being analogous to the Head Master's relationship to the Provost. In 1962 he became Headmaster of Tonbridge, and he acquired there a reputation for a commanding personality. Certainly he is in many ways the antithesis of Chenevix-Trench: he has exceptional ability to master issues and to make decisions; he is physically robust with a distinguished presence; it is hard to doubt that he would have reached a position of eminence in whatever career he had chosen.

Among the immediate problems to be tackled was the entry to the School. Though there was a chance vacancy list, known as the

General List, most boys were still put down at birth by individual Masters chosen by the Head Master to form house lists. This meant that parents, rather than boys, were selected, and that the Housemasters were not picked by the Head Master under whom they would hold their houses. Chenevix-Trench had appointed a committee to find ways of avoiding the shortfall of entrants, which had suggested that some boys on the General List, not necessarily put down at birth, could be guaranteed places when they were about 11 years old; parents without house places had been deterred by the uncertainty of chance vacancies and had taken safe places at their second-choice schools. The implementation of this recommendation before Trench left brought about a rapid improvement. A new committee on entry in 1972 had to consider whether it would be right to delay entry for all boys. This possibility attracted the Head Master, since he would have increased control over entry and appointment of Housemasters, and promotion to house lists later was in itself desirable since more Masters were being recruited after previous experience at other schools. It would be easier to select talented boys then than at birth. On the other hand, Masters were apprehensive of a longer wait in their careers before promotion. In the uncertainties of the inflationary times the School would lose the advantage of having a large number of boys firmly registered from birth. A compromise solution was adopted by which appointment to house lists was slightly delayed, and new Housemasters chose their first new boys from the General List. Inevitably there was a lag before the change took effect, but even in the 1970s there was a growing proportion of boys entering the School off the General List. Perhaps even more significant was the diminishing number of Old Etonians making house lists (only five in 1972); Old Etonian Masters tended to attract Old Etonian parents, who seldom changed their intentions to send their sons, whereas the others often started with a wider range of parents and subsequently drew more from the General List. Thus by 1980 there would be a few houses with up to 75% OE parents and perhaps only 10% off the General List, whereas others would have more like 25% OE parents and a majority of General List boys. The result has been a marked change in the composition of the School, despite Old Etonians being given some preference when the General List guarantees are offered, for many more parents from non-traditional backgrounds have been applying.

The system of guaranteeing places was to give the Head Master the opportunity to raise the Common Entrance standard. There was in any case an increased number of boys in the country as a whole at this time, and Eton quickly proved capable of attracting more. McCrum had been shaken to find on his arrival in 1970 that, despite the reforms of the 1960s, 10% of the boys completing their O levels in D Block had failed to obtain five O levels, regarded as a necessary base for the study of A levels. He determined to raise the Common Entrance level – a move unpopular with Old Etonians, who had often gone on to successful careers despite humble academic achievement. In fact the Common Entrance had sometimes to be used, not as was intended as a minimum standard, but as a competitive examination, for there were years when too many boys were promised places at Eton; the impact of inflation did not thin the entries as had been feared, and the reputation of the School soon recovered from its small dip in 1969–70. Unfortunately the Common Entrance is a very imperfect examination, and Eton rejected boys who subsequently achieved considerable academic success at other schools. Furthermore, preparatory schools scared a number of traditional Eton parents from even entering their sons for Eton Common Entrance. So this change also altered the social background of Etonians, possibly more than it actually raised the level of intelligence.

Even earlier, however, McCrum had secured a change in the Scholarship. He persuaded the Provost and Fellows to give five totally free scholarships, regardless of any means test (they had previously been free only to those who demonstrated need). This, and perhaps still more the rising reputation of the School, meant that the number of Scholarship candidates rose from just over forty on average to nearly seventy.* Also the Head Master induced the Provost and Fellows to part with their titular control over the Scholarship.

Furthermore, the Provost and Fellows agreed to follow the example of Tonbridge and institute Junior Scholarships for 10-year-old boys from the Home Counties in the State system. Those selected were given two or three years at preparatory schools before coming on to Eton. About half of them became King's

* The five automatically free places were dropped after 1992 following an agreement among schools about scholarships.

Scholars, and the other half were given free Oppidan places. For these boys the College incurred the extra expenditure of eight years' education; for those who became Collegers the additional cost was only the preparatory school years, for they replaced other boys in College. Up to six Scholarships p.a. were awarded, and the area of recruitment eventually enlarged. Junior Scholars and Music Scholars further extended the social spectrum of the School, even though the Hertfordshire bursaries ceased after 1974, as the County became unwilling to pay for them any longer.

The classical bias of the Scholarship Examination had been reduced when the classical papers ceased to be compulsory in 1967. The result was that the Collegers more frequently became Scientists. With the general rise in standards the number of Oxbridge awards continued to grow, reaching forty in 1979. In that year altogether eighty-four boys obtained admission to Oxbridge, about one-third; and another one-third went to other Universities. At the same time the O and A level results were improving – the pass rates at O level rising from 73% to 85%, and at A level from 86% to 95%. There can be no doubt that the academic performance of the School was improving, and Masters hoped that it was because Eton was doing a better job, not just taking in abler boys. It has to be granted that Eton's successes were gained at a time when the State system was offering less competition.

The increased numbers attempting to win Oxbridge places meant that more than half the boys stayed on after A levels to take the examination then held in December. The School became over-full, and rooms on private sides of boys' houses and in other Masters' houses were pressed into service. Furthermore, Eton welcomed a few girls to lessons from neighbouring schools which lacked the facilities for what was, in effect, scholarship teaching. Some boys were amazed that the Head Master should allow girls on the campus – an additional distraction at such an important juncture in their lives – but most were happy, even when girls who they knew to be weaker than themselves were successful at the traditional 'boys' subjects' and they were not. This so-called 'seventh-term' teaching was attractive and stimulating for Masters also. A few bachelors were nonplussed to find themselves without prior consultation facing a new problem – but they survived. At this time, too, there were occasional Masters' daughters admitted as day-girls for A levels – so few, however, that their condition was not really very natural: if some succeeded brilliantly, for others the stress was too great. Despite the economic attractions of a cheap Eton education, most Masters preferred to send their daughters to other schools.

The numbers staying on and the arrival of day-girls were naturally of substantial economic advantage to the School, which during the 1970s was obliged to raise its fees less than other schools. Yet the College contemplated this period of inflation with unjustified anxiety. Incomes generally kept pace with rising prices, and parents (and grandparents) were prepared to spend out of capital if necessary for what was seen to have lasting value. It was not, however, an easy period for Eton Masters. Initially Michael McCrum secured them a good salary rise, pointing out that the Eton scale was in some ways worse than that at Tonbridge; but periods of incomes policy hit Masters harder than most. Fellows, drawn from important positions in public life, would argue that Eton must be seen to be observing Government appeals for pay restraint. Despite occasional catching-up operations, Masters' salaries did not match the general increase of earnings in the country – though in this they fared no worse than other teachers. On the other hand Masters were helped with fringe benefits such as education allowances for daughters and reduced rents on their Eton accommodation. By a curious logic, it was believed that bachelors and Housemasters had a different rate of price rises from the rest of the staff, and at this period the extra payment for Housemasters, which had not in any case kept pace with inflation, was abolished. One aspect of inflation hit almost the entire staff – house price rises. Eton Masters are normally required to live in College houses so as to be accessible to boys at all times, and in the mid-1970s those who had no holiday homes found themselves very badly placed on retirement. The College responded by encouraging Masters to buy houses earlier with loans to top up mortgages. The consequences of Masters owning property away from Eton have been considerable, with hearts and bodies less wholly at Eton than was formerly the case.

The College's anxiety over inflation led to a number of economy measures which were unwelcome and felt by the Masters to be unnecessary.* Immediately on his arrival the Head Master had to give a view on a report which had been commissioned earlier on the feeding arrangements for boys. Much thought had been given to this question, and many 'solutions' had been rejected, before the proposals now propounded. The Head Master was against central feeding of a school, but the pressure from Provost and Bursar was considerable, and consequently in 1971 it was decided to build a hall capable of feeding half the houses, which could be extended to feed all the Oppidans should that be considered desirable. House-masters were almost unanimously opposed, and as a result the Head Master was reluctant to compel houses to move to central feeding. Also, rather more space was provided than pure regard for cutting costs would have decreed. As a result the building, discreetly built by Powell and Moya on one of the last green tongues reaching into the centre of Eton, failed in its primary objective of saving money. By the end of the decade it was still not cheaper to operate than individual houses. Gradually, however, its economics have improved: as Housemasters changed, more houses came in. Capital was saved when some of the last, and most difficult, houses to be modernized did not need to be given boys' kitchens and dining-rooms. Boys have been happy enough with the variety of food provided, but parents continue to regard Bekynton, as the complex is known, with disfavour. An education-al establishment should really insist that boys eat at least the main meal civilly together, rather than be processed in ten and a half minutes (as recommended by one of the School's more enthusiastic advisers). A bonus has been the provision at Bekynton of a Masters' Common Room, something which had never existed at Eton; this has proved a valuable meeting place at lunch-time for Masters whose wives were increasingly going out to work, or who were living alone. It has helped to prevent disunity which might

---

* Between 1932 and 1972 the number of boys increased from 1,124 to 1,228 and the number of Masters from 86 to 123. The Bursary computed the index figures for 1972 below (1932 = 100):

Retail prices	550
School fee	370
Payment per Master	340
Tuition costs	460
Boarding costs	290

These figures suggest that Eton did its best to resist inflation, to some extent at Masters' expense. In 1972, inflation was only beginning to gather pace.

easily have grown up in the staff, now that it is so much larger and private entertainment by Housemasters far less common.

Another economy which pained Housemasters, decided in 1975, was a reduction in the number of boys' maids. This at least made economic sense, since an extra room often became available for boys as boys' maids retired and were not replaced – the saving of wages was less significant. The move received a good deal of absurd press publicity, suggesting that Etonians for the first time would be making their own beds. The difference to the tidiness or cleanliness of boys' rooms was small, and to the boys' life negligible; but Housemasters, who valued the pastoral work of the best boys' maids, felt that a little less was fed back to them about boys' welfare. Altogether less controversially, the College at this time began to earn new income by using the facilities of the School in the holidays, and by charging tourists for admission; this last was as much to control a considerable nuisance as to make money.

A genuine economic casualty of this time was the School Stores. Small shops were suffering nationally, and Eton's shops with their limited season ceased to be viable. As a result the College established Eton College Services as a limited company to handle its commercial activities; and another company was soon formed to handle boat-building activities. The College has also been obliged to subsidize shops which it does not own but which are essential to the good operation of the School.

The Head Master had to tackle other immediate problems – one was the resistance to compulsory attendance at College Chapel, a symptom of the questioning attitudes of the young at the time. His solution was to make attendance at weekday services optional – with an Alternative Assembly held in School Hall. The intention was very much that this should not be a soft option – that the spiritual life of the boys should be catered for without the trappings of conventional religion. Lower Chapel remained traditional for the lower boys – and the problem of the School having grown too large for the two chapels was resolved by giving D Block its own programme, designed for 15-year-olds, in the Farrer Theatre. Success has been mixed. The assemblies in School Hall have sometimes been stimulating, and boys have had very valuable opportunities to put on their own programmes; but the spiritual content soon disappeared and often not very challenging fare has been provided to a passive audience. Meanwhile the hope that a better atmosphere would prevail in voluntary services in Chapel was partially disappointed. The clergy in their efforts to stimulate attendance seemed sometimes to regard novelty itself as a religious virtue. In the 1990s, boys are in Chapel more often, but the only elements of choice remaining are the C Sunday Communion introduced in the 1960s and a mid-week shortened Communion service. Otherwise different blocks of upper boys are assembled compulsorily on different days for services of varying styles.* At the time, in the 1970s, the change undoubtedly resolved a tension felt by older boys, but it is impossible not to review the religious scene with sadness. Eton does at least offer an experience of worship which is generally accepted, and a high proportion of the Anglicans are confirmed. The Choir sings beautifully and lessons are generally well read by boys, but the congregational singing seldom matches the volume or fervour achieved before 1960;† and whereas boys learned and loved the psalms, now only those of untaxing brevity are sung. In the 1940s Denys Wilkinson noted in his diary his dislike of Sunday early Communion if held in Lower Chapel – it was so crowded; that was a truly voluntary service on a day when each boy attended two compulsory services. Eton has clearly not escaped the malaise affecting the Church of England as a whole, and possibly the loss of confidence of those in authority was to blame in both cases. For Roman Catholics, however, now some 10% of the School, provision has improved. In the 1980s a resident chaplain was appointed for them; and in a new ecumenical spirit, they have returned to College Chapel for Confirmation services. Shortly before Cardinal Hume celebrated the first Mass there since the Reformation, College Chapel was struck by lightning, and this was interpreted by Provost Charteris as a divine exclamation mark in a spirit of approval.

The Head Master and the Governing Body were also confronted early on by a small eruption of discontent among the staff. This was largely a legacy of the fall of Chenevix-Trench. It was believed – in fact with only a touch of justice – that the Provost and Fellows blamed Masters, particularly Housemasters, for the troubles of the

---

* It is true that boys in B and C are entitled to attend services other than those for their own blocks, but very few do, and they are not encouraged to do so.

† It is fair to say that Chapel is less crowded; also the services occur sooner after boys rise, which apparently means they are in less good voice.

Head Master, and that McCrum had been told to whip Masters into line. Masters believed that the Fellows, distinguished but remote, had an inadequate picture of what they were thinking, and that some of the early moves by the Head Master were not addressing the real problems of Eton. A group of five senior and conservative Masters circulated a well-argued paper in 1972 to suggest that when Sir Michael Cary's term as Masters' Representative ended, two Masters should be elected to the Governing Body instead of a new outside Representative. A meeting under the chairmanship of the senior Assistant Master was hopelessly mismanaged – he made it so obvious that he felt nobody should support the dissident group that he united Masters behind the concept of at least some reform. The Head Master handled the situation skilfully – he persuaded the Fellows to introduce dinners before their meetings at which they could talk to Masters, and the traditional dinners on Founder's Day were resumed after forty years. Furthermore, a new openness about the agenda of the Fellows' meetings made it easier for Masters to make representations to the Head Master or to the Masters' Representative. When Sir Michael Cary died young in 1976 – much to the sorrow of Masters who appreciated his work for them – they found another Representative to look after their interests, David Hirst QC,* whose service now extends over more meetings than any other Fellow since the New Governing Body was created. This indicates in itself that a problem was solved.

To some extent, in everything mentioned so far, the Head Master was responding to problems brought before him. But in the middle of the 1970s he was able to initiate a reform of the curriculum at the bottom of the School, which had been left largely unchanged. In part he was responding to the demands of the specialist Divinity, English, and Geography teachers who had come to Eton to teach A levels, and who argued that they would achieve better results if they, rather than the Classicists, taught these subjects up to O level. He also was keen to improve the teaching of Music and Art, and to introduce Design into the curriculum other than as merely a voluntary option for specialists. An early battle was fought to provide a new School of Mechanics; it was doubtful whether the old building would have met the requirements of the Factories Act. Eventually a new, unglamorous

* Now Lord Justice Hirst.

structure funded by benefactors was erected, which was soon to fill up with busy boys solving problems of design and working in a variety of media, and to which the affectionate title 'School of Maniacs' was transferred. By the curriculum introduced in September 1977, Design joined with Art, Music, and Drama in providing a rotating programme of Creative Mornings for the bottom F Block into which all boys were now entering. Some boys' mornings were more creative than others, but at least boys had the chance to discover interests which could be pursued in E Block where an element of choice was introduced, and as one of the seven O levels in D Block. This new curriculum, which slightly increased the hours for English and Science, also in effect ended the old classical division, where one man taught some dozen varied periods. Classical Masters too became specialists, and inevitably fewer were needed. This rendered a classical Pupil Room no longer viable, and younger boys began to have Tutors who were not Classicists, and the main activity in the few tutorial periods still available changed from Latin to written English. Thus came about what was inevitable from the original Curriculum Committee's reforms under Chenevix-Trench: the demise of the system of classical division and classical Pupil Room on which Eton education had been based. The change was necessary, and has not damaged academic standards; but something of real value was lost. In the classical divisions Masters really saw the work across a broad spectrum and knew their boys as even exceptional teachers can hardly know them from three periods a week of one subject: the long perceptive classical reports which astonished parents new to Eton were an indication of this. And the classical Pupil Room provided a common fare upon which boys could be trained to methodical work under the Tutor's eye.

Acceptance that Classics was now just one form of specialist knowledge, with a little extra merit as a foundation of other disciplines, implied the end of the classical basis of the Newcastle Scholarship as Eton's most prestigious award. The Duke had intended to promote Divinity as well as Classics in the School, and from 1975 it was to be based on Divinity. But only in 1988 was a really satisfactory format found with a theoretical paper based upon an accessible text and touching on theology and ethics, and a paper dealing with topical problems in religion, morals, and politics. Now the Newcastle has again attracted the competition of a high proportion of the ablest boys for the first time since the 1940s. There is a Newcastle Classical Prize as well.

McCrum also made a big impact on the social life of the boys. Between houses there had been considerable differences in the minor regulations of matters such as possession of wirelesses and the times for lights-out. In his first year or two, in the face of some antagonism from Housemasters, the Head Master obtained greater uniformity. By the end of his reign, a new disparity was growing up over access to television, with some Housemasters accepting its fairly extensive intrusion and others restricting use to a Saturday evening opiate. There has been little positive educational merit in any of the media for Etonians, but some relaxation in long, busy weeks is permissible, and Housemasters occasionally find removal of a hi-fi or the closure of a house television useful sanctions.

Rather more important was the eventual achievement of at least paper uniformity over fagging. By 1980 the Head Master could say that personal fagging had been abolished. Messages could still be sent arranging games – an attempt to obviate the necessity even of this by installing an inter-house telephone had failed owing to the destructive ingenuity of the boys. The end of fagging had been so generally heralded that no great emotions were aroused, and the Head Master received little hostile mail from traditionalists.

A rather different series of changes was occurring spontaneously, with the growing importance of A levels. Boys at the top of the School were increasingly reluctant to carry out the simple chores necessary for the running of a house. More duties devolved on to Debate, from the daily checking of rooms for tidiness to the more educational activities of training and umpiring junior football teams or coaching Baby Fours on the river. The Captain of the House and the Captain of Games retained their responsibilities, and often had the welfare of the house as much in their minds as their predecessors. And stern words to a delinquent from the house Captain can still be quite effective, even if the ultimate penalty of a beating is no longer available. Discipline is less rigidly maintained than it was, but most Masters agree that the slight relaxation is justified. Possibly the need for unceasing vigilance by Housemasters is even greater, and the art of running an orderly house without too heavy a hand may require yet greater skill than it did of old. Curiously, in the 1960s and 1970s, as traditional rules disappeared, the boys themselves clung to rites of initiation, notably those attached to Debate elections, and Housemasters had to be more on guard against them: it would seem that certain basic tribal instincts survive even when boys themselves claim to be increasingly civilized.

It has been a greater problem to ensure that order is maintained outside houses. Michael McCrum continued the efforts begun by Tony Trench to make Pop more like effective school prefects; but if they took on some new roles successfully, other things they used to do – from maintaining dress rules to acting against those whose public behaviour reflected ill on the School – were now neglected; and Pop patrols designed to detect delinquents in Windsor pubs could end with Pops in the pub, their patrols suspended. McCrum did have a limited success in creating useful public activities for Sixth Form Select, and they were rewarded by a new distinctive element to school dress, silver buttons on their waistcoats.

The Head Master made some innovations in his own conduct of discipline. He did continue to cane boys, though he abandoned the use of the birch, which he characterized, not unreasonably, as medieval. He also introduced new penalties – detention on Saturday evenings and rustication. Although some problems of adolescent behaviour receded in the 1970s, drinking became more common among younger boys, and even writing out the conclusions of various reports on smoking failed to deter smokers. From 1974, boys with personal problems had access to a psychiatric consultant, Dr Philip Boyd, who acted successfully as a discreet counsellor until his death in 1993.

The Head Master also introduced some useful relaxations: he allowed weekend leaves for boys in their A level year (and post-A level), and he regularized Long Leaves in the Lent and Summer Halves. In 1979 early school was finally abandoned, even in the summer – thus saving Masters the temptation of setting boys to read in their houses during early school, and saving Housemasters the impossible task of ensuring that boys did not go back to sleep when they were theoretically supposed to be working. And reluctantly he made concessions over informal dress, though he never abandoned the fight against long hair. Elliott had liked what he called 'the Highland cattle look', but McCrum had no such tenderness.

The Head Master was also aware that Masters, intensely absorbed in their jobs, could be ignorant of what was going on in other schools, and that the boys not only wanted more contacts with the outer world but could benefit from them. For some Masters he arranged annual meetings with colleagues from eleven schools in what was called the Eton Group. The cross-fertilization was valuable, even if it chiefly emphasized that all schools were facing similar problems. For games-players there were many more matches, particularly with the transposition of soccer and rugger to the Michaelmas Half.* For a few boys there were opportunities for exchange visits to comprehensive schools. For rather more there were visits to the Eton-Dorney Project before Confirmation; this conference centre was backed financially to a small extent by Eton Action, which from 1973 ran annual Community Fairs, open to participation by local charities and popular with the public. Girls from nearby schools began to join in the Musical Society's choral concerts, and a few were brought in to act in theatricals.

Furthermore the Head Master was keen to speak more with parents, who had formerly been accustomed to see the Head Master only when sons were in real trouble. Addresses to the parents of new boys in College Chapel have been much appreciated; other discussion groups were less successful – parents sometimes feeling that they pay large fees for expert attention to their sons, and that they consequently accept the professional advice of schoolmasters as readily as that of doctors or solicitors. There is, however, more consultation with Housemasters and Heads of Departments about sons' academic careers as the variety of possibilities and the complexity of arrangements have grown. Michael McCrum also addressed the boys in two groups in School Hall more regularly than his predecessors had done; communication meant more to him than to any Head Master since Alington. He worried, rightly, about the low state of public speaking by boys at this time. And characteristically he set to reforming the *Chronicle*, when it showed some deterioration from the rather high level of the 1960s. In 1973 it became a roughly fortnightly paper, on white rather than yellow paper, with photographs; the hope was that with more time for production and a larger editorial staff, a higher-grade publication could be achieved. Certainly the initial impact was good, but the *Chronicle* has had further poor spells since its reform; and it has not been a reliable paper of record.

* The change in the football arrangements was also the occasion for ending a late Victorian institution, Old Boys' Day. It passed without regret.

The decade continued to see much building activity. Apart from Bekynton, two notable achievements were the reconstruction of School Library, from an ugly inefficient building to something altogether more attractive and workable in 1971, and the new heated pool for which McCrum strove hard, and which was opened just as he was leaving. It replaced the open Fives courts which, seen across the School Field, had looked to Lord Quickswood like elephants' latrines. A temporary structure, which managed to create almost as much ferment as some of the grander architectural projects, was raised in 1977 to mark the Queen's Silver Jubilee. This red, white, and blue pyramid, prefabricated at the Drawing Schools, was placed over the Burning Bush, an ornate lamp-post which had stood since 1864 as *the* recognized landmark in the centre of the Slough Road until in 1963 it was moved adjacent to School Library, permitting a more orthodox traffic island. The boys, from all but the house most involved in its construction, were outraged by the pyramid and petitioned for its removal – at least from the Burning Bush. But boys soon accept any novelty as traditional, and they were equally outraged when some days later in the middle of the night it was rammed to destruction by a car driven by young Old Etonians – and boys who had witnessed the assault were prepared to report the registration number of the car, which led to the apprehension of the offenders.

In that summer of 1977 Harold Caccia retired. He had presided over the continued renovation of Eton, as well as being Provost through some other striking changes in the Eton environment. The building of the Eton Relief Road in 1968, and the closure of Windsor Bridge to vehicles in 1970 made central Eton far more agreeable for pedestrians;* though what was gained on the ground was lost overhead, as air traffic grew and lessons were continually disrupted by noise which made teaching impossible. (During the 1980s traffic increased again, but aeroplanes became less noisy.) In the years from 1973 to 1976 the appearance of Eton was changed by Dutch elm disease. The College fought against this vainly by injections as well as by a policy of felling and burning. The appearance of the Thames Valley was changed, but the College

---

* Before the bypass opened over 26,000 vehicles daily passed along the High Street; this fell immediately to 11,000 and almost vanished when the bridge was closed.

grounds have recovered their well-furnished look through extensive replanting.

The Provost had been a considerable force for the modernization of Eton, as much by affecting the style of its management as by any particular decisions. He also created a better framework for the preservation and exhibition of Eton's treasures. Partly out of anxiety, which much occupied the College in the mid-1970s, that Eton would lose its charitable status, a Collections Trust was set up to safeguard the College Library, and so on; and outside advisers of distinction helped to direct policy. Over the last twenty years more has been done to make available to boys and to the general public Eton's heritage – assets which are a burden rather than an advantage from the narrow perspective of financing a School, but which the College has tried to look after responsibly.

To succeed Harold Caccia, the Fellows asked for the appointment of the Queen's Private Secretary, Sir Martin Charteris. Though it is too soon to pass judgement, there can be no questioning the wisdom of their choice. The new Provost, created Lord Charteris of Amisfield on his retirement from the royal service, was able to build on the foundations he inherited, guiding Eton with humour and wisdom through the 1980s; and the reader who would like to know more of his character need only look back to the perceptive sketch of him as a boy quoted in Chapter 8.

At his last College meeting Caccia was still lamenting that not enough Etonians were going into industry. Indeed for all the industrial conferences and business visits, despite the foundation of a Keynes Society by enterprising boys, and despite the popularity of Economics (taken at its peak year by just over half the specialists at A level), the 1970s were years when Etonians headed for careers in financial services; accountancy became the most common profession. It is possible that the more hostile outside world, sapping Etonian self-confidence, was inducing boys to look after themselves more aggressively than their predecessors; characteristics sometimes called Thatcherite were to be discerned at Eton before the 1980s.*

The competitive element was perhaps one legacy of McCrum's headmastership. It is again too soon to attempt a full assessment, but there was no doubt in anyone's mind when he left Eton in 1980

* Dr John Rae in his memoirs, *Delusions of Grandeur*, remarks on the same phenomenon at Westminster School.

to be Master of his old College, Corpus Christi, that the 1970s would be seen as very much his decade. His emphasis on promoting Eton as a centre of excellence had borne fruit in academic achievement. Sporting success was modest, but Music and Art flourished. The innovation of artist Tutors – young people to help part-time at the Drawing Schools – introduced useful diversity into the teaching skills, and the longer sessions available in the new timetable were also valuable. Other innovations had a more mixed reception: there were times when McCrum's desire to introduce the most up-to-date practices of other schools provoked almost automatic hostile reaction among Masters. There was much to recall the parable of the sower; the seed of innovation sometimes fell by the wayside – attempts to bring local schools into Eton activities failed because of a basic difference in objectives and in timetable; sometimes it fell on shallow ground – promising ideas such as a Police Cadet group, or talks for boys in C Block with Marriage Guidance Counsellors about personal relations, failed to take lasting root; but what has been written above shows that much fell upon rich soil. To the basic management of Eton, too, he brought greater skill than any Head Master since Dr Warre in his prime. His qualities were to bear further fruit in his years at Cambridge, where he was Vice-Chancellor from 1987 to 1989.

The Fellows were again fortunate to have a good candidate for Head Master and wise enough to identify him. Eric Anderson, Headmaster of Shrewsbury, had a varied background in independent education. A pupil at George Watson's College, he passed to St Andrew's University and then Balliol College, Oxford. His subject was English Literature, his hero Sir Walter Scott. He had taught at Fettes and Gordonstoun before becoming Headmaster of Abingdon School in 1970, going on to Shrewsbury in 1975, winning a considerable reputation all along the way. He has been notably assisted by his wife Poppy; Eton has once again been extremely fortunate in the Head Master's wife, and she has exceeded all others in the amount she personally contributed to the School: no other wife has been so well known to the boys. Their son had just completed a successful career in College, demonstrating the Andersons' regard for Eton. A technical problem, that the Statutes required that the Head Master should be a member of the Church of England, whereas Anderson was a member of the

Church of Scotland, was solved by amending the Statutes.* On appointment he was aged 44.

After all the activity of the Chenevix-Trench and McCrum years Masters were hoping for a more stable regime, and this they were granted: the School was to be run with good sense and a forward look, but without radical change. Nevertheless the Head Master did stamp his own mark on the curriculum, for instance in a new emphasis on modern languages and computing, and in the priorities for building. Some adjustments to the curriculum have been driven by external developments, notably the change from O levels to GCSE; thus English is no longer taken in E, but by every boy in D. Mathematics remains compulsory in D, but History no longer is. The very broad base and wide choice in D has been retained, and Etonians take normally nine or ten out of over twenty possible GCSEs. Some relaxation of the Eton week was achieved when the maximum number of periods taught, which had been only twenty-five in the week until Trench's time, was reduced from thirty-five to thirty-two. In the College's investment programme priority was given to another reconstruction of the Science Schools, and this was followed by modernization of other schoolrooms and the renovation of the Gymnasium. The most notable requirements still to be met are enlargements of the Drawing Schools and Music Schools to match the heavy demands made by the popularity of both these activities.

The capital position of the College had in one sense continued to improve – its assets had become more liquid. One sale, planned in the 1970s, matured in the 1980s, and made a considerable difference. Cippenham Farm, purchased by the Land Fund in the 1920s, was a small farm squeezed between Slough and the M4, and this was sold to Slough for development; one part of it unexpectedly, but certainly to Eton's advantage, received planning permission for a supermarket. On the other hand, by the end of the decade leasehold reform was leading to the continued diminution of the Chalcots estate as leaseholders are given the right to buy their freeholds. As a result of all these sales, Eton's income-earning assets in land are being continually reduced, but the College has been able to increase its share portfolio, and it has been tempted by the existence of ready cash to spend more on development than

* The Statutes had also been amended for Lord Charteris since he was not a graduate of any University.

was always justified. The College has felt that it should ensure that its income grows in line with earnings – since most of its expenditure increases with labour costs. In Provost Caccia's time the idea was to spend capital to save labour – not altogether wise since in practice new capital seems to require more labour for maintenance; now under Provost Charteris the temptation was to spend in the short run with the intention of retrenching in the longer run – also a delusion since the long run constantly retreats. However, aided by a battery of modern management techniques such as five-year plans, the College has recently rationed the demands for capital to what is available. As a result, Eton is better off than the generality of schools, but not rich by comparison with similar American foundations.

The culminating capital investment, the most expensive project that Eton has undertaken, was perhaps the best; and it was very much to the credit of Lord Charteris. For at least twenty-five years Eton had needed to replace its sanatorium; now the redundancy of the Eton parish church gave an opportunity which was brilliantly taken by the local architect, Philip Tilbury. Besides the sanatorium the building contains a medical centre for the town and for the School, several flats, and a chapel of the appropriate size for the parish of Eton – all preserving the overall framework of the Victorian church, with handsome proportions and amusingly recycled ecclesiastical ornament. This has been the most conspicuous example of what is now College policy – to make Eton's facilities available locally. Not surprisingly considering the size of the College in relation to the town of Eton, relations between town and gown have not always been easy. There was a slightly farcical dispute in the 1950s between the Town Council and the College over the quality of the street lighting, and a more serious quarrel fifteen years later about the rates which the College should pay. The College may have had the better arguments in each case, but was not sufficiently sensitive in its actions and did not gain the day. By contrast, Lord Charteris brought about a new harmony, and the College is now *perceived* to do more for the town either directly or through various charities than has been the case in the past.

Arguments of a different financial character disrupted the 1980s. Early in the decade once again Eton Masters felt their pay was being held back because of a type of unofficial incomes policy, and their salaries did not even keep pace with inflation. Eton fees certainly were rising fast, but not so fast as those of other schools. Masters particularly resented what appeared to be consideration for parents, many of whom are rich, at what they assumed to be their expense. Masters in general have favoured high fees with generous bursaries; but it is argued that parents cannot count on bursaries, and that some do not in any case like to ask for them – so that a high fee might discourage the less affluent regardless of the availability of bursaries. A more weighty argument was on the Masters' side; even in the mid-1970s Michael McCrum was pointing out to Fellows his difficulty in recruiting good Masters, and this problem certainly persisted until the end of the 1980s. In some subjects, nationally as well as at Eton, few candidates of any merit would offer themselves. There was a particular shortage of Old Etonians wanting to return as beaks; those with vocations to teach often entered the Maintained Sector. There may once have been too many OE Masters, but now there are probably too few (eleven). In the summer of 1986, Masters' pay was increased by 10% in real terms in return for Masters accepting appraisal (and a possible bar to progress up the salary scale) – which certainly gave the Head Master a valuable weapon for management. Subsequently further real increases were agreed, as the pay of the best Maintained Sector teachers rose. Also a payment to Housemasters has been restored. As a consequence Eton Masters can now all feel confident that they are better rewarded than when they were recruited – and this situation is very welcome after the long decline in salaries. The only cause for disquiet is that the rise in costs from a larger and better-paid teaching staff may not be tolerated by parents hit by recession.

Fortunately the College has had the resources to provide extra bursaries. It has also been able to increase the number of scholarships. Two new types have been created during Anderson's headmastership: first, Sixth Form Scholarships were created for a few boys from the Maintained System who wished to join Eton for the specialist years; secondly, carrying on a long tradition of welcoming a few foreign boys, in 1991 the College also offered a number of International Scholarships for foreign boys for one year. Thus more than one boy in five has his fees wholly or partly remitted. (It can indeed be said that under Anderson the School has become more internationally minded, with boys encouraged to reach a fair proficiency in two modern languages and having opportunities to learn Japanese, Chinese, and Arabic, as well as European languages. Besides Japanese* and Chinese teachers, and French, German and Spanish assistants, there is also an American Annenberg Fellow who comes for one year, funded by Ambassador Annenberg.†) Finally, the College at the Head Master's suggestion has financed its own Summer School for boys and girls hoping to try for Oxford and Cambridge from the Maintained Sector; this has been very popular and successful.‡ The Precentor appointed in 1985, Ralph Allwood, brought holiday choral courses with him from Uppingham, and oarsmen among the Masters started holiday rowing courses. In all cases what Eton does well has been made more widely available.

The arrangements for Oxbridge entrance changed in the middle of the 1980s with considerable consequences for Eton. It has to be said that schools like Eton contributed to the change by their very success. In 1981 for instance, Etonians won forty-seven awards, the most ever, and well ahead of even the great academic day-schools. The conclusion drawn at the Universities was that the examinations must be faulty. In the long run, they felt, Etonians did not perform at University up to the level of other schools; and indeed boys may lose the habits of industry inculcated at Eton. Furthermore they frequently are disappointed by less lively lectures, and they miss the often stimulating cross-talk between Etonians and their Masters or visiting speakers. The most successful Etonians have already enjoyed a more mature experience than they are sometimes offered at Universities, though certainly some boys who have not fulfilled their potential at Eton blossom at their University. Yet the proportion of Etonians gaining Firsts at Cambridge has increased from below the average overall to above the average – admittedly with a smaller number of Etonians going to Cambridge; and it seems that this has occurred elsewhere.¶

After 1985 there was no seventh-term entry to Oxford or Cambridge, and thus the A Block vanished and Oxbridge girls

* The Japanese courses and exchange visits are financed by the Sumitomo Trust Bank.

† United States Ambassador to the Court of St James 1968–74.

‡ Some help in the first years came from the Manor Trust, endowed by Arthur Villiers as an educational charity after the Eton Manor Clubs closed.

¶ In 1986 one Oppidan house achieved five Firsts – half an annual intake; all the boys had been entered at birth – not taken on as Scholars.

along with them. Boys no longer joined the School in January, and a summer intake of new boys had ceased in 1979. Etonians had tended to start at a younger age than other public school boys, but now it was felt that they would be at a disadvantage trying for Oxbridge as only 16-year-olds; consequently those due in January were mostly put back to the following September. Boys now normally arrive aged 13 and may be nearly 19 when they leave – a change of considerable social consequence, which the School has begun to meet by increasing the frequency of weekend exeats. It also caused a shortage of trebles for the Choir.

The arrival of all boys in September has also meant that houses are more clearly defined in year blocks, normally ten per house. This has also brought changes; for example Debate and Library have diminishing significance – what matters is that boys progress to the more privileged C and B Blocks.

A further consequence was that the mode of election to Pop had to be changed significantly. Boys leaving each summer simply did not know enough of their juniors to choose a new Eton Society. Now a sophisticated system selects the first ten members of Pop for the coming year: a small committee of three Masters and the outgoing Captains of the School and Oppidans and President of Pop choose from lists sent in by the departing Pops, by Captains of houses, Keepers of various activities and Masters forming house lists. After this Pop is self-elected as hitherto, but there is a pious hope that a core of reponsible boys will ensure that the Eton Society elects no irresponsible members. The Head Master is able to choose the new President, at last achieving a power that other headmasters take for granted. Needless to say, boys being boys, perfection will not be achieved and Head Masters will continue to deal with abuse of Pop privileges once or twice a decade. In the 1980s a cleaner alerted authority to a problem when he enquired innocently whether it would not be convenient to provide ashtrays in the Eton Society's room.

Disciplinary problems continue as ever in a school. In the mid-1980s, all corporal punishment quietly ceased before legislation was introduced (even though that did not apply to independent schools). Possibly there have been a few more boys rusticated and expelled than would have been the case had the sanction still existed. The Lower Master has missed this useful weapon against young delinquents more than the Head Master, particularly against those experimenting with alcohol. Drug offences are, however, the biggest anxiety and the main cause for boys making an early departure. Enforcement of routine regulations is more irksome than it was, but Eric Anderson has been fortunate to have three Lower Masters willing to shoulder much of this unpopular work. Housemasters still have to deal with self-indulgent boys anxious for the licence to behave with as little regard for traditional morality as many of their teenage contemporaries.

None of this has been affected by the changing social composition of Eton. By now only one-third of Etonians are the sons of Old Etonian parents, and parents are drawn from a far wider range of occupations than in the nineteenth century. There has been a notable increase of professional people living in the neighbourhood of Eton sending sons. Very many parents are based at least partly in London. Sadly there are fewer boys from Scotland (though Eton still has a magnificently turned-out pipe band).* More parents are resident abroad, and boys of African or Asian descent are almost as numerous as they are in the nation as a whole. Similarly there has been a growing diversity of occupations into which Etonians have gone – for instance, there has been a sharp increase in medics from a low base. Most recently many boys have been attracted to some aspect of the media. Despite all boys experiencing an industrial conference and a business attachment, Etonians still do not often aim for manufacturing industry. For almost every career they now wish to go to University, and there has been a similar widening-out of the Universities to which they are attracted; numbers at Oxford are well maintained, but fewer try to go to Cambridge. The overall proportion going to University is about 95%.

The Head Master's structure for controlling the School has become even more sophisticated. Anderson has replaced the Chairman of Committees by a Director of Studies, his academic adviser, who presides over the Curriculum Committee and the School Fund Committee (in charge of the budget for teaching aids, schoolroom staff, etc.), and a Senior Tutor who advises on

---

* Masters forming house lists used in the 1950s to be advised by their elders to enrol Scottish aristocrats if they wanted the aristocracy, on the grounds that Scottish boys would be given less to spend. Certainly many Etonian Scots turned out well. The kilts for the band were supplied in McCrum's day, thanks to the persuasive powers of Anderson KS, by Eric Anderson's family firm.

housemasterly matters and chairs the House Fund Committee (in charge of domestic budgets); while the Lower Master retains his responsibility for the bottom two years and is the Head Master's deputy. In all there are some forty permanent committees, about ten chaired by the Head Master, and a number of *ad hoc* committees to consider any current problem. By successful delegation, the last three Head Masters have somehow maintained contacts with the boys. They do not just meet the successful to be praised or the sinners to be punished, but continue to entertain many boys and to take leave of all – which is now a Herculean summer task. Paul Watkins, with an ambivalent view of Eton, recalls:

> I barely knew Mr Anderson and had almost never spoken to him before. But somehow he knew more than I had written on my list of grades and prizes. He recalled shaking my hand one rainy Saturday in June when I had won the school discus award out at the track. He knew that I had won a short story prize and even remembered the content of the story. It was only a handful of unimportant details but this caught me off guard.'[1]*

Eric Anderson was the star of the TV film, *Class of '91* made in 1990. At Eton there was disappointment that this film did not show a wider range of the activities Eton does well, but critics of Eton were also disappointed: the School was evidently run by a sane and reasonable man, and the Etonians showed themselves to be in no sense a class apart. The routine assumption of journalists that all Etonians are rich toffs was shown to be absurd.†

The year 1990 saw the 550th anniversary of the foundation, and it was celebrated with a style which was justified by the absence of a properly marked Quincentenary. The College Chapel organ and the School Yard were expensively restored; the International Scholarships were founded and more funds were dedicated to bursaries. Concerts were given and exhibitions mounted to show some of the achievements of Etonians, and to illustrate how

---

* Paul Watkins, American novelist, won the Peter Fleming Owl awarded for the best contribution to the *Chronicle*. He won the School discus on a Friday in March rather than a Saturday in June – his autobiography, *Stand Before Your God*, is not entirely accurate.

† The photograph still most commonly used to illustrate articles about Eton shows two Harrovians of the 1930s with two cockney children.

actively the College was managing its collections, and to show off the remarkable modern literary collection, built up by Michael Meredith, thanks to a mixture of enterprise and generosity, and used to enliven the teaching of English.*

There seemed to be much to celebrate. The School was experiencing unprecedented demand; in each of the last five years a successively greater number has applied for guaranteed places at 11, and very many have been reluctantly turned away. In 1990, something close to the McCrum plan for entry was adopted: in 2003 all Etonians will have been selected and given firm entry in their eleventh year. It is, however, still possible to register sons with prospective Housemasters from the age of 4, so that personal links can be forged; for some time now relatively few boys put down at birth have been going to the Housemaster selected, because of promotions to headmasterships and the like, and Housemasters have had fewer boys whose parents they had themselves originally selected; so little of value has been lost.

Academic results as measured by A level grades continue to improve; some of this is due to 'slippage' as the number of weaker candidates entered nationally increases and the percentages awarded A grades remain constant, but Etonians appear to have achieved improvements transcending slippage. Art and Music flourish; and if some might wonder whether this is because of the great musical gifts of the Music Scholars, they should hear the second orchestra with its fifty or so string players offering the same sort of programme as the School Orchestra tackled up to the 1950s.† Theatrical standards vary, but the best is very good, and Etonians have the chance to see some twenty productions of significant plays a year, together with one or two written by their fellows. Indeed house plays have something of the role in engendering house spirit that the Field Game had for a hundred years. Despite the frequent concerts and plays, innumerable societies still draw audiences, though the ones connected with academic programmes are more popular, and most depend on prestigious outside speakers instead of papers read by boys themselves – sad consequences of the pressures of A level. Etonians do seem, however, to realize that sport can be combined with

---

* Eton is rich in Browning material, and now owns the Brownings' apartment in Florence, Casa Guidi.

† About four Etonians a year play in the National Youth Orchestra.

work, and there has been greater success lately for Eton teams in most athletic fields; more boys have achieved county and national selection. The energy with which the best boys fill their days in varied activities is inspiring, and provides a justification for boarding education.

Some boys certainly complain that they miss the presence of girls on the campus – though most older boys contrive a close relationship with a girl-friend. Eton is often asked when it will become coeducational, but there is little likelihood at present when it has to disappoint so many would-be entrants. Many other schools have taken to coeducation to solve problems: at Eton coeducation would create problems. It would be hard to expand the School on its crowded site, and so the introduction of, say, five girls' houses would have to be made by closing boys' houses. The press, who take a prurient interest in all things Etonian, would also create a special difficulty that other schools are largely spared. Even when the School employed a French woman in 1980, great (and harmless) hilarity was caused in the papers by the news that Etonians had a French mistress. (It broke when Eric Anderson was attending his first Headmasters' Conference as Head Master of Eton, giving him a first experience of one of the additional hazards of his new job.) Women are, however, now fairly regularly appointed to the staff, and girls are often to be seen in the streets. Martin Charteris felt that this was one of the most striking differences between modern Eton and the Eton he had left sixty years previously.

The 1990 celebrations with their royal visits were in a sense the apotheosis of Provost Charteris. A year later he was to retire amid displays of universal affection. His portrait was painted by Michael Noakes, and it hangs amid the leaving portraits that he had begun to collect from boys in the eighteenth-century manner – the first (appropriately considering Eton's racial mix) of Harry Matovu, an African Colleger distinguished as an actor. The new Provost is Sir Antony Acland, formerly Permanent Secretary of the Diplomatic Service and Ambassador in Washington.

Then in 1993 Eric Anderson accepted the invitation to become Rector of Lincoln College, Oxford. He leaves in the summer of 1994. It is the end of a happy era for Eton.

CHAPTER FOURTEEN

Continuity with Change

WHEN PROVOST CHARTERIS preached to the Old Etonians assembled in College Chapel for the 550th anniversary service, he chose as his text: 'Except the Lord build the house, their labour is but lost that build it'. He was expressing a belief that must have been in the mind of King Henry VI in founding Eton College, and which would certainly have been accepted by the Victorian Provosts with whom this volume began. He was thus claiming a continuity of faith less fashionable these days, yet still precariously alive at Eton. There are other things which endure at Eton – first of all an understanding of what a school is about.

A boy goes to a great school not so much for knowledge as to learn how to acquire it, and how to develop his power of reasoning and his imagination. He discovers in himself abilities that might lie fallow in isolation. His ideas are challenged by his fellows, and he learns from them and his teachers to take a balanced critical view of himself and of others. Although the establishment of his own identity may justify some temporary self-centredness, he should become aware of the needs and claims at first of those close to him and then of the wider community. Ideally he should acquire not only the individual strengths of application and mental courage, of humility and readiness to learn, but the social virtues of probity, practical compassion and leadership.

Compare what is written above with William Johnson's definition given in Chapter 1 (p. 26). The only change of substance is in the last lines: Johnson did not stress practical compassion and leadership. Perhaps he took them for granted; in his Economics lessons he argued for compassion for the poorly paid and unemployed; and certainly his pupils were remarkably successful in moving to positions of leadership in society. There is a continuity in the role that Eton has tried to play. Eton is also fortunate in some of its persistent characteristics.

Undoubtedly one of the great advantages that Etonians have enjoyed is the beauty of its surroundings. When Robert Birley said farewell to the School standing on the north steps of College Chapel, he referred to rumours then current that Eton, taken over by the State, would relocate itself – possibly in Eire; Eton, he said, could not move – it would be inconceivable without 'all this', the range of buildings around School Yard, and above all the Chapel. Monty James, saying that 'Eton centres its magic upon the eye and the heart as well as the brain', had much the same in mind.[1] Perhaps Winchester is even more fortunate in the overall beauty of its site, but considering that Eton is largely a man-made environment, with only the river offering natural beauty (and that now less peacefully enjoyed than in earlier days), it is happy in its legacy of buildings and trees. Nobody at Eton would seriously wish the boys to grow up isolated in the countryside.

Secondly, a distinctive feature, now beginning to be matched in other schools, has been that boys have had rooms of their own from the moment they arrive at Eton. There are risks in single rooms: unsociable boys can be neglected; it is easier to break rules; sexual misconduct may be more likely. Nevertheless the gains are great: it is easier for a boy to be individual; it is possible for him to retreat into privacy if he feels the need; he can talk to his Housemaster privately on his own ground, which may encourage a closer relationship.

The tutorial system has often been said to be another distinctive advantage of Eton, but what is implied by that phrase has changed over the years. In 1860 Eton was 'tutorial', as opposed to 'monitorial' Rugby – the Tutor (always a Classicist) being both director of a boy's studies and the source of discipline and pastoral care. When later Eton developed a system of boy discipline, it was generated by the boys themselves, and based on self-electing oligarchies – distinct from Arnoldian prefects acting as chosen vessels through which a Headmaster's ideas could reach down to the younger boys. In the one hundred years up to the 1970s the tutorial system provided a mental training based initially on classical work in Pupil Room under the Tutor's eye, supplemented later by Private Business designed to broaden the boy's mind in more relaxed conditions; but it also implied, in Alington's words 'a closeness of intercourse and a permanency of relationship between boy and master, which does not, so far as I know, exist elsewhere'.[2] Now it means little more than that boys have two adults to whom they can specially relate, thus narrowing the gap between the teachers and the taught; for a boy still has a Tutor, normally distinct from the Housemaster, to whom successes and failures are reported, for whom he does some written work (not enough nowadays), and whom he sees in Private Business; until the GCSEs in D Block this man will have been selected by the Housemaster, but thereafter the Tutor will usually have been chosen by the boy. Meanwhile the system of boy discipline has returned towards its 1860 state – with the significant exception that there is now no fagging – but Masters are more numerous and more active to prevent the near-anarchy of those earlier years.

The closeness of the tutorial and house ties are illustrative of perhaps Eton's most singular success, that it has become a very large boarding school while retaining the intimacy of small houses. The advantages of large scale include the cheaper provision of facilities and the running of minority programmes which could never be economic in a small school. Eton's average cost per boy of, say, providing libraries or a heated swimming-pool is less; and the range of languages taught is unmatched. Naturally there are disadvantages of large scale, such as the ten minutes' interval needed between school periods to allow boys to cross the campus – though this should not necessarily be regarded as all loss because minds are cleared, bodies exercised, and conversations developed. Yet the most familiar disadvantages of large scale, lack of personal contact and mismanagement, have been avoided.

The houses are even now smaller than in most schools, and Eton has almost a federal constitution. A great deal is delegated to houses, though much less than it was when Housemasters were economically independent. Perhaps bad houses have been more of a problem at Eton; but in good houses boys learn to be effective members of small societies, and can grow to be effective members of the School, and later of the wider community.

The organization of Eton is very sophisticated from its Governing Body downwards. A small and distinguished group of Fellows gives wise counsel, but is not tempted to interfere with the everyday operation of the School. The extraordinary arrangement by which the Provost and Vice-Provost are resident, with houses on either side of the Head Master's, has worked well since the Clarendon reforms, except for the near-farcical rule of Provost Quickswood. There is a clear division of responsibility, with the Provost and Vice-Provost guarding the property, looking after the College's charitable work and collections, and acting as figureheads, while the Head Master runs the School. The traditional boys' definition of the Provost's role, that 'the Provost does nothing, and the Vice-Provost helps him to do it', can be taken as a tribute to the successful division of authority – to the boys only the Head Master counts. The Bursar and his three lieutenants – the School Bursar to look after salaries, fees, and so on, the Buildings Bursar, and the Estates Manager – are at the interface between College and School, answerable to the Provost and Fellows, but facilitating the operation of the School. At weekly meetings the Provost and Vice-Provost consider with them such matters as lettings of School Hall, the condition and security of the School grounds, or the sale of a property – thus sparing the Head Master problems which would come his way elsewhere. In the economic management of the School, the Bursars work with committees of Masters, so that their interests, and through them the boys', are constantly consulted.

The Head Master's position is crucial. He sets the targets of the School, even though the Fellows will need to approve the general drift of policy, and though he is subject to outside influences, most obviously the requirements of the Universities. Eton education has to be utilitarian in the sense that it equips boys for a subsequent career, but it must also have idealism if boys are to be valuable leaders of society. In 1860 Eton prided itself on providing a liberal education, as distinct from technical education aimed at a particular career; but its claims depended on a very high estimate of the value of Classics as mental training. Etonians could pass through Oxford and Cambridge to Parliament, to the law courts or the church; but they lacked numeracy and logical training, and were not well equipped for business careers – to which in any case they seldom aspired. There was an idealism, ultimately based on the wide acceptance of Christian duty – that they should be of service to their fellow men and to the State. This vision was most clearly expressed under Dr Warre, when Etonians could almost be said to have been educated to a patriotic death. But that Eton education fell short of a proper utilitarian standard was evident when Etonians needed to go to crammers to become army officers. The limited reform of the curriculum, and the steps taken by Dr Warre to raise the level of industry among the weakest boys did much to make Eton education an effective preparation. However, the scholastic enthusiasms of Etonians remained very variable, with an able and successful group, more industrious than they sometimes pretended, and a long tail of intelligent but intellectually unambitious boys and dogged academic dullards. This situation was only really radically altered over the last twenty-five years. Eton's utilitarian achievement with weaker boys was in showing them that they could succeed as people even if they were not academically talented. Robert Birley was in a sense the pivotal Head Master, with his reluctance to adjust to A levels and his belief that educational values transcended the utilitarian. Yet parents, Masters, boys – all wanted an Eton which saw boys through examinations, whatever else it gave in addition. Now Eton is evidently effective in preparing boys for varied future careers, but it has consciously to struggle to persuade boys that passing examinations is not the proper end of education.

It is for the Head Master to achieve this, above all in the appointment of staff and in the selection of those for promotion, tasks which take an increasing part of the Head Master's time. He has to stimulate serving Masters, some of whom have lost the old confidence in what Eton is doing; he has to be open to their ideas; he has to meet them each morning in Chambers – an institution essential to the management of a large school, but curiously unique to Eton. The Eton beak has traditionally been independent and self-confident, with strong views which he is not frightened to express, and perhaps therefore more awkward for Head Masters to control. They have been accustomed to receiving protests, often expressed in intemperate language. Michael McCrum relates receiving one such in his last year from David Simpson, a staunch defender of the classical traditions of Eton, when McCrum proposed the introduction of the Revised Psalter in College Chapel: 'I have often protested before against changes which you intended to make in Eton. This change, I believe, would be actually your worst. Can you not let us off it? Do you really wish to ride away from us with the scalp of Coverdale dangling with the others from your belt?' There is great value in a staff willing and able to challenge the dictatorship of Head Masters.

It is very hard to capture on paper the quality of something so transitory as a lesson or a tutorial session. And since the best instruction is a two-sided process, even for the most skilled Master success depends on the responses of a particular group. Eton has had its share of bad Masters, and other schools have had men and women as dedicated as Eton's best; yet those with experience of several schools have often asserted that Eton has had more men of ability, concerned to give more than they take from the place. Above all many Housemasters and Tutors have been wholly concerned for their pupils. Percy Lubbock wrote of Eton Tutors at the end of the nineteenth century: 'To give so much and to get so much, to give with mind and heart and to get so much in return to fill them both – and then to lose so much, to be always losing: it is the schoolmaster's portion, who stays behind while youth that is life and work to him is always in flight.'* There have been and are many heroes of Eton – unsung in this history, since it has to be of less than transatlantic length – honourable men, generous with their time and their talents, confident that the more they put into Eton the more they are ultimately rewarded.

The Assistant Masters have not been adequately chronicled; still less the many excellent Dames, domestic staff, and servants of the College. In the last decade, for example, Bill Bowles retired, over 80 years old, having been for much of his half-century at Eton the most eminent groundsman in England; and Gordon Lovegrove retired fifty-five years after he first came to Eton, having been the head Physics technician for most of that time. Such people add strength to any school, and Etonians have been made aware at all times of how much is contributed by anyone who performs a job faithfully.

The advantages conferred on Etonians should not be overrated. Schools only influence their pupils: natural abilities and family circumstances will count for more in almost every case. Even if school influences are constructive, there will be occasional boys who react against what is offered – perhaps just because it is

* He had William Johnson particularly in mind.

offered by adults. In fact Eton has set itself against any attempt to mould boys. Instead they have been given opportunities and an unusual degree of choice. Freedom has inevitably been abused, but the opportunity of behaving well implies the rejected chance of misbehaviour. Delinquency in adolescence can be understood, punished, and forgiven as something fairly common in the development of masculine aggression and its guidance into useful channels. Boys who make good use of what Eton offers help their fellows by demonstrating possibilities more effectively than Masters can.

By the end of the nineteenth century some boys did exercise great authority, partly because Masters left whole areas of life to the boys, partly by deliberate policy. On the river, where the influence of Dr Warre was strongest, the Boat House was run by a committee of boys and Masters which was properly constituted only if the boys were in a majority. Captains of houses had very great power in their own kingdoms, and not surprisingly this was sometimes abused. The President of Pop and the Captain of the Boats had the greatest power of all. Certainly there are Etonians who never built on social or academic success achieved as boys, but many more did. The multitude of distinguished Old Etonians include many who did not make a mark at Eton, but the majority were already showing promise at the School. In the last thirty years any danger either of the satiation of ambition by excessive success or of the arrogance of office has been much reduced. Boys have to a considerable extent abdicated their historical powers, and find the exercise of responsibility for a year almost too long. Maybe hindsight will show that what used to be criticized should have been praised.

Provost Charteris in his sermon stressed Eton's need to adapt as well as to continue what is best. An assumption often made by outsiders, and shared by some boys, is that Eton does not change and tradition rules all. Perhaps the venerable beauty of the buildings and the continuance of school dress bear some responsibility. Boys of course have a very short time span and readily assume that what happened in their time has always happened, so that 'traditions' grow with astonishing rapidity. In fact Eton is not particularly resistant to change; John Dancy, Master of Marlborough, remarked once with more generosity than was perhaps deserved: 'If you get a good idea in education, you find that it

became common practice at Eton years ago.'* Eton has adapted
over its history, at some times more readily than at others. The
danger has been rather more that some things of value have been
lost. Eton has adjusted to the recent changes in social climate and
public opinion. Etonians have adapted academically to a more
competitive environment, and are more consciously educated to
contribute to our culture. To some visitors Etonians seem more
civilized than other students, more visually aware, better able to
talk widely about the arts. Yet are Etonians now too narrowly
motivated by the need to cross the various hurdles on the way to a
lucrative job? Do they fail to value learning for its own sake? Are
they more hesitant in applying absolute moral standards, too ready
to take the relativistic view that what goes in society is all right? All
one can say is that at least they are reminded from time to time by
direct statement and by example that mental courage and probity
do matter, and that society's values should not be accepted
uncritically.

Some changes have been forced on Eton and would not always
have been welcome to Eton if regarded selfishly. Most obviously
Etonians have lost much of the privileged position that their
predecessors had acquired by the nineteenth century, and they
accept that such a change is right. It has also meant, however, some
loss of self-confidence, which used to be a particular strength of
Eton education, built on the wealth of possibilities for achievement
that Eton offers. Self-confidence is an aid to idealism, for those
who are less worried about their own position can more readily
concern themselves for others. Undoubtedly many Etonians did
accept the obligations of their social positions and education to
give service to the community. Now Etonians are more inclined to
feel guilt about their upbringing, and are more aware that they
need to fight to safeguard their careers – feelings that logically are
hardly compatible, but whose coexistence hampers their drive to
public service. It is also probably true that Etonians, though better
equipped educationally than at any earlier time, will find it harder
to give outstanding service than their forebears did – competition
has grown while the climate of opinion has become more hostile.
Yet they still may do the State much service. When Alexander
Solzhenitsyn spoke to the boys in 1983, he told them: 'Your

---

* Marlborough was about to introduce Business Studies as an A level course in
the 1960s, while Eton was already offering it as a General Study.

education will bear no fruit if you do not develop in yourself will, and the will to action.'[4] This message only restated what has always been a theme of Eton education, that boys should take initiatives and that there is no merit in passivity. Eton is a highly political school, not just in the sense that Etonians have been drawn to political careers, but more importantly in that they learn what initiatives can be taken, what conflicts resolved.

The sequence of Old Etonian Viceroys of India owed as much to their birth as to their upbringing. Even now it must be admitted that the same applies to the predominance of Etonians among Lords Lieutenant. Yet the idea of service was always there. The record of those who gave their lives for the country speaks for itself. Old Etonians have won disproportionately more Victoria Crosses than the old boys of any other school – the thirty-seventh in the Falklands War. The Corps no longer plays so big a part in Eton life, but the number of recruits immediately increased when that war broke out, as it had done in 1914. Those who have been treated well, and who realize that they should treat others as they have been treated themselves, are more likely to act to the benefit of their fellows. Etonians sometimes fail in imagination, and a less sheltered experience after school can be valuable; but over the years a high proportion has served the community voluntarily. Most may be instinctively on the right, but they have contributed to the politics and economics of the left – to almost every radical cause except feminism.* Mr Macmillan's government, with ten Old Etonians at one time in the Cabinet, did more for the aspirations of the ordinary family than any other recent government. It was no surprise that Old Etonians were to be found predominantly among the compassionate 'wets' when Mrs Thatcher came to power.

Etonians may be less well placed to influence public affairs than in the past, but even as recently as 1983 the Archbishop of York, the Lord Chancellor, the Chief of the Defence Staff, the Secretary-General of NATO, the Heads of the Home Civil Service and the Diplomatic Service, the Governor of the Bank of England, the Chairman of the Governors of the BBC, the editor of *The Times*,

---

* For example Mr Benn and Mr Scargill turned to Francis Cripps and Andrew Glyn for economic advice; Jeremy Sandford was the author of *Cathy, Come Home*, the seminal work about homelessness; Jonathan Porritt and Peter Melchett are leaders of the environmentalists.

the Chairmen of the National Trust and of the Nature Conservancy Council, and the Chairman of the University Grants Committee were all Old Etonians. The increasingly international Eton is spreading its influence more widely, and the next Old Etonian Prime Minister may well rule abroad.

It has been to the variety and richness of talent of Etonians, never greater perhaps than it is now, that the School ultimately owes its character. Their influence on each other has provided a stimulus renewed in each generation, and gives confidence for the future that Etonians will continue to develop a diverse individuality. There is a prayer used in Chapel for the Colleges of King Henry the Sixth in which the congregation asks 'that they may together serve thee to the welfare of this realm, the benefits of all men, and thy honour and glory'. History suggests the prayer has been fulfilled at least in part, and surely it still will be.

Glossary

ETON WAS NEVER so encumbered by esoteric local usages as Winchester, and the tendency in recent years has been to abandon distinctive words which might be taken to differentiate Etonians from their contemporaries. As circumstances change, words come in and out of favour; to some extent a glossary of Eton terms provides a small insight into Eton history.

Absence A roll-call which used normally to be held in School Yard, but is now generally held in houses. Boys prove their presence.

After Twelve A period originally from 12 to 2 in the winter, and to 1.30 in the summer, when upper boys would normally be free, but lower boys would be in Pupil Room.

Baby Fours Competition for first-year wet-bobs; the competition is based on an admirable mixture of aquatic skills, and has provided the stimulus for many fine oarsmen.

Beak A Master.

The Bill The list of boys required to see the Head Master at the end of the morning. If *a complaint* is made of a boy, he is placed *in the Bill* (now more commonly *on the Bill*).

Block (a) Boys are grouped in year blocks; currently they are promoted from F through to B Block. (b) Boys to be birched knelt on a block – now a museum piece.

Boy Queue Originally a queue of fags available for duty after meals; now more normally a queue of boys waiting to see the Housemaster to have order cards, show-ups, rips, and so on signed.

Burry A boy's desk: a bureau containing drawers, a desk, and bookshelves.

Capping A polite acknowledgment of Masters by raising a finger, which Masters should reciprocate. Sadly this civil practice is in decline.

Chambers Masters used to meet each morning in the Head Master's Chambers in the corner of School Yard. A larger staff now meets in School Hall or Upper School. Chambers means (a) this meeting; (b) the time allotted to it; (c) sometimes the food consumed by boys in houses at that time.

Change (a) Clothes worn when not in school dress. (b) Half-time at football when the teams changed ends (now obsolete).

Colleger One of the seventy Scholars who live in College.

Colours Test From the late nineteenth century until recently new boys were tested by the Library about the location of houses, the various colours worn by successful games-players, and so on. The aim was to ensure they could fag successfully, but it was also the most alarming initiation they faced. Now sanitized.

Commended for Good Effort A small reward for a good half's work in a subject. Ten commendations earn a prize. Introduced by Chenevix-Trench.

Conduct A priest who was hired to read the services in Chapel. Since the 1950s the Senior Chaplain.

Construe Translation of a Latin or other language text.

Cribs Aids to translation of construes, generally illegal. Hence *cribbing* – copying from notes or from a neighbour during a test or examination.

Dames Originally ladies who kept boarding houses for Oppidans. In this century, the house matrons, addressed by boys as 'ma'am' and still known sometimes as 'm'dame'.

Debate Junior house prefects, to some extent still self-elected but not debating.

Division (a) A class; thus the *division Master* is a form master. (b) A lesson; thus, 'I've a French *div* tomorrow'.

Election Saturday Until 1871 the Saturday celebration in July, marked by a Procession of Boats, when Collegers were elected to King's College, Cambridge, and young boys were elected to fill the vacancies created in College.

Eton Fives A game which originated between buttresses of College Chapel, played with gloved hands and a hard ball in courts modelled on the original. Taken up by other schools in this country, and in Northern Nigeria.

Extra Works (EWs) Work set to be done out of school.

Extras Originally tuition in subjects outside the main curriculum, or extra tuition in a subject because of a special examination need or a weakness. Obsolete – a modern Etonian would mean extra milk, yoghurt, etc.

Fags Younger boys who carried notes, fetched food, made tea, and the like. Besides working for a particular fagmaster, a fag would have to respond to a call of 'Boy!' – or if a Colleger 'Here!' Now fagging is restricted to fetching mail from School Office and other official house business.

Field Game An eleven-a-side game of football, one of the ancestors of Association Football. It originated in the open fields around Eton and is the one game at Eton universally played for over a hundred years, and still played by all but a few. Eight players are in a bully, a type of scrum, and there are three behinds who alone can kick the ball forward to their own side. The play is advanced by rushes and dribbling as well as by kicking.

First Fault Up to 1914 boys could ask the Lower Master (or occasionally the Head Master) for remission of punishment for a first offence.

First Hundred From 1870 the senior hundred boys in the School. Latterly the number expanded. They would be assembled for *First Hundred Lectures* given by distinguished outsiders. Obsolete.

The Foundation Those with a particular position in Henry VI's Statutes – the Provost and Fellows, Head Master, Lower Master, Bursar, Precentor, Collegers. Assistant Masters and Oppidans are part of the School of which the Provost and Fellows are the Governing Body.

Founder's Day 6 December, King Henry VI's birthday.

Fourth of June King George III's birthday, and the School's principal festival; now very seldom celebrated on 4 June.

Georgics Poems by Virgil about farming; the shortest, just over 500 lines, was often written as a poena.

Half A term – now falling out of use among the boys.

Head Man The boys' name for the Head Master.

Jackets Until the 1960s, the dress worn by shorter boys; for most of this century, by those under 5 ft 4 in.

Joby A seller of food and drink. Obsolete.

Kappa A boy who did not learn Greek. Derived from the curiously inappropriate use of the symbol, the Greek κ, in the School List to designate non-specialists who did not learn Greek. Obsolete.

Keeper The captain of a team, or the boy in charge of a game –

but the Captain of Boats, the Captain of the Eleven, and the Captain of Shooting are exceptions. Also each house has a Captain of Games, who appoints, for example, the keeper of the house junior football team.

King's Scholars (KS) Collegers. Now supplemented by Music Scholars (MS) and Music Exhibitioners (ME), by Junior Scholars, Sixth Form Scholars, and International Scholars.

Leave Away from Eton. There are now Long Leaves at half-term, and Short Leaves during the Michaelmas Half, supplemented by leave for special occasions and as a privilege for older boys.

Leaving books Boys used to give books to their friends on leaving, an expensive practice stopped by Dr Hornby. Now they give *leavers*, that is, photographs of themselves. Boys still receive a leaving book, normally Gray's *Poems*, as a gift from the Head Master.

Leaving money Boys used to give money to the Head Master on leaving, a practice stopped by Dr Hornby.

Library (a) The controlling boys in an Oppidan house. (b) The room where they can gather.

Lock-up When boys are required to be in their houses unless they have permission. The time varies through the year.

Lower Man The boys' name for the Lower Master.

Lower School (a) The younger boys under the Lower Master's jurisdiction – now those in Blocks E and F. (b) The fifteenth-century schoolroom, still in use.

Mesopotamia A playing field bounded by three streams.

Messing The habit of a few friends eating tea together in a boy's room; in the nineteenth century they might also have messed together for breakfast.

Mr Although titles are not used by Masters or boys in conversation, they are recorded in the School Lists and are used formally. Quaintly sons of peers are listed as Mr. Thus G.N. Curzon, son of Lord Scarsdale, was Mr Curzon.

Ninth Man The boy who rows number nine in the ten-oared processional boat, the *Monarch*, organizes internal rowing competitions.

Oppidan Any boy who is not a King's Scholar.

Oppidan Scholar (OS) Originally an Oppidan who could have been a King's Scholar, but opted to be an Oppidan. Now boys who prove themselves over the years equal to King's Scholars are awarded the title OS. Currently there are 91. They gain no financial advantage.

Ottoman A low chest with a padded top that also serves as a seat.

Passing A swimming test which must be passed before a boy is allowed on the river.

Poena A punishment which used generally to take the form of writing out Latin lines; for graver offences a boy would be required to write out one of Virgil's Georgics, over 500 lines. The term is obsolescent as Masters are appointed who know little Latin.

Pop The Eton Society, founded as a debating society, but later more of a social oligarchy. A *Pop* (or sometimes unattractively nowadays, a *Popper*) is a member of the Eton Society.

Pound A stock of second-hand work books.

Praepostors Originally appointed by Masters in each division to mark out boys absent, and so on. Now limited to two praepostors from Sixth Form Select who act as messengers for the Head Master, principally in summoning boys for his and the Lower Master's Bills.

Prayers Held in houses to mark the end of the day, after which the younger boys go to their rooms. Religious content is now frequently absent.

Private Business Tutorial periods held informally by boys' Tutors in their studies.

Pupil Room The room in which a Tutor had his pupils working under supervision, and hence the activity of working with the Tutor. Now almost obsolete – boys would be more likely to say that they had a tutorial.

The Ram In the Field Game, points are scored by conventional goals but also by *rouges*, when the ball cannons over the defenders' back line and is touched by an attacker. The rouge may then be converted by the attackers ramming it through the goal-mouth. When Dr Warre wished to increase the prestige of the Sixth Form, he caused them to process in and out of Chapel; there was a fancied resemblance to the Field Game ram, and thus the procession became known as the Ram. The Ram was part of the congregational services in College Chapel for seventy-five years. It was ended in 1970.

Remove (a) The intermediate E Block between Fourth Form and

Fifth Form was known until the 1960s as Remove. (b) Earlier boys spoke of gaining a remove if they obtained promotion.

Rip   Bad work is *torn over* or ripped by a Master, in which case it must be signed by the Tutors and the work normally repeated.

Sap   A derogatory term for a clever or industrious boy. All boys would *sap up* for Trials by revising. The word has become obsolete as Etonians have become more universally industrious.

Saying Lesson   Recitation of a piece learnt by heart, once a very common Eton activity, now obsolescent.

Schools   Periods. *In school* – attending a lesson.

Scug   A boy who had no games colour, and hence an opprobrious term for any young boy. Hence *scug cap*, the cap worn by all who had not obtained house or School colours. Obsolete.

Sent up for Good   A boy may be sent up for excellent work to the Head Master. The honour three times gained secures a prize.

Sent up for Play   This was an even greater distinction; the boy who earned it secured a half-holiday for all. Extinct since 1870.

Shirking   A boy missing any activity is said to be shirking it. Before 1865 shirking also referred to the requirement for boys in the High Street to go through the motions of evading Masters.

Shorts   Until the 1930s only boys who represented their houses at football could wear shorts: others wore knickerbockers. Hence a boy could win his shorts.

Show-up   A small reward: a Master can tell a boy that he may show good work to his Tutors.

Sixth Form   Originally the ten senior Collegers and ten senior Oppidans. Now officially known as Sixth Form Select in deference to the common use of Sixth Form; but Etonians still mean the élite if they use the term among themselves.

Sock   Food and drink. *Socking* means buying or consuming food or drink. 'Will you sock me an ice?' means 'Will you buy it for me?' Hence the phrase, now obsolete, 'Sock me my construe', meaning 'Translate it for me'.

Specialists   Those who had passed School Certificate.

Speeches   Recitations by Sixth Form before the Provost, notably on the Fourth of June.

Staying out   Missing school through illness.

Stick-ups   Collars worn with butterfly ties by Sixth Form Select, Captains of houses, and other such dignitaries.

Sunday Questions   Work on a religious theme set to be written on Sunday and shown up on Monday.

Swishing   In the nineteenth century a flogging from the Head or Lower Master; in the twentieth century the term changed to *swiping*. Beating in houses in the nineteenth century was known as *smacking*, in College as *working off*. Boys could be *pop-tanned* or *eight-tanned* for offences in the streets or on the river. Various canes were used. All these terms are now obsolete.

Tails   The morning coats which became the School uniform.

Taking leave   Bidding a formal farewell to the Head Master; the boy receives his leaving book.

Tap   The pub (since 1954 club) for senior boys.

Tardy Book   A book in School Office to be signed early in the morning by the persistently late.

Tickets   (a) Sanctions used by Masters for petty offences. For example a ticket might read: 'Jones. Rowdy. Two hundred lines for Thursday'; Jones has to have this signed by his Tutors as well as writing the poena. (b) Formerly there were *Yellow Tickets* for worse offenders, an invention of Dr Warre. (c) A *White Ticket* is given to a boy for persistent poor work or dishonesty: no leave is permitted, and the ticket has to be signed by all who deal with the boy before he is discharged.

Times   Period spent in some form of exercise. Houses displayed lists of boys below Debate on which boys were required to indicate the exercise they had taken: a Time might be football, a run, or a game of Fives, for example.

Trials   The internal Eton examinations at the end of a half.

Tug   A Colleger. This term was used by Oppidans offensively, but is now mostly used by Collegers.

Tutor   Formerly the Classics Master responsible for a boy's work. From the end of the nineteenth century a boy might also refer to his non-Classical Housemaster as a Tutor. Now the Master responsible for a boy's work, to whom he goes for tutorials. Less commonly the Housemaster, but the term 'M' Tutor's' may still be used to denote the boy's house.

Up to   A boy is up to a Master if he is taught by him.

Upper Boat Choices   The Captains of Upper Boats and Lower Boats. Thus the most distinguished oarsmen, normally the VIII plus four.

Upper Boats   The leading boats in the Procession.

Upper School (a) The senior boys. (b) The large schoolroom built at the end of the seventeenth century, which accommodated several divisions at once until the New Schools were built.

Verses Until the 1960s the composition of Latin and Greek verses was a major activity, latterly confined to abler linguists.

Wall Game A game of football originating alongside the wall between College Field and the Slough Road. It has points in common with the Field Game but is more complex, more cerebral, and above all more static.

Wet-bob A boy who rows.

Some new words and phrases have been coined. For example:

Bumped-back Means that a bad paper in Trials is returned to the boy to be done again. This derives from the earlier 'sending a bumf back'.

Busted Caught out law-breaking. *Busted for tabbing* or *busted on the piss* indicate caught smoking or drinking. There is some comfort that drug offences are not so common as yet to have attracted a vocabulary.

Readers Schools in which boys are meant to work on their own. A reading school may be planned by a Master or Head of Department, but may just possibly indicate a Master's failure to teach. In the latter sense it is replacing an older term, *a run*, among the senior boys.

Source Notes

Notes to Chapter 1

The principal sources used for 1860 are:

(a) the *Report of Her Majesty's Commissioners appointed to inquire into the Revenues and Management of certain Colleges and Schools and the Studies pursued and instruction given therein* (1864) referred to as the *Public Schools Report*. This is particularly useful for financial details.

(b) A.C. Ainger *Eton Sixty Years Ago* (1917) provides useful factual information, particularly on the curriculum; the author, who was at Eton from 1853 to 1860, became a Master from 1864 to 1901 and Secretary of the Old Etonian Association from 1899 to 1919. He wrote the words of two of the best School songs, the *Carmen*, still sung, and the *Vale*, sadly in abeyance.

(c) *Seven Years at Eton* (1883) is the most vivid account of life in the School. The author, James Brinsley-Richards, was actually R.T.S.C. Grenville-Murray, who was at Eton from 1856 to 1862.

1. Reported by Richard Martineau, whose father boarded at Evans's. No book explains why Evans was usually kept incommunicado.
2. *Eton School Register part II*.
3. John Maude *Memoirs of Eton and Oxford*.
4. *Collegers v. Oppidans* is thought by John Chandos to have been written by Grenville-Murray. It was first published in the *Cornhill Magazine* in 1871.
5. Bridges *Digby Mackworth Dolben, a Memoir* p. viii.
6. Radcliffe Memoirs.
7. Lubbock *Memories of Eton and Etonians* p. 119.
8. *Public Schools Report* para. 5090, evidence of Revd C.C. James.
9. *Journal of Education* no. 152 pp. 85, 86.
10. Johnson *Eton Reform II* pp. 6, 7, as adapted by George Lyttelton in writing to Rupert Hart-Davis.
11. Johnson Journal August 1867.
12. Johnson *Hints for Eton Masters* p. 19 and pp. 14, 15.

13. A.J. Balfour *Chapters of Autobiography* p. 9.
14. Maude op. cit. p. 59.
15. Johnson *Eton Reform* pp. 32, 33.

Notes to Chapter 2

Public Schools Report, Etoniana nos. 67–82 and 107–9, *Changing Eton* by
L.S.R. Byrne and E.L. Churchill, two Masters, and *Boys Together* by
John Chandos provide much material for the chapter. Dr Balston's
biography has been written by Thomas Balston.

1. *Saturday Review* 8 December 1960. Chandos believes that the author
   was Goodford.
2. 'Public School Education' a lecture.
3. *Eton Reform* and *Eton Reform II*.
4. *Westminster Review* April 1861.
5. Kegan Paul *Memories* p. 86.
6. *Public Schools Report* paras 1779–97 and 1803–11.
7. Ibid. para. 3128.
8. Ibid. para. 3739.
9. Ibid. para. 3689.
10. Ibid. para. 7025.
11. Ibid. p. 56.
12. *Cornhill Magazine* 6 July 1864.
13. *Etoniana* nos. 130, 131.
14. Esher papers.
15. ECL (Eton College Library).
16. ECL. The annual reports of the Finance Committee are preserved.
17. Browning *Memories of Sixty Years* p. 64.

Notes to Chapter 3

Parry's school diary is reprinted in *Etoniana* nos. 103–5. The Ascham
Society preserves its minutes. The journal of William Johnson is largely at
Eton, but one volume is with Reginald Brett's papers at Churchill
College, Cambridge (the Esher papers). Brett himself is the subject of a
valuable biography by James Lees-Milne. Johnson's biography has been
written by Brett and by Faith Compton-Mackenzie, but neither is
satisfactory. A pile of papers about Oscar Browning's dismissal is in the
College Archives. A biography of Browning by Ian Anstruther is to be
preferred to one by H.E. Wortham. Other useful sources on Hornby's

period are a manuscript recollection of his schooldays by Edward Lyttelton, *Eton in the Seventies* by Gilbert Coleridge, and *Eton Under Hornby* and *Memories of Bygone Eton* by Henry Salt.

1. An account of the origins of the Boating Song by John Carter is in *Etoniana* no. 118.
2. Lubbock op. cit. pp. 200, 201.
3. Johnson to Revd Wellington Johnson August 1868.
4. Johnson Journal 16 January 1868.
5. Ibid. 29 January 1868.
6. Ibid. 25 August 1868.
7. Johnson to Brett, written from the Williamsons, August 1868.
8. Quoted by Lees-Milne *Enigmatic Edwardian*. This volume of the diary has unfortunately now vanished.
9. Johnson Journal 31 July 1869.
10. Ibid. 26 September 1869.
11. Brett Journal 29 March 1872.
12. Ibid. 14 May 1872.
13. The final stanza of Johnson's *Academus*, written in 1858.
14. Edward Lyttelton MS.
15. Radcliffe MS.
16. Browning op. cit. p. 183.
17. Macnaghten *Fifty Years of Eton* p. 54.
18. Austen Leigh diary 4 October 1875 in *Etoniana* no. 99.
19. There is a substantial file on the tutorial question in the College Archives. Many letters on the subject were printed for circulation to all Masters.
20. E. Lyttelton MS.
21. Gambier Parry *Annals of an Eton House* throws some light.
22. An account is given in *Etoniana* no. 92. There is also a reminiscence in the ephemeral *Change* p. 16 by the Earl of Midleton.
23. Pilkington *An Eton Playing Field* p. 106.
24. Lyttelton *Memories and Hopes* p. 39.
25. M.R. James *Eton and King's* p. 47.
26. Coleridge *Eton in the Seventies* p. 119.
27. Quoted in Fletcher *Edmond Warre* p. 107.

Notes to Chapter 4

There is a biography *Edmond Warre* by C.R.L. Fletcher. The records of the Governing Body are more complete from Dr Warre's time onwards. A.C. Benson's diary throws much light on the second half of his headmastership, and the scrapbook kept by A.C. Heygate is useful. Both Benson and Heygate were Housemasters under Warre. Percy Lubbock *Shades of Eton* has much on his Head Master.

1. Fletcher op. cit. p. 140. He had the story from 'Jelly' Churchill, a long-serving and distinguished wet-bob Master.
2. A fragment of autobiography quoted in Fletcher op. cit. p. 47.
3. Fletcher op. cit. p. 136.
4. Benson diary September 1901.
5. Ibid. 9 October 1901.
6. The account of the fire is drawn from Benson's diary, from L.E. Jones *A Victorian Boyhood* and from the Captain of the Oppidans' Book, which confirms that Jones's memory in old age was accurate.
7. Pevsner *Buckinghamshire* p. 128.
8. Benson diary September 1903.
9. Lubbock *Shades of Eton* p. 15.
10. In a leading article after Warre's death 23 January 1920.
11. Lubbock op. cit. p. 20.
12. Benson diary 11 May 1902.

Notes to Chapter 5

1. Berners *A Distant Prospect* p. 38.
2. *A History of the Eton College Hunt* was written by a 17-year-old Etonian, A.C. Crossley, in 1922. A biography of the Grenfell twins was written by John Buchan.
3. Benson diary 23 Jan 1902.
4. Wingfield-Stratford *Before the Lights went out* p. 123. The author makes many errors in his passage about Eton, and it is clear that he was much influenced against Eton by Oscar Browning.
5. Lushington *The Eton We Knew* pp. 46–8.
6. Benson diary February 1903.
7. Benson diary July 1904.
8. Macnaghten *Fifty Years of Eton* p. 159.
9. Ibid. p. 179.
10. Benson diary January 1899.
11. Ibid. 9 October 1901.
12. Ibid.
13. *Etoniana* no. 127.
14. Recollections of Sir David Montagu-Douglas-Scott in his 100th year.
15. Jones *A Victorian Boyhood* p. 196.
16. Benson diary 16 March 1900.
17. Benson *Fasti Etonenses* p. 496.

18. Benson diary June 1904. He would have heard from the Vice-Provost.
19. Macnaghten op. cit. p. 91.
20. *Etoniana* no. 127.
21. Jones op. cit. pp. 208, 209.
22. Ibid. p. 237.
23. Ibid. p. 219.
24. Berners op. cit. p. 126.
25. Sir David Scott's recollections. See also *Arthur Villiers 1883–1969*.

Notes to Chapter 6

Memories and Hopes is Edward Lyttelton's own memories. C.A. Alington wrote an appreciation. Geoffrey Madan and Geoffrey Bridgeman wrote short sketches published in *Etoniana* nos. 121 and 127, and a manuscript commentary by Richard Martineau is in College Library. There is also the chapter about Lyttelton written by D.H. Macindoe: *see* Preface (above). The books about Etonians killed in the war are numerous and harrowing.

1. Benson diary volume 66 records the events of March 1905.
2. Luxmoore *Letters* p. 118.
3. Martineau MS.
4. Benson diary 6 April 1905.
5. Communicated by G. Chance.
6. Martineau MS.
7. M.D. Hill *Eton and Elsewhere* p. 112.
8. *Chronicle* 28 September 1911.
9. See for instance Anthony Eden *Another World* pp. 50, 51.
10. Marquess of Donegall in the ephemeral *Change* p. 39.
11. MS diary of Victor Cazalet.
12. His letters home are preserved by his family.
13. A file about the whole episode is in College Library.
14. Macnaghten *Eton Letters* p. 34.
15. Madan MS on C.A. Alington, Eton College Library.
16. Alington *Edward Lyttelton* p. 16.
17. Ibid. p. 18.
18. Recollection of Lord Home of the Hirsel.
19. Acton *Memoirs of an Aesthete* p. 75.
20. Burton *Cecil Spring-Rice* p. 205.
21. Luxmoore *Letters* pp. 218, 219.
22. *Letters of an English Boy* pp. 174, 175.
23. *Henry Dundas* pp. 230–2.

Notes to Chapter 7

There is no biography of Alington, but Richard Martineau's obituary in the *Chronicle* was supplemented by an MS note. College Library also has an MS by Geoffrey Madan. For M.R. James at Eton, Cox is more useful than Pfaff.

1. Martineau obituary *Chronicle* 27 May 1955.
2. Martineau MS.
3. Ibid.
4. Madan MS.
5. Ibid.
6. Martineau obituary.
7. Ibid.
8. Martineau MS.
9. Luxmoore *Letters* p. 110.
10. Madan MS.
11. Gowan paper to the Ascham Society.
12. Lord Home *The Way the Wind Blows* p. 56.

Notes to Chapter 8

1. Thesiger *The Life of my Choice* p. 70.
2. Connolly *Enemies of Promise* Chapter XX.
3. Ibid. p. 234.
4. Priestley *John Boughey* p. 215.
5. Elliott *Never Judge a Man by his Umbrella* p. 62.
6. Luxmoore *Letters* p. 280.
7. W. Douglas-Home *Half Term Report* p. 37.
8. Blunt *Slow on the Feather* Chapter 1.
9. Benson diary 15 June 1924.
10. *Chronicle* 1 March 1934.
11. Heckstall-Smith *Doubtful Schoolmaster* pp. 41, 42.
12. R. Byron *The Station* p. 143.
13. Ayer *Part of my life* pp. 48, 49.
14. *William Hope-Jones: A Memoir*.
15. Heygate *Decent Fellows* p. 70. Marten is disguised as Raven in the novel. Marten kept a raven at the back of his schoolroom to nip dozy boys.
16. D. Wright (ed.) *Walter Hamilton: A Portrait* pp. 37, 38.
17. Priestley op. cit. p. 180.
18. N. Byron *A Dame's Chronicle* p. 142.
19. For Mrs Hartley *see Grizel*, edited by P.S.H. Lawrence.

20. Hearnden *Red Robert* p. 72.
21. Longford *Five Lives* p. 43.
22. *Michael* pp. 89–90. Fleming writes in the Captain of the Oppidans' Book.
23. Lushington op. cit. pp. 99–109. First described in *Blackwood's* magazine January 1947.
24. Longson *A Classical Youth* p. 48.
25. H. Tennyson *The Haunted Mind* pp. 45–7.
26. Blunt op. cit. pp. 5, 6.
27. Connolly op. cit. p. 228.
28. H. Tennyson op. cit. p. 47.
29. Sir Charles Tennyson *Penrose Tennyson* p. 89.

Notes to Chapter 9

There is no biography of Elliott, but he did keep a file and made some notes for his grand-daughter. These have been used by his son Nicholas Elliott, in his entertaining book, *Never Judge a Man by his Umbrella*, which contains much about Claude Elliott. For Lord Hugh Cecil consult Kenneth Rose, *The Later Cecils*. The College Archives are rich on this period, and they contain the memoirs of B.J.W. (Bud) Hill, an amusing Housemaster.

1. N. Elliott op. cit. p. 16.
2. Elliott file.
3. N. Elliott op. cit. p. 46.
4. Hill memoirs.
5. N. Elliott op. cit. pp. 47, 48.
6. Elliott file.
7. Rose *The Later Cecils*.
8. N. Elliott op. cit. pp. 54, 55.
9. Elliott file.
10. *Chronicle* 7 February 1957.
11. Elliott file.
12. Elliott file – letter from Richard Martineau to Mrs Elliott.
13. N. Elliott op. cit. p. 38.
14. Elliott file.
15. Hill memoirs.
16. F.W. How 'Eton in 1940' is an Ascham Society paper reprinted in *Etoniana* no. 127. Also Hill memoirs.
17. Ibid.
18. Van Oss speech at Elliott's retirement.

19. How op. cit., *Chronicle* 6 December 1940 and 30 January 1941.
20. Elliott file.
21. Ibid. Quickswood's later view is in a letter to the Bishop of Oxford in 1947.
22. N. Elliott op. cit. pp. 55–6.
23. *Chronicle* 7 February 1957, where the final sentence of the speech reads 'And so I go to Bournemouth in lieu of paradise', but the less grammatical but wittier version is the author's recollection.
24. Elliott file.
25. Ibid.
26. Many reminiscences including some in Danziger *Eton Voices*.
27. A plaque in the Hopgarden commemorates this.
28. *Chronicle* 24 July 1941.
29. Elliott file.
30. Elliott file.

Notes to Chapter 10

There is a biography of Birley, *Red Robert*, by Arthur Hearnden, and a Festschrift assembled by David Astor and Mary Benson. For the architectural history *Eton Repointed* by J.D.R. McConnell is indispensable.

1. Hearnden op. cit. p. 163.
2. Elliott file.
3. McConnell *Eton Repointed* p. 32.
4. Pevsner op. cit. p. 125.
5. Elliott file.
6. McConnell op. cit. p. 37.
7. Ibid. p. 38.
8. Hill memoirs.
9. Austen Leigh *Eton Guide* (1964 ed.) p. 165.

Notes to Chapter 11

1. H.M. Inspector's Report (1955) p. 21.
2. Hill memoirs.
3. Ibid.
4. 'Guinea-pig' *Cornhill Magazine* Spring 1965.

Notes to Chapter 12

There is inevitably much less published material that can be quoted. On the other hand it is possible to draw on the memories of many who were involved in the management of Eton from 1963 to 1970. There is a confidential file on the dismissal of Chenevix-Trench, which includes the letter of 1968 in which Trench offered his resignation.

1. *Chronicle* 9 July 1965.
2. Ibid. 12 May 1967 and 19 May 1967.

Notes to Chapter 13

Again there is little published material. Among the papers of the Provost and Fellows is one written at their request by Michael McCrum, reviewing his headmastership; he also made available a paper setting out his reflections on the job. No such summary as yet exists for the Anderson years.

1. Watkins *Stand Before Your God* pp. 202, 203.

Notes to Chapter 14

1. In an address to overseas soldiers given at Eton in 1919.
2. Alington *Things Ancient and Modern* p. 98, quoted in Ollard *An English Education.*
3. Lubbock op. cit. pp. 87, 88.
4. *Chronicle* 3 June 1983.

Select Bibliography

I AM AWARE that I have not written down anything like all the books that I have consulted or quoted, but my work is primarily one of entertainment, not of scholarship. I have consequently limited myself to a Select Bibliography.

Manuscripts

1. Eton College Library (ECL) Archives
   Minutes and agenda papers of the Provost and Fellows
   Letters and journals of William Johnson
   Memoirs of B.J.W. (Bud) Hill: 'Eton Remembered 1937–75'
   Miscellaneous letters, scrapbooks, and documents
   Lyttelton MS
   Radcliffe Memoirs (transcript of part)

   Also at Eton: College annals, house books, Eton Society minute
      books, etc.

2. Churchill College, Cambridge, Archive Centre
   Papers of the 2nd Lord Esher

3. Magdalene College, Cambridge, Pepys Library
   Diary of A.C. Benson

4. Miscellaneous papers of C.A. Elliott

5. Diary of Victor Cazalet

Printed Sources

(Published in London unless otherwise stated)
Ainger, A.C. *Eton Sixty Years Ago.* (1917)
Alington, C.A. *Edward Lyttelton. An appreciation.* (1943)
Anstruther, I. *Oscar Browning.* (1983)
Arthur Villiers 1883–1969. (R.F.S.K.; privately published)
Austen-Leigh, R.A. Revised by R.C. Martineau. *Eton Guide.* (6th ed.,
      1964)

Ballance, Selina. *A Town called Eton.* [1982]

Balston, T. *Dr. Balston at Eton.* (1952)

Bankes, G. Nugent. *A day of my life.* (1877)

—— *About Some Fellows.* (1878)

Baring, Maurice. *The Puppet Show of Memory.* (1922)

Barlow, N. and Van Oss, O. *Eton Days.* (1976)

Benedictus, David. *The Fourth of June.* (1962) [A novel]

Berners, Lord. *A Distant Prospect.* (1945)

Birkin, Andrew. *J.M. Barrie and the Lost Boys.* (1979). (For the Llewellyn Davies boys and why Captain Hook was an OE.)

Blunt, Wilfrid. *Slow on the Feather.* (Salisbury, 1986)

Bourne, G.C. *Memoirs of an Eton Wet Bob of the Seventies.* (1933)

Brinsley-Richards, James. *Seven Years at Eton.* (1883)

Browning, Oscar. *Memories of Sixty Years at Eton, Cambridge and Elsewhere.* (1910)

Buchan, John. *Francis and Riversdale Grenfell.* (1920)

Byrne, L.S.R. and Churchill, E.L. *Changing Eton.* (1937)

—— *The Eton Book of the River.* (Eton, 1935)

Byron, Nora. *A Dame's Chronicle.* (1965)

Chandos, John. *Boys Together.* (1984)

Coleridge, G.J.D. *Eton in the Seventies.* (1912)

Coleridge, Sir John. 'Public School Education'. A lecture delivered at the Athenaeum, Tiverton 1860. (1861)

Compton-Mackenzie, F. *William Cory.* (1950)

Connolly, Cyril. *Enemies of Promise.* (1938)

Cox, Michael. *M.R. James. An Informal Portrait.* (Oxford, 1983)

Crossley. *See* Floyd

Danziger, Danny. *Eton Voices.* (1988)

Dixon, Mark. *An Eton Schoolboy's Album.* (1985)

Dundas, R.N. *Henry Dundas.* (1921)

Elliott, Nicholas. *Never Judge a Man by his Umbrella.* (Salisbury, 1991)

Eton College Chronicle (1863–1993)

Eton School Lists

Eton School Register

Etoniana. 131 numbers irregularly issued between 1904 and 1975, edited by R.A. Austen-Leigh, R.C. Martineau, and T.P. Connor

Fergusson, Bernard. *Eton Portrait.* (1937)

Fletcher, C.R.L. *Edmond Warre.* (1922)

Floyd, C.M. and Berry, M.F., eds. *A History of the Eton College Hunt.* (1968)

Franklin, Jonathan. *Two Owls at Eton.* (1960)

Gambier Parry, Ernest. *Annals of an Eton House.* (1907)

Gathorne-Hardy, E., ed. *Cornishiana.* (Cairo, 1947)

Green, Henry [Henry Yorke]. *Pack my Bag.* (1940)

[Grenville-Murray, R.T.S.C.] *Collegers v. Oppidans* by an Old Etonian. (Eton, 1884). First published in the *Cornhill Magazine.* (December 1871) [A novel]

Grenville-Murray, R.T.S.C. *See also* Brinsley-Richards

H.M. Inspector's Reports (1936 and 1955)

Hearnden, Arthur. *Red Robert. A life of Robert Birley* (1984)

Heygate, Sir John. *Decent Fellows.* (1930) [A novel]

Hill, B.J.W. *Eton Medley.* (1948)

Hill, M.D. *Eton and Elsewhere.* (1928)

Honey, J.R. de S. *Tom Brown's Universe.* (1977)

James, M.R. *Eton and King's.* (1926)

James, S.R. *Seventy Years.* (1926)

Johnson, W. *Eton Reform* and *Eton Reform II.* (1861)

—— *Hints for Eton Masters.* (1862)

—— *Ionica.* With biographical introduction and notes by A.C. Benson. Sesame Library [1905]

—— 'On the Education of the Reasoning Faculties' in Farrar, F., ed. *Essays on a Liberal Education.* (1867)

Jones, Sir L.E. *A Victorian Boyhood.* (1955)

Knox, R.A. *Patrick Shaw-Stewart.* (1920)

Lambert, Royston. *The Hothouse Society.* (1968)

Lawrence, P.S.H. *An Eton Camera 1850–1919.* (Salisbury, 1980)

—— *An Eton Camera 1920–1959.* (Salisbury, 1983)

——, ed. *Grizel.* (Salisbury, 1991)

Lehane, Brendan. 'Guinea-pig' in *Cornhill Magazine.* (1965)

Leslie, Sir Shane. *The Oppidan.* (1922) [A novel]

Letters of an English Boy (ed. M.S.L.). (1917)

Longson, Michael. *A Classical Youth.* (1985)

Lubbock, Alfred. *Memories of Eton and Etonians.* (1899)

Lubbock, Percy. *Shades of Eton.* (1929)

Lushington, Stephen, ed. *The Eton We Knew.* (1952)

Luxmoore, H.E. *Noblesse Oblige ... Some views and opinions of Sparrow on Housetops.* (Eton, 1885)

—— *Letters of H.E. Luxmoore* (ed. A.B. Ramsay). (Cambridge, 1929)

Lyttelton, Edward. *Memories and Hopes.* (1925)

McConnell, J.D.R. *Eton – How it Works.* (1967)

—— *Eton Repointed.* (1970)

——, ed. *Treasures of Eton.* (1976)

Mack, Edward C. *Public Schools and British Opinion since 1860.* (New York, 1941)

[McKenna, Pamela]. *Michael.* (Privately printed, 1932)

Macnaghten, Hugh. *Fifty Years of Eton.* (1924)

Macnaghten, Melville. *Sketchy Memories of Eton.* (Calcutta, 1885)

Maude, John. *Memories of Eton and Oxford.* (Privately printed, 1936)

Maxwell-Lyte, Sir Henry. *History of Eton College 1440–1910.* (4th ed., 1910)

Miscellaneous ephemerals in Eton College Library

Mosley, Nicholas. *Julian Grenfell.* (1976)

Newsome, David. *Godliness and Good Learning.* (1961)

—— *On the Edge of Paradise. A.C. Benson: the diarist.* (1980)

Ollard, Richard. *An English Education.* (1982)

Oneayama, D. *A Nigger at Eton.* (1972)

Parker, Eric. *Eton in the Eighties.* (1914)

Parker, Peter. *The Old Lie.* (1987)

Paul, C. Kegan. *Memories.* (1899)

Pfaff, R.W. *Montague Rhodes James.* (1980)

Pilkington, E.M.S. *An Eton Playing Field.* (1896)

Powell, Anthony. *Infants of the Spring.* (1976)

Priestley, Hermia. *John Boughey.* (1947)

Public Schools Commission. *Report of Her Majesty's Commissioners.* HMSO (1864)

Register of Old Etonians. Published up to 1919; further work is in progress

Robert Birley 1903–82. (Eds David Astor and Mary Benson). (Oxford, 1985)

Rose, Kenneth. *The Later Cecils.* (1975)

Salt, H.S. *Memories of Bygone Eton.* (1928)

[Salt, H.S.] *Eton under Hornby,* by O.E. (1910)

Stone, C.R. *Eton Glossary.* (Eton, 1902)

Sturgis, H.O. *Tim.* (1891) [A novel]

Tennyson, Sir Charles. *Penrose Tennyson.* (1943)

Watkins, Paul. *Stand Before Your God.* (1993)

William Hope-Jones. A Memoir by various friends. (Privately published, 1968)

Wingfield-Stratford, Esmé. *Before the Lights Went Out.* (1945)

Wortham, H.E. *Victorian Eton and Cambridge. Being the Life and Times of Oscar Browning.* (1927)

Wright, Donald, ed. *Walter Hamilton 1908–1988. A Portrait.* (1992)

INDEX

Note: Dates in brackets refer to time at Eton.